# THE SYSTEM OF PROFESSIONS

# THE SYSTEM
# OF PROFESSIONS

## An Essay on the
## Division of Expert Labor

## Andrew Abbott

The University of Chicago Press
Chicago and London

The University of Chicago Press, Chicago 60637
The University of Chicago Press, Ltd., London

© 1988 by The University of Chicago
All rights reserved. Published 1988
Printed in the United States of America

09 08 07 06 05 04 03 02 01 00      5 6 7 8 9

Library of Congress Cataloging-in-Publication Data

Abbott, Andrew Delano.
  The system of professions.

  Bibliography: p.
  Includes index.
  1. Professions—United States. 2. Professions—
Great Britain. 3. Professions—Europe. I. Title.
HD8038.U5A615   1988      331.7′12′09      87-30206
ISBN 0-226-00069-9 (pbk.)

For My Parents and in Memory of W. G. Abbott, Jr.

# Contents

# Preface

On a brave spring morning in 1973, I sat with two psychiatrists in the office of John R. Collier, superintendent of Illinois's Manteno State Hospital. After a year observing the use of psychiatric knowledge in an outpatient clinic, I was now ready to analyze the stranger world of the mental hospital. Friends had introduced me to David Turner and David Klass, consultant specialists at Manteno, the great chronic hospital that anchored the Illinois state mental health system. The place overwhelmed me. Dozens of ward buildings covered a square mile of prairie. So regular was their formation that when we had passed beside the northernmost ward on the way to the administration building, I had seen through its porch arches the concentric outlines of equivalent arches on ward after ward to the very end of the hospital. While Collier read my little letter of intent, I looked out at the briskly snapping state flag and thought of Foucault finding in those arches the triumph of regularity and order. Turner and Klass joked quietly. Finally, Collier glanced up. "I don't see why you need to go on the wards to study psychiatric knowledge," he grinned. "All the psychiatric knowledge in this hospital's sitting right here in this room."

I was later to see what Collier had meant. To care for its 3,500 patients, Manteno employed only one board-certified psychiatrist and indeed only three or four licensed physicians. Most medical care was performed by unlicensed foreign doctors, who were at that very moment dreading the brand-new Federal Licensing Examination. Turner and Klass, by contrast, had both been chief residents at the University of Chicago; in an official sense, they and Anne-Marie Rohan, the one board-certified staff member, did indeed possess all the psychiatric knowledge in the hospital.

"In an official sense. . . ." What is it to possess and control expertise? After five years at Manteno, I had spent more time with mental patients, seen more of their activities, and endured more of their jokes than most psychiatrists do in a lifetime. I had lost pool matches to manic-depressives and poker games to schizophrenics. I had dodged clutching fingers that had killed four less-agile people. I had conversed with an elderly man who lived what Wittgenstein wrote. I had helped administer several tons of thorazine, mellaril, and their cousins, and the pounds of cogentin and artane to control their side effects. Yet, "in an official sense," five years at Manteno did not make me an expert on the insane.

They did, however, make me wonder why I was not. I went on to write a thesis on psychiatry as a profession and then began to consider the general issue of how modern societies institutionalize expertise. I knew that the common form of that institutionalization was professionalism. Many writers had studied professionalism, but few, I felt, studied the basic conditions and contexts of the control of work. Most studied the organization and affiliation of practitioners, and, for most, professionalism was either a phenomenon happening to individual professions or a grand sea change in the occupational system generally. There was in this work little sense of the squabbles between the Manteno psychologists and social workers over who could interpret diagnostic tests, of the war between our attorneys and our doctors over the patients who were incompetent to stand trial, of the vast distance between Klass, Turner, and Rohan on the one hand and the foreign ward doctors on the other. Of course, all of these problems had been studied individually. But with the exception of some work by Everett Hughes's students—particularly Eliot Freidson, Rue Bucher, and Anselm Strauss—there was no theory about them. There was certainly no attempt to see these interprofessional battles as central aspects of professionalism, rather than as isolated movements and pathologies.

In typical Chicago fashion, then, this book grew out of my experiences as a participant observer. That the book's evidence is mostly historical should not obscure its fieldwork origins. My Manteno years, and the clinic year before them, forced me towards a theory that could reconcile the historical continuity of professional appearances with the day-to-day discontinuities of professional reality. I experienced this disjunction quite personally. Manteno psychologists eagerly participated in their profession's war with psychiatry, actively lobbying for third-party payment. Yet their everyday professional world was so insecure that they protested in vain when administrators placed my uncertified self into the civil service "psychologist" classification.

Yet these local vicissitudes reflect larger reality, and a serious theory of professional development must embrace and explain this larger reality as well. Manteno's professionals struggled within a historical environment of peculiar intensity. Deinstitutionalization of mental patients was in full swing, destroying professionals' jobs as it fulfilled their ideologies. Biological psychiatry was rapidly recouping the doctors' position against the counseling professions, although token economies were making a substantial counterattack. Within the counseling area itself, psychoanalysis was at last losing its monopolistic dominance, and the flood tide of nonmedical psychotherapy beginning to flow. It was a time of great hope and change.

Yet the prevailing feeling of the hospital was of decline. Around us stood mute witnesses to the death of the asylum. When I stayed at the hospital on summer evenings I would walk at sunset past rank on rank of empty wards, past swings and seesaws unused for decades. The thousand-acre hospital farms had been rented to sod and corn farmers. The great southern lawn had become a public golf course. The diesel switching engine stood idle by the power plant, behind the empty kitchens that had once fed ten thousand persons a day. Beyond the power plant, the railroad siding snaked two weedy miles towards the Illinois Central tracks, passing an orchard where a few hardy trees still produced worm-eaten fruit. On such an evening, the whole history of the asylum hospital gleamed on the signs naming the wards—the idealistic founders Pinel and Dix, the famous Europeans Kraepelin, Freud, and Adler, the great Americans Rush, Meyer, and Mitchell. There were buildings, too, for other professions important to the asylum hospital—Barton and Nightingale for the nurses, Addams and Wines for the social workers, James for the psychologists. If I have captured in this book a sense of professions' transiency, it owes much to this experience of the dying hospital.

This book, then, aims to show the professions growing, splitting, joining, adapting, dying. The objects of its analysis include a wide variety of professions in the United States, England, and, to some extent, France and the other nations of continental Europe. I have been catholic in my tastes, trying to offset the customary reliance on American law and medicine. (I have generally avoided writing about academic professions, hoping to escape charges of navel gazing from nonacademic readers and the sense of we-know-it-all-already among academics.) The breadth of examples requires the usual disclaimer a synthetic writer makes to area specialists. Few of these analyses other than those in my own primary research areas will seem sophisticated to specialists on individual professions. I have done my best in unfamiliar territories, but doubtless many minor errors remain. On the other hand, that I write such a book testifies to my belief that synthesis will prove more worthwhile than further area work. Readers can judge for themselves whether that belief is correct.

Since the roots of the book lie in my personal experiences and observations, my first debts are to those who got me into the field; to Morris Janowitz, who pushed me into field study in my first year at Chicago; to Jarl Dyrud and Dave Klass, who got me into Manteno; to Klass and Jon Steinmetz, who managed to support me there for five years. Like all field observers, I have great debts to my subjects. Unlike most observers, however, I have the pleasure, afforded by ten years' time and a book using little of their evidence directly, of thanking the most important of them by name. Eberhard Uhlenhuth and his clinic staff, particularly Rose West, Mark Moulthrop, Dave Turner, Polly Everett, Zanvel Klein, and Jeff Teich, helped me immensely. The Chicago psychiatric residents of the 1972–1974 classes put up with numerous bumblings, for the most part with unfailing good humor.

At Manteno my debts are more extensive, because my stay was longer and my participation more complete. For official authorizations and support I must particularly thank Jack Collier and his successor Ella Curry. For varying degrees of forbearance and helpfulness I must thank the professional staffs, particularly Solomon Noguera and Luis Palacios among the doctors, Henry Lin among psychologists, Nora Brashear and Bonnie Hellyer among social workers. Among ward people I owe great debts especially to Janet Tetrault, Penny Kneissler, Doug Baldridge, Raymond Marshall, Dennis Hopkins, Marge Curry, and Harold Spearin. Among the nonprofessional staff, Arvada Ruder, Doris White, and Charlotte Morgan were helpful and supportive, as were John Crayton and Mike Strizich among the Chicago-based consultants. Finally, I must thank friends whose personal support got me through Manteno's deadlier moments—Dave Rudolf, Margaret Kasper, Jon Steinmetz, and, *dulcissima*, Cindi Clyden.

Over the years, a number of friends in diverse professions have talked intimately about their work. For this I must thank in particular Scott Thatcher, Richard Kalb, and James Gill, lawyer, architect, and priest. I have learned much about engineering from talks with my father. My mother taught me about librarianship by making me work in various libraries she ran, and I have indulged my enduring interest in libraries with indexing theorist Jim Anderson. My firsthand knowledge of the military I owe to Richard Nixon.

Beyond these general debts, I have some more specific debts for ideas in the book. The notion that diagnosis and treatment are general modes of knowledge came from Donald Levine, and the vacancy metaphor that underlies chapter 4 from Harrison White. In most of the book I have softened the vacancy metaphor into a more ecological one so that the relative positions of professions might seem somewhat less exclusive. Although ecology is a fashionable metaphor in sociology today, the book's ecological flavor comes directly from Park, Burgess, Zorbaugh, and others of the old Chicago School. Reading this work in the early 1970s, I came to see social structures as fluctuating and geographic, conceptions that strongly underlie this book. They underlie as well the Chicago writers on occupations and professions, and the book thus lies very much in the Everett Hughes tradition. The book's comparative emphasis has diverse sources. Although I originally designed my dissertation study of American psychiatrists without much comparative knowledge, Joseph Ben-David shamed me into studying other professions and other countries. The comparative emphasis was reinforced when I was able to attend two years of sessions on the history of professions at Princeton's Davis Center. Although the Princeton historians had little respect for sociologists, they did examine an immense amount of information about various professions, and I would not have dared so broad a book without the exposure I acquired there.

Like any synthetic scholar, I owe much to past sociological and historical work. On the sociological side, Joseph Ben-David, Magali Larson, Eliot Freidson, and Terence Johnson have been particularly important theoretical sources, as have the earlier synthetic books of Geoffrey Millerson, W. J. Reader, and A. M. Carr-Saunders and P. A. Wilson. A number of sociological colleagues have talked professions with me for years, and I must thank them, particularly Terence Halliday and Michael Powell, for their insights and criticism. To the historians I owe a still greater debt, for theirs is the data that undergirds the book. Although sources are of course listed where relevant, I must thank here those historians who have personally shaped my ideas: Gerald Geison, Steve Botein, Nancy Tomes, Janet Tighe, Gerald Grob, Paul Miranti, and Robert Kohler.

A number of people have read the book manuscript, or pieces of it. Terry Halliday, Mark Granovetter, Doug Nelson, Eliot Freidson, Harrison White, and Susan Gal gave me very helpful, although often contradictory, comments. Two research assistants, Bruce Carruthers and Margaret Antinori, helped with material appearing in chapters 1 and 8. Ed Laumann was helpful at publication time. Financial support came in small amounts from faculty grants at Rutgers, and in large ones from my wife's real world salary from Bell Laboratories. Portions of the manuscript have appeared before, and I must thank the relevant journals for permission to reprint; chapter 9 appeared virtually in its entirety in the *American Bar Foundation Research Journal* and portions of chapter 10 in *Sociological Analysis*. I must also thank the Harvard University Department of Sociology, whose invitation in 1982 provoked my first formal discussion of the central argument of the book.

A first book is the proper occasion for acknowledging help of years ago that led, in its circuitous way, to this present. I thank, then, my parents, James and Rita Abbott, for fostering me in the life of the mind and some teachers who furthered that endeavor: Seaver Gilcreast, Sr., Robert Shields, George Best, Simeon Hyde, Dudley Fitts, R. H. Goodyear, J. P. Russo. I thank also those who exemplified for me what that life could be: Alston Chase, Roger Revelle, Morris Janowitz.

Lastly, I thank those who made life fun while I wrote this book. Among my present and former colleagues at Rutgers, Stan DeViney, Andy Szasz, Randy Smith, Rob Parker, and Judy Gerson have criticized, cheered, and supported, as did that anthropologist who is still my closest friend thirty years after we were third grade sweethearts.

Finally, by her support, threat, cajolery, and exhortation, Sue Schlough probably has as much to do with the appearance of this manuscript as I do. She did not read it, or type it, or prepare the index. But she interrupted her plane trips and experiments to do much more than her share of the dishwashing and cleaning (I think I've held up my end of the ironing and cooking). As any two-career couple knows, that's a big deal. We've had a great time while this book was being written, and that's an even bigger deal. Thanks.

A.M.D.G.                                         Phillipsburg, New Jersey
                                                 14 July 1987

Note for the reader: This is a long book, with long and often involved arguments. To make the argument followable, I have suppressed all citation in text. This makes the scholarly machinery harder to follow—something I resent when *I* read—but it makes the book much more readable. I apologize to those who want to check everything as they go along. James Anderson kindly assisted me with the index. Its unfortunate brevity was dictated by considerations of space.

# 1    Introduction

The professions dominate our world. They heal our bodies, measure our profits, save our souls. Yet we are deeply ambivalent about them. For some, the rise of professions is a story of knowledge in triumphant practice. It is the story of Pasteur and Osler and Schweitzer, a thread that ties the lawyer in a country village to the justice on the Supreme Court bench. For others it is a sadder chronicle of monopoly and malfeasance, of unequal justice administered by servants of power, of Rockefeller medicine men.[1] Beneath the impassioned contradictions of these interpretations lie some common assumptions. Most authors study professions one at a time. Most assume that professions grow through a series of stages called professionalization. Most talk less about what professions do than about how they are organized to do it.

These assumptions seem to emerge from our central questions about professions. Why should there be occupational groups controlling the acquisition and application of various kinds of knowledge? Where and why did groups like medicine and law achieve their power? Will professionalism spread throughout the occupational world? To answer such puzzling questions, it seemed necessary to adopt simplifying assumptions. The complexities of the individual professions forced case by case study. The fact that professions like medicine and architecture seemed more similar in organizational pattern than in actual work made organizational pattern the focus of analysis. The focus on pattern implied in turn a search for its origins and led to the idea of a common process of development, the idea of professionalization. But professionalization was at best a misleading concept, for it involved more the forms than the contents of professional life. It ignored who was doing what to whom and how, concentrating instead on associ-

1

ation, licensure, ethics code. In fact, not only did it miss the contents of professional activity, but also the larger situation in which that activity occurs.

By focusing on parallels in organizational development, students of the professions lost sight of a fundamental fact of professional life—interprofessional competition. Control of knowledge and its application means dominating outsiders who attack that control. Control without competition is trivial. Study of organizational forms can indeed show how certain occupations control their knowledge and its application. But it cannot tell why those forms emerge when they do or why they sometimes succeed and sometimes fail. Only the study of competition can accomplish that.

The professions, that is, make up an interdependent system. In this system, each profession has its activities under various kinds of jurisdiction. Sometimes it has full control, sometimes control subordinate to another group. Jurisdictional boundaries are perpetually in dispute, both in local practice and in national claims. It is the history of jurisdictional disputes that is the real, the determining history of the professions. Jurisdictional claims furnish the impetus and the pattern to organizational developments. Thus an effective historical sociology of professions must begin with case studies of jurisdictions and jurisdiction disputes. It must then place these disputes in a larger context, considering the system of professions as a whole. It must study such evolving systems in several countries to assess exogenous factors shaping systems of professions. Only from such portraits can one derive an effective model for understanding and predicting professional development in modern societies generally.[2]

The movement from an individualistic to a systematic view of professions organizes this book. I begin by evaluating the idea of professionalization and move on to theorize the systematic relations of professions. I then analyze external forces bearing on the system and close by discussing three important examples of contested jurisdictions. Throughout, I addresss the familiar questions about professions. How do professions develop? How do they relate to one another? What determines the kind of work they do?

But this summary slights a methodological theme that accompanies the substantive one as harmony does a melody. My substantive questions all involve generalizing about stories, such as stories of professionalization. My methodological concern is with how this generalization takes place. Traditional theories of professionalization argue that professions follow a certain sequence of development. This "careers" model is one way to generalize about sequences of social events. My theoretical scheme, particularly in Chapter 4, illustrates a different way of generalizing about sequences, one that makes them interdependent. Since jurisdiction is the defining relation in professional life, the sequences that I generalize are sequences of jurisdictional control, describing who had control of what, when, and how. Professions develop when jurisdictions become vacant, which may happen because they are newly created or because an earlier tenant has left them altogether or lost its firm grip on them. If an already existing profession takes over a vacant jurisdiction, it may in turn vacate another of its jurisdictions or retain merely supervisory control of it. Thus events propagate backwards in some sense, with jurisdictional vacancies, rather than the professions themselves, having much of the intiative. This simple system model shows how a set of historical stories can be analyzed without assuming a common career pattern, as in the concept of professionalization.[3]

Throughout the book, then, run two levels of analysis. Substantively, the book answers some questions about the evolution of professions. Methodologically, it considers the difficulties of generalizing about sequences of events and proposes a new way to address them. It both does historical sociology and asks how historical sociology ought to be done.

## The Professions Literature

Although the professions derive from medieval or in some cases ancient origins, the first systematic attempts to study them came in this century. In part this reflected the rise of the social sciences, but it reflected more importantly a great change in the professions themselves. The nineteenth century saw the first development of professions as we know them today. In England the merging of apothecaries with surgeons and physicians, the rise of the lower branch of the legal profession, and the appearance of the surveyors, architects, and accountants signaled the change. In America the triumphs of regular medicine over its various sects, the growth of the university professional schools, and the host of would-be professions all testified to the new form of occupation.[4]

The nineteenth century professions were important but peculiar social creatures. With the exception of accounting, they stood outside the new commercial and industrial heart of society. They were organized in a collegial manner that was distinctly anachronistic. On the Continent, to be sure, the professions were more hierarchical. But this hierarchy came not from the new capitalist forms of organization, but rather from the Old Regime, from which it acquired a civil servant quality quite peculiar in the modern occupational world. The professions, and in particular the Anglo-American variety, were therefore a great puzzle for social theorists. Weber spent many embarrassed pages confronting the wanton irrationality of the English Bar. Durkheim simply ignored the Anglo-American professions altogether and looked to more familiar French occupations for his neocorporatist future.[5]

It was the English themselves who perforce first analyzed these unusual occupations. Carr-Saunders and Wilson's *The Professions*, published in 1934, was the first such attempt.[6] The book gave historical background on every group that could then be considered a profession in England. Its theoretical discussion systematized a view of professions that had by then come to dominate the writings both of the professions themselves and of the social scientists examining them. Professions were organized bodies of experts who applied esoteric knowledge to particular cases. They had elaborate systems of instruction and training, together with entry by examination and other formal prerequisites. They normally possessed and enforced a code of ethics or behavior. This list of properties became the core of later definitions.

The Carr-Saunders and Wilson volume epitomized two methodologies characteristic of writing on professions, combining naturalism and typology. Early articles on the professions would summarize the life history of their particular case, review the then-current essential traits of a true profession, and decide whether social work or nursing or whatever really was a profession. Work in this genre rapidly built the stock of case studies, fitting each case into the procrustean bed of essential traits. But that bed was so often refinished as it passed from hand to hand that the case studies were never very comparable. By 1964, when Geoffrey Millerson attempted a new general analysis of professions, he had to treat earlier work as merely advisory and build on new data in a new framework.[7] Millerson recognized that trait-based definitions had often reflected political concerns. If one disliked social work, one easily found some trait excluding social work from the prestigious category of "professions." He himself avoided this by identifying only very general traits of professionalism (e.g., organization, education, ethics) and then permitting wide variation within them.

Other authors confronted this empirical diversity more directly. An early and parsimonious answer came from the theorists of professionalization. The diversity of the would-be professions arose because professional status was an end state that few had yet achieved. Diversity would disappear with time, as groups gradually acquired all the marks of true professions. The concept of professionalization thus consummated the marriage of naturalism and typology. Professionalization was a natural process, as in the case study literature, but that process entailed a series of types. In 1964 Harold Wilensky published an article that demonstrated such a regular sequence in the American professions. Professionalization seemed an established fact. The new conceptualization meant in turn a new theoretical question. Why did professionalization follow the sequence it did?

But just as professionalization became an established concept, the study of professions was suddenly reshaped by the new political climate of the 1960s. Early work on professionalization had rested on the functional assumptions characteristic of postwar sociology. It attributed the collegial organization of professions to their position as experts. The "asymmetry of expertise" required the client to trust the professional and the professional to respect both client and colleagues. These relations were guaranteed by various institutional forms—associations, licensure, ethics codes. But theorists rejecting functional assumptions disputed the whole picture. In a lucid analysis of professionalism as a form of control, Johnson argued that the professions did not serve disembodied social needs but rather imposed both definitions of needs and manner of service on atomized consumers. Writing on American medicine, Eliot Freidson argued that dominance and autonomy, not collegiality and trust, were the hallmarks of true professionalism. Another student of medicine, Jeffrey Berlant, attributed the structures of professionalism directly to the goals of economic monopoly. Berlant's work was the more striking in that the feature of professionalism whose monopolistic function he most carefully analyzed was ethics codes, whose altruistic nature had been assumed by earlier workers.[8]

By seeing monopoly rather than control of asymmetric relationships, the new theorists moved the focus of debate from the forms of professionalization to its functions. For the new theorists, the regularity of professionalization was not the visible regularity of school, then association, then ethics code, but rather the hidden one of successive functions for these professional forms. Ethics codes came late in professionalization not because they were a culmination of natural growth, but because they served the function of excluding outsiders, a function that became important only after the professional community had been generated and consolidated. Since ethics codes did not serve these earlier functions, they came late.

The new power literature thus unmasked earlier work as ideological. This unmasking reached its final form in Magali Larson's *The Rise of Professionalism* (1977). Here professions were explicitly market organizations attempting the intellectual and organizational domination of areas of social concern. Yet even while it reversed the traditional images of profession and professional, Larson's book drew on themes and assumptions standard throughout the Anglo-American study of professions. The old model was accepted for new reasons. Since she cast professions as market dominating organizations, Larson ruled out the professions of the Continent, where expertise was never formalized independent of the state. Like her predecessors in the power tradition, she explicitly excluded the organization-based professions— armed and civil service and clergy—that continue in the Anglo-American world the institutional forms of the Continent. Through her focus on dominance she ignored professions like nursing that had accepted subordination. The exclusions should come as no surprise. By accepting professionalization as the thing to be explained, the new power theorists accepted the assumptions behind the concept. These included not only the idea of a fixed sequence of events or functions, but also assumptions about the best examples of professionalism (American medicine and law), about its essential qualities, and about the character of the interprofessional world.

The split between the functionalists and the monopolists was thus not total. It was also not one-dimensional. First, the two groups emphasized different consequences of professionalism. Berlant and Larson were interested in the consequences of medical professionalism not for health, but rather for the status and power of the medical profession. These were external, social consequences that derived from professional status or activity; sickness was of little interest. Other writers emphasized internal consequences of professionalism, consequences affecting the area of professional work itself—healing, auditing, and so on. To Parsons, for example, the impact of professionalism on sick individuals was of central importance. Yet it was also central for Freidson, whose critical stance otherwise identifies him with Larson and Berlant. This contrast between Parsons and Freidson indicates the other dimension of the split, which concerns the locus of analysis; like Larson but unlike Parsons, Freidson aimed his analysis at the social level. He asked how the overall social handling of illness was affected by the existence and nature of professional groups. Similarly, Larson's concern with the external consequences of professionalism extended to the profession as a whole. She asked what professions got out of professionalism and how. Parsons and other functionalists, while concerned, like Freidson, with internal consequences, saw them at the individual level. How, they asked, does a social relation between client and professional have to be structured for healing (or some other individual professional act) to occur?

Of course, the crossing of these two dichotomies implies a fourth approach, one examining external consequences, as do Larson and Berlant, but at the level of individuals. This view has been argued at length by Joseph Ben-David and Burton Bledstein. Both emphasize the function of professionalism in protecting certain individuals—the professionals themselves—from the structured, rigid employment that emerged with nineteenth century capitalism. Beyond this independence, they both argued, professionalism also provided both an ideal metaphor for vertical mobility and the means with which to attempt it. This argument defines the chief implications of professionalism as its external consequences (status, money, power), but at the individual level. Professionalism was a matter of individual choices and corporate action taken to protect or extend them.[9]

The literature on professions has thus gradually moved from naturalism to theory. It began with case studies and typologies. The internal contradictions of these studies led ultimately to the idea of professionalization, in which a developmental typology generated the natural histories, producing an apparent variety of professions. For the process of professionalization there then emerged a variety of theoretical interpretations. For some, professionalism was a means to control a difficult social relation; for others, a species of corporate extortion. For still others its importance lay in building individual achievement channels, while a fourth group emphasized how it helped or hindered general social functions like health and justice.

Despite their substantive differences, authors of these theories took a surprisingly consistent view of what professions were and what about them must be explained. Certainly all agreed that a profession was an occupational group with some special skill. Usually this was an abstract skill, one that required extensive training. It was not applied in a purely routine fashion, but required revised application case by case. In addition, professions were more or less exclusive.

This consensus seems surprising in light of the squabbles characteristic of the period of naturalistic studies. For many years the definitional question was the focal issue of studies of professions, obscuring the substantive questions that made professions interesting in the first place.[10] But of course the surprising consensus of theoretical writers reflected the place of definition in theoretical work, where it is a means to substantive ends. The confusion over definitions arose mainly in writing that lacked theoretical intent. There, definitions were judged by their ability to regenerate common opinions. Since those opinions were organized around the familiar examples of American law and medicine, definitions excluded things that didn't look like law and medicine, such as automobile repair, and included things that did, like accounting and perhaps social work. There were and are fundamental difficulties with this test-by-example. First, American law and medicine do not in fact look like our images of them. Only half of each is self-employed. The vast majority of work in both is utterly routine. A surprising number of professionals, even in these fields, will be in another occupational classification in twenty years.[11] Second, many groups that obviously *are* professions do not look like American medicine and law at all. English barristers do not necessarily train in university but rather by apprenticeship and eating dinners "in hall." American clergy do not generally have ethics codes nor, until recently, associations independent of their ecclesiastical structure. Yet both groups are unmistakably professions. The underlying problem is that for many writers, calling something a profession makes it one. People don't want to call automobile repair a profession because they don't want to accord it that dignity. This unwillingness probably has less to do with the actual characteristics of automobile repair as an intellectual discipline—which are conceptually quite close to those of medicine—than it does with the status of the work and of those who do it. When definitions aim to distinguish groups according to such an external agenda, they are disputed. When used to answer theoretical questions, they are not.

Definitions, then, must follow from theoretical questions. The theory I sketched in the opening paragraphs implies the very loose definition that professions are exclusive occupational groups applying somewhat abstract knowledge to particular cases. It is important to show why this definition is chosen here. In doing so, I can further outline my fundamental theory.

My underlying questions concern the evolution and interrelations of professions, and, more generally, the ways occupational groups control knowledge and skill. I have already argued that the evolution of professions in fact results from their interrelations. These interrelations are in turn determined by the way these groups control their knowledge and skill. There are two rather different ways of accomplishing this control. One emphasizes technique per se, and occupations using it are commonly called crafts. To control such an occupation, a group directly controls its technique. The other form of control involves abstract knowledge. Here, practical skill grows out of an abstract system of knowledge, and control of the occupation lies in control of the abstractions that generate the practical techniques. The techniques themselves may in fact be delegated to other workers. For me this characteristic of abstraction is the one that best identifies the professions. For abstraction is the quality that sets interprofessional competition apart from competition among occupations in general. Any occupation can obtain licensure (e.g., beauticians) or develop an ethics code (e.g., real estate). But only a knowledge system governed by abstractions can redefine its problems and tasks, defend them from interlopers, and seize new problems—as medicine has recently seized alcoholism, mental illness, hyperactivity in children, obesity, and numerous other things. Abstraction enables survival in the competitive system of professions. If auto mechanics had that kind of abstraction, if they "contained" the relevant sections of what is presently the engineering profession, and had considered taking over all repair of internal combustion engines on abstract grounds, they would, for my purposes, be a profession.

My central questions and my framework thus determine my definition of profession. As we have just seen, they determine first its emphasis on the knowledge system and its degree of abstraction, since these are the ultimate currency of competition between professions. But they also determine its relativity, since the degree of abstraction necessary for survival varies with time and place in the system of professions. As social work and nursing have become collegiate professions, medicine has become postgraduate. How abstract is abstract enough to be professional? The answer depends on time and place. What matters is abstraction effective enough to compete in a particular historical and social context, not abstraction relative to some supposed absolute standard. I am interested not merely in the living, dominant professions like medicine and law, but also in the the moribund groups like mediums, railway surgeons, and electrotherapists. A definition too specific would exclude them from view. Yet they too have made their mark on the system of professions we see today.[12]

## The Concept of Professionalization

Having settled the definitional issue, at least temporarily, we may move on to examine past theories of professional development more closely. Probably the most common theme of past work is that professions tend to develop in a common pattern, called professionalization. Is there, in fact, a common story of how professions develop? To answer this question, we must first answer the preliminary one of what we mean by "common story." This question is quite complex. There have been many theories of professionalization, and they differ along two distinctly different dimensions—the formal and the substantive.

Let us consider formal differences among theories of professionalization by studying some versions of the professionalization story. In the 1964 article mentioned earlier, Harold Wilensky discussed what he called "the professionalization of everyone." Wilensky looked at the dates of "first events" in various American professions—first training school, first university school, first local association, first national association, first state licensing law, and first code of ethics. He found by inspection that the events usually fell in the order just listed. Reflecting on that order, he then made up a story to account for it. I shall paraphrase it as follows:

Professions begin when people "start doing full time the thing that needs doing." But then the issue of training arises, pushed by recruits or clients. Schools are created. The new schools, if not begun within universities, immediately seek affiliation with them. Inevitably, there then develop higher standards, longer training, earlier commitment to the profession, and a group of full time teachers. Then the teaching professionals, along with their first graduates, combine to promote and create a professional association. The more active professional life enabled by this association leads to self-reflection, to possible change of name, and to an explicit attempt to separate competent from incompetent. Reflection about central tasks leads the profession to delegate routine work to paraprofessionals. At the same time the attempt to separate competent from incompetent leads to internal conflict between the officially trained younger generation and their on-the-job-trained elders, as well as to increasingly violent confrontations with outsiders. This period also contains efforts to secure state protection, although this does not always occur and is not peculiar to professions in any case. Finally, the rules that these events have generated, rules eliminating internal competition and charlatanry and establishing client protection, coalesce in a formal ethics code.[13]

Wilensky's story consists of a series of narrative steps, each of which moves from situation to event to situation. What propels these steps? Here Wilensky is less clear. He tells who pushes for schools, but not why. Presumably he uses some commonsense theory like "people who are doing something full time want to do it well," or "see a need to do it well," or "begin to know what it is to do it well." Note that the causal models underlying the various links in this story draw on different general views of why things happen in social life. Schools arise functionally; they fill a need. Delegation of tasks, by contrast, arises in a historicist manner (success confers the power to delegate, which further enhances success), while ethics codes simply coalesce inevitably.

Who is the subject of this story? This, too, is problematic. Ethics codes happen to the profession as a whole. Yet at the beginning of Wilensky's story, the profession as a whole did not really exist. The initial subjects are "those who do full time the thing that needs doing." Through the story the profession gradually emerges as the new central subject of the narrative, although often the agents or occasions of change come from subgroups. At one level this seems obvious enough. One central process of professionalization is coalescence into a group. But there is an essential difference between demonstrating emergence as a process in the social world and presupposing it by means of a narrative structure. It is the latter that Wilensky has done; at least some of the "full-time doers" have in fact become defined as charlatans by the latter stages of the story.

Although Wilensky theorized a general process of professionalization, he saw variety in the actual sequences and advanced special explanations of deviations from his overall story. Theodore Caplow, in contrast, saw a more strictly universal story. We can paraphrase it as follows:

Professions begin with the establishment of professional associations that have explicit membership rules to exclude the unqualified. Second, they change their names, in order to lose their past, to assert their monopoly, and, most importantly, to give themselves a label capable of legislative restriction. Third, they set up a code of ethics to assert their social utility, to further regulate the incompetent, and to reduce internal competition. Fourth, they agitate politically to obtain legal recognition, aiming at first to limit the professional title and later to criminalize unlicensed work in their jurisdiction. (The growth of schooling Caplow sees as concurrent with this political activity, as he does the establishment of confidentiality rights and effective relations with outsiders.)[14]

Caplow's story differs from Wilensky's not only in chronology but in narrative structure as well. For one thing, it has a uniform central subject. The profession appears at the beginning of the story and undertakes all the activity in it. For another, all links of the story are functional. In fact, there is a sequence of functions. Exclusion is included in all four links, assertion of jurisdiction in the last three, internal control in the last two, and external relations only in the last. This sequence of functions is triggered by the need for professionalization, which Caplow derives from larger social forces in a separate argument. Yet despite these differences, Caplow's story shares with Wilensky's the assertion that there are clear sequences of professionalization.

This clear succession disappears in professionalization as described in English sources. Geoffrey Millerson's explicit denial shows the very different approach he takes to narrating professionalization.

Clearly all Qualifying Associations did not begin as straightforward attempts to gain professional status. Immediate causes, so far as they can be traced, reveal a variety of reasons for establishing an association; to co-ordinate the activities of workers within an occupation; to offer facilities not otherwise available; to provide for new technological development. Subsequently these associations introduced examinations and sought to improve members' status.

Foundation of associations often failed to follow a simple chain of events: technological advance and/or commercial advancement—demand for personnel—organization of personnel. More important, such a notion ignores the variable time-lag between first appearance of personnel and ultimate organization. Sometimes formation anticipated an expanding demand in an occupational area, the establishment of specialists and consequent need for 'qualified people'. Occasionally further development of association justified the founders' foresight. At times, slow development of the association suggested the evident inability of the association to satisfy requirements for qualified personnel, or a false anticipation of need for organization.[15]

Millerson here insists on a variety of possibilities. The organization may anticipate, it may follow a given demand; it may be too much too soon, it may be too little too late. That is, Millerson believes that the link between full-time work (i.e., demand) and association may be emplotted in a variety of ways. In an earlier discussion, after illustrating the impossibility of a single plot, he lists the possible models (all functional) for the link leading to a successful qualifying association—to achieve or consolidate status or prestige, to break away or react to an existing association, to coordinate existing practitioners, and to respond to utterly new occupational possibilities.

This diversity in part reflects the complexity of the British professions. But it also reflects several decisions Millerson has made about how to tell his story. First, he does not accept the implicit self-interest model that unifies the professionalization narratives of Wilensky and Caplow. Self-interest is but one among a number of theoretically possible motives for action. Second, he uses a different strategy to assemble his data. Wilensky looked at a set of first facts across professions and made up a story to fit them. Caplow's model is clearly based on much the same process, using the stories of journalists, undertakers, junk dealers, and laboratory technicians. Millerson, on the contrary, begins not with the bare details of first facts, but with individual narratives, profession by profession, complete with standard historical accounts of motivation. He looks at all his organizational histories and sees four or five reasons why organizations were set up. Since he has no fundamental model of self-interest to tie all these reasons together, he leaves them as independent versions of the link from demand to organization. He employs a similar strategy in studying the link between schools and examinations.

Millerson's analysis also reminds us of the complexity involved in ordered social processes. Sometimes we see the present as independent of the past, a position Millerson follows with regard to professional ethics. Sometimes we see the present as uniquely determined by the past; a profession has only one place to go next from where it is now, only one career to follow. This career model is the one chosen by Caplow and to a lesser extent by Wilensky. Millerson, on the other hand, generally uses the less-restrictive idea of contingent development. Even though the past shapes the future, there are several outcomes for any professional present. The next event after professional association may be licensing, examinations, or an ethics code. The important questions are which one and why.

Millerson despairs of finding a single story of professionalization. "The resounding impression is of individual uniqueness, tempered by an adjustment to the social and educational climate of the time."[16] For some authors, this "individual uniqueness" is in fact directly attributable to "the social and educational climate of the time." One such is Magali Larson.

Larson tells the story of professionalization in a new way. The difference lies in her use of time. For Wilensky, Caplow, and Millerson, professions develop in abstract time. With the exception of the "tempering" just mentioned, this time has no properties of its own that condition the development of professions. In contrast, for Larson such properties are central forces of professionalization. Some professions developed in aristocratic societies, some in democratic ones, still others under corporate capitalism and bureaucracy. The course of professionalization varies in each regime. The larger story determines the time, the conditions, and the structures through which professionalization takes place.[17]

In general form, Larson's stories follow not the convergence plot, but rather a stages-approaching-a-steady-state plot. The steady state is elite status. Larson's central subjects are elites of practitioners, which seek personal rewards through collective mobility. There is no particular content to her generic story of professionalization. Any organizational pattern (association, licensing, etc.) that furthers corporate reward is a logical next step, provided that it is possible within the larger context of the society. Thus the causal links are functional, but their content is determined by the societal context.

Despite Larson's unusual handling of time, however, her story of professionalization still draws on the standard repertory of techniques for telling the story. It is useful to summarize the alternatives available in that repertory. First, stories may assume a central subject of narrative and follow it, or they may chronicle the creation and dissolution of such a subject. Stories proceed by joining a series of specified situations with links that describe the successive resolution of each situation. These links are usually drawn from a limited set of basic models for why things occur in society—functional, historicist, evolutionary, and so on. Underlying these links is often a single simplifying assumption about why events occur, such as the self-interest model. In putting these links together, social stories take a variety of approaches to the order of events—making it sometimes essential to their outcome, sometimes irrelevant, sometimes partway in between. They also take a variety of approaches to issues of convergence and divergence—some of them recounting the emergence of a steady state like "full professionalization," others the development of oscillation or imbalance. Tellers of social stories also have metaphors for generalizing these stories. Some employ the metaphor of career or life course, searching for a single typical sequence. Others employ more open-ended link-by-link models, using an implicit metaphor of conversation or interaction as their model for sequences.

This somewhat literary analysis allows us to separate the formal from the substantive diversity of professionalization theories. Some of the choices made in analyzing patterns like professionalization we regard as substantive—the choice of an underlying self-interest model, or of functional models for links, or of particular structures (e.g., ethics codes) serving a given function. In past discussions of professionalization, these substantive aspects have sometimes been the focus of attention. But other choices we see as purely formal, like the choice of a central subject and a plot form, and it is important to recognize that many incompatibilities among theories of professionalization arise out of these formal decisions. The "proletarianization of professions" arguments are classic examples. Their central subject is professionals as an occupational class, rather than professions qua social groups. Yet they have been held to reject the concept of professionalization. What they have in fact rejected, or rather qualified, is a certain version of the professionalization argument, the version in which the motive forces of the story are the external rewards professionalization provides to individual professionals. Other versions, with different driving forces, are completely unaffected.[18]

These formal differences in theories of professionalization exacerbate the enduring substantive differences, some of which I noted in outlining the history of studies of professions. It is important to recall those substantive differences here. I earlier distinguished studies of professions in terms of their locus of analysis (individual or society) and the consequences of professionalism they studied (internal or external.) I shall classify substantive views of professionalization slightly differently, although again in four basic categories. The four versions can be called the functional, structural, monopolist, and cultural concepts of professionalization. The functional version was the first of these, dominant in the writings of Carr-Saunders and Wilson, Marshall, and Parsons. Profession was here a means to control the asymmetric expert-client relation. Professionalization was simply the evolution of structural guarantees for that control.[19]

In the structuralist writers—three of whom I have just discussed (Millerson, Wilensky, Caplow)—the functions disappeared and the structure alone remained. Profession was merely a form of occupational control; the content of work and the expert-client relation were less important. Professionalization here became an explanation of why the professions displayed such diverse properties; the answer was that some had not finished professionalizing. The explicit focus on structure and its evolution led to theories about the historical forces driving the structure, and hence the structuralists developed the explicit models of professionalization here analyzed.[20]

The monopoly school saw the same structural developments, but attributed them not to a "natural growth," but to a desire for dominance or authority. Professions were corporate groups with "mobility projects" aimed at control of work. For Larson and others, as I have noted, this control was interesting for its influence on the status and power of professions; Freidson was more interested in its effect on such social functions as healing or justice. This school attributed the pattern of professionalization to larger, external social processes—the rise of bureaucracy in Larson, the shift from professionalism to mediation in Johnson. The actual sequence of structures (association, school, etc.) became less important than the sequence of functions they served (identification, exclusion, etc.).[21]

Some recent studies have moved away from the focus on structural regularity that marked prior work on professionalization. Bledstein, Haskell, and others have emphasized the cultural authority of professions, returning to the Parsonian fascination with expertise as a social relation. By making cultural legitimation a central process in professionalization, these writers have set a new criterion for the "professionality" of occupations, replacing the old one of organizational similarity to law and medicine. As I noted before, Bledstein has connected this cultural authority directly to individual decisions for mobility.[22]

Given such diversity, both formal and substantive, it may seem hard to consider the validity of professionalization arguments in general. Wilensky's regular sequence of organizations is a far cry from Bledstein's rise of a "metaphor and means" for vertical mobility. But it is essential that we do consider whether the general professionalization argument can be successfully defended. The various views can in fact be synthesized into a general concept of professionalization, as follows:

Expert, white-collar occupations evolve towards a particular structural and cultural form of occupational control. The structural form is called profession and consists of a series of organizations for association, for control, and for work. (In its strong form, the professionalization concept argues that these organizations develop in a certain order.) Culturally, professions legitimate their control by attaching their expertise to values with general cultural legitimacy, increasingly the values of rationality, efficiency, and science.

This synthetic professionalization concept has some powerful successes to its credit. As sociological concepts go, it is relatively coherent and its terms relatively well-defined. In the strong (structural) form especially, the organizations and their sequence were particularly easy to measure and surprisingly comparable from case to case. The concept's focus on expertise referred directly to general theories of occupational control. Moreover, not only was professionalization well behaved theoretically and operationally, it also had no small empirical power. The major British and American professions seemed to follow it relatively well, although organization-based professions like the military and the clergy created some problems. As I noted, Wilensky tested the strong form on a sizable sample of American groups and found great regularity in the sequence of organizations.

At the same time, the professionalization concept has had some grave difficulties. First, it turns out that the results of Wilensky's strong form test were largely artifactual. Second, more than a decade of historical case studies shows that most of its underlying assumptions are false.

To test Wilensky's argument, I have studied the order of eight events in 130 American and British professions. My analysis splits occupations studied into three groups: recognized free professions (about 20 each in both America and Britain), subordinate professions (again about 20 in each case), and an "other" group containing various pseudo and would-be professions. The events ordered were:
1. First (national) professional association
2. First governmentally sponsored licensing legislation
3. First professional examinations
4. First professional school separate from some other profession
5. First university-based professional education
6. First ethics code
7. First national-level journal

8. First accreditation of schools (U.S.) or certification by association
   (England)

The data were gathered from a wide variety of sources and were, of course, incomplete in many cases. (Missing data does not, however, bias the results, given the methods used.) The analysis proceeded by finding mean "distances" between the events under a variety of metrics (e.g., real time, log time) and then using these distances to establish an "order of professionalization." I applied a simple one-dimensional scaling algorithm to find that order. The results were that there is possibly a regular order among the American free and subordinate professions, but none among the American other category or among any of the three British categories.[23]

Perhaps more importantly, analysis of the assumptions of this formalization of Wilensky's approach shows that the results cannot help but be artifactual. Since there is one major, national professional association but, in many professions, dozens of schools, it is inevitable by probability theory alone that the first school will precede the association. Similarly, Wilensky found university education to follow separate schooling not because it necessarily did, but because he included university schooling as a subset of separate education generally. Thus, the date of the first separate school was either that of the first university school or that of the first nonuniversity school, should one exist. It was therefore inevitable that the "separate school" event should appear, generally, before the university school event. There is in fact no real empirical support for the strong form hypothesis that the organizations seen in professionalization arrive in a particular sequence.[24]

The empirical problems of the strong form hypothesis of professionalization would not be so important were it not for the evidence accumulating against the underlying assumptions of the concept itself. There are five basic assumptions hidden in my synthetic concept of professionalization. The first is that change is unidirectional; professions evolve towards a given form, structurally and culturally. Second, the evolution of individual professions does not explicitly depend on that of others; professionalization can be treated case by case. Third, the social structure and cultural claims of professions are more important than the work professions do; the latter is unmentioned in theoretical studies of professionalization, although it makes obligatory appearances in case studies. Fourth, professions are homogeneous units; what internal differentiation they possess reflects contingencies of the "professionalization project." Fifth, professionalization as a process does not change with time; although a description of history, it lacks a history of its own. Of course particular writers have avoided various of these assumptions. Nonetheless, this summary captures the concept as it is generally used.

The assumption of unidirectionality has been attacked by both sociological theorists and historians. The theorists have come up with deprofessionalization and proletarianization to refer to the apparent decrease in professional legitimacy and autonomy on the one hand and to the lessening benefits of professionalism for the members of the professions on the other. The historians have studied numerous professional or pseudoprofessional groups that have stalled or even died on the high road of professionalization—psychological mediums, electrotherapists and railway surgeons, computer "coders," midwives. They have studied amalgamation, among British nineteenth-century doctors and among twentieth-century social workers, and also division, among twentieth century British doctors and among social and religious workers in America. In short, there are clearly a variety of directions for development, and development towards strong control is but one of them.[25]

The assumption that one profession's development is independent of another's is threatened implicitly but no less strongly. It is true that most work on professions continues to be done on a profession-by-profession basis. But evidence available in this very work questions such a procedure strongly. Much work on subprofessions in the medical area emphasizes the interdependence of professional development, as do the cases of American psychiatry and social work, of the various types of engineers, of law and accounting. Books on individual professions spend much of their time on interprofessional relations, but none draws the obvious moral that interprofessional relations are potentially the central feature of professional development.[26]

The assumption that structure is more important than actual work is, like unidirectionality, an aspect of the sociological theory challenged by historical work. Sociological work on professions, including much of the power literature of the last decade, pays little attention to the actual work that is done and the expertise used to do it. Freidson's work is a striking exception. Historical study, by contrast, has emphasized the actual work performed. In professions as diverse as librarianship, engineering, psychiatry, and the clergy, historians have shown the intimate relation of professional structure and culture to work itself. The sociological theorists have not learned from this that work must be the focus of a concept of professional development.[27]

Ignoring internal differentiation in professions has helped the professionalization concept simplify what it has to explain. But recent work implies that this assumption, too, is dangerous. Sociologists themselves have contributed analyses of differences in intraprofessional prestige, in locations of work, in access to professional power. While sociologists have not in general connected these internal patterns to patterns of professional development, historians have done so, in studies of the legal profession, of engineering, of medicine. The development of internal differences is bound directly to the development of professionalism. [28]

Finally, the assumption that professionalization is a general process without any history of its own has been challenged forcefully by the sociological theorists themselves, particularly Johnson and Larson. Both noted that the increasing involvement of the state reshaped professionalization, as did the general drift towards bureaucratic practice. These lessons were regarded as long overdue by both the historians and the sociologists studying Continental professions, for the changes described by Larson and Johnson brought the unusual professions of England and America more in line with the model of professionalism long dominant in France and Germany. [29]

On balance, then, the evidence argues for a new approach to professional development to replace the general professionalization concept. There is, of course, great diversity in professionalization theories. Much of it, as I have argued, is formal diversity. There are many theories claiming to be general theories about professional development that are in fact special theories of this or that aspect of it, and even the general theories often pose their analyses in fundamentally different narrative terms. And there are wide differences in the substance of these general theories—in the driving mechanisms they posit, in the pattern of causation they adopt, in the particular structures they emphasize. Yet most professionalization theories follow a common approach to their subject, what I called the synthetic theory. This synthetic theory, despite the strong support that many case studies give it, has profound shortcomings. A serious empirical test rejects it. More importantly, its basic assumptions have all been overthrown by recent empirical work. These problems imply that the case study support is more illusory than real.

In the chapters that follow I will propose an alternative theory that reverses the problematic assumptions of professionalization theories. The alternative assumptions begin with a focus on work. The central problem with the current concept of professionalization is its focus on structure rather than work. It is the content of the professions' work that the case studies tell us is changing. It is control of work that brings the professions into conflict with each other and makes their histories interdependent. It is differentiation in types of work that often leads to serious differentiation within the professions. By switching from a focus on the organizational structures of professions to a focus on groups with common work we replace several of the problematic assumptions at once.

The central phenomenon of professional life is thus the link between a profession and its work, a link I shall call jurisdiction. To analyze professional development is to analyze how this link is created in work, how it is anchored by formal and informal social structure, and how the interplay of jurisdictional links between professions determines the history of the individual professions themselves.

## Cases of Professional Development

To illustrate the complexities that any theory of professional development must handle, I shall give in the remainder of this chapter some examples of that process. These examples represent the much larger collection of case studies that I am trying to explain. Such exemplary vignettes embody a compromise between several ways of approaching the data. A positivist would reduce all these histories to coded facts and present them as dependent variables. A theorist would present an exemplary case at length and delineate the mechanisms at play within it. I wish to balance these contrary imperatives. On the one hand, the diversity of the professions warrants a narrative presentation of contrasting cases. On the other, we must abstract from such cases and generate testable ideas. My compromise is to illustrate the problems of explanation with these brief pictures.[30]

Let us begin with the familiar case of American medicine.[31] Like many American professions, medicine had two waves of professionalizing activity. The first, which began a little before the Revolution, saw the founding of a few early schools, the passage of some exclusive state licensing laws, and the creation and empowerment of some local and state societies. The Jacksonian era struck down this exclusivism and opened the gates of competition. A variety of sectarian and folk healers appeared. Among these were the homeopaths, who espoused, among other novel ideas, the practice of not killing patients with treatment. This practice, and the good results that attended it, made the homeopaths rather dangerous adversaries to "regular medicine." There ensued an intense war over who had the right to cure people. Each side claimed the legitimacy of science, debated the safety of the public, and attacked its opponents in editorials and speeches. The regulars devised exclusionary ethics rules requiring a dying patient to dismiss an attending irregular as a condition of their own attention. In this, its

darkest hour, regular medicine at last saw fit to found its national association. By the late nineteenth century, the regulars were fortified
by the new scientific medicine from Europe. Although concerned with
diagnosis, etiology, and pathology more than with treatment, European medicine claimed a few spectacular therapeutic successes that
underscored its abstract power. Thus reinforced, the regulars started
a national journal, revised their ethics, and began to reform their
schools. From the homeopaths they had learned to avoid heroic treatment, and the two groups united around the turn of the century to
fight off new outside threats—the osteopaths and later the chiropractors. In a whirlwind of reform from above, the nebulous world of proprietary medical schools, patent medicine, and unregulated practice
vanished under the clear organization radiating from a powerful, nationally united profession. The community general hospital, the foundation organization of modern medicine, developed rapidly. Although
generally fearful of state intervention, American medicine profited immensely from the formation of public and private insurance schemes,
which guaranteed its income and professional dominance. By midcentury it had assumed a position of social prominence and power envied
throughout the occupational world. Included in its vast organizational
empire were a host of subordinate professional groups.

The case of American medicine shows how complicated and interwoven are the questions about what professions do and how they interrelate. If one aims to "find the origins of" American medicine, then
the homeopaths are an outside force that enters the picture, fights with
the protagonist, and then unites with it. But such an interpretation
ignores the virtual dissolution of regular medicine under the Jacksonian onslaught. The "doing of healing" became a free-for-all. The protagonist itself is not a continuous entity. Development, activity, and
interprofessional relations are bound up together.

The medical profession's absolute control of bodily ills required de-
fensive work on a number of borders. Perhaps the most important of
these borders was the hazy one between bodily and mental ailments.
Here emerged a second professional group, organizationally a part of
medicine but intellectually and practically separate from it. This second sketch, of American psychiatry, shows again how complex and in-
tertwined is the web of professional development. (I will give a sustained analysis of this case in chapter 10.)[32]

Psychiatry began when a group of enterprising medical reformers
argued in the early nineteenth century that madmen ought to be removed from the jurisdiction of the legal authorities and placed under
that of the medical profession. Madmen are sick, they said; give them

to us and we will cure them. A new theory and therapy justified the shift, and private bodies and state legislatures were soon dotting the countryside with insane asylums. Psychiatry was the profession of the superintendents of these institutions. (Nonsuperintendents were finally admitted to the organized profession in the 1880s.) Like teaching and social work, and unlike its parent, medicine, psychiatry thus arose out of an organizational form—the hospital for the insane. An association, journal, and official principles sprang simultaneously into being in the mid-1840s, about the same time as the AMA was founded. Throughout the latter half of the century, psychiatry was an elite profession, its members exceeding most of their medical brethren in income, power, and prestige. But the latter half of the century also brought decline. The early hopes of cure proved illusory; the psychiatrists gradually became administrators of custodial warehouses.

Meanwhile, the jurisdiction that would ultimately become psychiatry's was being explored by other pioneers, the neurologists. From their bloody baptism in the field hospitals of the Civil War, these men emerged to become general consulting specialists, helping their medical colleagues with perplexing cases. They took from other physicians any patient whose otherwise untreatable illness could somehow be related to "nerves." Under this conveniently vague heading, they collected the misfits whose recalcitrant illnesses impugned the new efficacy of medicine. Heavily influenced by German medicine, they were skeptical of treatment in general, and when cures were discovered, as for the "nervous" endocrine diseases, they at once returned the diseases to general medical jurisdiction. The neurologists developed their association, journals, and university teaching positions during the second wave of medical professionalization.

But they soon found themselves overwhelmed by the horde of "nervous" patients other physicians referred to them. These patients had few but perplexing organic symptoms; for the most part the problem seemed to be "in their minds." As a result, neurologists and psychiatrists began to handle this jurisdiction together, the neurologists defining the patients by their lack of response to standard treatment, the psychiatrists seeing them as incipiently insane. For about twenty years after the turn of the century the two groups interpenetrated. Then in a sudden shift, they divided. The term "neurologist" came to refer to organic physicians generally working in hospitals. Psychiatrists took over the neurologists' old position as the outpatient border guards of the medical profession, handling the symptoms and diseases that seemed not quite real. At the same time, they began to accept direct referrals from the lay community.

The direct referrals reflected the psychiatrists' rapid, entreprenuerial expansion into areas of social control long dominated by other professions. With the help of a popular front organization, the National Committee on Mental Hygiene, psychiatrists in the twenties tried to seize control over juvenile delinquency, alcoholism, industrial unrest, marital strife, and numerous other areas. This brought them into violent competition with the clergy and the law among the older professions, and psychology and social work among the newer ones. Intellectually, the psychiatrists routed all but the law, although their numbers were too small to take more than a supervisory role in the jurisdictions they seized. The profession continued uncontested until the sudden expansion of demand for psychotherapy in the 1970s found it so understaffed that psychology and social work penetrated the third party payment schemes that had so long protected its monopoly.

The story of psychiatry is thus a different one from that of medicine generally. The profession began with an organization. It rushed through the formalities of professionalization—association, journal, code—in a decade. It changed jurisdiction almost completely over its 150-year history. Again we see that the central questions of how professions develop are tied up with questions of interprofessional relations and the content of professional activity. Professionalization occurs, to be sure, but in a context that helps determine its course. A comprehensive theory of professional life must deal with these complex facts of jurisdictional competition and interprofessional relations. This can be seen even more clearly in the British professions.

Unlike American professions of the late eighteenth century, their contemporaries in England were not dominated by a metropolis distant in space, but by traditions distant in time. Law in particular could trace its origins to the personal councils of the first Plantagenets.[33] The schools and associations of the Bar, the Inns of Court, had lost their records so long before that no one knew how old they were. Even less was known about the Inns of Chancery, in which were collected many members of the lower branches of the profession, the ancestors of the present solicitors. The profession had an intricate hierarchy, as befitted its semiofficial origins, but can be loosely understood as having three levels in each of a number of jurisdictions. The three levels were distinguished by function, the highest being that of judging, the next that of oral argument, the third that of representing or appearing for a litigant. Each court had its own jurisdiction and its own names for these levels—serjeants, barristers, and solicitors in common law; chancellor, barristers, and attorneys in equity; judges, doctors, and proctors in the civil law courts of Admiralty and Arches. (The last was the chief ecclesiastical court, which until the 1870s had jurisdiction over all family matters other than property.)

The common law and equity professions of the late eighteenth century were in some senses more appearance than reality. The Inns of Court, which had at times been vibrant, active organizations, were at low ebb. Education was moribund; barristers and others learned their work on the job. Discipline was exercised, very occasionally, by the courts and the administrative committees of the Inns, the Benchers. Despite this apparent indolence, the common lawyers of this period had just won a signal professional victory over the better-educated and more formally professional doctors of civil law. Under the leadership of Mansfield and the other great common law judges, they had over the preceding two centuries stolen the entire commercial jurisdiction from the Admiralty courts and made it part of common law.

The security of the barristers was upset by a revolution from below. The attorneys and solicitors built in the early nineteenthth century a national association (really a metropolitan one, for most legal business was done in London), which undertook what we would now call serious professionalization. It mandated a formal apprenticeship, prepared a careful list of authorized practitioners, imposed professional examinations, and began a serious and careful professional discipline. It also fought for, and won, a monopoly of the newly lucrative business of conveyancing (property transfer). The barristers responded by consolidating their own absolute monopoly of verbal pleading, which had been granted several centuries before over the intense objections of the lower branches. They removed their last competitors, the moribund serjeants, consolidated the jurisdictions of their courts, and reaffirmed the old rule that all judges be barristers. As for professionalization in the modern sense, they did less than nothing. By the mid-twentieth century there was still no single list of authorized barristers, no national association, no central disciplinary body. The educational activities of the Inns continued nonexistent. Although the English universities now gave bachelor's degrees in common law, passing the bar was still a matter of sitting terms at the Inns and enduring a vague apprenticeship. Unlike the physicians, their counterparts in the British nineteenth-century medical hierarchy, the barristers never made peace with or absorbed their competitors from below.[34]

The solicitors, as the more adventurous branch of the profession, faced numerous challenges after their formal professionalization. They early began to give general business and financial advice. Since their services were generally required for formal business activity, this area was a natural zone of expansion. The expansion had a number of interesting effects. First, the slow growth imposed on the profession by its own strict standards meant that it was overwhelmed by the welter of commercial and real estate work that was generated by business expansion. In consequence, its chief jurisdictional monopoly, conveyancing, had by this century been delegated to a subordinate professional group, the managing clerks, who did the work under the very loose supervision of solicitors. This internal subordination of routine work is a characteristic strategy of professions claiming more jurisdiction than they can effectively serve, American medicine being the best example.

From the outside, however, solicitors faced competition from a new profession focused directly on money itself. Emerging in the early nineteenth century, this new group, the accountants, began in Scotland as a branch of the legal profession, and in England as an outgrowth of laws requiring formal audits of the new joint-stock companies.[35] Sorting out the financial tangles of bankruptcy and liquidation was in fact the chief activity of accountants in those early days of entrepreneurial individualism. As commercial affairs became more regular and bankruptcies less frequent, accountants in England moved to monopolize the business of auditing. Unlike their later American counterparts, they did relatively little in the area of cost accounting—working within firms to tell managers how, why, and whether they were actually making money. In the area of financial advice and corporate restructuring, accountants and solicitors reached an uneasy truce. Each had its own home turf; this area between was often one of conflict.

The accountants developed national and local organizations simultaneously around 1880. Their journal dates from the same period, as do their strict disciplinary practices and their examinations for entrance. Accounting education was supervised and regulated by the national society, although it took place in the characteristically British setting of articled clerkship with a member of the profession. Like the solicitors, the chartered accountants in fact had far more business than their slow growth could handle, and soon were forced to tolerate at least one group of less educated and certified competitors, the Incorporated Accountants. (The continued exclusivism of the Chartered and Incorporated Accountants means that many other groups of accountants are organized outside these leaders of the profession.) In the present century, the profession underwent a further change, in this case a divergent one. Accounting firms continued to depend on corporate auditing work. But the conglomeration of industries led to the replacement of local with conglomerate accountants. There resulted a rapid division of the accounting world into a very few giant, transnational firms, auditing transnational commercial organizations, and a large number of individuals and small partnerships doing a completely different local business.

The case of English accounting provides a particularly good example of how professionalization in the narrow sense of acquiring an association, education, licensure, and even state-sanctioned monopoly is merely the outward form of successful professional life. The accountants profited from the earlier examples of the solicitors, apothecaries, and surgeons, and created all the proper attributes of professionalism in short order. What really determined the history of the profession was the development and shift of its jurisdiction—from bankruptcy to auditing, with gradual expansion into cost accounting and now into "management services." Here, too, we see a number of other characteristic developments of professional life—the competition from below, the gradual molding of profession to clientele, the maintenance of a strategic heartland monopoly. Yet at the same time accounting showed its willingness for head-on competition—with law over the definition of profit, with law and banking over the jurisdiction of business advice, with management over the provision of staff services. There is much more here than is told by the simple image of professionalization.

But even more troubling questions about the way professions develop and interrelate arise when one leaves the familiar Anglo-American success stories and studies either the continental professions with their civil-servant character or the failed professions that litter our own history.

In France, the new effects arise because professional life is overshadowed by the state. While independent competition still takes place, and independent professional evolution occurs, both aim immediately at the achievement of certain status with the state. The absolute, centralized, and rationalized character of French government led it to take a decisive role in organizing occupations both before and after the Revolution. As a result, developed professions all tend to look alike in structure. At the same time, protoprofessions tend to be ignored altogether; things unrecognized by the state seem unimportant.

Thus, the French legal profession, while in some ways reminiscent of the English one, differs from it in essential ways.[36] In the first place, it is broken up into a different set of jurisdictions, with different relations between them. (I am here presenting the profession in its pre-1972 form. The fusion of that year merged *avocats* and *avoués* and created a new group of *conseils juridiques* out of the old *agréés*.) *Avocats*, tracing their roots well back into medieval times, are roughly analogous to barristers. They are organized into bars under each different court, and their tacit monopoly of oral pleading in many courts was made formal in the Napoleonic Code. But they are unlike the English Bar in many ways. They share their self-disciplinary function with the courts, as the British have not since the Middle Ages. Indeed, the French courts have on occasion reorganized their bars completely. The Bar was abolished altogether during the early years of the Revolution and was reinstated with some reluctance by Napoleon, who detested lawyers. The *avocats* are also unlike the barristers in their requirement of university legal education and formal attendance at court, requirements for admission to the bar dating from before the sixteenth century. Under the Old Regime they seldom if ever became judges in higher courts, and in the modern French profession the *magistrats* are a separate group with separate educational requirements. This is precisely the opposite of the British situation, where barristers monopolize the bench in the higher courts.

Beyond the *avocats*, the French legal profession looked in 1970 as if it had no history. Its major branches all had the same structure and traced that structure to the lucid clarity of laws governing public officials. The various branches were separated by jurisdiction. The *avoués* appeared for their clients; they filed forms and motions and shepherded the cases through the court. The *notaires* recorded formal documents and conducted the transactions so recorded, thus controlling marriage, property transfer, probate, and other jurisdictions controlled by attorneys in England and lawyers in America. *Huissiers* served official papers and levied executions, both for courts and for private parties, combining what in America would be the functions of process servers, bailiffs, and collection agents. *Greffiers* kept court records and other official documents, particularly those pertaining to businesses. All of these jurisdictions were formalized in legislation or decree. So also was the professional structure. Each group (or *ordre*) was organized into local (*départementale*), regional, and national *chambres*. These bodies were officially charged by the state with keeping records and rolls, with originating disciplinary action and administering court regulations, with running the welfare systems for the *ordre*, and with governing conditions for subordinate workers. The Code also set educational requirements for the various orders. Perhaps the most astonishing aspect of the regulations of these professional groups, to the Anglo-American observer, is their formal provision for the purchase of office. Each member of these groups of *officiers ministériels* bought his position when he entered the profession and sold it (or bequeathed it) when he left it. The price was normally from four to ten times the annual income. The state thus had indirect control over the number of these officials, as well as over their behavior.

Two things happened as the legal profession evolved within this set structure. First, de facto changes reshaped the official structure. While *notaires* are not required to have law degrees, most in fact do. *Avoués* typically have the second (*licencié*), not the first (*capacité*), degree in law, as they are required. Second, informal groups have emerged serving new jurisdictions unforeseen in Napoleonic times. These have been regulated extemporaneously by the courts involved during the prolonged period in which practitioners agitated for state recognition. When state recognition came, these new groups became, overnight, indistinguishable in structure from the other branches. Among the groups emerging in this way were the *agréés*, a group of *avocats, notaires,* and *hommes d'affaires* who began to represent parties in the commercial courts in the mid-nineteenth century. They were accepted (hence the name *agréé*) and listed officially by those courts. Having arisen out of an open professional competition, they were formally regulated in 1941, acquiring an examination, court-shared discipline, purchased offices, and national, regional, and local governing bodies, like the other branches. Similar groups are the *commissaires-priseurs*, who monopolize judicially ordered appraisal and auction, the as-yet unregulated *arbitres-rapporteurs*, who examine accounts and attempt conciliation in commercial cases, and the *syndics administrateurs judiciaires et liquidateurs judiciaires*, who handle bankruptcy and receivership (regulated in 1955). In most cases, one individual can hold only one of these titles, although *avoués* and others may be enrolled as *syndics*. All of these groups possess voluntary associations that long antedate the state *chambres* that presently govern them, associations that indeed did the lobbying that brought state regulation about. With the coming of that regulation, however, the voluntary groups seem somewhat eclipsed.

The legal profession in France thus presents a different version of professional development and interrelations from what we have seen so far. Development here means development toward official status. Interprofessional relations means regulated jurisdiction. Yet before regulation and in the informal realities after it, professional development continues in hidden ways. These ways are channeled and influenced by state structures, but are in some ways independent of them. An effective theory of professional development must therefore be general enough to deal with the fact of intense state participation in professionalization.

It must also be wide enough to embrace the phenomenon of professional death. We are so fascinated with the success of American medicine, in particular, that we forget the specialized, knowledge-based occupations that have disappeared. Some have gone because the organization or technology that created them has disappeared. The railroad professions and protoprofessions—dispatchers, agents, surgeons—are one such example. Had they developed knowledge that abstracted beyond the world of the railroad, they might have survived its fall. But dispatching did not become what we now think of as operations research, even though its central task was essentially under the jurisdiction now held by that profession. Because they lacked abstraction, dispatchers died with their technology. Another such group are the itinerant entertainers—musicians, dancing masters, singing teachers—whose numbers have been decimated by the centralization of entertainment through the mass media. (Local entertainment resurfaced, of course, but only through finding a foundation in the profession of public school teaching.)[37]

A good case of professional death is that of the psychological mediums. Mediums flourished in the latter nineteenth century as the professional embodiment of spiritualism. After the turn of the century, spiritualism, insofar as it survived at all, became an organized church of the afterlife, complete with congregations and ministers. But for fifty years its banner was carried by a group of mediums several hundred strong.

The medium's skill was her ability to encourage, through passivity and openness, effective communication between her audience and the inhabitants of the spiritual world. The first followers of the calling began in the 1850s, although Mesmerism, Swedenborgianism, and a variety of other predecessors had prepared the way. The weekly journal of the mediums, *Banner of Light*, appeared from 1857 to 1907. The Mediums Mutual Aid Society, aiming at instruction and support of all using mediumistic powers, was founded in 1860. A variety of client and support groups such as the National Organization of Spiritualists flourished briefly and discussed, in vain, the problem of regulating the charlatans. An official school of mediumship was founded by Morris Pratt at Whitewater, Wisconsin.

It is important to realize that mediumship fits the basic definition of a profession very well. It applied a set of esoteric skills to particular cases. Certainly it possessed all the organizational paraphernalia of a profession—school, association, attempted regulation. It is important, too, to recall that many well-known Americans patronized mediums and that spiritualism was perceived as a kind of "scientized" religion. As R. L. Moore has pointed out, mediums enabled people to undertake major decisions without impugning existing states of social affairs or assuming full personal responsibility. It was a jurisdiction that psychiatry was later to stumble into, and indeed a number of psychiatry's early battles were fought with mediums and their descendants the spiritualist healers.[38]

In reflecting about the development of professions, then, we must develop answers that tell us why mediumship grew the way it did and why it died so quickly. The answers that spring to mind are not very helpful. It is useless saying spiritualism was a ridiculous waste of time since the mediums simply couldn't deliver results. Neither could nineteenth century medicine. Nor is it helpful to identify "external" factors —the rise of science, the liberalizing of Protestantism, the recognition of the psyche. For these are all intimately tied to other competing professions—the clergy, the psychiatrists and neurologists, the academic psychologists who took over psychic research. So that even while a model of professional development must take account of such external factors, it must also see their direct embodiment in interprofessional relations.

These brief examples show some of the breathtaking diversity of professional life. It has been easy to mistake American medicine for the paradigm. In reality the professions are a diverse lot—winners and losers, public officials and private individuals, autocrats and subordinates. Many a profession has gone from rags to riches, not a few the other way. Many claimants have never found a niche in the system at all. Yet all these are a part of professional life. Beyond this diversity, these examples show how the development of the formal attributes of a profession is bound up with the pursuit of jurisdiction and the besting of rival professions. The organizational formalities of professions are meaningless unless we understand their context. This context always relates back to the power of the professions' knowledge systems, their abstracting ability to define old problems in new ways. Abstraction enables survival. It is with abstraction that law and accounting fought frontally over tax advice, the one because it writes the laws, the other because it defines what the prescribed numbers mean. It is with abstractions that psychiatry stole the neurotics from neurology, the abstractions of its fancy new Freudianism. It is with abstraction that American medicine claims all of deviance, the abstraction of its allpowerful disease metaphor.[39]

Finally, these vignettes have introduced some of my cast of characters. Much of the book involves theoretical statements that make it easy to forget the historical events they abstract. To me these events, case by case, profession by profession, are the test of the enterprise.

One cannot build an argument that works in every case. But one must build an argument that works for most. Case studies of professions are both the raw material of the theory and the audience that says thumbs up or down. It is important that the reader begin to make their acquaintance.

# I  WORK, JURISDICTION
AND COMPETITION

In part 1, I will offer a theoretical alternative to professionalization
that accounts for idiosyncratic developments in individual professions
without invoking a societal trend. This theory is based on ideas already sketched in the Introduction. Each profession is bound to a set
of tasks by ties of jurisdiction, the strengths and weaknesses of these
ties being established in the processes of actual professional work.
Since none of these links is absolute or permanent, the professions
make up an interacting system, an ecology. Professions compete
within this system, and a profession's success reflects as much the situations of its competitors and the system structure as it does the
profession's own efforts. From time to time, tasks are created, abolished, or reshaped by external forces, with consequent jostling and
readjustment within the system of professions. Thus, larger social
forces have their impact on individual professions through the structure within which the professions exist, rather than directly. My
theory is thus partway between the old case study approach and the
"new class" approach. Professions are never seen alone, but they are
also not replaced by a single encompassing category of "the professions." They exist in a system.

   The next three chapters set forth this argument. In chapter 2
I show how professional work helps determine the vulnerability of
professional tasks to competitor interference. Since professions compete by taking over each other's tasks, it is essential to know how professional work constitutes those tasks and how that process determines vulnerability. In chapter 3 I discuss the social tie of jurisdiction
that binds profession and task—a recognized right, a legitimate link
between the two. I discuss this link in detail, replacing earlier sim-

plistic views of control with a more flexible model allowing for different types and levels of jurisdiction. I consider the actual claiming of jurisdiction—where the claims are made, what different kinds of claims are made, and how they depend on professional structure.

Jurisdiction is a more-or-less exclusive claim. One profession's jurisdiction preempts another's. Because jurisdiction is exclusive, every move in one profession's jurisdictions affects those of others. It is this interacting pattern that I take up in chapter 4. There I show how a variety of forces, some internal to professions, some external to the whole professional world, and some inherent in the system itself, lead to disturbances in the system. I investigate how these disturbances propagate, how they are absorbed. I discuss the conditions underlying amalgamation and division of professions, and the impact of the central variable of abstraction on interprofessional relations.

Throughout these chapters, I give short examples from relevant cases. In order to facilitate the theoretical exposition, I have reserved extensive analysis of particular cases to part III. Each of the chapters in part III considers a single case study and emphasizes concepts from a particular chapter in part I: chapter 8 draws heavily on chapter 4, chapter 9 on chapter 3, and chapter 10 on chapter 2. The analyses of part III do make extensive use of concepts from other chapters, however, and so are best read after the six theoretical chapters. However, those in search of extended illustrations may want to glance at the relevant chapter in part III after reading each of three following chapters.

# 2        Professional Work

For some, the relation between professions and their work is simple. There is a map of tasks to be done and an isomorphic map of people doing them. Function is structure. But the reality is more complex; the tasks, the professions, and the links between them change continually. To some extent, these changes arise beyond the professional world. Technology, politics, and other social forces divide tasks and regroup them. They inundate one profession with recruits while uprooting the institutional foundations of another. But one cannot analyze external effects without first studying the internal dynamics they disturb. We must therefore examine the tasks of professions, the groups that carry them out, and the changing links that bind one to the other. We shall see that the foundations of interprofessional competition are laid in the very acts of professional work itself.[1]

## Objective and Subjective

The tasks of professions are human problems amenable to expert service. They may be problems for individuals, like sickness and salvation, or for groups, like fundraising and auditing. They may be disturbing problems to be cured, like vandalism or neurosis, or they may be creative problems to be solved, like a building design or a legislative program. The degree of resort to experts varies from problem to problem, from society to society, and from time to time.

Some problems are officially in expert hands in most societies. Sickness is an example. Others vary in their degree of expert service. The problem of meaning in life is highly expertized in most societies, but completely laicized in others; the contrast of Catholic religious experts with the Protestant priesthood of all believers is repeated periodically throughout the history of Christianity and the other world religions. The problem of finding a spouse has sometimes been in the hands of experts, the matchmakers. At other times, the families or individuals involved have controlled it. Now, experts are returning in the guise of the computer dating services. There is, in short, wide variation in assigning problems to experts. In American society, while experts commonly seize new problems, indeed find and label them, they shed their old problems with equal speed. The passage of once esoteric system knowledge from high-level programmers into the hands of lay microcomputer owners is a good example. While a few problems are in expert hands whatever the society or epoch, most shift around perpetually.[2]

Some problems are close to others. Problems, that is, can be imagined in an abstract space. Two kinds of properties make problems alike. Some are objective, given by natural or technological imperatives. Others are subjective, imposed by the present and past of a culture itself. It is often difficult to distinguish the two. For example, we think that fixing a broken thumb is "closer" to curing typhoid fever than it is to building a bridge, because of the common object of the first two tasks, the human body. But in purely theoretical terms, broken bones are close to bridges because both involve the science of mechanics. Indeed, the physicians who handled the fever and the surgeons who fixed the thumbs had little to do with one another before the nineteenth century. It is by no means certain that the body is an objective entity here, despite our intuition of its importance.

Sometimes tasks seem determined by their objective nature. Thus, the expert tasks involved in running a railroad, from driving the trains to dispatching them, always remained tied to the object itself. Even such potentially abstract tasks as dispatching never got off the train. By contrast, other tasks seem more subjectively shaped. Theology and musical composition, for example, are pure projections of the mind, imposed definitions of the meaning of life and of beautiful sound. There is little in their objects that limits or shapes them; they are purely cultural constructions.

But the real difference between the objective and subjective qualities of problems is a difference in amenability to cultural work. In the preceding chapter, I argued that professions sometimes use their abstract knowledge to reduce the work of competitors to a version of their own. This is a basic mechanism of interprofessional competition. The objective qualities of a task are those qualities that resist such reconstruction. Despite the normal connotations of the word, objective qualities are not a reality that awaits discovery beneath the cultural images; they are an inertia that reconstruction must overcome.[3]

Alcoholism provides a good example.[4] With hindsight, one can see that alcohol was made a serious social problem by the new regularity of the early industrial world, with its factory time and its standardized production. There was no place here for the fuddled execution, slow work, and relaxation that resulted from the then customary consumption of alcohol during the working day. At the same time, the industrial revolution early succeeded in mass producing spirits, making them more widely available than ever. The coincidence of the rising supply and the culturally induced decline in legitimate demand created "the problem of alcohol." Like all such problems, this one needed a location. At first Americans defined it as a moral and spiritual problem; ministers were the relevant experts. The doctors soon attacked, substituting the claim of cure for the clergyman's mere condemnation and forgiveness. In the late nineteenth century, the problem was pronounced a legal one, although the lawyers and the police dealt with alcoholism simply by incarcerating it. The psychiatrists also claimed alcoholism in this period. Experts lost the problem altogether when laymen reclaimed it as a political problem that could be abolished by legislation.

Through all of this alcoholism retained certain objective qualities. It always involved individual consumption of alcohol. Consumption always produced central nervous system depression with loss of fine and, ultimately, coarse motor and sensory function. But these objective aspects were often invisible. The first American temperance movement preceded the scientific discovery that spirits and wine involved the same chemical, and opposed itself only to spirits, urging a transfer of allegiance to wine and beer. It was not then evident that the biological manifestations of spirits consumption were identical with those of beer and wine consumption. Between the objective facts of alcohol consumption at various rates by various people and the subjective definition of alcoholism qua problem there is thus a long and tenuous relation.[5]

There are two easy, and erroneous, views of this relation. The first holds that problems are given facts and that varying perspectives on them are errors or ideologies. The second argues that problems have no objective reality whatsoever and are the simple creations of self-seeking groups. Neither view works. To deny the objective aspects of the alcohol problem is silly. Those objective properties have changed little, although increasing body size and health may have increased tolerance to the drug. But it is just as silly to claim that these objective qualities determine (or should determine) the subjective perception of the problem. Alcoholism has been a biological disease, a nervous and mental disease, a personal problem, a moral delict, a sin. It has even been a "scourge of society"—a problem caused by poverty and injustice and hence not really an individual's problem at all. Yet all of these reinterpretations and reconstructions were bounded by the objective properties of alcohol consumption itself. There is no easy formulation for this bounding of subjective by objective dimensions.[6]

The further a reinterpretation takes a phenomenon from its objective foundation, the more energy that reinterpretation requires. While this energy comes originally from the redefining profession, it comes later from public acceptance. Reinterpretations are normally part of larger jurisdictional claims, claims not only to classify and reason about a problem, but also to take effective action towards it. The final tests of such claims are their practical results, whatever the criteria for efficacy may be in a given culture. Since public acceptance ultimately requires results, it follows that the greater the deviation from objective qualities, the more necessary are measurable results.[7]

This rule applies directly to alcohol problems. Nineteenth-century psychiatrists took the problem some distance from its objective character; they claimed that it was a psychological disturbance in which victims lost their ability not to drink. Although common enough today, the notion of such addiction contradicted then-dominant ideas of the individual will. Indeed, these ideas were in effect objective qualities in the phenomenon of alcoholism as then perceived. The psychiatrists had great difficulty making their reinterpretation persuasive, for not only had they strained the objective foundation of the problem, they had also developed only mildly effective treatments. Even further afield was the claim of the social reformers that alcoholism was not an individual but a social problem. In this reinterpretation, the individual lost his will, not to his own psyche, but to the larger social units of which he was a part. This was even harder for individualistic America to swallow. Given that the indicated therapy—serious social change— was out of the question for political reasons, it is little wonder that this particular reinterpretation of alcoholism never stuck.

Ultimately, of course, even the idea that alcohol consumption is an individual rather than a group activity is a cultural belief, not a natural fact. But for the purposes of most jurisdiction claims, such deep-rooted beliefs have an objective quality. They may change as the culture itself changes, but jurisdictional claims are made over a considerably shorter time scale, within which these cultural facts appear like objective facts. The opposition of objective and subjective in human problems is not between the natural and the mental, but rather between the movable and the fixed.

There are in fact several types of objective foundations for professional tasks. Some of them are technological. I have earlier noted the railroad as a technological system generating a variety of problems for experts. Computers are an excellent contemporary example. Another objective source of such tasks is organizations. Social work and teaching are professions based on such organizational foundations; neither would exist in its present form without the current mass welfare and educational systems. Psychiatry similarly looks back to its foundation as the profession of mental hospital superintendents. A third source of objective qualities lies in natural objects and facts. The body and the universe, water and weather, are all objective aspects of the work of medicine, astronomy, hydrology, and meteorology. The case of medicine to the contrary, the strength of natural objects as objective foundations should not be overestimated. For a long time it was not hydrologists but foresters who dominated American water resource management. Finally, there are, as I have noted, slow-changing cultural structures that have an objective character. Often these have passed through periods of rapid flux to a later objective existence. The concept of private property, a fundamental work area for the legal profession in England and America, once caused wild debates among narrators and other early English legal professionals. But it has been an objective aspect of Western legal work since the late Middle Ages.[8]

A profession is always vulnerable to changes in the objective character of its central tasks. Thus, in the immediate postwar period, computer professionals were generally electrical engineers or programming specialists expert in the hardware peculiarities of particular machines. The development of compilers and other forms of fixed software has freed computing professionals to develop rapidly towards the much more open applied software jurisdiction. The development of UNIX and other hardware-impervious operating systems will allow complete emancipation. Other examples are common—the removal of the psychiatrists from the financially pressed mental hospitals, the feminization of American teaching as education ballooned into a mass institution, the death of the railroad professions. In each case, autonomous change in the objective character of the task transformed the profession.[9]

A task also has subjective qualities. Like its objective ones, these too may make it vulnerable to change, although the change comes from a different place. Not the vagaries of external forces, but the activities of other professions impinge on the subjective qualities. Moreover, while the objective qualities of tasks may be discussed as if they existed in themselves, subjective qualities may not. The subjective qualities of a task arise in the current construction of the problem by the profession currently "holding the jurisdiction" of that task. The subjective qualities of alcoholism, which define it for the readers of popular magazines, are created by the work of the medical and psychological professions with the task. To investigate the subjective qualities of jurisdictions is thus to analyze the mechanisms of professional work itself.

In their cultural aspect, the jurisdictional claims that create these subjective qualities have three parts: claims to classify a problem, to reason about it, and to take action on it: in more formal terms, to diagnose, to infer, and to treat. Theoretically, these are the three acts of professional practice. Professionals often run them together. They may begin with treatment rather than diagnosis; they may, indeed, diagnose by treating, as doctors often do. The three are modalities of action more than acts per se. But the sequence of diagnosis, inference, and treatment embodies the essential cultural logic of professional practice. It is within this logic that tasks receive the subjective qualities that are the cognitive structure of a jurisdictional claim.[10]

## Diagnosis

Diagnosis and treatment are mediating acts: diagnosis takes information into the professional knowledge system and treatment brings instructions back out from it. Inference, by contrast, is a purely professional act. It takes the information of diagnosis and indicates a range of treatments with their predicted outcomes. Occasionally professions separate the three explicitly. In English law, for example, a solicitor diagnoses the legal problems of a client and refers those requiring formal litigation to a barrister, who may never see the client. The barrister deals with inference alone. As he litigates the case within the professional system, a variety of posssible treatments (pleas, settlements, etc.) emerge. The actual decision about these treatments is made by the solicitor and client, not the barrister. Medical consultants play somewhat the same role. When a primary physician diagnoses a patient but cannot make an effective inference to treatment, his request for consultation concerns only the medical aspects of the case. The patient's original human complexities—his contentiousness, his jogging ability, his pride in his daughter's tennis prowess—have been diagnosed away. It is a perplexing case that the consultant sees, not a human being.[11]

This example indicates the dual nature of diagnosis. Diagnosis not only seeks the right professional category for a client, but also removes the client's extraneous qualities. If the client is an individual, such extraneous qualities often include his or her emotional or financial relation to the "problem." If the client is a group, they include irrelevant internal politics, financial difficulties, and so on. (A diagnosed problem may still be ambiguous, but the ambiguity will be profession-relevant ambiguity—ambiguity within the professional knowledge system.) Thus, diagnosis first assembles clients' relevant needs into a picture and then places this picture in the proper diagnostic category. Following Whewell, I shall call these two processes colligation and classification. Colligation is the assembly of a "picture" of the client; it consists largely of rules declaring what kinds of evidence are relevant and irrelevant, valid and invalid, as well as rules specifying the admissible level of ambiguity. Classification means referring the colligated picture to the dictionary of professionally legitimate problems. A classification system is a profession's own mapping of its jurisdiction, an internal dictionary embodying the professional dimensions of classification.[12]

Like the larger pairing of diagnosis and treatment, colligation and classification are often tied together in strange ways. Classification can, for example, determine colligation; a diagnostic classification of psychosis leads psychiatrists to disregard further client evidence altogether. More importantly, the actual sequence of colligation is often dictated by the classification scheme, since the ultimate object of colligation is a classifiable object. When a doctor suspects a common disease, he or she asks a series of leading questions aimed at establishing its existence. So also generals must ask leading questions of civilian politicians who "don't know what they want," or architects make similar advances when their clients are similarly uncommitted. Although logically distinct, colligation and classification are seldom separate in practice.[13]

Colligation is the first step in which the professional knowledge system begins to structure the observed problems. For example, rules of relevance are often strict. A divorce lawyer does not want to hear about a client's lingering love for an estranged spouse; that is for the counselor, clergyman, or psychiatrist. (Not all professionals can enforce their relevance structures; an architect does not want to hear about costs but often does.) Rules of evidence may also be strict; for example, doctors make a careful distinction between symptoms, which a patient reports, and signs, which are externally verifiable.[14]

Information passing these exclusion rules is assembled into a picture that can be classified. The diagnostic classification system to which it is referred is of staggering complexity. Unlike most biological taxonomies, it is not organized in a simple hierarchical structure. If it were, there would be a standard sequence of questions, a proliferating diagnostic key, that would allow problems to be properly classified without colligation and indeed without reference to experts at all. But the classification system cannot be organized that way. The information available may be inevitably ambiguous or incomplete; a key without built-in redundancy will then mistake diagnoses. Yet even once the professionally irrelevant information is excluded, much of the information remaining will prove unimportant in a given case. There are, moreover, likely to be several plausible colligations. The art of diagnosis lies in finding which is the real one. This holds as much for a financial planner ascertaining a client's true financial picture as for a doctor divining a patient's illness. There are further problems with a key model. Within the classification system itself, there may be large areas of unclassified, residual problems. Problems may fall under several classifications simultaneously, or may be able to change from one classification to another. More importantly, many or even most clients lie in relatively few classifications, and so the majority of steps in a key approach to diagnosis can usually be skipped. Indeed they must be if service is to be efficient. A profession's diagnostic classification system is therefore actually organized not as a logical hierarchy from the general to the specific, but as a probabilistic hierarchy from the common to the esoteric. As it moves towards the esoteric, however, the system becomes more and more logically structured. This gradient causes a classic pattern of misdiagnosis in professions. A patient is discovered, after many diagnostic attempts, to have an esoteric disease absolutely identifiable by two or three unusual and easily accessible symptoms or signs. The successful diagnostician cannot understand why these were not discovered earlier in the process. The reason, of course, is precisely that early diagnosis is *not* key-based, and therefore skips many tests that "ought to be" performed if a key approach were followed from the start.[15]

The diagnostic classification system has two external relations that constrain it. First, it is related to the abstract foundations of professional knowledge, normally maintained by academic professionals who impose a logical clarity that belies the muddle of practice. Second, it is constrained by the treatment system, which classifies problems implicitly by lumping together problems that share similar treatments. This treatment classification is usually complex and probabilistic, and in absolutely pragmatic professions may dictate the diagnostic or academic one.

When coupled with internal complexity, these external constraints make diagnosis a very complex matter. Medicine, which provides the metaphor of diagnosis and treatment, offers excellent examples. The explicit separation of classification and colligation is illustrated by the statement that "pancreatic cancer (a disease classification) often presents as a personality change (a symptom picture)." The well-known complexity of medicine's diagnostic classification is illustrated by its diverse ways of labeling diseases: by the location and type of pathology (multiple sclerosis), by leading symptoms (epilepsy), by etiology (amoebic dysentery). A common by-product is that one disease usually has several names; thus, infantile paralysis = anterior sclerosis = poliomyelitis. Diseases are constantly shifting around in classification. The endocrine diseases, whose chief symptoms defined them as nervous diseases at the turn of this century, are now amorphously classified as functional diseases with anatomical bases. As one might expect, the medical diagnostic system is dominated by the treatment classification. Thus, when lithium carbonate turned out to treat many patients diagnosed by the old psychiatric classification system as manic-depressive, the disease was essentially reconceptualized as lithium insufficiency, and response to lithium treatment became its identifying sign. The century-old diagnostic entity of manic-depression simply disappeared, even though it is quite possible that there is a disorder presenting this picture but not generated by lithium insufficiency. Such cases are now considered mistaken diagnoses. As a by-product of this dominance of diagnosis by treatment, those aspects of a disease unknown when an efficacious treatment is discovered are never studied.[16]

A similar interaction of the three poles of diagnostic, therapeutic, and purely professional knowledge may be illustrated in architecture. A client's demand is for a building for a certain purpose and perhaps with a "designed" quality. Such a categorization has little place in formal theories of architecture, where buildings are classified by aesthetic, by general social function, by material, by openness to redesign, by spatial flow, and by a number of other attributes. The treatment classification, by contrast, is often dictated by cost, site, local codes, and the trade-offs between them, particularly between various costs. The architect cannot move from the client's need for a "nice-looking warehouse" to the resulting structure by means of a key-based diagnosis and a treatment that "applies to that box" in the classification system. The practicing architect juggles the various dimensions of architectural knowledge, the limiting structures of treatment, and often the character as well as the demands of the client.[17]

Like the objective qualities of the problem, the subjective qualities given to it by the diagnostic transformation strongly affect the openness of the jurisdiction to redefinition and reconstruction by other professions. To the extent that a profession restricts the relevant information or specifies the admissible types of evidence it risks competition with groups whose standards are less restrictive. Many of architecture's professional tribulations reflect its insistence on an extremely strict relevance structure that many clients will not accept. Builders who do whatever the client wants threaten the livelihood of architects who don't.[18]

The classification system, too, affects the openness of the jurisdiction. Vulnerability begins not with the most commonly treated professional problems, but with the peripheral ones. Diagnostic classification implicitly claims any problems sharing features with the standard professional problems and, more generally, any problems identifiable by the underlying dimensions of the diagnostic classification system. Such implicit claims often include vast areas of residual problems not conceptualized in clear types like the standard professional problems, but loosely labeled as "nervous exhaustion," "emotional difficulties," "marital troubles," "financial difficulties," "tax problems," or whatever. These residually conceptualized areas are a standard site of interprofessional poaching. Since they are not claimed explicitly by a specific picture on the main list of professional tasks, but rather implicitly by the dimensions of professional jurisdiction, they are held only weakly. Redefinition under a new system of abstractions can easily remove them.[19]

Diagnosis, then, begins to assign subjective properties to the objective problems with which professions work. The problems become more than simply objective tasks. They are related to various underlying conceptual dimensions, guarded by rules of evidence and of relevance, and located at the ends of various diagnostic chains. The clarity, the strictness, and the logic of these subjective definitions of the problem make it more-or-less open to the intervention of other professions. But the properties assigned in diagnosis are only part of the subjective aspect of jurisdiction. A different set of properties arises in treatment.[20]

## Treatment

The effects of treatment parallel those of diagnosis. Like diagnosis, treatment imposes a subjective structure on the problems with which a profession works. Like diagnosis, treatment is organized around a classification system and a brokering process. In this case brokering gives results to the client, rather than takes information from the client; colligation is replaced by prescription.

The treatment classification system occupies a space defined by the various possible treatments. Problems are clumped together if they share a common treatment. This classification often differs from the diagnostic one, although, in some ultimate sense, the aim of every profession is to reconcile the two. Thus, excessive vomiting and schizophrenia are quite different diseases diagnostically, but may involve similar drug treatments. Again, whatever may be the cause that takes a lawyer to litigation, the formalities of civil procedure are invariant across them all. Professions are ambivalent about the isomorphism of diagnosis and treatment classifications. On the one hand, identifying the two would clarify and simplify professional work, at the same time making it more comprehensible to outsiders. Yet it would also make professional work more easily downgraded.[21]

In many cases, of course, the two systems coincide. Like the diagnostic classification system, the treatment system is organized around the common cases that make up the majority of professional work—bacterial infections, wills, preparation of IRS Form 1040, amplifier design. Most of these problems have trivial diagnoses, and for each the profession involved has a purely conventional treatment. Often the treatment is delegated to subordinates, as conveyancing is by solicitors to managing clerks in England, as working drawings are by architects to draftsmen, as much of primary medical care is by doctors to nurses and others. Beyond these conventional cases, however, the treatment system and the diagnostic system are not isomorphic. Indeed, the treatment system often suggests a combination of treatments for a particular diagnosis, or a sequence of treatments conditional on prior results.[22]

The treatment classification not only lumps together problems with similar treatments, it also associates with each problem a likelihood of successful outcome under a given treatment. For some standard problems, this likelihood is near 1.0; such treatments are uniquely tied to antecedent diagnoses. In most problems, the chance of success is much lower, and often much less clearly known. In medicine, the literature specifies formal morbidity, mortality, and complication rates for all sorts of procedures, often specified by age, sex, and other qualities of the patient. A good lawyer has an equally solid, if less universal, sense of the probabilities associated with settling a case or trying it, often specified by which side he is on, which judge he is likely to get, and how proficient the opposing counsel is, as well as by the facts and legal merits of the case.[23]

Clearly many properties of this treatment classification system influence the vulnerability of professional jurisdiction to outside interloping. I have already noted that too absolute an association between diagnoses and particular treatments may lead to demands for delegation or deprofessionalization. Another variable, of course, is efficacy itself. Treatment failure obviously makes a jurisdiction vulnerable, although a variety of forces, as we shall later see, weaken this effect.

Another variable affecting vulnerability is the measurability of the results. As results become less and less measurable, there is less and less need to prefer one treatment to another, and thus a weaker professional hold on the problem area. Since the results of psychotherapy are famously difficult to measure, psychotherapeutic schools have become interchangeable and the problems they treat have become an interprofessional battleground. On the other hand, results that are too easily measurable lead to easy evaluation from outside the profession and consequent loss of control. They may also make it easier for competitors to demonstrate treatment superiority if they have it.[24]

Treatments, like diagnoses, can range from very general to very specific, and this too influences the amenability of the jurisdiction to seizure. "Get lots of rest" is one kind of injunction; "take two of these tablets three times a day, give up alcohol and cheese aged over ninety days, and see me in two weeks" is quite another. Normally, the more specialized a treatment is, the more a profession can retain control of it. Control over certain kinds of treatment may be central to a profession's jurisdiction, as law and medicine's monopolies of litigation and drugs make very clear. That control of treatment may be central and that specialized treatments are easier to protect suggests that professions may defend jurisdiction by specifying treatments even where the results of specification may be unmeasurable and where general treatments in fact suffice. For example, at the turn of this century, treatments proposed for nervous diseases were arranged in concentric circles, from general treatments aimed at the overarching "predisposing causes" to highly specific (and quite dubious) ones aimed at the particular "precipitating" cause, which was more often than not unknown. The complete lack of efficacy for the specialized treatments did not prevent their elaboration, which indeed was competitively necessary to protect medicine's control over these problems from the incursions of the faith healers.[25]

The professional interested in effective treatment must worry about many client characteristics that influence treatment efficacy. Just as the diagnostic system removes the human properties of the client to produce a diagnosed case, so also the treatment system must reintroduce those properties to make treatment effective for real clients, human or corporate; this is the process of prescription. Sometimes the client cannot comply; schizophrenic outpatients are given long-lasting shots of fluphenazine because they will not remember to take daily dosages of shorter-lasting drugs. Sometimes a client's daily routines oblige prescription; doctors schedule pills around minimizing their side effects (e.g., sedation during the day) as much as around maintaining blood titer. The same decisions must be made by a lawyer who knows what his client will look like "in the box" or by the architect who knows how his client is likely to alter the building after it is designed. Who the client is thus determines much of what he or she gets. And most professions—American medicine is the great exception here—have treatment cost as a central problem in prescription. Each treatment fits uniquely into the life of a particular client, and that in part must determine whether it is preferred.[26]

The impact of client characteristics on prescription and treatment is felt both within the profession itself and in its relations with competitors. Within the profession, the ability of clients to handle prescriptions is an important stratifying mechanism, generating forces I shall discuss in detail in chapter 5. One factor that makes certain clients more attractive to professionals is their ability on the one hand to pre-diagnose their problems and on the other to understand their treatment in relatively professional terms. For example, this quality makes upper class people more attractive clients for psychotherapists. A similar difference makes corporations more attractive than individuals as clients for lawyers. Brokering, whether in diagnosis or prescription, is a dirty business, and intraprofessional status often reflects the amount of it a professional must do.[27]

But client ability to handle prescription also has effects on interprofessional competition. These effects are analogous to the effects of rules of relevance in diagnosis. A profession clearly derives general social prestige from meeting clients on *its* own, rather than on *their* own, grounds, just as it derives prestige from strictly enforced rules of relevance. But a profession that forces clients to take treatment completely on its own terms risks heavy competition from those who talk to the clients in their own language. Many of medicine's nineteenth-century competitors followed this approach, as does chiropractic today. Only when a profession possesses absolute monopoly can it afford to ignore this arena of competition. Even the British barristers, whose clogged courts monopolize legal dispute settlement, have seen administrative tribunals emerge to handle disputes to the expeditious liking of corporations, unions, and other social groups. So it is that many professions meet clients on their own grounds—phrasing their treatments in common language, offering advice on professionally irrelevant issues, indeed promising results well beyond those predicted by the treatment structure itself. If they didn't do it, clients would take their problems to someone who would. A similar process forces professions to keep a weather eye to treatment costs. Professions can easily price themselves out of markets, as psychoanalysts have discovered over the last few decades.[28]

The move from diagnosis to treatment is not necessarily one-way. As I noted at the outset, treatment is often a means to diagnosis; its failure may falsify the diagnosis on which it was based. Yet professions vary in their temporal structuring of diagnosis and treatment. Many professions allow an unlimited sequence of diagnoses and treatments; psychotherapists and clergymen get a second or third or fourth chance. A few professions, like forestry and other renewable-resource specialists, get an infinite number of chances, since their work is to manage a relatively constant situation. For law and architecture, however, there is one chance and one only. In both cases, of course, the reality is much more complex. A good lawyer can switch treatments in mid case, just as a good architect can correct some problems even after a building is completed. But in principle, there is only one chance. Doctors are in the same position when they work with precarious cases.

The time structure of the diagnosis-treatment relation determines the resort to the intermediate, purely professional task of inference. Where costs of failure are low and the professional is assured of a second chance, he or she prescribes the most likely treatment and sees what happens. It is curious that this approach, common among professionals, is held by many to be a definitive sign of nonprofessionalism in the stereotypical nonprofession of automobile repair. Even though careful professional inference is possible in car repair, the costs of failure are low—failure is indeed profitable to the expert—and there is nearly always a second chance. As a result, the standard diagnostic procedure in expert auto repair is to replace something. But where costs are prohibitive or there is no second chance, a professional must set a strategy of treatment from the outset. Only professional inference can do this.

## Inference

Professional thinking resembles chess. The opening diagnosis is often clear, even formulaic. So also is the endgame of treatment. The middle game, however, relates professional knowledge, client characteristics, and chance in ways that are often obscure. Nonetheless, like diagnosis and treatment, this middle game—professional inference—has qualities that make a profession's work more or less accessible to competitors.[29]

Inference is undertaken when the connection between diagnosis and treatment is obscure. The composite of diagnostic and treatment classification cannot narrow the range of outcomes acceptably. Acceptability depends, of course, on the costs and reversibility of failure on first trial. High costs and near-total irreversibility make inference a necessity in military tactics. Minor chronic illnesses demand less of it.

Inference can work by exclusion or by construction. Medicine, for example, tends to work by exclusion. If a case is unclear, doctors maintain a general supportive treatment while ruling out areas by using special diagnostic procedures or watching the outcomes of "diagnostic" treatments provided beyond the general maintenance. Classical military tactics, on the other hand, work by construction. The tactician hypothesizes enemy responses to gambits and considers their impact on his further plans. Since in general the flow of forces can be affected only marginally once a battle is begun, the tactician constructs a plan allowing as many winning scenarios as possible. Sometimes, of course, a tactician is mainly interested in not losing—like Jellicoe at Jutland—but there too the emphasis is on constructing possible battles ahead of time, rather than on fighting little ones to find out what doesn't work. [30]

As these examples show, reasoning by exclusion is a luxury available only to those who get a second chance. The impact of reasoning by exclusion on a profession's vulnerability to outside interference is thus conditional on the effects of time structuring. Multichance time structuring, curiously, is more vulnerable. Other things being equal, an incumbent profession with several chances to work on a problem will have more failures than will a profession that gets only one chance. For multichance professionals may be conservative, taking short-run failure in exchange for a greater chance of long-run success (which will help them in terms of the efficacy competition). Even where a profession makes its best effort from the start, there will be more failures with multichance problems from simple probability. Given one hundred clients and a success rate of 50 percent, a profession generates fifty failures on the first chance, twenty-five on the second, and so on. Even if the success rate rises with the number of trials, there will still be more failures in absolute numbers when there are more trials. Since treatment failure is the first target of attacking professions, professions with multiple chances are generally more vulnerable, ceteris paribus.

Within the world of multichance problems, however, there are clear differences in vulnerability by type of inference, although again we must distinguish two cases. Incumbents' rate of success can be measured either by successes achieved or by catastrophes avoided. There is no question that exclusion is a more effective strategy under the latter measure. It will not, however, reach success as fast as constructive strategies. To the extent that nonfailure is the dominant measure, then, exclusion protects an incumbent's jurisdiction over a problem. After a problem has bewildered a profession for some time, however, it tends to become fair game for outsiders, because nonfailure no longer satisfies. Success is demanded. Both early neurology and chiropractic founded themselves on jurisdictions largely made up of patients who had bewildered the regular medical profession despite repeated attempts at therapy.[31]

Inference also varies in the length of the logical chains it permits. Again, in the case of one-time problems, these chains are "as long as they need to be." Tacticians or architects, who must construct decisions no matter what, extend inferences until they afford conclusions. Like doctors or social workers, they associate with each step a probability of error or difficulty, and with the whole chain a total probability compounding these single probabilities. Doctors and social workers, however, have a freedom tacticians and architects lack. They can terminate any chain in which the total likelihood of error reaches a certain level, waiting for further information and following up other chains in the meantime. The higher this tolerated level, the more open a profession's jurisdiction is to outside interference. This is true not only because higher errors imply lower probabilities of success, but also because higher overall errors reflect longer chains, which allow more places for outsiders to intervene.

This process is most evident in architecture, whose time structuring forces constructive inference and consequent inability to limit overall errors in inference. In any particular architectural problem, the chains of inference from a diagnosis of what the client wants to a prescription of actual designs are long and involved. Even though the elements of these chains are all logically subordinate to the design task, the chains in fact traverse the jurisdictions of many other groups—engineers of several kinds, lawyers, accountants, and, of course, builders. Each of these occupations takes its toll of the autonomy of architecture's inference, and in fact the architect often becomes a broker negotiating a general design through a maze dictated by others.[32]

Another aspect of inference that influences the course of external poaching is the use of stopgaps. Each profession has has some well-recognized problems for which it knows it lacks effective treatment. Since these are very vulnerable to external attack, they are secured in various ways. They often become the province of elite consultants, or are academicized as "crucial anomalies." The academicization may be connected with a conveniently vague public labeling, which serves as a stopgap against dangerous questioning. The study of viruses, for example, is an important and advanced area of medical research. Nonetheless, the common culture believes with some reason that physicians label "viral" a wide variety of diseases whose chief common property is their therapeutic intractability. While such stopgap labels protect a profession's jurisdiction in the short run, they are often signs of long-run weakness.

The most important aspect of professional inference in determining jurisdictional vulnerability is actually external to inference itself; it is the degree to which inference predominates, rather than the routine connection of diagnosis and treatment without inference. Any profession has rules dictating when a professional must resort to complex inference, and learning these rules is central to learning the profession. Yet whatever these rules may be, either too little or too much use of inference will ultimately weaken jurisdiction.

Too little inference is a familiar part of the larger phenomenon of routinization. Of course, routinization occurs not only to the diagnosis-treatment connection, but also to once-esoteric diagnostic and therapeutic procedures; palpation, sight testing, administration of medicine, and preparing working drawings were once specialized procedures for dominant professionals. Indeed professions sometimes routinize whole procedures, from diagnosis to treatment; conveyancing and preparation of certain kinds of audits are examples. While such procedures are sometimes delegated to subordinates, to the extent that they are not they are an obvious target both for poaching by other professions and for compulsory deprofessionalization by the state. The only defense is the argument that such routine cases may be indistinguishable from less routine ones, an argument long used by psychiatrists to protect their jurisdiction against incursion by lay psychotherapists, who "might not recognize organic brain syndrome." No such argument was available to protect the railroad auditing work of CPAs when the Interstate Commerce Commission imposed a rigid "scientific" account structure on the railroads. Much of the work has been done by government-paid nonprofessionals since the 1910s.[33]

But just as professions doing mostly routine work risk jurisdiction incursions, so also do professions that refer nearly all their cases to formal inference. For one thing, the claim that all problems are nonroutine does not persuade external critics. For another, the profession cannot reinforce its legitimacy by showing how, in simple cases, the professional knowledge system leads ineluctably from diagnosis to treatment. While it may successfully demonstrate efficacy, a profession that is purely esoteric has trouble demonstrating the cultural legitimacy of the basis for that efficacy.

For example, in the early days of American psychiatry, Adolf Meyer and others argued that each case had its own unique logic. After dominating American psychiatry in the twenties, this system was gradually destroyed by the Freudian one, which made some problems more routine than others and offered relatively clear rules for the decision to invoke formal inference. Freudianism succeeded because the routine aspect of the system made it comprehensible to laymen, while the nonroutine aspect justified the creation of a specialized corps to apply it. To an outsider, Meyer's system seemed like a mass of personal judgments, well-informed, but ultimately idiosyncratic. It was effective, to be sure, but only because Meyer and those he trained were good therapists individually. There was no abstractable, portable system independent of those individuals, and hence no scientifically legitimate basis for efficacy.[34]

Like diagnosis and treatment, then, professional inference has a number of qualities that help subjectively define a profession's area of work and thereby shape the jurisdiction it exercises over its tasks. These properties are closely related to the temporal structuring of professional work, in particular to whether a profession gets one or many chances with its problems. Professions with only one chance per task approach it constructively, developing chains of inference that choose a single treatment that maximizes chances of success or minimizes chances of failure, depending on the context. Professions that get second chances can minimize failure by exclusionary reasoning, which may protect their jurisdictions to some extent, but this strategy ultimately opens certain jurisdictions—those for which they have no answers—to direct attack. Irrespective of the mode of inference or the temporal structuring of the problem, long chains in professional inference seem more vulnerable than short ones. Finally, it seems clear that professions cannot afford to invoke either too much or too little inference. Too little makes their work seem not worth professionalizing. Too much makes their work impossible to legitimate. In either case, their jurisdiction is weakened.

## Academic Knowledge

Diagnosis, treatment, and inference are aspects of professional practice. In most professions, that work is tied directly to a system of knowledge that formalizes the skills on which this work proceeds. Some writers have viewed the knowledge system as equivalent to the profession. They separate professional knowledge from its use, and either disregard use altogether or relegate it to a minor role, on the argument that knowledge in practice deforms knowledge in the abstract. By contrast, I have begun with a theory of professional knowledge in use, since application is its main purpose. But professions do in fact develop abstract, formal knowledge systems from their first origins. We must understand those systems and their effect on a profession's jurisdictions.

A profession's formal knowledge system is ordered by abstractions alone. Like any knowledge it is organized into a classification system and an inferential system. The classification, however, is quite unlike the diagnostic and treatment classifications. It is not organized from common to esoteric or from treatable to recalcitrant. Rather it is organized along logically consistent, rationally conceptualized dimensions. In medicine there are etiology, gross pathology, micropathology, presenting pictures, treatments. In law there are rights, duties, procedures, and so on. While these resemble the dimensions of the diagnostic classification, they are in fact more formal and rationalized.[35]

Within this academic sector of the profession, entities are defined not in little bundles, like the syndromes of the diagnostic classification system, but rather as disassembled pieces. Academic medicine is not interested in tuberculosis as the intersection of a certain micropathology, a certain gross pathology, a characteristic picture, a characteristic disease course, and a characteristic physiological response system; it wants to understand different kinds of physiological responses or micropathologies on their own, their form in tuberculosis being merely one instance among many. The entities of diagnosis are disassembled into their components in order that those components may be rationally theorized. Thus, in academic library studies, indexing can be seen as independent of the thing to be indexed, and more importantly, of accessibility or collection structure. A working librarian knows that indexing must reflect collection structure to be of use, and that many published indexes are so thorough as to obscure the information they would retrieve. But that is not the problem of the indexing theorist. Similarly, in psychiatry an academic aims to understand the dynamics of a particular defense mechanism rather than to identify it in a particular case. The character of the abstract classification system is thus dictated by its custodians, the academics, whose criteria are not practical clarity and efficacy, but logical consistency and rationality. Professional knowledge exists, in academia, in a peculiarly disassembled state that prevents its use.[36]

The ability of a profession to sustain its jursidictions lies partly in the power and prestige of its academic knowledge. This prestige reflects the public's mistaken belief that abstract professional knowledge is continuous with practical professional knowledge, and hence that prestigious abstract knowledge implies effective professional work. In fact, the true use of academic professional knowledge is less practical than symbolic. Academic knowledge legitimizes professional work by clarifying its foundations and tracing them to major cultural values. In most modern professions, these have been the values of rationality, logic, and science. Academic professionals demonstrate the rigor, the clarity, and the scientifically logical character of professional work, thereby legitimating that work in the context of larger values.[37]

This task exists even in professions where the central values are not of efficacy but, say, of beauty. Thus the musical profession of Europe, a well-organized and cosmopolitan group from at least the fourteenth century, acquired by the seventeenth a fairly strong body of academic work on the writing of counterpoint and harmony. Although often disregarded in practice, this theoretical work unified the profession's musical ideals and tied them to values of harmony, rationality, and structure that dominated seventeenth century high culture. While one might argue that patrons, after all, didn't need Fux's textbook to tell them that the *Kapellmeister* produced legitimate music, in fact the coherence of their judgment rested on a well-developed training and exchange system that unified European musical culture from before the Baroque. The training system in turn rested on the crucial texts, which in fact defined music quite explicitly in relation to central cultural values. Today this function has been taken over by critics, who tell the larger audience why and how the activities of artists of various kinds constitute legitimate art, a task that in some cases takes considerable effort. The canons of taste promulgated by Dryden, Johnson, Boileau, and their latter-day imitators rationalize the theory of art in order to demonstrate its legitimacy. It is interesting, but not surprising, to note that this criticial function is increasingly carried on in universities, as is the rationalizing academic work in most professions.[38]

That demonstrable legitimacy protects jurisdiction should be obvious. Societies have little time for experts who lack cultural legitimacy, irrespective of their success rates. This issue ultimately undid the homeopaths in their competition with regular medicine, although medicine's recent narrowing of its legitimation to science and technology has proved dangerous, since late twentieth-century cultural values increasingly conceptualize health as quality of life. Legitimacy is responsible, too, for the persistence of a "gentlemanly" army long after its inefficacy received decisive demonstration in the Revolutionary and

Napoleonic wars. That war could be scientific, beyond the realm of military engineering, was a lesson that Europe took a century to learn.[39]

That abstract knowledge serves to legitimate professional work should not belittle its other functions. The most important of these is the most familiar, the generation of new diagnoses, treatments, and inference methods. Academic knowledge excels at invention precisely because it is organized along abstract lines, rather than syndromic ones. It can make connections that seem nonsensical within practical professional knowledge, but that may reveal underlying regularities that can ultimately reshape practical knowledge altogether. Examples from medicine are legion, but the importance of law review articles in reshaping legal doctrine is equally evident in the citations of appellate court reports. In professions where practice is rare, academic knowledge may become peculiarly influential. Modern military commentators routinely spend interwar periods interpreting past errors and recasting tactical practice around the latest technological innovations. For the last century, academic military writing has been extremely influential in practice, as Liddell Hart and Mahan show.[40]

The academic, abstract knowledge system is thus universally important throughout the professions. It is therefore not surprising that jurisdictional assaults are often directed at the academic level. For example, the attempt of psychiatry to take over criminality in the twenties was a largely academic assault on the concept of responsibility. The attack had then, as it has now, very little to do with defense counsel's treatment question—is the insanity defense a good gamble? Rather it was a general assertion that the whole category system by which crime is classified, the typology of personal responsibility for action, was in fact a system about which psychiatrists knew more than lawyers. The psychiatrists actually won a number of intellectual battles in this conflict, but ultimately lost the jurisdictional war, partly because they didn't have the numbers to turn every criminal court into a psychiatric clinic and partly because the public believed too deeply in the lawyers' version of personal responsibility. But the case illustrates that the academic level of professional knowledge is by no means invulnerable. Indeed its very strain towards clarity makes it one of the more vulnerable parts of a profession's knowledge structure. As Weber argued, the British lawyers protected their jurisdictions effectively indeed with the antirational procedure of founding law on cases rather than on formally constructed statutes.[41]

In principle, of course, the various aspects of a profession's abstract knowledge system can be assembled into a full and fully rational system. Ideally, they would be mutually consistent. In such a consistent system many possible inferences would lead to the same conclusion, and therefore, though different aspects of a problem might become known at different times, any path would still lead to the same conclusion. An effective abstract system would also be, in principle, complete. It would classify every relevant problem, even those problems residual at the diagnostic level. Most importantly, any effective abstract system would define the borders of professional jurisdiction with utmost clarity. It would be obvious what is and what is not part of the professionally claimed universe of tasks.

In reality, this perfected abstract knowledge system exists only in the world of professional textbooks. By contrast, researchers operate within the disaggregated, rationalized system of single problems and aspects, while working professionals operate with the use-based diagnostic and therapeutic classification systems already discussed. It is only students and teachers who work in the arbitrarily complete classification structure just discussed. Since teachers and students occupy a peculiar role in an actual profession, however, it is not clear how the properties of this perfected abstract system influence the vulnerability of a profession's jurisdiction. (This is unfortunate, since the artificially pure information of the texts is one basic source of information on past professional jurisdiction.) In general, however, the pattern is the same as in diagnosis. Redundancy will increase efficacy and will thereby help a profession control its jurisdictions. Inconsistency between different ways of construing problems will lead to specialization and possible differentiation in the profession. Large uncategorized residual areas are certain to encourage extraprofessional invasion.[42]

Finally, the clarity with which professional borders are defined towards other professions may affect the jurisdictions' vulnerability. Under some conditions, clarity is a good defense. Certainly it has served lawyers well against psychiatry's attacks on the notion of responsibility. A similarly sharp border has generally been effective in defending American medicine from the invasions of faith healers. At the same time, clarity does give an easy target for attempts at "seizure by absorption." Thus, hydrologists in the United States have been very clear about what exactly is their area of expertise. But they lost jurisdiction over many of the country's water problems because their clear claims were made subordinate to the foresters' much more vague conception of "good resource management." For many years foresters dictated the entire jurisdiction, with hydrologists essentially as subordinates.[43]

In summary, the academic knowledge system of a profession generally accomplishes three tasks—legitimation, research, and instruction—and in each it shapes the vulnerability of professional jurisdiction to outside interference. Legitimacy provides a central foundation for jurisdiction, and its absence provides a central line for attack. General shifts in culturally accepted values can thus be expected to reshuffle the system of professions dramatically, a topic I return to in chapter 7. The academic knowledge system also provides new treatments, diagnoses, and inferences for working professionals; if it fails in this function, professional jurisdictions gradually weaken. These effects are usually visible secondarily, through loss of practical jurisdiction, although there are cases of dominant professions becoming dependent on other professions for new means of treatment and diagnosis. (Generally, as in the case of medicine and the pharmaceutical houses, joint control is worked out.) Finally, the instructional system, with its hyperrationalization of professional knowledge, provides yet another ground for professional attack. Few dominant professions lose the ability to instruct themselves, although subordinate professions often lose it to dominants, this being an important means of domination. Again, as in the case of research, dominants co-opt other necessary instructors into their own system—as accountants and others have lawyers—but retain control. More generally, the vulnerability of the instructional system varies like that of diagnosis.

To investigate the relation of a profession to its work is no simple task. To be sure, the tasks of professions have certain objective qualities that resist professions' efforts to redefine them. But many basic qualities of tasks turn out to be subjective qualities assigned by the profession with current jurisdiction. These objective and subjective properties have a dynamic relation in which neither one predominates. On the one hand, a task's basis in a technology, organization, natural fact, or even cultural fact provides a strong defining core. On the other, the profession reshapes this core as it pulls the task apart into constituent problems, identifies them for clients, reasons about them, and then generates solutions shaped to client and case. Through this reshaping of objective facts by subjective means there emerges a fully defined task, irreducibly mixing the real and the constructed.

As I have shown throughout the chapter, both objective and subjective qualities of tasks and of work with them determine the vulnerability of the tasks to intervention by other professions. Each of the three modes of professional work—diagnosis, treatment, and inference—helps create ties that connect profession and task. Various aspects of each mode make those ties more or less strong. In inference, the crucial aspects are the logical structure, the tenuousness of inferential chains, and the balance of inference against routine professional processing. In treatment, the important properties are the measurability of results, the specificity of treatment, the acceptability of the treatment to clients, and, of course, efficacy itself. In diagnosis, central aspects are the restriction of relevant information, the clarity of the diagnostic classification, and the degree of residual categorization by the classification system. All these are signs and attributes of the profession's making something of a problem. That "making something"—by categorizing a problem, thinking about it, and acting towards it—may strain the objective qualities of the problem. It may, for example, say that fixing a broken bone really is a matter of mechanics, and really is closer to building a bridge than to curing a fever. To generalize a point made earlier, the more strain put on the objective qualities of the problem by the interpretation implicit in this professional work, the more strong the subjective ties between profession and task must be. Not only efficacy, but all of these other variables are involved. Vulnerability comes in many places.

Thus the actual conduct of professional work determines many of the parameters of interprofessional competition. But as we have just seen, these parameters are also affected by the academics. For behind the world of professional work lies a rationalizing, ordering system that justifies it with general cultural values, at the same time generating new means for professional work. As custodian of professional knowledge in its most abstract form, this academic center is uniquely situated to claim new jurisdictions. But the claims it makes are cognitive only. They cannot become recognized jurisdictions without concrete social claims and legitimating responses. Interprofessional competition, that is, takes place before public audiences. To that process of claim and response we now turn.[44]

# 3    The Claim of Jurisdiction

Diagnosis, treatment, inference, and academic work provide the cultural machinery of jurisdiction. They construct tasks into known "professional problems" that are potential objects of action and further research. But to perform skilled acts and justify them cognitively is not yet to hold jurisdiction. In claiming jurisdiction, a profession asks society to recognize its cognitive structure through exclusive rights; jurisdiction has not only a culture, but also a social structure. These claimed rights may include absolute monopoly of practice and of public payments, rights of self-discipline and of unconstrained employment, control of professional training, of recruitment, and of licensing, to mention only a few. Which of them are actually claimed depends in part on the audience. Claims made in the political and legal systems generally involve much more than do those in public media. The claims also depend on the profession's own desires; not all professions aim for domination of practice in all their jurisdictions. Finally, they depend on the social organization of the professions themselves. This indeed was the focus of the professionalization literature. To understand the actual claims, then, it is less important to analyze their particular content than their location, their general form, and the social structure of the claiming professions themselves.[1]

## Audiences

Jurisdictional claims can be made in several possible arenas. One is the legal system, which can confer formal control of work. Another is the related arena of public opinion, where professions build images that pressure the legal system. An equally important, but less studied,

59

arena is the workplace. Claims made in the workplace blur and distort the official lines of legally and publicly established jurisdictions; an important problem for any profession is the reconciliation of its public and its workplace position.[2]

Perhaps the most familiar arena for professional claims is public opinion. In America it is ultimately through public opinion that professions establish the power that enables them to achieve legal protection. By contrast, on the Continent the state itself has traditionally been the professions' public—what I am here calling public and legal realms are run together. For purposes of this discussion, we can think of a continental profession's public as the state in its informal sense—the common opinion of state officials. The legal arena is then the state in its formal legal activities of professional control.

A jurisdictional claim made before the public is generally a claim for the legitimate control of a particular kind of work. This control means first and foremost a right to perform the work as professionals see fit. Along with the right to perform the work as it wishes, a profession normally also claims rights to exclude other workers as deemed necessary, to dominate public definitions of the tasks concerned, and indeed to impose professional definitions of the tasks on competing professions. Public jurisdiction, in short, is a claim of both social and cultural authority.[3]

Authority often confers obligation. But jurisdictional claims entail only secondarily an obligation to in fact accomplish the work claimed. Lawyers have a right to perform legal work as they wish, but only a hazy obligation to guarantee that all the needs of justice are served. Such general social obligations are more formal among continental professions than among Anglo-American ones. The relative power of continental governments has allowed them to place and enforce such obligations on the professions; in America these obligations are merely paraded in the preambles to codes of professional ethics. The different relation between authority and obligation is one of the profound differences between continental and Anglo-American professions.[4]

Claiming public jurisdiction of tasks is a pervasive activity. The advice columns of newspapers and magazines are familiar vectors of these claims, as are the perennial "what laymen need to know about the law" (or medicine or taxes) handbooks published by or for professional associations. By revealing to the public some of its professional terminology and insights, a profession attracts public sympathy to its own definition of tasks and its own approach to solving them. Since the Second World War, television has played a central role in this public image making, both through fictional programs and through talk shows, although magazines and newspapers remain crucial. In the last century, individual professionals played a larger image-making role. Professional organizations often concentrated on making members aware of their personal effects on public perception. Early professional ethics codes emphasized this aspect of professional behavior, and to this day it is violating the public image of the profession that draws the heaviest ethical censure. Finally, in the earlier years of this century, and for the less prestigious professions even today, the professions' presentation of self in vocational guidance manuals has considerable importance in this public image making, as, of course, does the extensive media presentation of heroic professionals—the Pasteurs, the Darrows, the deBakeys.[5]

Public claims to jurisdiction develop over a period of a decade or more. Professional images do not change suddenly. Today, for example, when the vast majority of professionals are in organizational practice, and indeed when only about 50 percent of even doctors and lawyers are in independent practice, the public continues to think of professional life in terms of solo, independent practice. Similarly, the ideas that lawyers spend large amounts of time in court, or doctors in hospitals, or that architects spend most of their time actually designing buildings persist long after the realities they imply disappeared. To some extent, of course, this archaism is self-consciously maintained, since it provides the older professions with a legitimating link to the romanticized past. (Professions that lack this history cannot cultivate it.) In addition, the public seems to remember professionals in the image in which it first saw them; "Ben Casey" is still alive for many Americans. For whatever reason, public images of professions are fairly stable.[6]

In the public arena, the nature of discourse about jurisdiction is sharply constrained. Public discourse must concern homogeneous groups. All doctors are equivalent, all nurses are equivalent. There is no distribution within the groups—no variation by skill, by specialty, by training. The phrase "doctor-nurse relations" refers to relations between archetypical individuals. It does not concern relations between medicine and nursing as whole professions, in America at least. Nor does it concern relations between a particular doctor and a particular nurse in a particular place of work. Public jurisdiction concerns an abstract space of work, in which there exist clear boundaries between homogeneous groups. Differences of public jurisdiction are differences between archetypes.[7]

Another assumption of public discourse about jurisdiction is that tasks are objectively defined. When medicine claims jurisdiction over children who are so active as to be social-control problems in current settings of child life, it claims that such children *are* hyperactive; they are not merely behavior problems, but have a disease that makes them behavior problems. Past perception mistook their appearance for their reality. The previous "reality" (of behavior problems) is reducible to a new one over which medicine, the claiming profession, already has jurisdiction. Of course, such claims-by-reduction assume that further reduction is not possible; otherwise yet another profession might receive jurisdiction. The reductionist profession, that is, claims to replace subjective with objective definitions of the task. The claimant's domain is assumed to be more objectively coherent than the present incumbent's, and this objectivity justifies the jurisdictional transfer. Thus the public content of jurisdiction claims tends to assume and to imply that professional tasks are or should be objectively defined, that they should have none of the subjective qualities that are in fact among their inevitable constitutents.[8]

The public arena, then, shapes the jurisdictional relation in important ways. By limiting the forms of discourse about jurisdiction, it limits the forms public jurisdiction can take. It assumes exclusive jurisdictions by homogeneous groups. It assumes given tasks without subjective elements. These public images of jurisdiction typically last for decades. Professions contest them in a variety of places—in the various mass media, but also in such crucial recruitment settings as the schools. At stake is public legitimation of professional jurisdictional claims—the right to define certain problems culturally and to dominate the social structure dedicated to solving them.

These qualities of the public arena are heightened in the second arena for jurisdictional claims, that of the legal system. Here the contents of the claim of jurisdiction are considerably more specific. They may include a monopoly of certain activities, a monopoly of certain kinds of payments by third parties, and control of certain settings of work. They often include formal control of certain kinds of language, not only language that describes the tasks at issue and the groups attempting to perform them, but also even the language used to conduct the work. Accountants, for example, not only control the definitions of auditing and other such tasks, they also have exclusive legal rights to certain names (e.g., Certified Public Accountant in the United States, Incorporated Accountant in England) and fairly complete legal control of the meaning of words like "depreciation" in formal financial contexts.[9]

Contests for legal jurisdiction occur in three places. The first of these is the legislature, which in America and Britain grants statutory rights to certain professional groups. The second is the courts, where such rights are enforced and the actual boundaries of loose legislative mandates specified. The third is the administrative or planning structure, which has always dominated the legal structuring of professions in France, and which increasingly does so in England and America. In France, the *Conseil d'Etat* has controlled the legal positions of French professions since the time of Napoleon. The general structure of professions is set in statutes, but the specifics of jurisdiction and professional function are set from time to time by the *Conseil*, with extensive assistance from various ministries (which also propose statutes). In England and America, legislatures have traditionally dominated in the legal establishment of professional rights, the American legislatures having been considerably more profligate in the number of rights so established. Parliament has generally refused to register professions and grant them monopolies. It has left registration to private bodies and has granted monopoly only of certain welfare state payments, as in the case of medicine. Of course, this may be equivalent to monopoly of tasks, but it leaves openings that are unavailable to competing professions in the more rigidly structured American professional world.[10]

As one might expect, legal jurisdictions for professions are even more durable than are public jurisdictions. Serjeants maintained their monopoly of the judiciary in England for five hundred years. In America, legally established jurisdictions for professions have not been disestablished in significant numbers since the Jacksonian era. Of the various specific rights established at law, rights to payments seem to be less enduring than absolute monopolies of treatment. Thus, psychiatry has in the last decades lost to psychologists and even, latterly, to social workers, its exclusive right to third party payment for psychotherapy. Since relatively few professions work in the third-party milieu, however, this weaker side of legal jurisdiction has less importance than might appear. Overall, legally established jurisdictions are extremely durable. It took centuries for *avoués* to breach the *avocats's* monopoly of pleading; English attorneys and solicitors never achieved the same success vis-à-vis the barristers except in the lower courts.[11]

The legally established world of professional jurisdiction also exaggerates the rigidity of discourse noted in the public arena. Since all terms must be rigidly defined, reification is absolute. All members of the legal category of doctor are indeed exactly the same in legal eyes. All tasks are rigidly defined as well, with definitions normally taken from the dominant professions involved. This absolute necessity to abolish uncertainty leads to virtually arbitrary definition of the margins of professional jurisdiction. Boundary areas are firmly delineated with formal definitions that are in fact uninterpretable in actual situations. Thus, a crucial boundary between law and psychiatry concerns the point where legal definitions of responsibility give way to psychiatric ones, the point at which the insanity defense becomes tenable. To mark this point, the McNaghten rules were established in 1849 by the highest authorities of the common law. Yet these rules have been decried throughout the subsequent history of the defense. Their very clarity makes them inapplicable to concrete situations.[12]

As a result of this extreme formality, the legally established world of jurisdiction is a fixed, static world that rejects the living complexity of professional life. Most importantly, its insistence on rigid definition forces it to ignore the ambiguities that professions can successfully enshrine in their public images. As a result, legally established jurisdiction comes slowly and endures forever. Professions often attempt legal jurisdiction early in their development, as we saw in the analysis of American medicine. But by the time a profession actually achieves legal establishment, it has usually long since won its public position. The legal arena for jurisdictional claims was perhaps a living, active one over a century ago. Sittings of itinerant magistrates and of legislatures were then spectacular public events rather than the routine matters they later became. The legal arena was a public one, and its decisions had unique power in a world unstructured by large corporate actors. But though mass media have again made legal developments a matter of "news," the legalities of professional jurisdiction today reflect outside forces, rather than determine them.[13]

I have already discussed one arena where those forces conflict, the arena of public opinion. The other, and equally important, arena is the workplace itself. In the workplace, jurisdiction is a simple claim to control certain kinds of work. There is usually little debate about what the tasks are or how to construct them. There is normally a well-understood and overwhelming flow of work—alleged criminals waiting to be processed, buildings to be designed, welfare clients to be handled. The basic question is who can control and supervise the work and who is qualified to do which parts of it. My example implicitly (and correctly) assumes that the typical professional worksite is an organization, although in some cases, professionals work in solo or small group practices in open markets.[14]

Professionals in open markets and in organizations control jurisdictional relations in different ways. In open markets, jurisdictional boundaries between competing professions are established by referral networks and similar structures. Occasionally, advertisements are used, either by official groups or by individuals, to establish for the public and for the referral sources the exact contribution of this or that profession. "Let the financial planning professionals at XYZ Bank help you find the money you need." More often, professionals simply establish rules for the kinds of things they do and the kinds of things they don't do, and refer the latter out. Small-town attorneys and accountants, for example, generally operate this way. They are enmeshed in a referral network maintained by club life, personal acquaintance, and a constant flow of business. Since such networks draw so directly on personal relations in fairly tight social systems, interprofessional relations in small towns have a fixed, enduring quality. In large cities, by contrast, several excellent studies have shown that interprofessional relations in open markets range from chaos to open warfare.[15]

Within an organization the situation is quite different. Here such a referral structure would crosscut the logic of the organization. The standard interprofessional division of labor is replaced by the intraorganizational one. More often than not, this locates professionals where they must assume many extraprofessional tasks and cede many professional ones. To be sure, the organizational division of labor may be formalized in job descriptions that recognize professional boundaries, but these have a rather vague relation to reality. In most professional work settings, actual divisions of labor are established, through negotiation and custom, that embody situation-specific rules of professional jurisdiction. These actual divisions of labor exist over relatively short time periods—perhaps a few months to a couple of years. They are extremely vulnerable to organizational perturbations. Professional staff are often replaced by paraprofessional or untrained staff without corresponding change of function. The division of labor must then be renegotiated, with the common result that boundaries of actual professional jurisdiction change to accommodate organizational imperatives.[16]

It is in the workplaces, then, that the actual complexity of professional life insists on having its effect. Here, for example, the diversity within professions must be recognized. If a professional is incompetent, organizational function demands that his or her work be done by someone else who is probably not officially qualified to do it. Or if there is too much professional work, nonprofessionals do it. Boundaries between professional jurisdictions therefore tend to disappear in worksites, particularly in overworked worksites. There results a form of knowledge transfer that can be called workplace assimilation. Subordinate professionals, nonprofessionals, and members of related, equal professions learn on the job a craft version of given professions' knowledge systems. While they lack the theoretical training that justifies membership in that profession, they generally acquire much of the diagnostic, therapeutic, and inferential systems discussed in the preceding chapter. This assimilation is facilitated by the fact that professionals are not in reality a homogeneous group. In the jurisdictional system of the workplace, it is the real output of an individual, not his credentialed or noncredentialed status, that matters. Since some professionals are much more talented than others, the best of the subordinates often excel the worst of the superordinates; certain individuals in closely related professions end up knowing far more about a profession's actual work than do a fair number of its own practitioners.[17]

The reality of jurisdictional relations in the workplace is therefore a fuzzy reality indeed. To be sure, in the elite workplaces—the university teaching hospitals, the Wall Street law firms, the leading architectural houses—the blurring is minimized. Since each group is represented by its best members, vertical and horizontal assimilation can be minimized. (On occasion it is encouraged on the grounds of facilitating organizational function, even in elite firms; the great architectural firms are examples.) But in most professional worksites, the mix of workers is so broad that assimilation is considerable. It reaches its maximum in publicly funded worksites specializing in pariah clients—mental hospitals, jails, criminal courts—where few elite professionals venture, and where attendants, guards, and clerks effectively conduct such professional work as is done. Of course, it makes some sense that attendants prescribe medications in mental hospitals. After all, they are the ones who spend eight hours a day with the patients and see how the medications work. But on the other hand, they have strong interests in certain results of the medications, interests less in the patient's personal improvement than in quieting down the ward. Nor do they have disciplined knowledge about the course and treatment of the diseases involved. When a seasoned attendant tells the unlicensed mental hospital doctor "He's doing fine on that Thorazine, Doc, but maybe he could use a little more," there is generated a real threat to the psychiatric profession's jurisdiction of mental illness.[18]

There is a profound contradiction between the two somewhat formal arenas of jurisdictional claims, legal and public, and the informal arena, the workplace. If the public knew the extent of workplace assimilation, it would profoundly suspect professionals' claims of comprehensive jurisdiction. Clearly then, the professions themselves must reconcile the sharp contrasts between the various settings of jurisdictional relations. These efforts sharply affect the workplace itself. In the first place, every new worksite begins by accepting the clear jurisdictional relations of the public arena as a preliminary model for its own division of labor, and existing worksites are periodically reshuffled to reflect them more closely. Organizational reality, of course, soon undermines these efforts. In small organizations, divisions of labor are too simple to support ideal interprofessional differentiation. In large ones, differentiation within professions leads inevitably to jurisdictional overlap between them. Even where the public division of jurisdiction seems directly applicable, the reciprocal assimilation necessary for effective functioning still undermines jurisdictional boundaries.

Even from the best beginnings, such forces would soon eclipse the public picture of jurisdictional relations were it not for active maintenance. Thus, the public picture is continually reemphasized in the workplace, although, curiously, it is reemphasized only in part. The exclusionary clarity of the public image is normally applied only to subordinates. Thus, since doctors dominate the medical division of labor, they invoke their clear *public* relations with everyone else in the hospital. Nurses, on the other hand, emphasize their formal separation from *their* subordinates, but emphasize, vis-à-vis physicians, the functions and knowledge that both groups share. Public clarity applies below; workplace assimilation applies above. The actual methods for emphasizing jurisdictional boundaries and professional differences in the workplace are of course diverse. They include disfunctional monopolies (as medicine's of prescription), distinctions of dress and speech (the use of white coats and honorifics), the maintenance of artificial educational distinctions (the teaching of unnecessary basic sciences), and so on. It is also the custom to define overly assimilated workplaces (and by implication the professionals who work in them) as shady or unethical. This is one reason why mental hospitals, criminal courts, and even solo legal practice are regarded with some suspicion by the professionals not involved in them.[19]

The tremendous inconsistency between the public and workplace realities of professional life has grave implications, not only for professional life in the workplace, but also for the public jurisdictional structure. The diversity of professional workplaces must be reduced, in public, to a clear, simple picture of straightforward jurisdictional relations between undifferentiated wholes. Some aspects of this reduction recall workplace jurisdiction maintenance. Thus, where professions exist in public hierarchies, superordinates emphasize clarity of jurisdictional boundaries towards subordinates, while subordinates emphasize assimilation. In public settings, nineteenth century British apothecaries and surgeons emphasized what they had in common with physicians, while physicians emphasized what was different. In most public settings, however, since the dominant professions are superordinates, exclusionary strategies are the most prevalent. Thus, in public presentations, professions emphasize theory rather than practice, for they control the former much more than the latter. Similarly, the central public argument against workplace assimilation holds that subordinates lack the theoretical education necessary to understand and use what they know by assimilation. This is often a fiction, since the theoretical education in the dominant profession is often irrelevant to practice. The practicing physician has no use whatever for his fading knowledge of biochemistry, any more than practicing lawyers have for theoretical training in constitutional law. Practice is in fact made up of the formulaic problems discussed in the preceding chapter, and training for it is usually conducted on the job, in internship, residencies, and associateships. But the argument seems to work very well in public contexts, and the irrelevant learning continues to be a central part of professional education.[20]

Dominant professions also form setting-based associations within themselves—for example, the American Academy of Matrimonial Lawyers, the American Society of Hospital Attorneys—while undermining interprofessional societies that are based on particular settings of work, such as the American Orthopsychiatric Association. Yet another strategy for maintaining the publicly clear picture of jurisdictional relations is media manipulation, a tactic most effectively utilized by the American medical profession. The committee on media portrayals of the AMA passed judgment on every episode of *Dr. Kildare* before it went into production. Clarity of jurisdictional portrayal was one of the central criteria.[21]

It is difficult to judge the long run relation of the two major spheres of jurisdictional claims. Dominant professions seem to be successful in hiding from the public the excessive assimilation of professional knowledge in the workplace. The public fiction survives that only doctors can do certain kinds of things, when nurses and others are in fact doing them all over the professional world. On the other hand, it is clear that assimilation occasionally intrudes into the formal jurisdictional system, restructuring it fairly completely. The psychotherapeutic revolution is a good example. Social workers and psychologists worked under psychiatrists in early child guidance clinics; they mastered the arts and the literature of psychotherapy on the job. Although this assimilation was increasingly exchanged for formal instruction from 1930 onward, it was assimilated professionals who moved into solo practice and eventually broke the psychiatric profession's monopoly of third-party payments.[22]

The relative importance of the various arenas for jurisdictional claims has clearly changed with time. In the nineteenth century, when professional work generally took place in small solo offices, assimilation was less extensive. Workplace relations meant market relations. The public arena for jurisdictional claims was clearly the most important. The public in the nineteenth century was a narrow, often elite group. Indeed, the debates for public recognition moved very quickly into the legal arena, since institutions like Parliament were in fact both public forums and legal institutions. But the rise of a mass communication system has meant the explicit separation of legal and public spheres, just as the rise of professional work in organizations has created new problems of assimilation. The relations of the three arenas of jurisdictional claims have therefore changed considerably. Even within any given period, the balance of power between them is a matter of empirical inquiry.[23]

Before we can investigate that balance, however, we must confront another issue, the actual settlement of jurisdiction envisioned by a claim. The claims assumed so far have been comprehensive claims. The implicit models have been the full jurisdictions of medicine over sickness and of law over social disputes. But in fact there are many other jurisdictional settlements. Every profession uses most of them. In fact, the different types of settlements play different roles in the three arenas just discussed. We now know the kinds of legitimacy claimed in each arena, the time period of a claim's duration, and the nature of discourse about claims. Now we must specify the alternative solutions envisioned by the various jurisdictional claims themselves.

## Settlements

The claim to full and final jurisdiction is only one of the possible settlements of a jurisdictional dispute. There are at least five other important settlements. Each can serve as a transition to some other form, although there are characteristic relations between them. Professions can settle a jursidictional conflict through the subordination of one under the other. Sometimes the subordination is merely intellectual, the dominant profession retaining only cognitive control of the jurisdiction, while allowing practical jurisdiction to be shared more widely. Alternatively, professions can form a final division of labor that splits the jurisdiction into two interdependent parts, and occasionally they share an area without a division of labor. Another solution is to allow one profession an advisory control over certain aspects of the work. Finally, professions can divide their jurisdictions not according to content of work, but according to nature of client. As we shall see, the last of these is often the most important.

Certainly the standard image for a professional claim, in the minds both of the professions and of most of those who have written about them, is what may be called full jurisdiction. A full jurisdictional claim is normally made in the public, then later in the legal arena. It is based on the power of the profession's abstract knowledge to define and solve a certain set of problems, which may or may not already be under the full jurisdiction of some other professional group. Ordinarily claims assert the efficacy of the profession's social organization in applying or further developing its knowledge or in controlling its work. These subsidiary claims will reflect the current status of the jurisdiction, emphasizing the weakest aspects of the incumbent. If the incumbent's efficacy is poor, efficacy will be emphasized by challengers. If, on the contrary, theoretical efficacy is high, but discipline is poor, a challenger will argue that its disciplinary power augments its overall efficacy enough to offset any advantages of the incumbent's theory. This was, for example, an important aspect of the apothecaries' challenge to physicians in early nineteenth-century Britain.[24]

Since the advent of associational professionalism in the nineteenth century, the claim to full jurisdiction is nearly always made by a formally organized group. Certainly this has been true since the advent of the formally organized profession in the later nineteenth century. No unorganized challenger can hope to unseat an organized incumbent. To be sure, claims often begin as public speculations by highly placed members of the challenging group. When W. A. White, superintendent of the national government's insane asylum and a generally prominent psychiatrist, wrote books and articles claiming that all criminality was essentially mental disease and the proper business of psychiatrists, he was merely driving an entering wedge. But for that claim to have amounted to anything more than a nuisance, it had to be backed by extensive formal proposals for organizational alternatives to current criminal procedure, not to mention some sort of demonstration of efficacy. In general, then, claims of full jurisdiction must be made by organized groups.[25]

Claims to full jurisdiction must also be explicit because of their location. Since they are made in public and legal arenas, they have no real effect as long as they are implicit. Public attitudes may be somewhat shaped by implicit professional claims; the public long granted to prominent nuclear scientists an implicit jurisdiction over policy relative to nuclear weapons irrespective of their political knowledge. But such claims seldom develop any depth. They do so only when other factors have brought about explicit, organized action.[26]

Claims of full jurisdiction are maintained by a variety of means. Once successful, they are backed by legal rules prohibiting either work with the claimed task or the collection of fees for such work. Within organizations, they are backed by organizational rules. Professions particularly sensitive about professional invasion may maintain vigilante groups to guard the borders—the "unauthorized practice of law" committees of America's bar associations being the best examples. The lawyers, of course, also directly control the means of enforcement, which may explain why they get away with such groups. Other professions have to depend on the law to back up their claims of full jurisdiction.[27]

Full jurisdictional claims are, in general, the goal of all other types of settlements. Every profession aims for a heartland of work over which it has complete, legally established control. This control should be legitimated within the culture by the authority of the profession's knowledge. It should be established in the law. It should determine the structure of referral that brings work to the profession. It should shape, indeed, the very public idea of the tasks that the profession does. Every profession aims not only to possess such a heartland, but to defend and expand it. The few who are content with limited jurisdictions—actuaries, veterinarians— are quite atypical.

Since there is a system of professions, however, there are only so many full jurisdictions to go around. Some have been claimed from time immemorial. Others have been grabbed willy-nilly by old or new groups as they emerged as potential jurisdictions. To develop themselves, professions may have to accept limited mobility within this circumscribed environment. A variety of alternatives to full jurisdiction provide the limited settlements that make this possible.[28]

The most familiar of these limited settlements is subordination. Nursing is the classic case. The profession Miss Nightingale envisioned was an administrative and custodial equal with the medical profession, with independent authority and training. Nursing was to create an environment within which effective medicine could take place. Ultimately, however, that vision proved unacceptable to the medical profession, partly because of the interprofessional relations implied, partly because Miss Nightingale was unable to find enough of the proper recruits necessary. The result, familiar enough today, was the subordination of nursing under medicine. The latter controls a complex division of labor in which a number of such subordinate groups take their places. Similarly subordinated divisions of labor lie under architects, solicitors, and lawyers today, and lay under clergymen and psychiatrists in the past.[29]

Like full jurisdiction, subordinate jurisdiction is generally a public and legal settlement. It often results from an unsuccessful attempt to subdivide a full jurisdiction, as in the case of nursing. In the legal and public arenas, medicine argued successfully that custodial care in and the administration of hospitals were tasks subordinate to the medicine conducted in them. Often, these attempts at subdivision arise originally through workplace assimilation, which leads the challengers to think themselves equal to the incumbents on the basis of workplace-acquired skills. Turn-of-the-century general practitioners in England feared with good reason that on-the-job trained nurses were successfully invading the primary-care market that was their bread and butter. Today subordinate groups are often directly created as the divisions of labor below dominant professions elaborate, and so subordination without contest is more common. A host of subordinate groups have emerged under medicine's domination in this way—physicians' assistants, laboratory technicians, X-ray technicians, and so on.[30]

The direct creation of subordinate groups has great advantages for the professions with full jurisdiction. It enables extension of dominant effort without division of dominant perquisites. It also permits delegation of dangerously routine work. Most importantly, it settles the public and legal relations between incumbent and subordinate from the start. This is of course essential; subordination assumes a complex division of labor, with extensive workplace assimilation creating consequently fuzzy workplace jurisdictions. This would be a threat were not the public and legal relations firmly established ahead of time.[31]

Subordination, then, is an explicit settlement between formal professional groups. It is an inherently uneasy settlement, partly because it is undercut by workplace assimilation and partly because subordinates become absolutely necessary to successful practice by superordinates. Draftsmen, nurses, managing clerks, and paralegals have become essential parts of architectural, medical, and legal practice. This combination of assimilation and necessity reaches its peak in complex professional workplaces, which usually cannot function without extensive assimilation between the subordinates and the dominant incumbent. Maintenance of subordination therefore emphasizes formal—legal and public—subordination, which is less vulnerable to challenge than the assimilated realities of the workplace. Since the public believes that nurses are subordinate to doctors, it believes that all nurses know less than all doctors about all medical things. This kind of reasoning is permitted, and indeed enforced, by the nature of formal discourse about professions. But maintenance of subordination in the workplace requires bringing all this public clarity to bear. It requires on the one hand the complex symbolic order noted above—the use of honorifics, the wearing of uniforms and other symbols of authority, and countless similar behaviors. But it requires as well countless acts of exclusion ("nurses don't need to know why") and of coercion ("we do it because the doctor ordered it"). Subordinate professions are in some sense contradictions in terms. Maintenance must be constant.[32]

Occasionally, a contest in jurisdiction results in a standoff. Such drawn contests are often followed by division of the jurisdiction into functionally interdependent but structurally equal parts. I shall call this situation a settlement by division of labor, as opposed to subordination within a fully controlled division of labor. Very rarely, two groups may hold full jurisdiction equally in a particular task area. The practice of accountants and lawyers before the Internal Revenue Tax Courts in America is, in theory, one such case, although in practice the situation is one of functional differentiation. Another good example is marital counseling, where clergy, psychiatrists, social workers, psychologists, and others have made common cause since 1941 in the American Association of Marriage and Family Counselors. There, too, there is often an informal division of labor between the kinds of cases the various groups handle.[33]

Generally there is a clear distinction of areas of responsibility within such a division of labor. This is virtually required when conflict arises between two professions that already hold secure full jurisdiction of other tasks. Such functional divisions of labor arise most commonly when changes in the objective qualities of tasks force together professions that had been apart. The clearest examples come from architecture. Although architects retain full jurisdiction over the design of buildings, they increasingly divide their work with lawyers, various types of engineers, and even accountants. Each of these groups— particularly the engineers—takes full responsibility for its part of the assembly of a buildable building. The architect retains control of design and overall oversight of the project, and normally negotiates the construction itself with the builder and the client. This apparent reduction in the jurisdiction of architects—who one hundred years ago did their own engineering—reflects the developing complexity of the task. By bringing together groups with preexisting and secure full jurisdictions, such change generates settlements by division of labor. Another solution is the creation of architectural firms that employ members of all the relevant professions under the supervision of architects who have actually become managers and entrepreneurs; Skidmore, Owings and Merrill is the prototypical example.[34]

The move to division of labor is gradual, because the task changes that generate such settlements are gradual. They first become evident in the workplace, where one profession may find itself increasingly relying on another's advice in handling particular parts of its task. This creates an implicit claim for the advisors, a claim that may gradually become more and more explicit. Again the case of tax practice is a good one. Shortly after the original income tax amendment, the law became so complicated that lawyers found themsleves relying on accountants' advice. Accountants reasoned that they might as well share the jurisdiction. The result, settled legally by the tax court itself, was a fully shared legal jurisdiction, although the workplace has to some extent retained its informal division of labor by different types of cases.[35]

Maintenance of a settlement by division of labor is difficult. The degree of assimilation between the two groups is normally great, and boundaries correspondingly obscure. There may be specialization within each field, in turn followed by fusion of the two specialties into a merged new profession controlling the old shared jurisdiction. This process was more common when the dominant professions had not yet established such complete organizational hegemony. Accountants themselves emerged in England as an amalgam of solicitors, bankers, and others who had shared during the middle nineteenth century the jurisdiction of bankruptcy and receivership. Such differentiation is less likely today, when specialists tend, in America and England, to retain their original professional identification. (In France, formal subdivision is encouraged by the state, and such processes have created several of the special forms of *officiers ministériels*.) More current patterns in America and England are the joint specialty association, which admits members of more than one profession (e.g., the American Academy of Forensic Sciences), and more recently the joint professional, who holds both qualifications (e.g., the attorney-CPA).[36]

In part, the formal settlement of jurisdictional disputes by division of labor reflects the regularity with which tasks involving the two groups occur. Sometimes such tasks are intermittent and represent a tiny fraction of work for professionals of either kind. The legal responsibility of the insane is such an example. Although this topic has given some psychiatrists an excuse to invade the legal jurisdiction of responsibility, in fact the insanity defense is a rare matter and the responsibility of the insane a minor concern for both psychiatrists and lawyers. With such tasks, the division of labor is indeed much less institutionalized. Since the issues are practically unimportant, they do not command the kinds of institutional maintenance that regularize other situations of divided jurisdiction. On the other hand, since those institutions aren't present, the borders are open for invasion should one of the groups decide on it. Yet another example of such an infrequent but shared jurisdiction is the control of riots. Riot control has been claimed in the last fifty years by the military, by the police, by private police agencies, and occasionally by social scientists. Each group has its own version of what to do and how to do it, but in America at least, riots have been rare enough that interprofessional conflict over their jurisdiction has been uncommon. This has not, of course, made the disputes any less vicious, and there is in fact no effective division of labor between the various claiming groups.[37]

Midway between subordination and division of labor stands an unstable but common settlement that can be called intellectual jurisdiction. Sometimes a profession retains control of the cognitive knowledge of an area but allows (or is forced to allow) practice on a more-or-less unrestricted basis by several competitors. This has been the situation of psychiatry since the Second World War. Psychotherapy has become increasingly the province of psychologists, social workers, and even clergymen, although the chief ideas in the field continue to come from psychiatry (and psychology). Such a jurisdiction is extremely unstable, since there is little preventing the outsiders from developing academic, cognitive programs of their own, and indeed psychology has done that extensively. For several decades psychiatry maintained its preeminence only through a peculiar mechanism. Psychoanalysis was the dominant psychotherapeutic school, and the proper psychoanalytic therapist underwent a "training analysis" under a qualified analyst. But since the accidents of psychiatric history in the United States meant that all analysts were psychiatrists (i.e., doctors), the psychiatrists retained a measure of control through the analytic system. Social workers and psychologists could undergo analysis and could be supervised by analysts in administering what was called psychoanalytically oriented psychotherapy. But they could not, at least officially, become analysts. The rise of new therapies—many within psychology—and the surge of demand in the seventies upset this mechanism and left psychiatry with its currently precarious intellectual jurisdiction. The recent rise of biological psychiatry is an obvious retreat to the secure professional heartland.[38]

The gradient from subordination through intellectual jurisdiction to full division of labor can be continued to a yet weaker form of control. Again this settlement often arises to solve a jurisdictional dispute between two professions already possessing independent full jurisdictions. This is advisory jurisdiction. It is a weak relation, in which one profession seeks a legitimate right to interpret, buffer, or partially modify actions another takes within its own full jurisdiction. The classic examples of advisory jurisdiction are the relation of the clergy to medicine and psychiatry, and of law to accounting and banking. The recent rise of "clinical pastoral education" reasserts the clergy's right to interpret a patient's illness to the patient. This interpretation, seen by the clergy as expressing their full jurisdiction over the ultimate meanings of things, is seen by many physicians as an invasion of the doctor's final jurisdiction over what illness is. The clergy, of course, do not aim to take back the full jurisdiction of sickness they once had, but nonetheless are insisting on an advisory jurisdiction over it. With psychiatry, however, the clergy conflict is much more overt; the distinction between calming psychological distress and interpreting the ultimate meanings of things is often obscure.[39]

That law enjoys many advisory jurisdictions indicates that advisory jurisdiction is not merely a protective device for a once-dominant profession that is losing jurisdiction to others, like the clergy, but is also an offensive device. Indeed, medicine itself has expanded its jurisdiction again and again by advancing advisory claims. The expansion of medicine into child behavior occurred in this way, led by such figures as Dr. Spock, who expressed along with their medical expertise the gratuitous advice generations of doctors had given confused parents. It was a short step from this advisory jurisdiction to the disease concept of hyperactivity and its drug treatment.[40]

Public claims are particularly essential to advisory jurisdiction, although, as the development of pediatrics from the late nineteenth century to Dr. Spock indicates, these public claims may be accompanied or preceded by implicit claims in the workplace. But the pediatricians' implicit claims occurred in a relatively unconstrained market. Now, such advisory claims must be made—like the claims of the clergy over sickness—within a system of professions that exhaustively claims most conceivable professional tasks. It is inconceivable that such claims could endure without strong public support. Thus the clergy's practical invasion of hospitals originated as much in a public feeling of the hospitals' inhumanity as in the clergy's own jurisdictional claims. The feeling was fueled by some clergy, of course. But the practice of clergy visiting in hospitals was already well-established from the nineteenth century. What was new was the popular revulsion against the technological mechanism of the hospital.[41]

Advisory jurisdiction is thus sometimes a leading edge of invasion, sometimes the trailing edge of defeat. It is in some ways the bellwether of interprofessional conflict. Where there is advice today, there was conflict yesterday or will be conflict tomorrow. An explicit, public claim, it is maintained normally against a workplace control of jurisdiction that clearly favors the full incumbent. It is maintained only by constant attention. Indeed, since the public expects professions to solve particular problems, not advise about them, advisory jurisdiction is unlikely to last for a long period.

All five of the settlements so far discussed—full, subordinate, intellectual, divided, and advisory jurisdiction—are or eventually become formal, explicit claims in the public or legal arenas. The last form of settlement is purely a workplace settlement. Indeed, it often exists in contradiction to the officially established structure of jurisdiction. It is jurisdictional settlement by client differentiation. Examples of such settlements are legion. In nineteenth century England physicians had formally full jurisdiction over sickness, a jurisdiction justified by their education, their training, and their knowledge system. Under them were the surgeons, mere sawers of bones, and the apothecaries, who were in official terms peddlers of drugs. In fact, they were all doctors, long before the Medical Act of 1858. The physicians treated the upper classes, the surgeons some fraction of the middle classes, and the apothecaries the remainder of the middle and the entirety of the lower classes. In American law today, two virtually separate legal professions handle on the one hand the problems of large corporations and a few wealthy individuals and on the other the problems of small corporations and the mass of individuals. Accountancy is even more radically divided. Chiropractors, the despised quacks of American medicine, in fact specialize in a particular clientele, middle- and lower-class people with insoluble medical problems. In psychotherapy the division is extremely clear, with psychiatrists treating the high end of the socioeconomic scale, psychologists the middle, and social workers such of the rest as get treated. As should be clear, client differentiation goes on not only between professions, but also, as in law, within them.[42]

Such divisions are not, of course, absolute. But they are regular, determinate features of professional life. It is clear that they offer a potentially disastrous critique of the public and legally legitimate systems of interprofessional relations. They are jurisdictional claims implicit in an actual task division of labor. It is obviously essential to the incumbents of full jurisdiction that the public and legal arenas remain completely unaware of such client differentiation.

Client differentiation settlements usually reflect the relation between the size of the profession and the available demand for its services. Normally differentiation appears when demand suddenly outstrips available professional numbers. This was certainly a contributor to the psychiatry–psychology–social work client differentiation, although the structuring of the three as a division of labor subordinate under psychiatry dates from the twenties. Demand characteristics certainly defined the three-level British medical hierarchy of the nineteenth century, as it did a similar hierarchy in British accounting around the turn of this century.

Situations of excess demand can have several outcomes, depending on the prior settlement. One such outcome is complete jurisdictional reconstruction. This seems to be imminent in psychotherapy. Psychiatrists retain only two vestiges of their prior control. To some extent they still lead the field intellectually and culturally. They also continue to serve as consultants to the other professions, partly on the basis of their monopoly of medication, partly on the status of their more extensive education.

Another outcome of client differentiation can be division of labor in some formal sense. This has been the result in British accountancy, where municipal accountants and cost accountants have separated from the rest of the profession, forming strong independent groups. To be sure, there continues a general sense of identification and common knowledge among the British accountants, not to mention a strict sense of the relative status of the various groups. But the sudden influx of clients led first to the partial amalgamation of Incorporated and Chartered Accountants, then to emergence of the rest of the profession in differentiated bits.[43]

But undoubtedly the most common outcome of a sudden demand influx combines retention of public and legal jurisdiction by the incumbent with an elaborate workplace differentiation by client type. The most common criterion of differentiation is client status. Although social work has public jurisdiction of "social problems" in America, the vast majority of the welfare system is not served by licensed social workers but by unlicensed ones. Licensed social workers are therapists for the middle classes or supervisors. Similarly, for many years there have been very few board-certified psychiatrists working full time in American mental hospitals other than those for the upper classes. Such client-based settlements are, of course, implicit rather than explicit, and are maintained by a number of simple, hidden mechanisms. The most important is pricing. Another is the construction of referral networks that screen and assort clients by social status.[44]

How can such workplace settlements, which grant implicit jurisdiction to subordinates and outsiders, coexist with public and legal full jurisdiction by a particular incumbent? Clearly one important mechanism of this maintenance is the prevention of information exchange between the two spheres. The full incumbent focuses public attention on elite workplaces, and more generally on the theoretical, cultural basis for its jurisdiction. The world of actualities disappears behind that of potentiality. The incumbent may also subordinate groups serving the lower-status clients. This was certainly the approach of psychiatry in the early days of child guidance in America, when psychiatrists ran the clinics and consulted with the psychologists and social workers who actually saw the juvenile delinquents. Subordination works because the workplace settlement by client differentiation implicitly admits that the lower professions have the ability to carry out the task involved. The alternative to subordination is an open fight. Client differentiation can lead to overwhelmingly strong claims by lower groups, as the British physicians found out in 1858.

The settlements of jurisdictional disputes by client differentiation are thus settlements of a fundamentally different kind than the other five discussed. They involve the workplace. They are implict rather than explicit, although they can develop into explicit challenges. Most importantly, they reflect forces external to the system of professions itself—large swings of demand. As a result, client differentiation settlements typically coexist with patterns of formal jurisdiction that crosscut them.

## Internal Structure

In chapter 2 we saw how professions perform their cultural work—the application of knowledge in practice, the making and teaching of knowledge in the academic world, the legitimation of work in cultural values. Earlier in this chapter we have seen this cultural structure transformed into practical claims for various types of social control in various kinds of settings. In order to specify fully the jurisdictional relation, we must conclude by discussing briefly the social structure of the groups that make the claims—the professions themselves. Although some qualities of these groups have been examined in earlier chapters, here we must examine their impact on the jurisdictional tie.

A profession's social organization has three major aspects—groups, controls, and worksites. Professional groups have diverse forms and functions. Local groups usually emerge early in professional history and later amalgamate into larger ones. Some groups are lobbying groups, some informational ones, still others aim at practitioner control. Some are organized around mere professional membership, while others embody a wide variety of special interests within that membership. The mature profession typically has hundreds of professional associations, many or most of which are open only to members of some large, dominant association.[45]

Under the heading of professional controls can be placed the schools that train practitioners, the examinations that test them, the licenses that identify them, and the ethics codes they are presumed to obey. There are in addition a wide variety of informal controls, usually specific to various professional worksites. Empirical studies of professions show that attempts at licensure seem to come early and ethics codes late in professional development. Examinations and formal schooling tend to come in the middle of professional development. Once begun, however, all develop continually. The typical profession has one ethics code, but usually dozens or hundreds of schools. Although recent years in America have seen consolidated licensure structure across state lines, licensure and examination have characteristically been state based in America, and the politics of license maintenance consequently continuous and complex. In England and Europe, professions are more centralized, although in France the legal professions, for example, have a fairly strong local and regional character. It is important to note that licensure alone, of these controls, has direct implications for others beyond the profession involved. Licensure normally carries certain preemptive rights over outsiders, particularly in the United States and France. That a profession has an ethics code does not keep another closely related profession from having one. With licenses, the reverse is generally true; where one profession has a licensed right to do certain work, others are excluded.[46]

Professions operate in a bewildering variety of worksites. Some professions have consolidated, exclusive worksites whose divisions of labor they dominate. The hospital is the most familiar, but large law, accounting, and architectural firms are also examples. Many professions, as we have noted, are identified by their organizational location—social work, librarianship, and teaching being among them. Here the worksite is usually the origin of the profession. Characteristically, the work organizations involved are controlled by groups outside the profession. Finally, a few professionals work alone or in small group worksites, but these are in fact the minority in current professional life.[47]

A profession normally has some worksites that are not involved in practice, but only in the purely professional work of maintaining and furthering professional knowledge. These include not only the academic settings discussed before, but also journals, research institutes, and other such organizations. In the United States, such cultural organizations are nearly all affiliated with universities, with a few journals and research institutes being tied to the larger professional associations (e.g., the American Bar Foundation), to industry, or to government agencies. In Europe, the ties with the government are generally stronger and those with the universities correspondingly weaker. In all countries, these specialized cultural worksites involve only a tiny minority of the profession.[48]

The strength with which individual professionals are tied to this organized structure varies considerably. Some are central members tying elite worksites to elite schools and dominating major professional associations. Others are totally peripheral, passing their entire careers without contacting any of the central institutions of professional life beyond a few journals. This internal stratification of professions is often confounded with specialization. Often professional tasks are so complex as to require considerable specialization, and individual professionals develop enduring identification with specialty work. In medicine particularly, the process is far advanced, but similar specialization structures exist in law, the various business management professions, accounting, and architecture. These specializations generally fall in a status order of their own, although there is within each an internal hierarchy.[49]

The basic social organization just sketched is clearly an ideal type. Many functioning professions have only certain segments of it, as we have seen. Given this, it is clearly of some interest when a group of workers can be said to have coalesced into "a profession." Here we return to one of the original typological debates. Like many other things in professional life, this too is in fact part of the jurisdictional claim. It is by their claims that groups identify themselves; to claim a jurisdiction is to claim it for someone. Perhaps this explains why Wilensky defined professionalization as a "convergence" plot, and why Caplow and others have made the change of name so important an event in professionalization, even though it is not all that common. By the change of name, the group identifies itself as "the profession of x." To say a profession exists is to make it one.

Yet at the same time, it is unclear whether we should identify professions by the group claims (and the social structure supporting them) or by the functional realities. Psychiatry is officially a part of the medical profession, but I have followed what I see as functional reality in calling it a profession here. To say it is not a profession but a specialty is simply to define the interesting questions about it out of existence. Yet on the other hand there are important consequences to psychiatry's membership in the medical fraternity; it grants the profession crucial controls over unruly subordinates by granting access to medication, to medical referral networks, and to other structures of the medical profession.[50]

The same problem is again confronted in analyzing professions like the military, engineering, and social work that openly include several levels of training and experience under a single professional canopy. In many ways, the distinctions between Ph.D.-level and B.A.-level engineers parallel those between doctors and physicians' assistants, but in other ways they do not. Advancement across these lines is considerably more possible, although not necessarily more likely. The control of subordinates in such occupations is largely an intraprofessional matter, meaning that jurisdictional battles between subordinates and superordinates are fought within the professionally dominated segments of worksites and within the professional organizations themselves. The distinction between this "internal" jurisdictional conflict and the "external" one assumed heretofore is subtle but important.[51]

The contradiction between defining professions by their claims or by their functions is resolved by recalling that the importance of professional social structure lies in its effect on professions' abilities to maintain themselves within a competing system. It is clear that the claim to be a profession is essential, since only by that claim can a group enter the competition in the first place. However, once a group enters the competition, what matters for us is not what it claims to be, but what it actually is. Of course, its claims are important as mechanisms of jurisdiction change. But our real interest is in how it competes. Psychiatry, despite its partial alliance with medicine, competes for itself alone and within a jurisdiction largely separate from the medical one. Engineering, despite the single name given to its practitioners, in fact competes largely by specialty—civil, mechanical, and so on—and should really be treated as several professions. That is, the level of professional identification that matters is the one at which the group competes as a single unit. This same generalization holds for the rest of the internal social structure of professions. What matters is not having or not having an ethics code, but whether having or not having one influences competition for jurisdiction at that particular moment.[52]

We must therefore consider how the social organization of professions affects the kinds of jurisdictional claims they make and their success in achieving those claims. First, other things being equal, the more strongly organized a profession is, the more effective its claims to jurisdiction. This holds particularly in the public and legal realms, but extends to the workplace as well. The organized profession can better mobilize its members, can better direct media support of its position, and above all, can better support the effective academic work that generates cultural legitimacy for jurisdiction. It may also dominate powerful organizations that maximize professional efficacy—integrated architectural firms, large law and accounting firms, hospitals, and so on. It also possesses, at least in principle, the means to control its members, and can therefore reassure public fears of untrustworthy work. In contests between professions, the profession with more extensive organization usually wins. Thus medicine defeated nursing in the hospital administration area. Thus psychiatry dominated social work and psychology in child guidance. Thus teaching has effectively resisted the efforts of computer scientists to take over classroom teaching. This generalization holds only when the remaining aspects of the contesting professions are roughly equal. The clergy, although generally well organized, has lost numerous jurisdictional battles—to psychiatry over everyday life problems, to social work over social welfare, to lay teaching over control of the classroom—where its antagonists have possessed more current cultural legitimacy.[53]

Second, professional organization, in particular the existence of a single, identifiable national association, is clearly a prerequisite of public or legal claims. By national here, I mean embracing the whole societal task; in some cases this may be localized, as was eighteenth-century English law in London. (The Society of Gentleman Practisers in Courts of Law and Equity, the forerunner of the present Law Society, was effectively national since the London solicitors and attorneys it included comprised the majority of their professions nationally.) It is noteworthy that neither national organization nor even significant local organization is necessary to effective claims of jurisdiction in workplaces. These are inevitably local at first, and national organization in fact builds upon them. It is, however, certainly true that organized professions stand much better chances of maintaining workplace claims against competitors. They may have public or legal claims to fall back on, and may possess resources to pressure heteronomous work organizations into acceptable positions. The outcome of these pressures reflects relative power. Large industrial corporations cannot be pressured by the engineering profession, despite its size and extensive organization. But smaller ones are much more open to influence.

Third, in a peculiar way, relatively less organized professions have certain distinct advantages in workplace competition. Because they lack a clear focus and perhaps a clearly established cognitive structure, they are free to move to available tasks. This kind of freedom has been a striking feature of the evolution of the computer professions. Computer professionals have typically possessed only limited cognitive resources—knowledge of certain programming languages or of assembly language. But this has translated into control over the algorithms programmed, and thereby into control over the nature and extent of the information generated. Numerous groups of computer specialists have used this freedom to float out from programming into planning and operations. In most cases, the very lack of an identity as "the computer profession" or of programmers as anything more than people with a fairly limited but necessary skill has proved a distinct advantage.

The extent of structuring also affects a profession's ability to deal with attack. Thus it is common in professions to create rigid entry standards, coupling extensive education with several levels of examination prior to formal entry into the profession. This is part of a structure of control that seems utterly advantageous to the profession. It protects recruitment, controls professional numbers (and consequently professional rewards), and guarantees a minimum standard of professional ability. This strategy seems perfectly monopolistic in effect. Yet it is clear that several professions have nearly lost jurisdictions because sudden expansions in demand found them committed to standards that would not permit rapid expansion. Thus the upper groups in British accounting lost control over the municipal accountants, cost and works accountants, company accountants, and various other groups. Thus psychiatry lost its hold on psychotherapy. The only defense in such conditions is rapid and effective creation of subordinate groups to handle the business, the strategy that led solicitors to develop the managing clerks' role in conveyancing and, above all, medicine to proliferate its subordinate nurses, pharmacists, and others. But except in the case of medicine, this has not been a terribly effective strategy. The British lawyers have in fact lost jurisdiction over many of the important aspects of dispute settlement in Britain precisely because they are too few to service demand and their divisions of labor have not been sufficient, a subject I shall examine in depth in chapter 9.[54]

The social structure of professions is thus neither fixed nor uniformly beneficial. As we saw in the Introduction, the fundamental assumption of the professionalization literature is incorrect; there is no fixed limit of structure towards which all professions tend. It is clear from the brief discussion here that the mature profession is constantly subdividing under the various pressures of market demands, specialization, and interprofessional competition. Some competitive conditions favor the less, some the more organized.

The central organizing reality of professional life is control of tasks. The tasks themselves are defined in the professions' cultural work. Control over them is established, as we have seen, by competitive claims in public media, in legal discourse, and in workplace negotiation. A variety of settlements, none of them permanent, but some more precarious than others, create temporary stabilities in this process of competition. Those settlements reflect in some ways the social structures of the professions involved, but also depend on the many variables making for strength and weakness of jurisdiction. When taken together, all these factors tell us more than how a profession defines and acquires its jurisdictions. They imply that the professions as a group will develop in the structured pattern that I shall call the system of professions.

# 4    The System of Professions

The link of jurisdiction embodies both social and cultural control. The cultural control arises in work with the task and is legitimated by formal knowledge that is rooted in fundamental values. The social control arises in active claims put forth in the public, legal, and workplace arenas. This social and cultural control differs from the classic hallmarks of professionalism in a simple and profound way. It is exclusive. A profession is not prevented from founding a national association because another has one. It can create schools, journals, ethics codes at will. But it cannot occupy a jurisdiction without either finding it vacant or fighting for it.[1]

Since jurisdiction is exclusive, professions constitute an interdependent system. A move by one inevitably affects others. In this chapter I consider the formal structure of such a system. I first analyze the general character of systems with exclusive positions. I then consider the internal and external sources of disturbances for the system of professions. This leads to a consideration of how disturbances propagate from one jurisdiction to another. While the discussion of propagation builds on my earlier analysis of the sources for jurisdictional strength, it also introduces a new and central variable—the relative abstraction of a profession's knowledge.

## The Implications of Exclusion: A System of Professions

Early theorists of professions did not emphasize their exclusive qualities, even in analyses of power. For Parsons a professional's power over clients was necessary to successful treatment and did not prevent other professional powers. It was grounded in expertise, guaranteed by professional control, and offset by the trust between professional and client. For Ben-David and Bledstein, power was an aim of professionalism, but was not achieved at the apparent expense of others. There were simply fixed social categories of wealth and power to which individual professionals aspired. Later theorists, however, have viewed professional power in exclusive terms, as power at others' expense. Larson and many others emphasized the professions' use of organized power to achieve wealth and prestige. On the one hand, powerful professions attacked and destroyed the "charlatans," whom this literature romanticized as the underdogs of the professional world. On the other, the powerful professions extorted concessions from their unorganized clients and from the state. A more specifically interprofessional power was central for Eliot Freidson. In studying "professional dominance," Freidson took the subordinated division of labor under the medical profession as his model and made power explicitly exclusive.[2]

Of the various exclusive properties of professions, jurisdiction is the most important. More general than the dominance Freidson analyzed, it includes it as a special case. Although jurisdiction is not as exclusive a property as dominance (I have, after all, identified several jurisdictional settlements allowing sharing of work), in general it still remains true that one profession's jurisdiction preempts another's. Because of this interdependence, the analytic approach appropriate for the professionalization concept—assembling a group of comparable careers—cannot sustain a comparable study based on jurisdiction. We can't compare careers that aren't independent. What should replace the idea of a common career? One alternative is implicit in the concepts of the professional power school. Perhaps professions are carnivorous competitors that grow in strength as they engulf jurisdictions. The more they have, the more powerful they become. Such a system would rapidly evolve towards two or three dominant groups, each maintaining a host of subordinates to serve as prey. The subordinates, that is, would develop new areas of jurisdiction, only to lose them to the dominants once they were sufficiently developed. This model seems to some extent appropriate for medicine.[3]

On the other hand, the jurisdiction medicine exercises over areas like juvenile delinquency is in fact metaphorical. Doctors do not provide the service; their knowledge system provides an abstract model for those who do. As such a metaphor spreads more and more widely, it becomes less and less the property of the originating profession. The widespread use of "the medical model" does not, ultimately, affect the medical profession much. It may maintain medicine's legitimacy and perhaps foster its cultural prominence in the public mind. But it means less for the future of the medical profession than do changes closer at hand.

Since the carnivorous professions model does not recognize the actual limits on professional dominance, we must find a model that does. Indeed, the example of medicalization implies an inclusive complement to the exclusive rule that two professions cannot usually occupy the same jurisdiction at once. No profession can stretch its jurisdictions infinitely. For the more diverse a set of jurisdictions, the more abstract must be the cognitive structure binding them together. But the more abstract the binding ideas, the more vulnerable they are to specialization within and to diffusion into the common culture without. Only rarely has a single set of abstractions been appropriate to all specialized tasks and at the same time limited to a single group of experts. Such was the knowledge of the Chinese mandarins, who applied their Confucian abstractions to salt mining, tax collecting, and adjudication, among many other things. The clerics of the Middle Ages and the Imperial Civil Services of Britain and other colonialists provide other examples. But such infinite jurisdictions are obviously rare.[4]

There are thus two basic constraints on jurisdiction in the system of professions. The first limits occupancy of a particular jurisdiction by various groups. The second limits occupancy of various jurisdictions by a particular group. In the extreme case, this model takes a very strong form; one profession, one jurisdiction. Although this limiting form oversimplifies reality, it offers a useful heuristic.

Models in which particular individuals occupy particular places are called vacancy models. The name reflects the nature of mobility in such systems. No individual can move except to a vacancy, and therefore vacancies have the causal initiative, rather than individuals. Common in studies of housing, vacancy models received their most elegant application in Harrison White's studies of clergy mobility. No one could become Bishop of Boston until the present Bishop transferred, retired, or died. Should the rector of Saint Andrew's become Bishop, the vacancy then moved to Saint Andrew's, and perhaps thence to another church before "leaving the system" through the entry of a recent seminary graduate.[5]

Vacancy models contrast with the careers models of the professionalization literature in several ways. First, they interweave sufficient and necessary conditions of events. The necessary conditions are, on the one hand, the vacancies themselves, and on the other, the positions involved, since some vacancies may require incumbents with certain prior experience. In contrast, individuals' qualifications are the sufficient conditions that get them the jobs. The vacancy model thus neatly combines the two types of causes.[6] In vacancy models, further-more, the chains of events have no history. It doesn't matter where a particular vacancy came from (i.e., where the old incumbent went) but only where the vacancy is now. The effects of an initial event like a bishop's retirement propagate in ways determined only by the require-ments of the positions and by the qualifications of the potential incum-bents. Finally, external forces have their most important effects on a vacancy system by creating or extinguishing vacancies. These effects are not limited to the incumbents immediately affected; one new va-cancy may cause ten moves in the system, by drawing an incumbent whose vacancy draws another incumbent, and so on.

We are here concerned with professions, not professionals. Cer-tainly the professions and their jurisdictions do not form a strict va-cancy system. Even in the formal arenas of professional jurisdiction—in the law and in public opinion—tenancy of multiple jurisdictions exists, as well as, occasionally, multiple tenancy of single jurisdictions. But at the same time the system of professions and jurisdictions much resembles the strict vacancy structure. Many or most jurisdictions are uniquely held; the tenancy of one profession generally excludes that of another. Professions cannot hold more than a few substantially differ-ent jurisdictions.

The vacancy model can therefore indicate the important questions to ask about interprofessional jurisdictional relations. The fact that va-cancies have the initiative indicates that our first questions must be about how jurisdictional openings are created and destroyed. The idea of "vacancy chains" suggests that we study how effects move through the system. The limited length of chains implies that we should con-sider how effects eventually dissipate, whether they are absorbed through professions or professionals leaving the system, as the vacancy model suggests, or are absorbed internally, by change within a profession.

There are, however, important differences between disturbances in the strict vacancy model and in the system of professions. In the latter, vacancies can be created by brute force; a profession can attempt to dislodge a current incumbent by direct attack. Such "bump chains" can begin with groups entering the system for the first time or with old groups seeking new turf. They can also be started with the eradi-cation of a current jurisdiction by external events.[7]

That bump chains exist indicates another general difference be-tween the interprofessional world and a true vacancy system. Jurisdic-tional change inevitably involves interprofessional contests. In bump events those contests arise when one profession attacks another; in vacancy events, contests arise as professions moving to vacancies open themselves to invasion elsewhere. In either case, the outcome of these contests is determined largely by the variables discussed in the two preceding chapters, including aspects of the knowledge systems involved, of the arena in which the contest occurs, and of the internal structure of the fighting professions. By determining individual contests, these variables determine how effects propagate through the system.

In summary, chains of effects in the system of professions start in two general ways—by external forces opening or closing areas for jurisdiction and by existing or new professions seeking new ground. Whether begun by vacancies or bumps, the changes lead to chains of disturbances that propagate through the system until absorbed either by the professionalization or deprofessionalization of some group or by absorption within the internal structure of one or more existing professions. At every step in these chains occur jurisdictional contests, determined in large part by variables studied in chapters 2 and 3. The central questions about this system are what forces initiate the disturbances, how and how far those disturbances propagate, and how they typically end.[8]

This system model radically shifts our overall conception of the development of professions. First, it recognizes the interdependence of professional development that is obvious in the historical record. This reverses the false assumption of the professionalization concept and its successors that professions develop independently of each other. Second, the new model makes the internal structure of professions one among many determinants of jurisdictional contests and system position. Structure is important not in itself, but in its effect on relative jurisdictional position. This, too, remedies a basic defect of earlier theories—the excessive attention to structure that led to their ignorance of actual professional work.

Third, the system view differentiates and conceptualizes the various mechanisms through which external social forces affect professions, mechanisms seen by many theorists as undifferentiated social pressures. In the present model, the system structure mediates the effects of larger social forces on individual professions, not only through vacancy creation and abolition, but also through changes in the locus of competition (e.g., the dominance of competition in the public or legal-state arenas) and in the public criteria of efficacy and legitimacy. External changes may also favor or hinder monopoly and oligopoly in interprofessional relations, affecting the packing of professions into the space of tasks.[9] This complex representation vastly improves on models that treat general social forces either as affecting each profession individually or as affecting professions as a kind of corporate group, for it allows such general changes to have idiosyncratic effects depending on the system position of a given group. Finally, the present model openly embraces the lack of long-run equilibrium in the professional world. Tasks are continually changing, jurisdictional weaknesses continually being challenged. The ensuing disturbances propagate through the system, sometimes a little way, sometimes a long way. If we can understand the beginnings and endings of these disturbances, the ways they propagate, and the conditions determining them, we will have an effective model of professional development.

## Sources of System Disturbances

### EXTERNAL SOURCES FOR SYSTEM CHANGE

External forces directly disturb the system by opening new task areas for jurisdiction and by destroying old jurisdictions. A new task appears, and some profession achieves jurisdiction over it, at the expense of weakening its other jurisdictions. Those others become vulnerable to invasion, and the changes propagate on through the system. Likewise, a professional task can disappear and the group that held it may contest and win another jurisdiction, or may strengthen other jurisdictions it already holds.

Not only tasks can enter or leave the system, but also groups of professionals. Some occupational groups have simply withered with time—the serjeants of the English courts. Usually, however, a group of professionals disappears only when its tasks disappear. The replacement of the early computer "coders" by software compilers is an example. New groups enter the system in two ways. The first arises out of what I called in chapter 3 a clientele settlement. A powerful profession ignores a potential clientele, and paraprofessionals appear to provide the same services to this forgotten group. These paraprofessionals later attack the dominant group for the jurisdiction. This was the means by which apothecaries, homeopaths, osteopaths, and, potentially, chiropractors entered the system of professions. In the other case, which I shall call enclosure, a group claims jurisdiction over a task previously common to a number of professions. Examples are the emergence of marital therapists, gerontologists, and, perhaps less familiar, English land agents, surveyors, and auctioneers.[10]

In general, externally induced changes in tasks have been more influential than the appearance and disappearance of groups performing them; tasks usually antedate groups. Of the four "objective" sources for professional tasks noted in chapter 2—technologies, organizations, natural facts, and cultural facts—the last two change too slowly to provide the sudden expansions of demand that reshape the system of professions. While cultural facts—particularly cultural criteria for professional legitimacy—can have profound general effects on the system, and while culturally defined jurisdictions can be hotly contested (e.g., property), new cultural facts demanding professional attention do not appear suddenly. The same argument applies to natural facts, although sudden change often occurs in technologies giving access to those natural phenomena. By elimination, then, changes in technologies and organizations provide most new professional tasks. Correlatively, the two are the central destroyers of professional work.[11]

The creation of new tasks by technologies is familiar. Engineering, for example, arose out of the increasingly technical quality of machinery and physical structures. Civil engineers designed fortifications and siege machinery, bridges and canals in the civil and military service. As these problems became more technical, the requisite education increased correspondingly, and civil engineering achieved professional status by the late eighteenth century in France. The mechanical engineers were a later, artisanal group transformed into a professional one as manufacture became more and more complicated. Electrical engineers appeared similarly, although later and much more rapidly.[12]

Today new technologies create potential jurisdiction both rapidly and often. The succession of computer "professions" is indeed so rapid that few such groups have any stable existence. Jurisdiction creation and transfer clearly takes time, particularly if a new profession must be organized to hold a new jurisdiction. New technological jurisdictions are therefore usually absorbed by existing professions with their strong organizations. Yet not always. The technology of airplanes revolutionized the tasks of war. Yet the air arm of the American military became separate from the Army only after an internal battle of several decades, and it lost a similar fight with the Navy.[13]

Just as technology creates jurisdictions, so also it destroys them. The American railroads provide striking examples. The railway surgeons, an active medical specialty of the late nineties and the turn of the century, disappeared without a trace. The railroads' hospitals and contract medical systems vanished, along with a body of medicine based on "railway spine" and similar ailments. Likewise, the railroad dispatchers and booking agents did not become the operations researchers and travel agents of today, but shriveled as the technology that supported them weakened. In part, of course, this happened because these various positions were organized into a set of career steps, rather than a set of lifetime careers. (One was first a brakeman, then a dispatcher, then a stationmaster, and so on.) But it also reflected the dependence of such groups on a single technology and organizational structure, on knowledge that was not abstract, but rather tied to the particular task before them. Among the sole survivors were those railroad telegraphers who followed the path of abstraction towards modern electrical engineering.[14]

Similarly, when computers first began to show their potential, programmers were called coders and wrote simple algorithms for routine processes. As transistors and the magnetic core rapidly increased the computer's capabilities, demand for programmers rose suddenly. The result was their replacement not by less qualified professionals (as in the case of nineteenth-century accounting, for example), but by technology itself. Yet the compilers that replaced them—FORTRAN, COBOL, and so on—in fact created new areas of expertise. The abstract skill remained the construction of efficient algorithms, but the algorithms were now written in the more flexible high-level languages. The old jurisdiction of machine code became a small area for the few experts responsible for maintaining and upgrading the compilers.[15]

The other major source for creation and destruction of jurisdiction is change in organizations. New organizations often create new professions. People who occupy equivalent positions in equivalent organizations band together, pool their knowledge, and organize occupational groups that ultimately become independent of the originating organization. The American Psychiatric Assocation began life as the Association of Medical Superintendents of American Institutions for the Insane. For forty years thereafter neither the superintendents' assistants nor their colleagues in private practice could join this professional association, despite the knowledge and skills they obviously shared with its members; organizational position defined the profession. Similarly, American social work began when the charities organization movement turned to permanent, paid supervisory personnel. The individuals hired for these positions gradually accumulated knowledge of "social diagnosis" and created a profession on that basis. In England, the organizational roots of social work are even more clear; the profession was divided until the 1960s by the organizations within which practitioners worked—the almoners in hospital, the probation officers in the courts, the family workers in welfare agencies. Similar organizational foundations exist for teaching, librarianship, and numerous other groups, not the least among them business management. Some of these professions have been more successful than others in defining and controlling their jurisdictions, but all originate in waves of new organizations.[16]

Although, unlike technologies, organizations object to being replaced, many a profession has been threatened severely by organizational destruction. When the late-nineteenth-century welfare-reform movement brought mental hospitals under statewide control, the glamour and power of the psychiatric superintendency began to fade. Aspiring young psychiatrists left the hospitals for private practice, and some never worked in the hospitals at all. The profession preserved its identity and independence only by leaving the organizations nearly completely. A similarly longstanding, but less complete, exodus has taken social workers out of organizations into private practice. In both cases, of course, the organizations concerned did not disappear, but were transformed in a "deprofessionalizing" manner.[17]

A more subtle example involves British accounting in the late nineteenth century. Accounting's original jurisdiction was created by organizational change. Nineteenth-century bankers and lawyers devised the joint-stock company to bring the mobilization of capital out of the family world and into their professional world. In France, joint-stock companies were monitored by the *Conseil d'Etat*, whose cautious councillors permitted very few to exist. The English, however, created them with abandon and with inevitable result. Most of them failed. There was a need for individuals expert in both law and money to wind up their affairs. This need brought accountants into existence, drawing them partly from the law, partly from the world of finance itself. The era of bankrupt stock companies was, however, short. English capitalists grew more skilled, and fewer companies failed. Accountants were forced, in the last quarter of the nineteenth century, to find new work; an organizational change—the virtual disappearance of the office of receiver—had forced the profession to seek another jurisdiction.[18]

The creation and destruction of organizational jurisdictions complements the creation and destruction of technological jurisdictions. But there are also external effects on the system generated by groups of workers, who may enter by attack or enclosure. In external attack, the new groups are usually generated by clientele differentiation. English medicine is the best example. Despite their legal and public jurisdiction of the science of medicine, the physicians were too few and too proud to care for the vast majority of the population. As a result the surgeons and apothecaries came to service the middle and lower classes. The apothecaries then began internal reforms designed to justify an attack on the public and legal jurisdiction maintained by their superiors. Their project was successful, culminating in the merger of all three groups under the Medical Act of 1858. Other excellent examples come from the clergy, where paraprofessional groups commonly emerge to serve clienteles ignored by professions.[19]

While the pattern of attacking groups emerging from the paraprofessional periphery, serving ignored clienteles, and urging reform is the most common, attackers may also appear from other countries by transplantation. The homeopaths thus appeared in America from Germany. Not all such groups enter at the bottom of professional status hierarchies. American accounting began as a branch of British accounting and spent forty years living down its British heritage. In general, however, such transplanted groups ultimately play the same role as locally generated ones: they attack weak jurisdictions or serve unnoticed client groups.[20]

Where legal monopoly of service is the rule, as in the United States and France, external attack is not common. The dominant incumbent can employ state apparatus both to defend itself and to prevent the attackers from developing the internal structure necessary for sustained attack. Only in England, where legal jurisdiction is generally less complete, is attack by external groups common. Since names rather than tasks are legally protected, client differentiation is an officially legitimate jurisdictional settlement, and attacking groups have room to develop.

Enclosure is a similar process, although it seldom initiates changes in the system, but rather completes changes begun within individual professions. Typically, there emerge specialties in several professions, performing similar sorts of work but retaining their original allegiance. Eventually these groups make common cause and consider forming a new profession, enclosing their common work as a single jurisdiction independent of their parents. A good example is the struggling field of marital therapy. In the years since treatment for disturbed marriages became formally legitimate, professionals from a variety of fields have undertaken it—psychiatrists, social workers, clergymen, psychologists, uncertified caseworkers, and others. The area could clearly be construed as a separable jurisdiction with its own expertise, but in fact the American Association of Marriage and Family Counselors (founded 1942) has not been able to successfully defend the jurisdiction against the prior claims of the environing professions, from which most marital therapists are drawn. Marital therapy is an enclosure that failed.[21]

Enclosure has indeed become less and less common in the American and British systems of professions. The dominant environing groups are too well entrenched to allow anything but dual certification or joint membership in a common specialty association. Certified public accountants who are also lawyers are one example, lawyers with M.B.A.'s another. It is not yet clear whether such groups will split off from their parents. (The variables involved in decisions to split are considered later in this chapter.) The French system, however, has made enclosure a quite common practice. Thus, the *agréés près des tribunaux de commerce* emerged precisely as did marital therapists. People from a number of groups—*avocats, avoués,* uncertified *hommes d'affaires*—simply began to practice in front of the *tribunaux,* which eventually started to publish certified lists of practitioners. In time the professional groups of these *"agréés"* took over the functions of certification from the courts, although the content of certification was specified by statute. In France, as we shall see again and again, the state imposes fairly narrow and prescribed task differentiation; dominant incumbents do not have the protection against subdivision available to them in England and America.[22]

On occasion a jurisdiction is enclosed and seized by a group which comes into existence for that purpose. This occurs only when dominant individuals or organizations direct the process. The classic example is nursing. Miss Nightingale defined a potential area of work, seized it from the military (and later civil) authorities, who weren't really doing it in any case, and created schools, association, and knowledge to serve it. It is not a performance often repeated; Melvil Dewey's role in American librarianship is perhaps the only equivalent. Such enclosure tends to have little effect on the system unless the tasks enclosed were in fact significant areas of work for preexisting groups. Nursing's work was not. The system-wide effects of the creation of nursing began only when nursing started to expand out of the hospitals into primary health care, invading the doctors' heartland jurisdiction.[23]

INTERNAL SOURCES FOR SYSTEM CHANGE

The external sources for disturbances in the system of professions are complemented by sources within the professions themselves. Unlike external sources, these do not create or abolish whole jurisdictions. But they can so strengthen or weaken current jurisdictions as to produce similar results. Generally they strengthen jurisdiction; in the next chapter, we shall see how internal stratification and other kinds of internal differentiation can undermine jurisdictional strength. But here I am assuming professions to be internally homogeneous, and jurisdiction is seldom weakened by internal forces involving the unified profession.

First, the development of new knowledge or skill may consolidate jurisdictional hold or may facilitate expansion at others' expense. The classic example of consolidation is the development of American medicine in the late nineteenth century, based on the new "scientific" medicine of that time. Another consolidation is the developing theory of narcissism, through which the psychoanalysts have tried to retain their jurisdiction of the psychotherapeutic world. A good example of expansion through new skills is the one given a few pages ago—the lawyers' perfection of the joint-stock company, a device that enabled them (and the bankers) to take over and control capital formation. This expansion created a large jurisdictional field that lawyers left mostly to old and new financial professions, although retaining advisory jurisdiction over crucial aspects. Other examples of expansion by knowledge are legion. Operations researchers and economists have tried to capture an increasingly lucrative evaluation jurisdiction with the technique of cost-benefit analysis. The similar attempt of engineers to apply their new efficiency concepts to human labor led to the vogue of Taylorism in the 1910s and 1920s. Insofar as new skills consolidate a jurisdiction, they do not originate disturbances but stop them. When used for expansion, however, they are one of the basic disturbing forces in the system. At their most extreme, claims based on new skills are frankly imperialistic. The claims of the social psychiatrists of the twenties—that they could "cure" strikes, alcoholism, and juvenile delinquency, that they could raise industrial production and solve people's everyday problems—attacked a host of professions at once. Although such general expansions may seem overambitious, the psychiatrists succeeded in at least one of these areas—juvenile delinquency.[24]

A second set of internal effects arises in the social structure of a profession, including among other things the changes normally called professionalization. One competing group raises its standards or organizational efficiency and thereby threatens the public and perhaps legal jurisdiction of its environing competitors. Such structural change may be the initial move in an external attack, as with the apothecaries and the solicitors of England. In each of these cases, the subordinates' new professional society and effective examinations challenged the legitimacy of the "higher branches"—physicians and barristers respectively. But new standards for professional control may also respond to changes in other groups; they may be necessary for competitive parity. There often results a spiral of structural developments; as subordinate professions institute formal degree programs, dominants pile on fellowships and specialty training. This spiral does not occur with organizational innovations; subordinates generally have great difficulty forming independent organizations for professional work to compete with hospitals or architectural firms. Therefore, dominant professions emphasize organizational innovations, which tend to be exclusive, rather than the usual control structures of professionalization, which are not.[25]

Internal changes prepare professions to consolidate old jurisdictions or to invade new ones. They thus have the same system effects as the external destruction of old jurisdictions; they create professions on the prowl. In each case a profession has a certain ability to hold jurisdiction, an ability dependent on both its professional knowledge system and its internal structure. Any change in that ability—whether by freeing some of it from an old jurisdiction or by increasing it internally—makes the profession ready to claim new jurisdiction.

## The Mechanisms of Jurisdiction Shift: Abstraction

External and internal forces create vacant task areas and greedy professions. In the first case, environing professions and new groups will contest the open task. In the second, professions will search for new work at the expense of old neighbors. A variety of conditions determine the outcome of the interprofessional contests involved. In the preceding chapters, we have reviewed many of the general variables affecting them. Now we must examine the mechanisms of the contests themselves.

### COGNITIVE STRATEGIES FOR CHANGING JURISDICTION

Like jurisdictions, contests for jurisdiction have cognitive and social-structural aspects. Just as the cognitive components dominate the structuring of jurisdictions, so also do they dominate the conduct of jurisdictional contests. A few standard rhetorics justifying jurisdictional attack constitute the basic mechanism through which the disturbances induced by external and internal forces propagate.[26]

One such rhetoric has already been mentioned, the device philosophers call reduction. An attacking move made by secure professions, this argument shows some new task to be reducible, in principle, to one of the attacker's already-secure jurisdictions. Child misbehavior is reduced to the disease of hyperactivity, and hence to the jurisdiction of medicine. Industrial disturbances are reduced to a collection of individual behavior disorders, and hence to the jurisdiction of psychiatry. Urban planning is reduced to a problem of design, and hence to the jurisdiction of architecture. Although sometimes specific, reduction can also be very global, the limiting case being the all-embracing professional metaphor. In general, the more global the aim, the less substantial the jurisdictional settlement that results. But when reduction is applied to a particular problem, as with hyperactivity, it can have decisive effect. This effect is multiplied when an "effective" therapy is appended, as was the strong sedation of ritalin in that case.[27]

Reduction can take many forms. They can be distinguished in terms of Kenneth Burke's "five key terms of dramatism": Act, Scene, Agent, Agency, Purpose.[28] Jurisdictions are often organized around one of these terms. For example, organizational jurisdictions are first defined by their scene, but later by acts or purposes, after early professionals seek a knowledge base free of the organization; librarianship attempts to become information processing. Professions founded on particular technologies of treatment are founded upon agency—radiologists, electrotherapists, physical therapists. Professions based on custody of certain individuals are organized around agents—early psychiatry, social work. Reduction is often a redefinition of another profession's jurisdiction into the dramatistic structure of one's own. Thus, in the case of industrial disorders, psychiatrists denied the relevance of scene—which made the problem part of business management—on the grounds that the acts involved were individual behavior disorders. In urban planning, again the relevance of scene was denied, but in this case the relevance of agency (design) was asserted.

Each culture prefers certain ways of organizing jurisdictions over others. In the United States, scene is generally the weakest means of legitimating a jurisdiction, although the actual power of the organizations involved may buttress it. Agency, too, is relatively weak, since it addresses treatment alone, rather than the full triad of treatment, diagnosis, and inference. Acts and purposes, by contrast, seem the most powerful bases for organizing jurisdiction in American society. Agent is powerful only when identified with act, as is generally the case in American definitions of deviance. The hierarchy may reflect not only cultural differences, but also the relation of individual professionals to the dramatistic pentad. A profession based on scene is organizationally dependent, while acts and purposes are portable. Thus while scene is more important in France (there is a vast array of organization-based professions there), professions free of the constraints of scene are still generally the most powerful—witness the elite managers who move from the Ecole Polytechnique to government services to public companies.[29]

The limiting case of reduction—the global professional metaphor— is a weak means of jurisdiction extension, although surprisingly common. Medicalization has distracted us from the many other such metaphors. In fact, legal metaphors permeate the professional world, as in the "therapeutic contract" of the psychotherapists. Surgeons use cost-benefit metaphors drawn from professional policy analysts. The efficiency metaphor of Taylorism seized business, education, and even conservation in its day. But metaphors provide ineffectual attacks on jurisdiction. Partly their weakness bespeaks their origins; they are more likely to result from cultural dominance than to create it. Their appearance may therefore simply signal public respect or, as in the case of Taylorism, a kind of fad. But more importantly, metaphors simply promote ways of imagining problems; they do not provide the full system of diagnosis, inference, and treatment that can maintain jurisdiction. These ways of imagining do have powerful effects. Medicalization, for example, locates the origin of problems beyond both the individual's and society's immediate volition, thereby absolving both of responsibility. When applied to deviance, then, the medical model is profoundly conservative. But while such consequences may have profound importance elsewhere, as far as the system of jurisdictional relations itself is concerned, metaphors have little effect.[30]

Reduction replaces one profession's diagnosis of a problem with another's. Metaphor extends one profession's models of inference to others. A third rhetoric of jurisdictional change contests neither diagnosis nor inference, but treatment. The attacking profession claims simply that its treatments apply to problems diagnosed by others. The best recent examples come from the clergy and reflect the peculiar position of that profession in modern times. Possessed of a large and solid set of professional institutions and a cognitive heritage unsurpassed in age, complexity, and profundity, the clergy has found the twentieth century relatively uninterested in its central jurisdictions—salvation, meaning, ultimate concern. As a result, it has taken its treatments— pastoral care, supervised church attendance, and the like—and aimed them at other kinds of problems. The first of these were social problems, which were largely unprofessionalized at the end of the last century. But the secular profession of social work split fairly rapidly from its clergy tutelage, and even the United States census separated social workers from religious workers by 1930. Clergy then tried to invade the problems of everyday life that psychiatry had successfully defined as neuroses, to which they argued they could make unique therapeutic contributions. Again they enjoyed only equivocal success. More recently, the clergy have argued similarly concerning medical problems, with the same mixed results.[31]

In all these developments, clergy have accepted the diagnoses of others, but recommended treatment along religious lines. They have never claimed exclusive jurisdiction. Indeed, these claims have been opposed by many or most clergymen, who argue that using religious treatment for nonreligious problems is not professionally proper ("idolatrous"). This opposition may explain why jurisdiction expansion through treatment claims alone is rare; it concedes too much to be effective. But treatment expansion may also be weak because, as I have already noted, our culture does not consider agency an effective basis for jurisdiction in general.

A particularly important argument for jurisdictional change is the gradient argument, a special case of reduction. According to the gradient argument, those who hold jurisdiction of the extreme versions of a problem should also hold jurisdiction of the mild ones. The argument usually makes claims about prevention, and appears when the jurisdiction of extreme versions is under threat. Again, changes in psychiatry and accounting provide good examples. In psychiatry, as we have seen, the increasing state control over the mental hospitals in the late nineteenth century made them a less attractive organizational jurisdiction. Psychiatry had also come to recognize that it could not cure chronic psychosis. The profession escaped the hospitals through a rhetoric of prevention. The chronic cases had "gone too far"; psychiatric cures would work only with "acute" cases. It was necessary to find and treat psychosis as it emerged. According to the psychiatrists, this emerging state was what the neurologists were then calling neurosis. While this last assertion had little basis in fact—neither then nor since has the evidence shown that untreated neurosis degenerates into psychosis— the argument allowed psychiatry's successful departure from the ever-less-attractive hospitals.[32]

In accounting, the threat to the jurisdiction of extreme problems came, as we have seen, through their disappearance. The English capitalists got so good at what they were doing that there were few bankruptcies for accountants to settle. Yet the businessmen were helped in this by a form of preventive treatment—the annual external audit of corporations openly traded on the stock exchanges. Audits were fairly effective prevention, since they made it much harder to water stock. For the accountants, this shift to prevention had profound implications; it changed their market from certain corporations at one point in their existence to all corporations every year. Although the practice of annual audits expanded slower than the accountants may have wished, it still provided a way out of a limited jurisdiction of extreme cases.[33]

That prevention arguments are usually responses to external threats is evident. Professions whose jurisdictions over extreme problems are neither threatened from outside the system nor insufficient for professional existence do not invoke prevention arguments. Public health and arbitration, for example, embody important aspects of prevention for medicine and law, respectively. And public health, at least, has been responsible for much of what is publicly perceived as medical efficacy. Yet these two areas are low-status medical and legal specialties, and are both largely supported by organizations and groups out-side the medical and legal professions. While the gradients exist for professional expansion, neither profession has found it necessary to use them.[34]

### ABSTRACTION AND JURISDICTIONAL STRENGTH

Gradient claims, reduction, and so on are the justifications of juris-dictional changes, the cultural medium by which effects propagate through the system of professions. The study of these media makes it evident, at last, why abstract knowledge is the foundation of an effec-tive definition of professions. Many occupations fight for turf, but only professions expand their cognitive dominion by using abstract knowl-edge to annex new areas, to define them as their own proper work.[35] My theory of professional development thus creates my definition of professions. As is traditional, abstract knowledge is central. But the justification for it is new; knowledge is the currency of competition. Only the move by treatment contradicts this rule, and it has, in the clergy's case at least, proved remarkably ineffective. The recent expan-sion of expert systems research illustrates the rule about abstraction perfectly. Practitioners of artificial intelligence argue that *all* profes-sional inference follows a certain form, which can be generated by a suitably programmed machine. This is in some sense the ultimate ab-straction, reducing all professional inference to one form and all juris-dictions to a single unit.[36]

There are, however, limits to expansion. As jurisdiction expands and as the ideas unifying it necessarily become more abstract, jurisdic-tion attenuates. To defend this assertion, I shall first distinguish two kinds of abstraction. One abstraction emphasizes mere lack of content; that is abstract which refers to many subjects interchangeably. A sec-ond abstraction emphasizes positive formalism, which may in fact be focused on a fairly limited subject area; that knowledge is abstract which elaborates its subject in many layers of increasingly formal dis-course. The two abstractions are often the same, since formalization is one route to the abolition of particular content. But they may be clearly distinguished in practice. The medical model for deviance ex-emplifies abstraction in the first sense; the wide applicability of this general metaphor reflects the subtraction of its particular content. The discipline of physics, on the other hand, embodies abstraction in the second sense. It is limited in subject, but extremely formal in treat-ment. It is true, of course, that physics and physical models could be applied to explaining politics, for example, but physics normally deals with what we consider a fairly narrow subject area. It could be abstract in the first sense, but in practice is not.

This distinction allows us to clarify the relation of abstraction to jurisdictional strength. Abstraction in the second sense makes a jurisdiction quite secure, particularly if it is associated with effective treatment. No one tries to explain particle interactions without mastering the abstract knowledge of physics. More practically, no one offers insurance companies advice on underwriting without having mastered actuarial theory. Formalization without effective treatment is not so secure—the elegant diagnostic practice of nineteenth-century medicine did not prevent people from patronizing other professions when the doctors could not cure them. But in general formalization—the elaboration of knowledge at several levels of abstraction—uniformly strengthens jurisdiction.

By contrast, extreme abstraction in the first sense—lacking content—can make a jurisdiction weak. Even if there are effective treatments, the abstractions may not appear to be connected with them unless a long and effective chain of formalizations ties the two together. With no effective treatments, abstractions are simply generalities without legitimacy. The task area is open to other groups with other generalities. For example, despite numerous efforts, the area of business management has never been made an exclusive jurisdiction. In part this reflects recalcitrance to treatment. The Taylorists and others since have proposed numerous formalizations for the area—jurisdictional claims abstract in the second sense. But none of them has worked well. The formalizations that *have* worked were immediately routinized or seized by limited groups—cost accounting and operations research being the best examples. But the real problem with business management is the tenuous connection between the various abstractions applied to the area and the actual work of managers. As a result of this disconnection, the management area has numerous claimants, a degree (M.B.A.) that covers extremely diverse forms of training and knowledge, and an equally diverse body of abstractions about how the work ought to be done. Psychology, sociology, administration, economics, law, banking, accounting, and other professions all claim some jurisdiction in business management, each by extending its own abstractions, emptying them of content, and claiming that they cover the whole field.[37]

The first kind of abstraction—the abstraction inherent in the medical model—can therefore make jurisdictions weak. But paradoxically, too little abstraction can make a jurisdiction weak as well. In fact, this generalization holds for both kinds of abstraction. Expert action without any formalization is perceived by clients as craft knowledge, lacking the special legitimacy that is supplied by the connection of abstractions with general values. While clients appreciate the simple case that shows them how professional knowledge works, they will not treat as professional a skill whose knowledge is *all* obvious to them. (Such a skill is also likely to be easily routinizable.) Effective jurisdiction also requires more than minimal emancipation from content, because jurisdiction bound to a particular content is excessively vulnerable to external forces, as we have seen earlier.[38]

Contrary forces thus push abstraction in professional knowledge towards an equilibrium between extreme abstraction and extreme concreteness. Since increasing formalization has generally beneficial effects, the main form of abstraction involved in this equilibrium is freedom from content. The equilibrium level of content varies with the general area of tasks involved. In the main task areas—sickness, disputes, building, finance, and the like—public ideas about legitimacy will combine with public perceptions of efficacy to create an optimum level of abstraction that lies between the extremely general and the extremely concrete. Since legitimacy in different areas may refer to different values—rationality, logic, self-actualization, efficiency, justice, beauty, success—and since criteria of success may vary with task, the optimum level of abstraction they determine will naturally vary. Medicine, for example, has a very narrow and particular object of work, the body, but a deep and formally rich body of knowledge about it. Medicine's jurisdiction is thus compact, although surrounded by imperialistic abstractions. Law, with an equally rich body of knowledge and an equal dominance in its area of work, has a much more general object of endeavor—a subject more abstract in the first sense. Since we can safely assume that these dominant professions have each approximated the level of abstraction suited to public culture in their areas, it is clear that optimal levels do indeed vary.[39]

Since these optima lie in the middle of the abstraction scale, contests for jurisdiction have different consequences for different winners. A profession that has yet to grow out of a limited area of work, possibly in tutelage under a dominant profession, will strengthen its current jurisdictions if it wins a new jurisdiction that justifies and encourages its developing a more abstract foundation. On the other hand, a profession already widely spread will, as I have argued, lose strength in its current jurisdictions if it claims yet another one, forcing its justifying abstractions to the limits of vagueness. Thus it is that medicine stops short of grasping every personal problem. Thus it is that law left so much of finance to the new finance professions. At the same time, parts of telegraphy strengthened themselves by merging with power engineering, and medicine in its earlier years did the same by absorbing surgeons, apothecaries, and homeopaths.

## MAINTAINING OPTIMUM ABSTRACTION

A variety of mechanisms help professions maintain this optimum level of abstraction. The most obvious are amalgamation and division. Sometimes professional groups join into single units. This event often terminates a chain beginning with threat from subordinates or outsiders. British medicine absorbed surgeons and apothecaries in 1858, as American medicine was later to absorb homeopaths and still later osteopaths. By contrast, the British barristers and chartered accountants held firm against their subordinates, both at some cost in jurisdiction. In other situations, merger has followed recognition of common bodies of knowledge and practice by groups that began as organization-based professions. British social work, its long-lived specialty groups finally unifying in 1960, is an example. Amalgamation may also terminate the process of enclosure, when environing specialties merge into a new profession. Such a process may be occurring in the information science area, as portions of librarianship, data processing, programming, and other professions draw together into a coherent group.[40]

Amalgamation often fails, through a variety of conditions. Subordinate groups may lack the power to coerce superordinates, as in British law. More commonly, as in American engineering, distinct professional heritages and tasks prevent a unified cognitive and social structure. The different varieties of engineering had established extensive professional institutions by the end of the nineteenth century, and modes of thought in the various branches proved resiliently different. Attempts to unify the profession failed because the required level of abstraction led to an ineffectual vagueness. Specialists in electrical engineering would still have done only electrical engineering; the unity would have been merely formal. Engineering illustrates an important distinction between the real level of professional unity, the level at which individual professionals are to a large extent interchangeably competent, and the titular level, at which the profession takes its name. Groups of professions whose members are not interchangeable may federate for political reasons rather than because of common knowledge. This indeed was the impetus in American engineering— the political issues being the increasing domination of engineering work by management (in the campaign for the Association of American Engineers 1918–20) and the ability of engineering to create an efficient, waste-free society (in the Hoover-led campaign against waste of the Federation of American Engineering Societies). In most cases, the true and titular levels are the same, but in some—for example, American engineering and British social work—they are not. The National

Association of Probation Officers remained outside the British Association of Social Workers for precisely these reasons.[41]

The obverse of amalgamation is division. It commonly proceeds within professions, as the phenomenon of internal specialization, and less often leads to official division. The forces behind the process are the same in either case. Specialization most commonly arises because the skills applicable to a given task area develop beyond the ability of single practitioners. Individual professionals lose interchangeability. Less commonly, specialization arises not through complexity of professional knowledge, but through differentiation in an exogenous social structure shaping the profession—divergence in worksites or in client groups, for example. Since a parent profession usually provides specialists with the full protections of professionalism, specialties do not in general leave that parent, but develop special education and certification structures within it. This holds true only if the parent has a strong internal structure; American mechanical engineers lost large numbers of electrical engineers in the late nineteenth century in part because they lacked such strong internal structure. Among professions with internal specialties, the degree of formal organization varies. While specialization of practice has nearly the same extent in American law as in medicine, the legal specialties lack the strong internal structures of the medical ones. Architectural specialization is similarly informal.[42]

The chief cause for formal division is the presence of other groups—either specialties within other professions or strong outsiders—performing the same tasks as the professional specialists. Thus, the English lawyers specializing in receivership split off from law to join others in building accountancy, while dermatologists and other medical specialists do not leave the protective umbrella of medicine, because there are few external groups in their area. Such competitive groups are more likely when specialty task areas lie not within a profession's heartland but on its periphery. This accounts for the secession of American mining from civil engineering, the competitors generally being nonprofessional entrepreneurs.[43]

Division is also a strategy for upwardly mobile groups seeking to set themselves above their current peers. Here the separation is vertical rather than horizontal; difference in status is involved, rather than in task. Such processes divided educational administrators from teaching, and, long ago, surgeons from barbers and apothecaries from grocers. Surgeons may again split from physicians on these grounds. A similar attempt to explicitly separate the corporate and local legal professions failed narrowly in America in the 1920s, despite the nearly absolute separation of educational institutions, sites of practice, and type of work between the two groups. Thus division, like amalgamation, can take place either horizontally or vertically, and, like amalgamation, is not always achieved when attempted.[44]

Even on the periphery, however, pressures against division may be strong, particularly within a dominant profession. Retaining the affiliation may confer power against competitors. Such considerations have kept psychiatry within medicine, even though interchangeability between psychiatrists and other doctors vanished many years ago. Division is also restrained by large, professionally dominated work organizations that organize specialized professionals into an overall division of labor. Hospitals were among the earliest examples, and they are now joined by the growing law, accounting, and architectural firms. The rewards of interdependency in such organizations are so great that specialized professions cannot consider withdrawing from them. Such organizational control over division exists only in the United States, where the size of professional partnerships is not usually restricted and where in recent times professionals have acquired the tax and liability benefits of incorporation. In Britain and particularly France, strict regulation of the size of partnerships and the extent of salaried work has prevented professionally dominated organizations with internal divisions of labor. Thus, there are solicitors' firms of up to twenty partners, but barristers may not form partnerships at all. In France, the *avocats* have been allowed, since 1954, partnerships with up to five members.[45] Even in the United States, the existence of professionally dominant organizations does not always prevent division. In the late nineteenth century, clergymen following the social gospel founded "institutional churches" as large scale social welfare operations. But these organizations were unable to prevent the loss either of the social welfare jurisdiction, over which the clergy then had loose control, or of the subordinate professions, most of whose members moved out into the secular profession of social work.[46]

Both amalgamation and division play a peculiar role in the system of professions. Each involves both a task and a group to do it. Amalgamation absorbs jurisdiction as well as groups. Division creates both a new jurisdiction and the group to occupy it. Their effects are thus not like changes in technology or organization, whose creation or abolition of tasks opens or closes opportunities for groups. Rather, they change the quantitative strengths of various jurisdictions, thereby blocking or facilitating further change. Often amalgamation ends "embarrassing" situations where groups that apply the same knowledge to two different sets of clients are incumbent and quack at law. In such a case—nineteenth century British medicine, for example—amalgamation clearly strengthens the overall hold of the newly joined incumbent; in other situations it may be less beneficial. Division has likewise diverse effects. It may strengthen jurisdiction, particularly when the preceding unity reflected a weak, abstract synthesis. Thus the jurisdictions of law, medicine, and other groups were clearly strengthened by their emancipation from the clergy in the early modern period, as the defeat of the clerical lawyers of Admiralty and Arches by the common lawyers in Equity and Law shows. In other cases, however, division may reduce jurisdictional strength. As throughout the system model, the actual effects of an event are determined by its context at the time.

### SYSTEM PROPERTIES

As the effects induced by internal and external changes work their way through the system, they follow a logic dictated by several factors. The way jurisdiction is embodied in professional work, the location and type of jurisdictonal claims, and the social structure of competing professions all affect the strength of jurisdiction and the outcomes of jurisdictional conflict. But the chains of effects also reflect a system's character as a complete structure.[47]

The first system property is connectivity. The space of tasks has a topology. Some tasks are near others objectively; some jurisdictions are brought close to others by common subjective properties or by jurisdiction under a common profession. Connectivity measures this closeness; in general, the longer the chains of effects generated by disturbances, the more connected we say the system is. One variable affecting this connectivity is the degree of state control; where state control of jurisdiction is strong, as in France, connectivity is low and disturbances propagate little. Connectivity also reflects the relative dominance of abstract over concrete knowledge. Powerful abstractions connect a system strongly, bringing more problems under single sets of organizing ideas. Particularly important agents of connection are professions holding jurisdictions of several different types or in different task areas. Among such professions, defeat in a particular contest is likely to result in further contests in unexpected places; therefore such professions provide important connecting links. The clergy and social work are examples.[48]

Detailed empirical description of the topology of professional tasks is impossibly complex. At the first level, the various jurisdictions of a single profession are closely connected. Beyond these lie the hazier units that I have called task areas. These are areas like health, justice, emotions, and business that are domains of professional work. Theoretically, these are functional units, although to specify them directly is to fall into imperative functionalism. Operationally, they are regions whose boundaries limit the interprofessional effects I have been discussing, although that is a purely empirical definition. Alternatively, they are regions within which Freidson's professional dominance model holds, although many large task areas lack a clear dominant profession—business administration, psychotherapy, financial advice. Within a task area, there generally appears dominance, division of labor, or some other formal interrelation of jurisdiction. Between them, professions exercise a distant respect, coupled with serious border disputes and occasional restructuring. The strength of task area boundaries is a central and problematic property of systems of professions, and forces affecting it (e.g., the emergence of expert systems) can have drastic effects on interprofessional relations.[49]

Another important system property is dominance. In some systems, there may be a few dominant groups; in others there may be many less dominant groups. Dominance may vary within task areas or within the system as a whole. Dominance may be structural—control of organizations and institutions. It may be cultural—control of dominant ideas. It may indeed be both.

In general, the more connected and competitive a system is, the more it will have a uniform degree of cultural dominance. This happens because connectivity is in part determined by the external audiences for professional claims. These external audiences may attach legitimacy to different values in different task areas, but high connectivity implies more common values across task areas, and competition hastens the system's approach to jurisdictional sizes optimal in terms of those common values. Professions far exceeding this size will seem in need of specialization; those far below it will seem craftlike. Therefore, serious disparity in dominance or in level of abstraction between two task areas signifies sharp separation between them. Since interprofessional competition takes place in real time, however, disparity in dominance may also signify the novelty of some areas relative to others. Equilibrium levels of dominance may take so long to achieve that other perturbations prevent their ever arriving.

A similar argument holds for structural, as opposed to cultural dominance. In general, the various task areas in a given system will be dominated by groups of equivalent structural power, because competitive conditions are to some extent set by general social forces, which are largely the same from task area to task area. This particularly holds for work organizations like hospitals and law, accounting, and architectural firms, since their size is usually subject only to governmental constraints and reflects general cultural judgments of "efficiency." It is unlikely that there will be two kinds of work organizations in a given task area, since the organizations of dominant professions will drive out others, even as the nonexclusive qualities of dominant and subordinate professions (associations, schooling, etc.) expand simultaneously. This process means that competitive conditions will produce patterns similar to those Larson predicted simply on the basis of general social changes—for example, the emergence of bureaucratic professionalism—with the difference that the present model allows better for exceptions like psychotherapy.

Another important system property is residuality. Systems may have all of their problems tightly claimed or they may have a good deal of slack. Residuality is high where dominance is high. The higher the level of dominance, the more abstract the ideas holding the dominant jurisdictions together. This abstraction ultimately weakens the ideas' hold on jurisdictions generally, and gives them less ability to define specific, peculiar jurisdictions. Thus, paradoxically, the bigger the dominant professions, both in structural and in cognitive terms, the more numerous the jurisdictions open for attack. Again, the pattern of causation is self-equilibrating, since excess expansion will lead to increased poaching and consequent division.

This argument assumes limits on the dominant groups' abilities to co-opt state power. It is to some extent true that dominance brings the power to subvert these processes. But even midcentury American medicine could not dominate all task areas. Its power extended to certain limits and then attenuated. Nor is it necessarily the case that such power is always available. In France, for example, the state has insisted on fairly narrow jurisdictions, has limited the size of professionally dominated work organizations, and has linked professional self-government to state control. The power available to American medicine is in some sense the level of dominance compatible with American expectations.

Another property of systems of professions is the degree to which professional knowledge is systematized. Extreme systematization is a likely consequence of serious competition for jurisdiction. Competing professions claim jurisdictions by arguments like reduction and establish legitimacy by demonstrating rationally grounded and effective treatment. This forces opponents to clarify their own positions, a clarity that then rebounds on the original attacker. Given such competition, obfuscation is an effective long-term response only where absolute monopoly is a possibility. The English Bar is the only real illustration of this technique.

Systematization has decisive consequences for service. Where professional knowledge is highly systematized, complex problems are likely to be ignored. Parts of them will be handled by various professions, but there will be no service to them as unified wholes. A good example is the problem of death. Clergyman, lawyer, and doctor gradually extricated formal jurisdictions from the general problem. The residual was seized by the struggling profession of funeral direction, which sought to transform the craft of embalming and burying into the profession of grief maintenance. More recently the area has been reinvaded by high-status professionals from social welfare and psychotherapy, who have started the field of death and dying. The competition among American professions has made the *general* handling of death a residual task, and it is perhaps this very fact that has drawn the counseling professions back into the fray.

## Conclusion

In summary, chains of effects in the system of professions begin sometimes in external events, sometimes within the professions themselves. Tasks can be created or destroyed by changes in technology and organizations. New groups can emerge through client differentiation or through the forces leading to enclosure. There are also forces within professions that strengthen or weaken jurisdictions—the development of new knowledge and skill and the structural changes like professionalization and organizational development. Disturbances that begin in these ways then propagate. Standard cognitive strategies move them through the system. The cultural media for the system, these strategies function by changing the relevant level of abstraction. They may lead to amalgamation and division, processes in which both task and group are simultaneously created or absorbed, and which sometimes lead to further changes in the strength of jurisdictional ties.

These various effects propagate until the balance of forces stops them. The seizure of vacant jurisdictions ends when some profession is able to make a new claim without weakening its other jurisdictions to the point of vulnerability.[50] As I noted in the preceding chapter, each contest terminates in one of a variety of settlements, ranging from full jurisdiction through division of labor to subordination and intellectual and advisory jurisdiction. Chains may also terminate in clientele differentiation or occasionally in the destruction of some particular professional group. As the examples I have used imply, most chains are not long. Unlike the strict vacancy model, the present one does not expect a single technological change in one area to generate a chain of successive shifts throughout the system, terminated by a vacancy destruction in some totally unrelated area. The effects of a given initiating event usually work themselves out in a single general task area, through the rearrangement of jurisdictions, the strengthening of some, the weakening of others. Occasionally these effects may reach another general area as an expansive profession like medicine is recalled from its furthest outposts by threats to its heartland division of labor.

This model for professional life remedies the basic defects of the professionalization concept. Its fundamental postulates are (1) that the essence of a profession is its work not its organization; (2) that many variables affect the content and control of that work; and (3) that professions exist in an interrelated system. Change in professions can therefore best be analyzed by specifying forces that affect the content and control of work and by investigating how disturbances in that content and control propagate through the system of professions and jurisdictions. The proper unit of analysis is the jurisdiction, or more generally, the larger task area.

Other analysts have, of course, investigated the defects of the professionalization model, and it is helpful to locate the present model in the context of their work. Some have simply replaced professionalization with new kinds of career models—the deprofessionalization literature abounds. Others have changed the unit of analysis from the individual profession to the professions as a whole and have made bureaucratization their central focus. But perhaps the oldest tradition attacking the strict professionalization model is that of Hughes and his students, which has tended to concentrate on workplace studies of professionals and to emphasize the negotiated character of professional dominance. For the Hughes tradition, the problem with professionalization was the functionalist logic that ultimately lay behind it. The Hughes school felt that professions evolved, to be sure, but that their evolution was interactional, negotiated by the group in an environment. The proper metaphor was that of natural history, where both functional nature and environmental nurture shaped the evolving group.

The present model arises, essentially, by extending the Hughes logic to its limit and focusing on jurisdictional interactions themselves. Interactionist students of professions have continued to treat the profession as the unit of analysis, although they have treated it quite flexibly and have investigated its interactions in the work environment. I have gone one step further. Moreover, by treating jurisdiction not only in the work environment but also in the much more formal public and legal environments I have tried to handle what I regard as the classic problem of interactionism—its inability to explain the evident stability of many interactions over time. My solution, and again it is a familiar one, is to demonstrate several layers of interaction, each operating at a different speed, such that the slower ones afford stability to the elements that are negotiated in the faster ones.[51]

# II  THE SYSTEM'S ENVIRONMENT

The system model so far sketched assumes that professions are internally homogeneous. Of course they are not, and internal differentiation can both generate system disturbances and absorb them. I have also assumed that competition for jurisdiction is in some sense free. Yet perhaps acquisition of several jurisdictions confers advantages in public and legal contests for further ones.

Likewise, I have not yet investigated the social and cultural trends that environ the system. On the one hand, social change opens and closes jurisdictions, provides new, bureaucratic models for practice, changes the basic audiences for professional claims, and creates new powers for co-optation. On the other hand, cultural forces reshape professional knowledge, change the currency of legitimation, and build the universities within which professional knowledge and education are transformed. These external forces provide most of the actual, historical events that drive change in professional life; to study them is to move from system structure to systematic content.

The following three chapters take up these topics. Chapter 5 considers internal differentiation and the problematic power assumption. Chapter 6 discusses the basic history of social changes surrounding the professions, addressing at the same time synchronic variation in social variables, particularly the role of the state. Chapter 7 examines changes in the cultural environment, both in knowledge and in legitimating values.

# 5    Internal Differentiation and the Problem of Power

I have so far treated professions as if they were individuals. There is a system, to be sure, but a system of archetypes. In fact the professions are not archetypical units of archetypical individuals, but organized groups of individuals who do different things in different workplaces for different clients. These diverse individuals have equally diverse careers.

How does internal differentiation affect the system of professions? Like other properties of professions, it has its effects through a profession's position in the system. Thus, internal differentiation can generate or absorb system disturbances; a challenged profession can respond not only by fighting a contest or changing its level of abstraction, but also by changing internally. Conversely, internal changes can generate such system disturbances.

Secondly, internal structure affects the interconnections between professions. Careers may be structured so that one profession recruits from another—as business administration does from engineering or librarianship from academics. Differentiation of worksites may bring members of professions into closer interaction with members of related professions than with their own. Finally, internal differentiation mediates the separation of the fluctuating workplace relations between professions from the relatively stable legal or public relations between them. It makes the formalized public and legal pictures of interprofessional relations two among many versions of professional life, so that the rapid changes of most professional life have few disturbing effects. Without internal differentiation, this decoupling of the formal and informal worlds of interprofessional relations cannot occur.

Internal differences thus have profound consequences. These consequences vary with the internal structure involved. There are four important ones, embodying differences by intraprofessional status, by client, by organization of work, and by career pattern. These structures are by no means separate. Indeed, they are often so mutually reinforcing that analysts have derived one from another—internal status from client status, for example. But it is easiest to understand them by viewing them separately. In each case, I shall consider both the effects a structure can send into the system and the effects it can absorb from the system. I shall also consider how that structure interrelates members of different professions and how it decouples the formal and workplace settings of interprofessional relations.[1]

## Internal Stratification

Undoubtedly the most interesting source of internal differentiation is a phenomenon I have elsewhere called professional regression. Professions tend to withdraw into themselves, away from the task for which they claim public jurisdiction. This pattern results from internal status rankings. The professionals who receive the highest status from their peers are those who work in the most purely professional environments. They are professionals' professionals who do not sully their work with nonprofessional matters, consultants who receive referrals only from other professionals. Barristers and modern-day surgeons are examples. Such high-status professionals may have exceedingly high incomes and extensive professional education, but their distinguishing mark is their work in purely professional environments.[2]

That such workers should enjoy the highest status before their peers is not surprising. A profession is organized around the knowledge system it applies, and hence status within profession simply reflects degree of involvement with this organizing knowledge. The more one's professional work employs that knowledge alone—the more it excludes extraneous factors—the more one enjoys high status. On this argument, the most pure professional work is academic work, which has nothing to do with clients at all, and, indeed, academic professionals generally enjoy high status within their professions. Conversely, the front-line professionals who make the first professional contacts with clients, and whom the public usually venerates, are generally at the bottom of status rankings within their professions, precisely because they work in environments where professional knowledge must be compromised with client reality. There is thus a peculiar paradox.

Professionals admire academics and consultants who work with knowledge alone; the public admires practitioners who work with clients.

Since professionals draw their self-esteem more from their own world than from the public's, this status mechanism gradually withdraws entire professions into the purity of their own worlds. The front-line service that is both their fundamental task and their basis for legitimacy becomes the province of low-status colleagues and para-professionals. This is the mechanism that withdrew the barristers into the Inns of Court, that staffs most American hospitals with foreign medical graduates, and that leaves state mental hospitals without board-certified psychiatrists. This mechanism means that the general public receives psychotherapy from psychologists and social workers who are themselves the clients of psychiatrists. Such professional regression clearly weakens jurisdiction, opening a potential vacancy in the system. In the psychotherapy case, the "lesser" professions of social work and psychology have successfully invaded the jurisdiction of dominant psychiatry. In the case of the British serjeants-at-law, professional regression meant professional death.[3]

The mechanism of professional regression is irreversible. Even under clear threat, regressing professions do not eradicate the internal status distinctions that cause regression. Rather, they attempt to control their heartland jurisdictions by other means. They may structure the professional career so that it begins in the heartland and, in elite cases at least, works its way out. In American medicine, for example, all doctors begin as front-line specialists—house staff in hospitals. Those who can, become specialists and consultants, moving towards practice in a purely medical and often academic environment. Alternatively, professions create divisions of labor in which some professionals are supported in purely professional environments by others who mediate with the client world. Thus, the design partners of the great architectural firms don't bother with client negotiations at all, which are the task of the business partners. The latter are all of them architects, to be sure, but not of the same professional status as the design partners.[4]

In contrast to professional regression, which originates a system disturbance, professional status changes can also serve to absorb external disturbances. If demand for professional services is insufficient, the relegation of some professionals to a lower or even a deprofessional status will maintain demand sufficient for the professional elite. The late-nineteenth century separation of black and female doctors from the white male medical profession in America can be seen as an attempt to advance one professional segment over another in a context of fixed demand. The closing of the American Psychiatric Association to assistant physicians in the mid-ninteenth century is similar. Since there was a relatively fixed demand for senior psychiatrists, superintendents created a subordinate group rather than share their perquisites with the juniors who shared their professional knowledge.[5]

Internal stratification in professions thus both generates system disturbances and absorbs them. It also drastically affects interconnections between professions, through the problem of status ambiguity. Internal status differences combine with differences in clients and in work organizations to create wide disparities in income, power, and prestige within professions. At the same time, the various professions involved in a task area generally fall into a stable status hierarchy: medicine, nursing, pharmacy, physicians' assistants, laboratory technicians, and so on, in the medical area; psychiatrists, psychologists, social workers, clergymen, and so on, in the psychotherapeutic area. As the range of prestige within these professions grows, there must eventually result status overlap between neighboring professions. Among professions tightly connected by work area or referral networks, this leads to serious status ambiguity, both within professions and within the public perception of professions.[6]

This status ambiguity in fact has little or no effect. First, status hierarchies are perceived in two limited worlds. One world is that of the profession; the status perceived there is the intraprofessional status just discussed. The other world is the workplace. While professionals working together are well aware of the public and legal status relations between their respective professions, they are considerably less aware of the internal hierarchies of other professions. But overlap is perceived only if intra- and interprofessional status are ultimately referred to a common linear scale. The reciprocal ignorance of internal hierarchies, an ignorance carefully maintained by the superordinates, at least, serves to prevent this reference to a common scale.

The effects of overlap are also dulled by the strong relation of intraprofessional status and worksite. Only in the workplace may superordinates regularly encounter members of officially subordinate professions who enjoy higher status on some general social scale than they do themselves. But low-status superordinates seldom work with high-status subordinates. Quite the contrary. All the professionals who work in mental hospitals and criminal courts have low status within their professions—the doctors, the lawyers, the nurses, the judges, the social workers—because the workplace is professionally "dirty" for all of them. The clients' problems require them all to make fatal compromises between their professional knowledge and the morass of human affairs, with a consequent loss of intraprofessional status. By contrast, at elite teaching hospitals, the doctors, the nurses, and the social workers are all high in their respective professional hierarchies; the best in one profession are talking down to the best in another. Thus it happens that interprofessional hierarchies in each workplace tend to follow the publicly accepted model, because workplace partly determines intraprofessional status. Strain arises only when elite members of subordinate professions invade dirty workplaces in an attempt to take over jurisdiction, as psychologists and social workers did mental hospitals during the years after the Community Mental Health Act of 1963.[7]

Such status strains might be expected to communicate their effects to public images. But the strains in fact disappear in public images. In theory each profession should emphasize its best, most "professional" work in the public discourse about professions and by contrast should portray competitors as highly differentiated, emphasizing the lower ends of competitors' scales. But the leading members of professional organizations—who are the individuals actually voicing these ideologies—are themselves likely to come from high-status workplaces and therefore to be relatively ignorant of the skeletons in other professions' closets. Consequently, pariah professionals disappear from formal interprofessional discourse altogether. At the same time, the extreme upper elite is deemphasized in formal discourse, since such individuals (academics, consultants, etc.) have little or no appeal to the public.

As a result, the breadth of intraprofessional status narrows to a nearly uniform picture of the typical social worker or doctor or architect. This typical picture is of course but one of many possible models for actual work in the profession. But nothing in public discourse about professions specifies where that model fits in the internal hierarchy. As a result, the status hierarchy itself fluctuates freely without affecting the public image of the typical professional. Internal stratification allows the publicly typical to become the intraprofessionally atypical. For example, large sections of a profession can be ghettoized—as mental hospitals were by psychiatry, and increasingly house staff is by medicine—without public perception. Only when the American public began to notice that emergency-room physicians often had difficulty with English did the vast changes in the medical status structure become publicly evident.

## Client Differentiation

As we have seen, client differentiation is often important in inter-professional relations. Two professions in superordinate-subordinate relation may occupy a common jurisdiction, with the superordinate generally serving the higher-status clients and the subordinate the lower-status ones. A similar sort of differentiation can take place within a profession. Client differentiation can be contrasted with task differentiation (specialization), which has already been considered. The latter changes the strengths of jurisdictions, usually increasing them, but does not generate a vacancy in the system. Client differentiation, on the other hand, can have profound system implications.[8]

Although I am more concerned with the effects of client differentiation than with its origins, why client differentiation emerges and endures is an important question. It may result from the exercise of power by those with high-status clients. Alternatively, it may reflect efficiency or some other "natural" force. Interprofessional power seems the best explanation in the special case of differentiation purely by client status, without any admixture of differentiation in task or in client structure. Thus, some doctors have only wealthy clients and others only middle-class ones. But in other cases—the differences between lawyers working for corporations and lawyers working for individuals—there are clear grounds for the professional differences in the differences of client structure.[9]

Client differentiation has some system effects by reinforcing the intraprofessional status differences of the last section. Several factors ensure this relation. In the first place, a doctor, clergyman, or lawyer who serves high-status clients receives some reflected glory, just as one who serves charity cases receives some reflected opprobrium. In the second, high-status clients pick high-status professionals to the extent that they can. But third and perhaps most importantly, high-status clients often aid in their own diagnosis and treatment. Often professionals themselves, they may well have some grasp of the profession whose aid they seek. At the least, they understand and recognize the basic professional rights of diagnosis—the restriction of relevant information and so on—and know how to present their problem properly for professional work. As a result, they themselves preprofessionalize their problems and the professionals they patronize thus have less need to compromise their professional knowledge, with consequent high status among their peers.[10]

This relation is strengthened by workplace status. As I have argued, high-status professionals are likely to work in high-status workplaces, and these generally have high-status clients. This parallel holds strongly in American law, and is also spectacularly evident in religion, as Liston Pope's study of Gastonia tells us. But there are exceptions. During American medicine's most rapid development, from 1880 to 1920, it was the great public hospitals, with their overburdened administrations and poverty-stricken clients, that were the high-status institutions of professional life, precisely because the clients' lack of power made the institutions ideal centers for the purely professional activity of research. The "society doctor" of that age enjoyed great public status, but found his ability to exercise his profession hampered by the irrelevant demands of clients for other services.[11]

Differentiation in clients also affects interprofessional relations directly, through differences in the clients themselves. Clients can be individuals, or disorganized groups, or highly organized groups. While all three can have similar problems, their service breeds great differences, and professionals generally specialize in serving one of them. Hence come the familiar differences between law, accounting, and architectural firms serving corporate clients and those serving individual clients, those serving corporate clients being "more incorporated" themselves. Librarians are similarly differentiated by clientele—school children, academics, industry, government, the public. Although libraries as social structures are reasonably constant, the type and flow of demands shifts sharply from client to client.[12]

Structure of client affects professional practice in several ways. First, large and organized clients can preprofessionalize issues; for example, large commercial concerns generally have their own legal departments, although they take major legal projects to outside firms. Organized clients are also likely to demand more constant levels of service, as well as a more predictable mix of specialized work. Both forces feed the internal divisions of labor among professionals serving such clients. Organized clients also require services peculiar to their organized status—corporate tax and securities law, corporate accounting requirements, corporate requirements in building structure.[13]

The system implications of client differentiation are considerable, but complex. Most importantly, it may lead to specialization, with the consequent possibility of division. Certainly in both American law and American and English accounting this has been an important outcome. But further implications are not easy to specify. For example, can client specialization vacate a jurisdiction or create a loose group with no jurisdiction? It may do so by making certain aspects of jurisdiction less defensible. Thus, the fact that a large segment of the legal profession never handles routine transfers of home ownership means that that work is more susceptible to routinization (and consequent deprofessionalization) or seizure by other groups than it would otherwise be. But here client differentiation is mixed with task differentiation.

The central problem is that client-specific professionals are vulnerable to the fates of their clients, which fates are established outside the system. This connection is particularly strong when client differentiation has led to task differentiation, as in the case of primary versus secondary and college teaching. There, client specialization is so complete that mobility between professional subgroups is minimal, even though demographic forces regularly shift the balance of demand, with catastrophic effects. Indeed, one general system effect of client differentiation is simple absorption of market fluctuations. Client differentiation gains when demand for professional services exceeds capacity, and shrinks when it falls. Well known from ecological theory, this argument predicts that the rate at which demand fluctuates should determine the degree of client specialization. But since these rates vary considerably from situation to situation and from period to period, there is no chance of general prediction.[14]

Sometimes members of different professions serving common clients generate bonds through their clients. Dickens paints such a bond between Mr. Merdle's friends "Bar" and "Physician" in the later chapters of *Little Dorrit*. But this bond is usually mediated by work in common settings. What builds bonds or strains between different professions is common work or common work place, not common clients. Doctors who see "green card" welfare cases do not thereby build bonds to the social workers who issue the cards. But if both work in a community clinic or neighborhood center, then the common clientele emphasizes the bond between them. Such interactions may then feed into the status strains of the last section.[15]

Client differentiation facilitates the decoupling of public and workplace images of interprofessional relations in much the same way as does intraprofessional status. The existence of differentiation means that considerable change can occur in workplace reality—in the percentage of total professional output dedicated to a particular group of clients, for example—without requiring corresponding changes in the public image. Since individual, private law still exists, for example, the public can continue to believe it to be characteristic of the profession, even though the corporate lawyers thought of shedding it altogether as long as fifty years ago.

## Workplace, Workplace Structure, and
## Internal Divisions of Labor

Within a given profession, professionals work in a wide variety of settings. In the United States and Britain, the traditional distinction is between independent and salaried professionals, and it is well known that there has been a sharp decline in independent professionals in both countries. However, one must first distinguish autonomous and heteronomous professionals; the latter are employed by organizations not headed by others of their own profession, the former work either for themselves or for professional peers. Within the autonomous category one can then distinguish the salaried and the unsalaried, and, among the latter, between solo practitioners and small, medium, and giant partnerships. The heteronomous category has expanded rapidly since the Second World War, as have the salaried and the medium and giant firms. This is particularly noticeable in law, accounting, and architecture. Medicine and veterinary medicine follow more slowly, although the former has the advantage of a peculiar hybrid—the hospital—largely controlled by the profession but administered by others. Dentists remain the major solo practitioners of America. In France, large professional firms have until very recently been restricted or prohibited by administrative law, and the Anglo-American tendency to gigantism has been averted.[16]

Most professionals, of course, have always been heteronomous. This category includes the clergy and the military among the older professions, and social work, teaching, academics, engineering, librarianship, forestry, and many others among the more recent. These professions have, of course, their solo practitioners—the revivalist, the mercenary, the social work "counselor," the test coach (English "crammer"), the engineering consultant, and so on. But these are exceptions; their professional peers usually lack control of their own settings of work.[17]

The important variable in workplace social organization, however, is not really size or control, but rather the thing that size and control indicate—the division of labor in professional work. This division of labor may reflect intraprofessional status forces; professionally impure work may be given to particular members of a profession. It may also reflect client differentiation. But the most important divisions of labor divide fully professional work into routine and nonroutine elements, with the two falling to different segments of a profession or even to paraprofessionals. Clear examples are the gradual delegation of conveyancing and costing to managing clerks by solicitors and of drafting to draftsmen by architects, as well as the separation of curriculum planning from classroom teaching, and that of systems design from computer programming. In every case, the eventual result has been the degradation of what had been professional work to nonprofessional status, sometimes accompanied by the degradation of those who do the work. Although theories of the "proletarianization of professionals" and of "deprofessionalization" see mostly recent degradation, degradation of work is in fact an old and familiar process in professional life. It was by drawing the line between compounding medicines and prescribing them that the British apothecaries left their brother chemists out of the unification of the British medical profession in 1858. Similarly, although social work began with "social diagnosis" and "casework," routine management of American welfare cases has for decades been the province of untrained social welfare workers, while the professionally certified social workers do only administration or individual therapy.[18]

Degradation ultimately results in the explicit division of the groups involved. This rule fails only when the division of labor is tied to career patterns, and then in appearance only. Professionals in training often do delegated work. Thus, medical students do "scut" work—routine, delegable medical functions such as giving shots, cleaning sores, taking histories—that they will generally escape in later career. This degraded work serves partly as an intiation ritual in which the ontogeny of the individual career recapitulates the hierarchy of the medical professions. But it also reinforces medical dominance by retaining a formal presence in an area of work almost completely delegated to nurses and others. Similarly, senior practicing lawyers spend remarkably little time doing research; most legal research is done by law students and associates. In each case, much routine work has left the profession altogether, and what remains remains only because it is tied to career patterns.[19]

Degradation is an essential mechanism for absorbing shifts in demand, in organizations, and in technologies that may affect a profession's jurisdictions. An excellent example is the rapid degradation within computer programming. In the early sixties, computer programmers were ebullient mavericks of the corporate world, handling payroll and accounting automation from the initial stages to final system design. Since only large companies and universities could afford the relevant hardware, systems were usually customized. When minicomputers, time-sharing, and simple microprocessors slashed computing costs, new clients appeared desiring either simple automation of data processing or implementation of simple logical structures. At the same time, large firm and university demand for software exploded. The inchoate profession of programming met this tremendous demand by increasing its internal efficiency. Just as the compilers had routinized the writing of machine-language instructions, now general algorithms routinized basic bookkeeping and calculating tasks, such as sorting under various data constraints. Since the performance of these routines could be calculated without actual implementation, their adaptation to a particular application was straightforward. The real professional expertise lay in knowing which set of algorithms would operate with maximum efficiency on specified data. The sudden expansion in demand thus led to the rise of superprogrammers—the systems analysts—who designed systems and specified algorithms. The details were left to others, the rapidly expanding subordinate group of programmers, who carried out the designs of systems analysts much as nurses carry out treatment plans designed by doctors.[20]

The success of computer programming required the development of knowledge that permitted a division of labor to increase professional output. Other professions have not found such knowledge. The British accounting houses of the late nineteenth century were unable to invent such a division of labor, with the result that municipal accounting, cost accounting, and so on grew up completely outside the early accounting establishment. Other professions have had middling success. In the early years of "efficient education," American superintendents of schools tried to take curriculum planning from teachers. As in the other examples, this movement reflected a sharp increase in demand—enrollments in American schools expanded by 50 percent between 1890 and 1920, and enrollments in high schools by more than 1,000 percent. Although the superintendents were only partly successful in centralizing curriculum work, they saw clearly that internal division of labor is one way drastic demand changes can be handled.[21]

Degradation can arise either through the degradation of the work (and status) of given individual professionals or through the recruitment of new professionals to positions embodying the degraded work. It is not clear, for example, which has happened in computer programming, although large numbers of B.A.-level programmers are currently being hired as "programmers" in the degraded sense.[22] Degradation of work is perhaps more familiar, from cases like nursing, librarianship, and teaching. The move of medical care from home to hospital destroyed the former independence of the private-duty nurse and placed her in a subordinated division of labor. A similar change occurred in librarianship, through the creation of subordinated specialty positions under directing librarians, a process repeated with slight variation in the teaching example just given. But in all three cases, recruitment changed as well. In nursing, recruitment of higher-status women declined; in librarianship and teaching, recruitment of men declined. Although feminization is perhaps the most familiar form of degraded recruitment, it is not the only one, as the class change in nursing shows. A similar decline in recruit status occurred with the huge expansion of mechanical engineering in the late nineteenth century.[23]

In summary, degradation has profound implications for interprofessional competition. Successful degradation, when not based on career patterns, generally leads to division between an upper, "truly professional" group and a lower, subordinate one. It inevitably leaves the lower group open to invasion by outsiders and paraprofessionals. By contrast, it tends to enhance the jurisdiction of the superordinate group, which has rid itself of dangerously routine work.

Divisions of labor often exist between professions as well as within them, and therefore, as we have already seen, workplace organization strongly affects the network of interprofessional connection. It is joint participation in common worksites that creates the strongest bonds (and strains) between professions. It is within the heteronomous worksites that hold most professionals that the status forces analyzed above work themselves out, just as it is within such organizations that the official division of labor between professions receives its practical shape.

Finally, the implications of workplace organization, and particularly of internal divisions of labor, for the relation between official and actual professional lives seem much the same as those of differentiation in clients and in intraprofessional status. The official image of professional work usually involves one among many possible settings of professional work. As long as some significant fraction of the profession works in such a setting, the official image remains in place irrespective of other changes. Thus, the medical profession had long since moved to office-based practice when the public expectation that doctors should make house calls finally disappeared. But in another sense, internal divisions of labor challenge this decoupling. Internal divisions of labor are typically vertical divisions of labor, and their result is often vertical division. Vertical division leads to particularly bitter fights within professions, fights that inevitably become public, as did those between upper and lower branches of the British medical and legal professions in the nineteenth century. The lower group has to defend its "professional" status, and since its superiors will not listen, it inevitably seeks other audiences. The realities of professional life then become publicly apparent. In computer programming, the first signs of this process are already evident. Surveys based on occupational titles show that there are more systems analysts than computer programmers in the United States, while detailed studies of actual work show that people doing what I have called systems-analyst work are in fact vastly outnumbered by those doing programming. Since the name systems analyst is not protected, the subordinate group has claimed it, both at work and in public. In contested cases, the carefully cultivated separation of workplace reality and public presentation does not survive.

## Career Patterns

Every profession has typical careers. As in most aspects of professional life, there is one official pattern and a variety of unofficial ones. Career differences often reflect status differences. Careers aiming at high intraprofessional status generally have longer training periods and are more fixed in form than other careers. Law students aiming at major firms "must" make law review, and later must march along the junior-associate, senior-associate, junior-partner path to senior partnership. Oswald Hall has outlined the similar patterns in medicine, and the phenomenon is equally familiar in academics.[24]

But quite exclusive of differentiation in careers, the general career line itself is an important differentiator within professions; it too means that professionals are not interchangeable. Some are young, some are old; some have training and experience, some training only. The structure of this career line both generates effects within the system of professions and absorbs them. Change in career structure has a catalytic role; it does not generally seize or abandon jurisdiction, but profoundly affects a profession's relation to system fluctuations.[25]

Let us first consider a pattern that I shall call demographic rigidity. A profession is demographically rigid if its current size and reproductive mechanisms prevent its expanding or contracting rapidly. This situation has grave consequences. Individual professionals can migrate between modes of professional practice, although, of course, this freedom varies from profession to profession; such migration handles shifts in relative specialty demand. But changes in overall demand may require sudden production of more or fewer professionals. Demographic rigidity prevents this.[26]

A central aspect of demographic rigidity is the length and nature of the formally structured career. In some professions the specified career is long: several levels of training, several stages of practice under increasingly emancipated conditions, perhaps several mutually exclusive forms of practice to which the various training pathways lead. The length of such a formally specified career generally implies early entry. Law, medicine, and academics are familiar examples of this pattern. Although less familiar, the military is the most fascinatingly rigid of professions, extending the rigid career period to retirement. Bureaucratic structure is, however, *not* the cause of demographic rigidity, for the various clergies, in many cases among the most bureaucratically structured of professions, are by no means characterized by career rigidity.[27]

Rigidity also arises when the future size of a profession is tied to current size, as, for example, when apprenticeship is part of training. British solicitors have traditionally served five years of articled clerkship with a certificated solicitor. From 1843, solicitors were forbidden to have more than two clerks at once, and in fact most solicitors preferred managing clerks, who took less effort to train, to articled clerks. The actual ratio was about one articled clerk for every three solicitors. The solicitors were thus ill equipped to deal with the sudden expansion of demand at the end of the nineteenth century, because their reproduction was tied too closely to their current size.[28]

In other professions, careers take much looser forms. Training is brief. Learning occurs on the job, and careers are entrepreneurial. The profession's current size is only loosely linked to its future one. Librarianship and social work, for example, are characterized by entry at many ages and by relatively short formal training. Such professions are often of lower status than the demographically rigid ones, although the clergy, at least in its Protestant versions, may belie this generalization.[29]

Demographic rigidity profoundly affects the response of professions to sudden shifts in demand. Since rigidity increases the time of response to change, it leaves the new demand or jurisdiction open to invasion until new cohorts are produced. The classic example of this is nineteenth-century British accounting. The sudden expansion of accounting to municipal and nonprofit bodies, decided by legislative fiat, found the Incorporated and Chartered Accountants completely unprepared. I noted above that they invented no divisions of labor to extend their services, and rather than restructure their career patterns or recognize other patterns as legitimate, they surrendered these new jurisdictions to other groups. Precisely the same mechanism can work in reverse. The American academic profession spent the sixties recruiting new members and pushing them through a lengthy fixed career. By the time these recruits were ready for practice, demand had fallen catastrophically, for purely external (demographic) reasons, and there resulted a cohort of highly trained professionals with nowhere to work. By contrast, demographically unrigid professions deal easily with demand fluctuations by simply absorbing new individuals, as social work did thousands of unemployed white-collar workers during the depression.[30]

Thus, demographic rigidity decreases professions' ability both to take up excess demand and to restrict excess service. Why should a mechanism so disfunctional survive? In part, it is enforced on professions by the structure of their knowledge. The more knowledge there is, the longer training has to be. Longer training means a higher investment in individual trainees and requires more certain recruitment. But this does not explain the large sections of medical and legal training in the United States that are irrelevant to practice, such as organic chemistry and constitutional law. (British doctors receive much less basic science training than American ones.)[31] Nor does it explain the relative prohibition on late entry. Demographic rigidity may be a luxury of dominance. The surplus individuals can find their way into other occupations—as unemployed academics found their way into librarianship, industrial engineering, and a variety of other professions in the sixties, and as unemployed physiologists found their way into philosophy in nineteenth-century Germany. Surpluses can also disappear through individuals' officially remaining members of one profession while in effect practicing another. Large numbers of nonparochial clergy work as counselors, social workers, businessmen, schoolteachers, and so on, but retain official membership in the clergy. Demographic rigidity also facilitates defense of the professional group itself, making it a more coherent, homogeneous group; its disfunctions may be endured for that benefit.[32]

Permeable professions handle system demand fluctuations quite easily through flexibility in age of recruitment and length of training. There are also "pool" professions, where specialized professionals work while awaiting new demand in their own. Teaching has become such a pool profession in the United States. It supports several groups whose parent professions lack sufficient, steady demand, in particular music and the arts. Local entertainment employed many musicians prior to the rise of radio and television. When the mass media took over much of that work, employing relatively fewer musicians to do it, local musicians became the music teachers and the band and choral directors of the schools, who still play occasional commercial jobs, teach a few students, and direct church choirs. The existence of such a pool profession allows the music profession to exist, outside major cities, largely on a part-time basis.[33]

Career paths also play an extraordinary role in the network of interprofessional connections. At first glance, this notion seems silly; the central idea of a "career" is remaining in a single occupation for a lifetime. Professionalism arose to make individuals' careers invulnerable to the instabilities of capitalist employment. But central as it was to the nineteenth-century conception of professionalism, the concept of career did not represent reality. Since the lifelong career severs the contemporaneous link between professional supply and demand, it has often been necessary for professionals to leave their careers and enter other professions. In some nineteenth-century professions—like psychiatry—turnover was truly astonishing. The few men who held American hospital superintendencies for twenty- or thirty-year periods cannot obscure the many who stayed but two or three. There was also high turnover among the clergy. At present such out-mobility is high in nearly every American profession except pharmacy and dentistry. By age forty-five, about 10 percent of a beginning cohort of pharmacists has left active practice, about 30 percent of physicians, 25 percent of lawyers, 30 percent of architects. Rates for clergy, engineers, social workers, and teachers are around 50 percent. (The image of lifetime career is thus another of the public appearances belied by the occupational realities of the professions.) This turnover is largely an American phenomenon. On the Continent, the professions draw their character *as careers* from their quasi-civil-service origins. Within such a formal structure, mobility is difficult.[34]

The individuals leaving the American professions must, of course, go somewhere. Many enter administration and management. Some enter government service. Others move into teaching, often in professional schools. But many simply enter another profession. The general flow is from professions with demographic rigidity to those without, and indeed, management, teaching, social work, and librarianship are among the characteristic targets. While little detail is known about this mobility, it clearly helps bind professions together. In the nineteenth-century United States, such ties bound schoolteaching to law, medicine, and clergy, because schoolteaching was generally a career stage on the way to all three. Today, such ties bind a large number of professions to administration, and indeed, perhaps the reason that business administration has never successfully managed to "professionalize" is that it commonly recruits from other professions, particularly law, accounting, and engineering.[35]

Career and mobility structures have a strong impact on the decoupling of public images and occupational realities. In occupational reality, fluctuations in individuals' career patterns are the chief means through which professions deal with local fluctuations in their environments. In the demographically rigid professions, these induced career fluctuations have become increasingly important as more professionals work in salaried and heteronomous settings, where administrative considerations dominate. The less-rigid professions have long used personnel flow to stabilize supply and demand.

In systems like the French one, where professional training is absolutely specific and interprofessional mobility is low, these mechanisms for handling demand fluctuations are unavailable. It is therefore necessary that there be formal and public planning of professional numbers, and indeed the government generally regulates the numbers of the various professions with some care. There, the lack of internal differentiation forces public and workplace images together. In America, when a major profession finds itself with excess members, the result is usually a brief flurry of public concern, but mobility generally removes the problem from public visibility quickly. Only the individuals affected need worry about it. The famed plight of the aircraft engineers in the early 1970s and the "Ph.D. glut" of the late 1970s are good examples. Such out-migration enables the comfortable perpetuation of the public picture of the lifelong professional, for without it the gluts would be serious social problems, as they are in France. By contrast, a sharp demand for a demographically rigid profession creates a public crisis in America, as did the demand for trained scientists after Sputnik. This situation, however, offers no threat to the public picture of professional life, and is not treated as such. On the contrary, it normally affirms a positive, romanticized picture of professional life—in the Sputnik case the hero-scientist saving his society from the Russian menace.[36]

The various forms of internal differentiation thus have profound effects on interprofessional relations. In the first instance, these are effects generating or absorbing system disturbances. Internal status differences can seriously weaken jurisdictional control; status changes can also absorb fluctuations in demand for professional services. Client differentiation may weaken jurisdictional control, but its main role is passive, increasing as demand increases, decreasing as it falls. Internal divisions of labor also handle demand shifts, particularly sudden increases. By degrading some professionals and elevating others professions can vastly increase their output. The internal differences created by careers, in contrast, reflect other forces than demand and consequently often impair a profession's ability to deal with demand shift. Professions with rigid career structures and reproduction systems resort to simple out-migration when facing insufficient demand and cannot respond at all to sudden increases. Those with flexible career structures handle these matters more easily, perhaps at some cost in status.

Internal differentiation also affects connections between professions. The division of labor, both within and between professions, plays the most important role in creating workplace links. The workplace contact occasioned by the division of labor leads to the potential strains of interprofessional status overlap. But these are dissipated, since professions in a given worksite have similar positions in their respective status rankings. Client differentiation has less importance for interconnection, merely reinforcing the common-worksite effect. Professions are also linked by recruitment. In summary, while professions are generally in system competition, many aspects of internal professional differentiation paradoxically help bind different professions together.

Internal differentiation also provides the basic mechanism that keeps the public picture of professional life separate from the workplace one. Were there only one professional status, workplace, and client type in a given profession, any shift in these actualities would at once become publicly evident. But since there are many varieties of each, great changes can occur in their relative importance without forcing any great shift in the public image of professional life. These changes in fact lead to radical career shifts, particularly for individuals in demographically rigid professions, but these shifts remain relatively invisible to the public eye.

The internal structure of professions thus limits the effects discussed in the last chapter. In a strict vacancy system, vacancy effects propagate through the system until they pass out of it. But the internal differentiation patterns of professions in fact absorb most system disturbances before they have gone very far. In physical terms, jurisdictional collisions are not perfectly elastic. Forces of jurisdictional change often deform the professions themselves rather than simply passing through them to the next.

## Power

I have derived the strength and weakness of jurisdiction from the various acts and structures of professional work, from the abstraction of professional knowledge, and from the degree of differentiation. None of this allows for the professional power discussed by Eliot Freidson, Magali Larson, and others. Cannot dominant professions consolidate a power that confers distinct advantages in jurisdictional competitions?

Furthermore, to found jurisdictional success on client choice is to make the assumptions of classical pure competition: that clients know about the various service alternatives, that the services are in fact substitutable, that there are no investments or sunk costs in present client choices. Yet patients may continue with private doctors because finding out about HMOs takes time and energy, because private doctors and HMOs deliver slightly different kinds and qualities of services, and because actually making the switch means writing off an investment in a particular doctor's familiarity with their problems. Beyond such workplace choices, in the legal arena the weight of both case law and statute gives an even greater conservatism to the system. Surely, a profession with legislated privileges is more likely to gain further privileges than is another profession to overthrow them. In summary, may not these conservative qualities undermine the kind of competition I have assumed?

The existence of dominant power and of system conservatism is not to be doubted; the issue is of their degree. Like any competitive, equilibrating model, this one recognizes forces retarding equilibrium in the short run. But in the long run it believes the equilibrating forces prevail, assuming that no profession delivering bad services can stand indefinitely against competent outsiders, however powerful it may be. Whether this assumption is correct rests in part on the definition of the short and the long run. Over the one-month short run, system conservatism dictates jurisdiction. Conversely, few dominant groups have survived a century of impotence or inactivity. Where should the intermediate boundary be drawn? In chapter 2, I have already specified boundaries I believe are empirically verifiable. Jurisdictions are renegotiated in workplaces over two- to three-year periods, in public over ten- to-twenty year periods, in the law over twenty- to fifty-year periods. These assertions imply that equilibrating forces dominate over the time periods specified.[37]

Ultimately, of course, the choice between an equilibrating model and a power model makes a political distinction by dividing phenomena into things-to-be-explained and things-to-be-ignored. I have here chosen a structural and equilibrating model because I saw a class of phenomena (interprofessional conflicts) that others had always treated as incidental—either incidental to the development of single groups, as in functionalist views of professions, or incidental to the preeminence of dominant ones, as in power theories. By taking these conflicts as to-be-explained, I consciously forego explanatory power lodged in each of the other models. The following discussion of power, then, can be seen at one level as an analysis of how and how much system conservatism retards the processes already discussed, and at another as a reasoned defense of my assumptions.

Professional power can be operationally defined as the ability to retain jurisdiction when system forces imply that a profession ought to have lost it. It has two aspects. The first is an ability to win jurisdiction by means not connected with strength of subjective jurisdiction (the variables of chapter 2), but rather by "interprofessional force." Such force is illustrated by dominant professions keeping subordinates in tutelage after a settlement by functional division of labor is appropriate, as English solicitors have managing clerks in the areas of conveyancing and costing, for example. But power is not only a matter of winning contests, but also one of preventing some contests from arising at all. A profession can, for example, exercise its subjective jurisdiction to so define its work that outsiders cannot see that treatment fails. By publicly emphasizing the germ theory of illness, the medical profession long minimized its failures with chronic problems like arthritis, heart disease, and cancer.[38]

As this example shows, professional power has several sources. Subjective jurisdiction itself constitutes a form of power, conferring prerogatives that help in jurisdictional contests. To the extent that the public accepts an incumbent's definitions of its problems, the incumbent acquires an enormous power over opponents whose case rests on new definitions. A good example is the legal profession's long battle with accountants over whether income-tax work involves legal problems or accounting problems. Before the general public, lawyers enjoy undoubted jurisdiction of the law, including the ability to define legal phrases. The publics more immediately concerned with tax work—the Tax Court, the Treasury, and much of the business community—have usually preferred coequal jurisdiction between lawyers and accountants. In a celebrated case, the lawyers argued that deciding what was legitimate "carry back loss" must be treated as a legal question, since the phrase appeared in the tax code. The accountants, who had invented that phrase and hundreds of others like it, viewed its definition as *their* business. But as incumbents, the lawyers successfully made the issue of defining such phrases a legal matter, even though the government and the businesses for whom the code was written saw such definitional questions as matters for themselves and their accountants.[39]

Other aspects of subjective jurisdiction produce power as well. The diagnostic classification system makes some problems residual ones, placing groups that specialize in them at a disadvantage in competition with the incumbent. Perhaps more important, the incumbent's definitions of what constitutes successful treatment are commonly accepted by the workplace and the public as legitimate. The early-nineteenth-century medical profession had the public convinced that the success of a treatment was best measured by the shock it gave the patient, and it was surprisingly hard for the public to see that the homeopathic doctors, who did not produce such tremendous reactions, were in fact less likely to kill their patients. Since treatment success or failure critically affects the outcomes of interprofessional competition, the power to define success is peculiarly important. Incumbents possess a special power, too, over problems to which treatment can be applied only once, for here the incumbent's performance can never be directly compared to that of a competitor. The incumbent can always argue that "circumstances were different."[40]

These incumbent powers to define a problem, to measure its treatment, and to escape comparison are preliminary weapons of professional force. Power may also arise from the objective aspects of the professional task. One objective aspect of lawyers' work is its association with the machinery that enforces legal jurisdiction. In the United States, lawyers staff the courts and dominate the legislatures; in Britain the two branches dominate the upper courts. It is clear that lawyers often call their brethren of the bench to their aid against professional interlopers. A similar power flows to journalists, who have not been slow to use it against such interlopers as publicity agents.[41]

Power may also be drawn from outside the system altogether. Some professions invoke state assistance in competition, usually under the rhetoric of putting down dangerous quacks or of creating a seriously disciplined professional body. Others co-opt institutions of the upper classes—in the United States often a foundation—to provide money, publicity, and legitimacy with which to pursue a competition. This certainly was the strategy of the psychiatrists in the 1910s and 1920s who parlayed the money of the Commonwealth Fund and the Rockefeller Foundation into a serious invasion of the various social-control jurisdictions. More recently, a crucial target for such co-optation is the university.[42]

A final means for drawing power from without is alliance with a particular social class, a strategy usually pursued by elite professions. In such a case, a profession draws both its recruits and its clients from the upper classes, locates its training in elite universities or similar settings, and affects an ethic of stringent gentlemanliness. The upper branches of the nineteenth-century English professions are excellent examples—the physicians and the barristers. In America perhaps the best example is psychoanalysis. Like the pattern itself, the exercise of power under this strategy is diffuse, but nonetheless effective. The affiliation gives preferential access to more direct power—to wealthy clients, to the state, to foundations, to universities, and so on. A similar alliance can be made with the elite corporate sector, as accountants and one section of American lawyers have shown. In that alliance, recruitment works in reverse, although its effect is the same; the profession sends its superfluous members into the corporate world, as well as drawing its members from (the children of) that world. (The case of architecture, however, shows that an upper class alliance does not always serve a profession well.)[43]

Class alliances are occasionally made by nonelite professions, although they seem to be ineffective. Class alliances provide power by permitting preferential access to resources for interprofessional competition, and nonelite groups command these resources only through standard political channels, which are easily short-cut by elite groups. American social work offers an interesting case. It began by recruiting members from the upper classes—the early friendly visitors were society women—and recruiting clients from the lower classes. As it split from clergy tutelage and became more strongly organized, the elite recruitment slowed, although elite ties were retained through foundations and universities. In the thirties, the profession allied strongly with the various dependent classes of the society, but that alliance does not seem to have helped in competition with other professions. In fact, with the exception of attempts by its elite to break the dominant hold of psychiatry on counseling, social work entered only areas of work in which other professions were not interested.[44]

The power built up in incumbency, task, and external co-optation is exercised in all three settings of jurisdictional endeavor—before the state, before the public, and in the workplace. Before agencies of the state, power is exercised by lobbying legislatures to establish licensing boards, by using those licensing boards against competing professions, by seeking statutory or judicial monopoly of service or of payment for services, by legal pursuit of unauthorized or unethical practitioners. Before the public, power is exercised through various forms of media coverage—advice columns, feature material, personal appearances, and enforcement of standards for media presentations of professionals. In the workplace, power is exercised through attempts to enforce legal jurisdiction, through control of professional language, through direct and symbolic subordination. Different sources of interprofessional power affect different arenas of exercise. Alliances and other forms of external co-optation clearly have their greatest effect in the legal arena, where external actors can assist a profession directly through pressure on the state apparatus. In contrast, incumbency has its greatest effects in the public and workplace arenas, where the ability to define the problems and measures of success allows a profession to make its work appear both more coherent and more effective than it might seem on impartial appraisal.[45]

Power flows through the three arenas in a very specific way. Suppose a profession "should" be losing jurisdiction, perhaps because opponents can show it no longer provides the most effective treatment. In such a case, its legal jurisdiction appears as pure power in its negotiations for workplace jurisdiction. Public jurisdiction plays somewhat the same role, but with less effect; it is one thing if the law says only architects may sign plans and quite another if the public believes that insurance agents are the best people with whom to talk about financial planning. Conversely, while workplace jurisdiction (won in whatever manner) can persuade the state to alter legal jurisdiction, it is not power in the sense I have here used. For the workplace is empirically the most freely competitive of the three arenas, the one in which the forces of subjective jurisdiction, abstraction, and differentiation have their freest play. The effect of workplace jurisdiction on jurisdictional contests in the legal realm does not retard the working of the system forces but rather furthers them.

This pattern of power assumes, correctly, that jurisdictional invasion generally begins in the workplace, then moves to the public mind, and then into the law. Power as conceived in this section—power of incumbents to slow or thwart processes of jurisdiction interchange—flows against this invasion, running from legal to public, or from legal and public to workplace realms. Only rarely does an incumbent hold workplace and public jurisdiction without any sort of legal protection, although older professions (the solicitors, for example) were occasionally in that position in some of their less specialized jurisdictions (in that case, collection work). In general, the exercise of power is directed either at defeating an invasion of legal or workplace jurisdiction or at preventing such a contest from arising. Defeating an invasion means in this case achieving a "better" jurisdictional settlement than would otherwise be achieved "on the merits of the case." Roughly ranking the settlements of chapter 3, a dominant jurisdiction is the best, then a jurisdiction with sharing through subordination, then a jurisdiction by division of labor through differentiation of function, then a jurisdiction by simple division of labor without differentiation, then advisory and intellectual jurisdictions, and finally, complete loss. Settlement by clientele differentiation differs in desirability depending on the amount of the clientele retained.[46]

No one familiar with the history of professions can ignore the importance of power in jurisdictional competitions. Such examples as the conflict of homeopathic and regular physicians in America, of doctors and nurses in Britain, of accountants and lawyers in tax practice, all show the ability of incumbent professions to mobilize resources unrelated to their subjective jurisdiction in order to win contests. On the other hand, there are even more examples of incumbents losing some or all of their work—the American lawyers losing trust work to trust companies, the neurologists losing neurosis to the psychiatrists, the solicitors losing bankruptcy to accountants. While power clearly affects jurisdictional conflict, in the long run power alone does not suffice, even when buttressed with absolute monopoly. The serjeants and the barristers are the best examples. If professions fail to deliver service, eventually clients go elsewhere.

Why is interprofessional power so unsuccessful? There are several possible reasons. The chief one is the presence of other powerful actors in the world of professions—the other dominant professions, the clients or payers, and the state. Each restricts the power of individual professions in jurisdictional contests.

Some argue that the dominant professions are oligarchs who divide the territory among themselves. They generally avoid each others' areas of endeavor and support one another against underlings and interlopers. Others feel that dominant professions compete like all professions and will fight each other if it proves rewarding or practicable. There is considerable evidence on both sides. Professions have in fact often cooperated in a general defense of professional privileges against rising groups. But on the other hand, lawyers self-righteously pursue medical malpractice work, accountants fight lawyers over tax work, and bankers organized trust companies explicitly to take over legal work. Many of a profession's competitions are against other professions of its own size and power. Since other dominants generally themselves have class alliances and other forms of external power, the countervailing powers are here of little use.[47]

Since jurisdictional contests are often decided by client choice, client power also restrains professional power, particularly when there are powerful clients or powerful payers, such as large commercial organizations or governments. As clients they purchase services from dominant professions. As payers they pay the bills that individual clients incur, as has been the case in American medicine. In either case, they confront dominant professions as powerful or monopsonistic groups that can overthrow their attempts to thwart jurisdictional competition. Thus the British lawyers lost the business of the City of London to arbitrators, because the businessmen would no longer adjust to the lawyers' slow justice. Thus American doctors face DRGs and other cost-containment practices imposed by a coalition of insurers and governments overwhelmed with medical bills. The dominant professions can be only as powerful as their clients will let them be. Finally, the state limits the power of professions. In countries like France, the state controls interprofessional competition directly. In both the United States and England, the state plays an important role, particularly as monopsonistic client in the medical field, but also in law through its capacity to create and control regulatory and welfare tribunals, in accounting through its control of taxation and other regulations, and in various other professions. Perhaps most surprising, the state is itself a serious competitor to dominant professions, providing various of the services they sell, usually through untrained officials at fractions of the prices professionals charge. (We shall see a detailed example of this in chapter 9.)[48]

These external forces—the power of other dominants, of clients and payers, and of the state—limit the exercise of current power by dominants considerably. All undermine dominants' ability to maintain their positions while providing unnecessary, ineffective, or excessively expensive services. But perhaps most important, a profession is not able to utilize its dominant position to build up a large reserve of power against the day of its trial by invasion. Dominant position confers short-run power, not long-run imperium. No profession can stand forever. American medicine, which looked so successful for so long, is now crumbling before a combination of invaders and external forces—business administrators, the various medical professions, the insurance companies, large corporations, and the government. Nor has medicine simply lost administrative appendages that were not properly part of its jurisdiction of "problems of the body." It has lost much of the flexibility it enjoyed in treatment. It has lost much of its right to police itself. It has seen its actual classification systems invaded and formalized by DRGs. The triumphant success of the medical profession at midcentury does not help it now. There is structurally determined power in the system of professions, and medicine has enjoyed that power for some time. But as the coalition of forces arises against it, medicine proves to have surprisingly little ability to withstand them.[49]

While power plays an important role in interprofessional competition, the long run of professional development reflects the equilibrating forces discussed in preceding sections and chapters. At any given time, professions have differing degrees of dominance reflecting the strength of their jurisdictions, the conversion of those jurisdictions into legal and public power, and the co-optation of external forces. This dominance helps them in small-scale jurisdictional conflicts and in the short run of jurisdictional change. But it does not immunize them from long run shifts and cannot be stored for later use. Like much power, it seems immeasurably strong when least exercised and surprisingly weak when most needed.

# 6      The Social Environment of Professional Development

The preceding chapter began to examine the forces that impinge on the system of professions. Some arose within the professions themselves. Others were external forces used as sources of power. In this chapter and the next I shall look at external forces more generally. The great social changes contemporary with the rise of professionalism often reshaped interprofessional competition. Analysts have generally assumed that their weight fell directly on individual professions. Books commonly study how profession $x$ bureaucratized or how profession $y$ rationalized its knowledge. But bureaucratization may help one profession while hindering another; its real effects are mediated by the system as a whole. General changes must therefore be examined, not in their effect on individual professions, but in their effects on the structures that make up the system of professions.

Some of these structures constitute the social organization of the interprofessional world: for example, the jurisdictional map itself. Technology in particular has created large new fields of potential professional work. General changes have also reshaped the internal organization of professions—both organization for work and organization for occupational advancement. The rise of bureaucracy is a well-known phenomenon here. Audiences for jurisdictional claims have also been remade. Mass media have changed how professions advance and buttress their claims by creating a substantial public discourse about professions, while the state itself plays an ever-increasing role as audience. Finally, a number of changes involve the system structure as a whole—its level of differentiation, domination, and competition. Many have seen the rise of oligarchy among the professions, and, linked to it, a steadily increasing use of the extra-professional power discussed at the end of the preceding chapter.

Like these social structures, the cultural structures that relate professions to their work have also felt the impact of powerful changes. Most important are the structures of professional knowledge itself; the progressive rationalization of knowledge has had important effects for some professions, and the rapid growth of knowledge has often built, and sometimes undermined, others. Scarcely less important, however, are the moral foundations of jurisdiction, the grounds of legitimacy for professional claims. The replacement of gentlemanliness by scientism, efficiency, and accountability has drastically reshaped the contents and results of interprofessional competition. Finally, no study of the changing cultural environment of professions can ignore the emergence of the modern university. By speeding the production of both knowledge and knowledgeability the university has transformed interprofessional relations.[1]

As I have argued, the effects of general changes on these social and cultural structures are not the uniform impacts described in the past. They are conditioned by historical accidents: which professions were dominant, which were losing jurisdiction, which were overstaffed. The aim of these chapters is, then, to introduce a real historical environment to the abstract model I have just posed. What have been the basic disturbances and changes that have worked their way through the system of professions?

## Forces Opening and Closing Jurisdictions

Our longstanding fascination with law and medicine has obscured the blunt fact that most professional work is new work. The social and technological changes of the last two centuries have opened enormous areas of professional endeavor. They have closed others, but the creative forces predominated. Two of these were particularly important; the rise of the large-scale organization and the rise of technology.

By technology I mean, first, the machines themselves. They created the areas of work that became mechanical, electrical, and chemical engineering. They vastly expanded the work available to civil engineering, from military and large public works to a vast array of civilian projects. These new and increased demands in turn vastly increased the demand for work in the professions of pure science. They also supported the expansion of such subordinate professions as engineering technicians and draftsmen. This expansion has even affected areas dominated by non-machine-based professions; machines created laboratory technicians within the medical division of labor, for example. Technology has also brought new specialties, if not new professions, to such areas—radiologists, data-processing executives.[2]

But machines have also closed jurisdictions. The creation of general public media lessened the need for local and regional entertainment, and thereby shrunk the music profession in particular and the arts professions in general. In the case of professions specialized to one machine or machine type, the gradual supercession of that machine has threatened professional ruin, although often such groups move to adjacent areas. The eclipse of the "telegraph electricians" by the new electrical engineers in the latter nineteenth century is an example. For many of the older group the new world of power and lighting offered no foothold; only a few made the transition successfully.[3]

Beyond the machines themselves, the rise of technology embraces a technological frame of mind, one that insists on measuring its world. This fascination with measurement opened jurisdictions for groups as diverse as optometrists, actuaries, geologists, and surveyors. In England, several different professions emerged for setting numerical values on various forms of property—valuers, quantity surveyors, chartered surveyors.[4]

As much as technology has reshaped professional work, the rise of large organizations reshaped it more. In both private and public sectors, large organizations have generated work both internally and externally. Internally, they have required administration and management. In England, where the rise of an interventionist government preceded that of giant corporations, this demand came first in the government. A quasi-professional civil service emerged in the mid-nineteenth century, although training for it remained quite unspecialized until well into the twentieth. In America, by contrast, the giant firms emerged well before a giant government, and the management jurisdiction began within private organizations. In both cases the potential demand for management was immense, since large organizations require coordination and planning of a hitherto unimagined complexity. Management in turn required information, which created the fields of work currently occupied by management and cost accounting, management information services, and operations research, as well as unclaimed task areas like program evaluation.[5]

Externally, too, the new organizations demanded enormous quantities of professional services. The interventionist governments required social workers to administer their welfare programs, and doctors, pharmacists, lawyers, and still more social workers to staff them. They required accountants, doctors, and others to staff the regulatory agencies that governed commerce, foodstuffs, transport, and a host of other areas. Private commercial organizations required the public accounting profession to certify them for the investing public, architects to design their magnificent commercial buildings, advertising artists to sell their products, public-relations professionals to hide their malfeasances. In addition they were, of course, the owners and operators of most of the technology that built the jurisdictions discussed above.[6]

Unlike the technology-based jurisdictions, these organization-based ones have nearly always endured. Organizational demand for services seems insatiable, although the recent conservative attempts to dismantle welfare states in England and the United States would have profound effects were they to succeed. However, like technology-based professions, organization-based ones face a continual revision of their tasks, often because of technological change. The development of the Hollerith tabulating machines at the turn of this century, for example, revolutionized cost accounting by multiplying the amount of available information. This undoubtedly hastened the split of bookkeeping from cost accounting and its establishment as a subordinate profession with a professional division of labor.[7]

The direct effects of technological and organizational change on the professions are generally positive. They have created vast areas of work for professions and have destroyed relatively few. The indirect impacts, however, are both more subtle and more far-reaching. The first of these is the commodification of knowledge.

Commodification pervades the history of professions. Esoteric professional activity can be embodied in commodities, which can then be bought and sold without the involvement of jurisdictional professions. Many early examples come from the law. For centuries there have been attempts to develop fixed legal forms (for wills, contracts, land transfers, and other legal actions) that will obviate the involvement of lawyers in such simple legal matters. (In France, one branch of the legal profession, the *notaires*, specializes in such forms.) Lawyers have always argued that such fixed forms encourage later litigation through their ambiguity. But lawyer opposition did not prevent English law stationers from issuing reams of fill-in-the-blanks legal forms, used by accountants, agents, and others in their competition with solicitors, a phenomenon repeated in the United States. Such early commodification spread well beyond the law; it was the embodiment of doctors' knowledge in pills that made apothecaries and chemists potential competitors of nineteenth-century medicine.[8]

However, commodification has become more important in the twentieth century. In particular, the computer has worked and will con-

tinue to work a commodifying revolution in professions. Forms of esoteric expertise can easily be reduced to keystrokes. Computer-assisted
design (CAD) programs in architecture are a familiar example, but social science itself produces another excellent one. Statistical procedures such as multiple regression and factor analysis were regarded as
esoteric expertise as recently as the early 1960s. Today they are easily
performed by those who understand neither inversion nor eigenvec-
tors. Esoteric statistics has become routine, nonprofessional work; today's esoteric statistical knowledge is knowing the comparative properties of Gaussian elimination with pivoting, the Crout and Cholesky
decompositions, and the QR algorithm—the various procedures that
do the commodified calculations. The location of expertise has thus
shifted from statistics (before 1960, when social scientists didn't know
these techniques) to social science (from 1960 to 1975, when these
procedures were democratized beyond statistics and became state-of-
the-art social science) back to statistics (from 1975 on, when SPSS and
other canned programs made "quantitative social science" possible for
those with merely a folk knowledge of statistics).[9]

These examples concern treatment commodification. The computer
can invade diagnosis and inference as well. Artificially intelligent diagnostic algorithms in medicine are the first of many such systems.
Thus, while the technological revolution has created large numbers of
professional jurisdictions, it has also created the tools for turning professional knowledge into commodities at an ever-increasing rate.[10]

The second indirect effect of the rise of technology and organizations on the professions occurs through the dominance of organized
capital. Modern societies invest much or most of their effort in the
production, consumption, and distribution of commodities. The commercial apparatus associated with this effort has distinct interests in
certain kinds of professional work, and distinct opposition to others.
It is striking that banking—a central function in the commercial
world—has never become effectively professionalized in either the
United States or England. This failure in part reflects the rapid turnover of bank personnel and the hybrid nature of many banking activities. But it also reflects the unwillingness of organized capital to admit
the existence of an even partially autonomous group of individuals governing flows of capital through some "scientific" knowledge of their
own. Other professions are opposed for other, equally obvious reasons.
Safety engineers were very late arrrivals to the professional world, and
pollution engineers, although a perfectly possible specialty, have yet
to appear.[11]

The dominance of capital may also explain why business administration has never developed into the profession envisioned by many founders of business schools. The inner logic of capital, whatever it is, is not subject to rationalization as professional knowledge. It cannot or will not be made a scientific or quasi-scientific discipline. The failures first of scientific management and later of operations research to dominate American industry show that interdiction clearly. Of the three countries here studied, only in France, where the longstanding migration of highly trained civil servants into dominant management positions (*pantouflage*) makes business leadership an extension of the state bureaucracy, is there any coherent "professionalization" of business management.[12]

In short, corporate capitalism has built certain kinds of professions and has blocked others. That corporate capitalism supports a more professional labor force in general cannot be doubted; its creation of professional work is prolific. But its own imperatives have shaped its results in specific ways. Indeed, they have occasionally made it a direct competitor with professions, as we shall see below.[13]

The final secondary impact of the corporate society is its creation of the problem of adjustment. The developing organizational society uprooted the work and personal lives of individuals and therefore required professionals who could adjust individuals to life within it. This problem of adjustment has been peculiarly poignant in the United States, where the symbolic ethic of rugged individualism enjoys incongruous persistence in a highly organized and structured society. The chief professions of adjustment have been the psychiatrists and the psychologists. The psychiatrists have made the problem of adjustment an individual emotional problem. They assist individuals whose achievement drives run afoul of organizational reality, whose personal dignity rejects their obligations as employees, whose cries for help echo through hollow bureaucracies. They assist as well the women trapped by the organizational society in the newly necessary role of housewife. Both psychiatry's jurisdiction—of defusing the individual's rage at the organizational society's impositions—and its individualistic approach are central creations of the organizational society itself.[14]

As important as this work of psychiatrists is, psychologists serve a function at once more pervasive and more important, that of preventive adjustment. The psychological profession tracks individuals into places where they will "most effectively realize their potential," or, to put it from the organizational society's point of view, where they will least disrupt the flow of organizational life. (The jargon for this task is international; the French phrase for the psychologists' goal is *assurer son dévelopement optimal et l'épanouissement de ses potentialités*.)[15]

Psychological tests, both intelligence tests and personality tests, have been a central part of organizational America since the 1920s. They track students into schools, trainees into jobs, executives into leadership. In a world where personal connection provides only the fine tuning of an individual's life course, professional psychology provides the general preventive adjustment of individuals to life chances without which modern organizational life would be impossible. Of course, psychology does its share of dealing with active problems—industrial psychology has worked with strikes and strike potential, for example. But its major function is tracking, a jurisdiction that, like the psychiatrists', is a secondary creation of the organization society.

Psychiatry and psychology are helped in their adjustment of the individual to corporate existence by numerous other groups. Much of social work consists of moving bewildered individuals through the maze of modern society, not excepting the maze of agencies designed to help the individual. In addition, since organized society must be orderly society, the corporate society has set a very high standard for personal orderliness, and professions enforcing that orderliness—law enforcement officials, guidance counselors, alcoholism specialists, and others—have profited immensely thereby.[16]

Technology and organization are thus the chief forces opening and closing areas of work for professions in the last two centuries. Without question, their direct effects on professions have been more positive than negative. The jurisdictions closed by technological change are far outnumbered by those opened by that same technological change and by the organizational revolution that accompanied it. But beyond their direct effects, technology and organization also exercise profound indirect effects on professional jurisdictions. Commodification steadily absorbs expertise, and thereby work, from professions. The dominant forms of production encourage the growth of certain professions while hampering or preventing others. Finally, the organizational society creates an insatiable demand for adjustment. On balance, these indirect forces, too, have been more positive than negative. The computer has so hastened the pace of commodification that they may turn negative in the near future, but for the time being, creation of work outweighs destruction.

Beyond technology, organizations, and the organization society that accompanies them, other social factors have also created and abolished professional work. In particular, social movements often identify social problems, which later become potential expert work. Professionals are often leaders in these movements; in other cases lay leaders gradually turn into professionals. The American public library movement is one example, and indeed American public education is to some extent another, powered as much by nativism and populism as by the direct demands of the organizational society. But social movements may also deprofessionalize problems—the temperance movement's wresting of alcoholism from the doctors, psychiatrists, and social workers being an excellent example.[17]

Social change thus has a dialectical effect on professional work. It simultaneously creates and destroys it. The actual location of these changes is often a matter of historical accident. Technologies and organizational forms appear unpredictably, and commodification, itself often dependent on technological change, is equally haphazard. There is no uniform pattern of "professionalization" or of "deprofessionalization." There are some regular trends, but they appear only when professional work is treated as an undifferentiated whole. For individual professions, the jurisdictional results of general social change depend on their particular situations.

## The Internal Organization of Professional Work

The organizational revolution of the latter nineteenth century not only shifted the jurisdictions of professions, but also changed their organization. Some evidence of this comes from the old professionalization literature; in the United States, for example, national associations and, later, certification of schools and ethics codes were structural forms that came simultaneously to many professions. There is, in fact, a succession of general organizational styles among Anglo-American experts. In the early modern period occupational organizations were corporatist and guildlike, both in work and in association. Under nineteenth-century liberalism, these strong groups were succeeded by looser associations of professionals generally practicing on their own. In the twentieth century, the characteristic organizational form of professions is more bureaucratic, a change particularly noticeable in professional workplaces, but also characteristic of professional associations. While the bureaucratic form was new to some professions—medicine, law, architecture, accounting—many other professions, including engineering, social work, and teaching, were bureaucratic from their beginnings.[18]

The competitive implications of this bureaucratization are not theoretically obvious. It may have affected professions' ability to provide service, to distribute services to those needing them, and to draw boundaries between professional jurisdictions. At the same time, the bureaucratic form correlates with other aspects of professional structure which change these effects. For example, the professions originating in bureaucracies have tended to include several levels of professionals within themselves: from bachelors to doctors in engineering and social work, for example. The nineteenth-century associational professions, in contrast, generally maintain the fiction that all professionals are equal. As a result, they usually have implicit status structures that do not reflect official divisions of labor and responsibility, a situation I have argued makes their jurisdictions vulnerable in the long run. Yet in fact the traditionally associational professions, perhaps simply because of their age, have generally held their jurisdictions strongly. Thus the implications of bureaucracy are bound up with the contradictory implications of its correlates—youth and inclusivism.

Past studies have seldom examined the competitive implications of bureaucratization. The effects of bureaucratization on professions have rather been seen as falling on individual professionals. Many authors have pointed to the rise of alienation and heteronomy, to the generation of invidious status distinctions. This focus on individual professionals in bureaucratic environments ignored the shift towards the bureaucratic organization of work within the professions themselves. The hospital tentatively began such organization, soon to be followed by large law firms, and later by accounting and architectural firms, each with internal hierarchies of professionals. This internal bureaucratization is compounded by a second major trend—the emergence of the *multiprofessional* environment. Welfare bureaucracies, criminal courts, business consulting firms, and information services divisions illustrate less the contrast of bureaucratic and professional authority than the conflict between the many forms of professional authority.[19]

Bureaucratization within single professions has swept the nineteenth-century associational professions to such a degree that even American medicine and law are 50 percent salaried today. Yet the connection of this change with competition between professions seems very tenuous. For example, although the hospital organized doctors into a bureaucracy, they participated on a free-contract model that largely preserved professional autonomy. Doctors themselves were not extensively bureaucratized, although the hierarchy of training did place interns and residents below attending and consulting physicians. Moreover, while the hospital division of labor granted the doctors domination, this domination was not achieved by using the hospital to produce more effective services than (subordinate) competitors could. Domination was achieved by other means and was imposed by transforming existing hospitals. There *were* entrepreneurial hospitals designed to compete with other medical providers—the specialty facilities of Victorian London and the sanitaria of turn-of-the-century America—but these lost ground to community hospitals in both countries, and furthermore were owned by other doctors. Hospitals, that is, had profound implications for competition, but mainly for competition between doctors. It may, however, be argued that the hospital's bureaucratic structure makes it easier for medicine to *maintain* its domination of other health-care professions, a point to which I shall return below.[20]

The other major intraprofessional bureaucracies follow slightly different patterns. The large law firm had little impact on traditional legal work in property and business, but did enable the seizure and control of the massive new work for big business and interventionist government. Other organizations couldn't do the work as fast and effectively as a firm with an internal division of labor among lawyers. The losers here included both solo and small-firm lawyers and competitors in other fields. That English lawyers lost more government work to alternative professions, administrators, and nonprofessional representation than did American lawyers undoubtedly reflects the new capabilities of the large American firms. At the same time, interprofessional organizations like trust companies and collection agencies made serious inroads into traditional American legal work precisely because the lawyers who did most of that work persisted in individual, rather than organized, practice.[21]

In architecture, the giant firm enabled the invasion of such jurisdictions as urban planning. But again, while the firms that accomplished this invasion were controlled by architects, they involved members of several other professions; one of the founding partners of Skidmore, Owings and Merrill was an engineer. The large firm was also, of course, capable of designing the giant buildings modern clients desired, and thus was competitively efficient against smaller architectural firms, as well as against outsiders.[22]

Accounting shows yet another pattern. The consulting divisions of the major accounting firms exemplify the multiprofessional workplaces we shall study below. In the larger accounting and auditing divisions, however, accountants themselves fall into a hierarchy that originates in the massive nature of the clients. When commercial firms merge, the accountants of the smaller partner lose their client because the joint firm is audited by the auditors of the larger. Inevitably, then, the merger of commercial firms has gradually meant the expansion and bureaucratization of a few giant accounting houses at the expense of the medium-sized ones. (Small firms and solo workers do small-business and personal work and hence are not involved in this competition.) Here again size and bureaucracy confer competitive advantage *within* the profession. The main force driving the bureaucratization of the nineteenth-century associational professions was therefore competition within profession. In medicine, architecture, and accounting, this force dominated, although size in some cases conferred competitive advantage against outsiders as well, as it did conspicuously in law.[23] The effects of the trend towards multiprofessional workplaces are much more thoroughgoing. The general trend to bureaucratic workplaces was fueled both by the competitive trends just described (which drove the associational professions towards bureaucracy), and also by the generation of dozens of new professions within other bureaucracies (teachers, social workers, librarians, nurses, and so on). Even within the new work organizations of the associational professions, proliferating divisions of labor soon expanded the bureaucracy beyond members of one profession; law firms filled with paralegals and managing clerks, architectural firms with engineers, accountants, and draftsmen, and accountancy firms with information scientists, programmers, and so on. In other bureaucracies, the tendency was the same; without formal limitations, (as exist for many professional organizations in France) bureaucracies generally became large and multiprofessional. The preponderance of multiprofessional bureaucracies among professional workplaces made the workplace contest for jurisdiction an increasingly important part of the overall competition for control of work.[24]

In the era of associational professionalism, professionals had tended to practice alone or in small groups. Their immediate workplaces were small offices, and their extended workplaces often neighborhoods, small towns, or cities whose various professionals were tied by networks of referrals, club membership, and public reputation. In such a setting the negotiation of jurisdiction was strongly public; workplace and public arenas for competition were closely identified. In the bureaucratic workplace, typical work environments were both heteronomous and multiprofessional, consequently separating the public competition for jurisdiction, increasingly conducted in general and even national media, from the workplace one, normally conducted within a complex workplace overseen by managers and bureaucrats with their own professional imperatives.[25]

This shift vastly reduced the power of professional associations in negotiating jurisdiction. When jurisdiction is contested in public media or the courts, professional associations can easily dominate. But when the battle must be fought by isolated groups of salaried professionals enmeshed in large organizations, an association's ability to control its turf decreases sharply. An early example of this problem was the inability of the late-nineteenth-century railway surgeons to form a coherent profession. Although the group developed an active professional life, with journals, societies, and meetings, the railroads insisted that only their chief surgeons really needed to meet to share ideas and allowed only those surgeons free travel to meetings. The group could not draw its members effectively together and build a coherent line around its expertise; its rapid disappearance was guaranteed.[26]

The consulting divisions of the accounting firms provide a current example. By hiring at the B.A. level, these firms reserve the recruit's loyalty to the firm rather than allowing it to an occupation. Training, usually internally provided, may be exactly equivalent to some profession's training—in computer work, accounting, information or data processing. But the association of work with profession is broken, and with it much of the professional association's power. In such settings, jurisdictions must be contested within a supposedly single-function firm by individuals whose attachment to the profession claiming their expertise has been already broken at the very outset.[27]

Professionalization—in the sense of creating a coherent occupational group with some control of an abstract expertise—is not impossible within workplaces made up of multiprofessional bureaucracies. The cases of operations research, information science, and engineering belie such a conclusion. But the internal structure of a profession successful under such conditions differs strongly from that of a profession successful under the earlier arrangements of audiences for professional claims. Such professions are more inclusive than medicine and law—including several levels of active professionals. They are much less committed to rigid definition of jurisdiction or membership, since they must be flexible enough to move in directions that enable organizational survival. To some this may mean that such groups are less professional. But surely engineers have an expertise, an enduring existence as a successful occupational group, and have many times taken over new areas of work from potential competitors. That they do not have full autonomy does not make them less interesting as cases of institutionalized expertise.[28]

The multiprofessional workplace makes even more central a problem that plagued the nineteenth-century associational professions: articulating the various settlements negotiated in local enclaves with a general public or even legal claim of jurisdiction. Under associational professionalism this articulation was partly accomplished by the ethics codes' detailed instructions to individual professionals about their appearance, their rectitude, their professional behavior, and their exact delineation of professional boundaries. The problem becomes much more difficult when the local enclaves exist, not within the unorganized setting of a town or city, but within a large commercial or public organization with its own goals. This embeddedness might seem to imply a distinctly attenuated interprofessional competition, but the long French experience with professions similarly embedded in state organizations doesn't show much attentuation. Indeed, the interservice squabbles of the American military provide another example. The competition merely changes in quality.

Bureaucratic organization among professions enabled them to meet the challenges of the modern world and transformed the nature and location of interprofessional competition. In two areas, however, the professions come into direct confrontation with the larger bureaucracies of the commercial world, a confrontation with distinct implications for interprofessional competition itself: in the gradual loss of administrative work to commercial organizations and in the increasing dominance of physical capital in professional life.

A number of authors have noted that professionals have lost work to the organizations themselves. Typically this has been labeled as loss of autonomy. Thus one might interpret the teachers' loss of curriculum planning to supervisory personnel as professions' losing work to their organization. In fact, however, professional jurisdictions are always amenable to subdivision, and this kind of division—in which planning or administrative work is divided from more short run functions—can be viewed as simply another subdivision within the professional world. Often, indeed, the organization members who steal the administrative work themselves try to professionalize—as did the school superintendents in the curriculum example. In such a case, work is lost, not to the organization, but ultimately to another occupation.[29]

Moreover, if we interpret professions' loss of administrative work as loss of autonomy, how are we to analyze situations in which administrative work is divided from "purely professional" work in competition *outside* of organizations? The American lawyers lost most of their work as trust administrators to trust companies in the early years of this century. This loss took place on an open market that involved both professionals and organizations, the trust companies usually being organizations of bankers and lawyers. It is better, then, to separate true loss of autonomy from loss of work and to recognize the latter as the more common phenomenon. The false opposition of organization and professional ignores the fact that often those members of the organization doing the pilfering themselves are members of or themselves are creating another profession. The loss of work does not in fact depend on the move of professionals into bureaucracies, but rather takes place outside them as well. Finally, this loss of administrative work is roughly uniform across the professions. It can affect professions' relative standing only to the extent that professions differ in the amount of organizable administrative work they retain in their jurisdictions. This is considerable in some areas—law and social work being good examples—but quite small in others. To the extent that a profession has such work and loses it, it may become predatory on its immediate neighbors in the system. As chapter 9 will show, law is indeed a good example. The competition of corporations and organizations thus reshapes interprofessional relations only under certain conditions and in certain places.

The second confrontation between professions and the corporately organized society arises through the increasing role of physical capital in professional work. Professional work may seem dependent on human capital alone; indeed Marxists generally argue that professions metamorphose expertise into property. But physical capital has become steadily more necessary to professional work in the last century. There have always been churches and libraries and hospitals. But modern medicine with its machinery, computing (for a while) with its mainframes, engineering with its gadgetry, and musicians with their studios all require vast investments in physical material. Once these materials were owned by small local governments, or professional or nonprofit organizations—county law libraries, community hospitals, local churches. The earliest large-scale piece of professional capital was a state property—the mental hospital—without which no nineteenth-century doctor could call himself a psychiatrist. But in the twentieth century, this capital, most of it absolutely necessary to successful professional practice, is normally owned by either governments or commercial organizations. This ownership of the means of professional production has vastly increased the dependence of professionals on organizations. There have long been professions working with others' physical capital, and among many other studies, Rosselli's elegant study of opera impresarios in Italy shows the difficulties of organizing such an occupation; turnover is high, intraprofessional competition is great, and work is externally dependent. Increasing dependence on organizational capital will clearly weaken professional organization.[30]

At the same time, some professions have succeeded in cutting loose from physical capital. Psychiatry is one such, as we shall see in chapter 10. The rise of microcomputers promises a similar emancipation for substantial sectors of computer programming. And engineering again exemplifies the alternative of adaptation, to capital dependence as well as to organizational location. The external benefits of that adaptation for engineers—their income and power—may indeed be less than those flowing to American doctors and lawyers from their independent and rigid forms. Nonetheless, engineers maintain considerable authority over their work patterns, as well as over their work itself, and fall well above center in economic terms.

The rise of highly structured work organizations has thus had diverse effects on professions and their competition for work. The creation of professional organizations with internal divisions of labor has largely affected competition within professions, although on occasion such organizations have favored certain professions over others. The rise and dominance of multiprofessional organizations, on the other hand, have had the distinct effect of separating workplace from public competition for jurisdiction, and have thereby changed the characteristic form of competitively successful professions. This change of form has been furthered by the increasing dependence of professions on others' physical capital, although a few reverse this dependence. Finally, bureaucracies have stolen substantial amounts of work from professions, particularly administrative work, thereby increasing competition for remaining work and damaging those professions, particularly law, that had held large amounts of administrative work within their jurisdictions.

## Changing Audiences for Jurisdictional Claims

Time makes now one, now another of the three basic audiences the dominant arena of interprofessional competition. The split of workplace and public jurisdiction, just discussed, is one such change. Another is the emergence of the legal apparatus, defined broadly to include administrative as well as legislative authority, as central professional audience in both Britain and America in the last fifty years. The legal arena has long dominated on the Continent; countries like France are well along a path that Britain and even the United States are beginning to follow. A static comparison of audiences for professional claims in the three countries therefore provides a shortcut to dynamic analysis.[31]

Interprofessional rivalry has as long a history in France as elsewhere. Under the Old Regime, for example, a wide variety of healers competed for work with diseases—physicians, surgeons, pharmacists, "empirics," "operators," *spagiristes*, and above all, the various members of the clergy, particularly the rural *curés* and the sisters who staffed French hospitals. This competition continued into the nine-

teenth century, with various bonesetters and empirical healers contesting rural medical work with the *curés* and the *officiers de santé* so
despised by the official medical establishment.[32]

This melee recalls the open competition for clients within quasi-free
markets characteristic of Anglo-American professions. But French occupational groups, when pressing claims for jurisdictional control,
pressed those claims directly before the state. Thus, the provincial
"communities" of French surgeons in the Old Regime were brought
under the king's first surgeon and regulated by general statutes. This
regulation was *welcomed* by the profession, because it provided higher
status, independence from medicine, and policing rights against the
charlatans.[33] What distinguishes the French system is not the recourse
to state authority, which is characteristic of professions everywhere.
But in France the state was already powerful when organized occupations first sought professions' perquisites, and this more-powerful state
required, in exchange for jurisdictional protection, far greater authority over the professions than the English and American states could
or did.

The interventionist approach went back to Richelieu, Mazarin, and
Colbert, that is, to the very foundations of absolutism. The Old Regime had graded and regulated occupations, explicitly associating particular occupations with particular areas of work. By contrast, such an
architectonic structure never existed in the United States, while in
England various forces weakened it fatally in the eighteenth century.
Although the old mapping of occupations and work did not survive the
Revolution, the interventionism of the French state did. Briefly dis-
mantled, the old institutions governing medicine and law were recon-
structed rapidly and firmly, again legitimated by strong claims of responsibility for public welfare. As before, too, state authority over
French professions affected professional jurisdiction and competition
not only directly, but also through state control of the professional
structures that secondarily determine competition—professional organization, professional discipline, and profession-client relations. This
pattern, continuing to the present, makes the state by far the central
audience for professional claims in France.[34]

The early nineteenth century established both the parameters of
proper professional organization and the mechanisms for governmental
authority over it. An 1803 law creating a two-tiered medical system (of
*médecins* and *officiers de santé*) showed the state's intention to au-
thoritatively define both the names and the functions of professional
groups. The state began all of the early-nineteenth-century initiatives
towards medical self-regulation, and directly controlled medical edu-

cation, at one point dissolving the Paris Medical Faculty. The Napoleonic Civil Code defined medical malpractice, and the Penal Code governed professional confidentiality (as it still does—violations carry sentences of one to six months in jail and fines of Fr 500–8,000). The Napoleonic and early Restoration regimes also created, in their laws and regulations for the *avoués* and other *officiers ministériels*, an organizational pattern that gradually became standard for professions. Central to this form was a national official body (an *ordre* or *chambre nationale*) to regulate important aspects of professional life—credentials and registration, professional discipline, relations with other professions, and relations with employees. As in the Old Regime, this national organization was a summit of separate local societies (*barreaux* among *avocats*, *chambres* among many other groups). The whole structure operated along loosely democratic lines, with representative bodies and elected officials.[35]

Separate from these official bodies, however, there also emerged, as time passed, voluntary professional associations, at first as local mutual support groups, which rapidly began lobbying state organs in the professional interest —in medicine, for example, for the suppression of charlatans and clergy-healers. In the mid-nineteenth century these local associations gradually merged into such national organizations as the Association Générale des Médecins de France (AGMF). In the last years of the century, the great tide of French syndicalism created in addition professional unions, which are, again, locally organized collective-bargaining agents with national coordinating bodies (e.g., the present Confédération des Syndicats Médicaux Français [CSMF] and Fédération des Médecins de France [FMF]). As a result, the three functions that are in America and Britain unified under a single national organization—professional control, professional mutual support, and professional bargaining—are in France dispersed among three types of organizations. These three are sharply separated; the *Ordre des médecins*, for example, is not allowed to cosign the economic agreement (*convention*) between the state (the general sickness funds) and the medical profession (represented in this situation by the CSMF and FMF). (The situation is similar in Germany, where the local compulsory disciplinary bodies [*ärztekammer*] are organized into a voluntary national lobbying association [*Bundesärztekammer*], while collective bargaining is done by Associations of Insurance Doctors.)[36]

The tripartite structure of modern French professions faces an equally complex array of controlling government agencies. The *Conseil d'Etat* grants official recognition of professional bodies (e.g., the two medical unions). In addition, each profession faces two particularly important ministries. The first is a substantive ministry that governs its area of work, as Justice does that of the law and Public Health does that of medicine and social work. The other is the ministry of Public Instruction, which has controlled professional education since the Napoleonic period, and, since licensing was early made a function of education, which controls licensing as well. This division has profound implications for professional development. In the nineteenth century, for example, the ministry of Public Instruction developed most proposals for medical reform, emphasizing in the process values usually ignored in professional politics elsewhere. The ministry aimed as much to open medical education to all classes (thereby providing at least limited social mobility) and to widely distribute medical services (thereby serving the general good) as it did to improve the quality of medical education in particular. Later projects of professional reform have usually been the projects of several ministries; the great 1892 reform of French medicine, which finally abolished the *officiat*, came from the four ministries of Interior, Justice, External Affairs, and Public Instruction. More recently, attempts to reform social work education have come from Public Health and Education, and have been aided by the *Conseil d'Etat* as well.[37]

Yet Public Instruction is not a profession's only governing ministry. The great power of the substantive ministry is well illustrated by the ministry of Justice. In 1972 the ministry was able to impose, against sustained bar opposition, the unification of *avocats*, *avoués*, and some *agréés*, and in the process to command both the acceptance of certain clerks as *avocats* and the indemnification, from bar funds, of the *avoués* who lost through the reform a dearly purchased position as *officiers ministériels*. Such reforms also delineate jurisdiction itself, in that case the exact limits of the jurisdiction of the new profession of *avocat*, as well as the nature and extent of every exception to the lawyers' monopoly of representation, agency, and pleading. The 1972 law attempted to define as well the contrasting task of "drafting and counsel," which was to be the monopoly of the *conseils juridiques*, a (then) unofficial but powerful group of business-legal advisors, often organized into large consulting houses, who inherited the old functions of the *agréés*. Although the *conseils'* monopoly failed in the Assembly, the law as passed brought this entire group under official regulation, specified the form its companies could take, and set limits on its involvement with private capital. This legal reform thus reshuffled the formal definition of legal functions that began with the *avoués*, *avocats*, *huissiers*, and *notaires* in the early nineteenth century and continued with *agréés* (1941) and auctioneers (1945). To be sure, certain areas of French legal work were defined as nonmonopolies (e.g., receivership), but overall the government exercised an unchallenged right to define and subdefine areas of professional work on its own initiative. Included in this power, but unused in this particular case, was the power to define a jurisdiction as jointly held, as the *Conseil d'Etat* did medicine in the nineteenth century, granting the pharmacists and *curés* substantial jurisdiction in healing.[38]

The French state not only organizes professions and structures their jurisdictions, it also displays an endless ability to create professional work. While other governments share this ability, France surpasses them in attaching certificate programs directly to particular functions. Thus, when the government made payment of family allowances conditional on evidence of their effective expenditure, an ad hoc "profession" grew up of individuals training families in proper administration of the funds. These *délégués à la tutelle* gradually took on more general social-work functions, aimed at "a mission of moral support and education." The government has recently established courses in the area and specified the area of work. Of course, this penchant for subdivision does not necessarily reflect reality. Many French social workers perform similar functions under different names; as a consequence, a crystal-clear system of legal jurisdiction overlies an often murky workplace one. But specificity and legal detail of jurisdiction characterize the French approach.[39]

The French state plays other central interprofessional roles as client or third-party payer. The state is, first, a planner and distributor of services, and distribution has always been a central criterion of French jurisdictional policy. The century-long preservation of the *officiers de santé* in the face of determined medical opposition rested largely on distributional arguments; if the *officiers* were not in the rural areas, no medical help would be available there. More recently, medical and other social planning has become a central theme in the French five-year plans. Similar concerns have lain behind the French program of legal aid; like the English, the French traditionally (from 1851) obliged lawyers to provide services at their own cost in charity cases "that seem meritorious." A Treasury advance covered court costs, which were ultimately assessed against the loser. When this system, like the English one, failed because only easy cases were taken and only apprentice *avocats* took them, the government (unlike England's in similar circumstances) moved to pay the *avocats* and set specific monetary levels for guaranteed aid. Again, the state played a central role in enforcing an actual level of service.[40]

Perhaps more striking is the French government's role in setting prices. Although *avocats'* charges remain free from restraint except for the legal prohibition of contingent fees, the fees of the *officiers minis-tériels* are all set by decree. Doctors' charges also are with few exceptions set by agencies of the state; price agreements (*conventions*) are made between the sickness funds (*caisses d'assistance-maladie*), which pay the vast majority of the bills, and the organized medical profession, which in this case means the *syndicats*. The situation in Germany is similar: the doctors' bargaining agents are local "associations of insurance doctors," with specific obligations to provide care. In Germany, in fact, even lawyers have statutorily set fees.[41]

The history of French pricing agreements illustrates this government's role very well. When Social Security was founded in 1930, the doctors achieved a settlement like that of American medicine post-medicare: no capitation, no collective contracts, freely set fees-for-service. After the Second World War, the government sought a new settlement, and the doctors achieved a situation of voluntary and regional *conventionnement*. If physicians and regional funds agreed on a fee table, the funds would reimburse at 80 percent; if not, at less. A series of special clauses allowed higher fees for wealthy patients, difficult cases, and eminent doctors. This system penalized the cities, where organized medicine blocked *conventionnement* and fund reimbursement was as low as one-quarter that in some rural departments. Among the solutions proposed within the government, that of the Ministry of Work prevailed, in 1960. Regional agreements were to be permitted, but had to respect government-set ceilings. Requests for higher fees were to be examined by a mixed board, not a physician board. Most importantly, individual agreements with the funds were allowed, thereby breaking the power of the unions. As a further pressure, the sickness funds were prohibited from developing health centers with salaried doctors in the *départements conventionnés*, but were left free to do so elsewhere. The reaction was enormous; the doctors held a one-day strike; a splinter union (the FMF) opposed *conventionnement* violently. As costs continued to rise in the 1970s, however, the doctors realized that only a national *convention* would preserve any form of fee for service. The 1971 *convention* was thus easily imposed. It subjected all doctors to national rates unless they appealed for release. The mixed boards continued to judge higher fees. In addition, the *convention* created *profils médicaux*, a set of quarterly clinical statistics on individual doctors, with provisions for removing doctors from the *convention* if self-discipline failed.

Not only does the state determine distribution and pricing—crucial variables in interprofessional competition—it also often referees disputes, not only between different professional groups, but also between professions and extensions of itself. Thus, the *caisses d'assistance-maladie* are in fact state agencies, administering redistributive insurance schemes funded by taxes. Yet their agreements with the doctors are subject to revision and constraint from central state authorities, including not only the ministries, but perhaps more importantly the *Conseil d'Etat*. The situation is similar in Germany, where both the sickness funds and the organizations of insurance physicians are bodies of public law (*Körperschaften des öffentlichen Rechts*), privately based associations made into public ones by the delegation of specific state powers. There also central ministerial power oversees and regulates a negotiation process between other state agencies and professional bodies.

The French pattern epitomizes the continental systems of professions. The government, rather than the public or the workplace, is the dominant audience for professional claims. The portion of the government most closely tied to public opinion—the legislature—plays a relatively minor role; policy is largely ministerial. Multiple ministries are involved—Public Health, Work, Social Assistance, Finance—as well as general administrative bodies like the *Conseil d'Etat* (which eventually annulled the 1971 *convention*). Claims of exclusive jurisdiction are made conditional on effective service at reasonable price; the government does not hesitate to redefine modes of practice—fostering the detested *salariat*—if service is not forthcoming.

These, then, are the central aspects of the interventionist state as an audience for professional claims: the dictation of professional organization and discipline, the direct control of jurisdiction, the control of prices and service delivery, and the hierarchical control of lower state involvements by higher ones. There are other, minor aspects as well. The interventionist state may hasten the various external forces discussed in this chapter, as the French state has bureaucracy in medicine and social service. It also occasionally creates agencies subject to the professional co-optation, a process that has made American medicine so dominant; in France the local hygiene councils of the early nineteenth century are an example. (I have deemphasized the state's enormous role in professional discipline and similar areas, because such authority falls equally on most professions and so has little competitive effect.)

To argue that the interventionist state has been the dominant audience for professional claims in France is not, of course, to ignore public opinion altogether. An extensive medical press has kept "biopolitics" in the public eye since the middle of the last century. Public concern with the high cost of medicine played a central role in the *conventions* of the postwar period. But during extensive periods of the nineteenth century, censorship restrained the public culture that would come to dominate the American politics of professions. For many reasons, then, the determining arena for professional claims in France has always been the state.[42]

This state dominance requires recasting my original theory of the relative roles of state and workplace competition. As in my original conception, the state jurisdictions are clear in France and the workplace ones murky. But here the early recourse of professions to state intervention exacerbates the difference, at the same time negating my *temporal* assessments of jursidictional arenas. Since the legal arena sees active competition as well as active ministerial policy, jurisdiction there by no means has the enduring, fixed qualities of legal jurisdiction in the Anglo-American setting. Ministerial decrees may change jurisdictions over fairly short intervals. Thus the dominance of the legal arena raises important problems about the relation of workplace and legal-public jurisdiction. Unfortunately, there are few studies of workplace jurisdictional competition among French professionals.[43]

The American case reverses the French one. In the United States, a strong public arena for jurisdictional claims preceded a strong legal one. Partly this reflected American federalism. Since jurisdictional battles were fought not one but up to fifty times, professions were well served by creating general positive sentiment among a literate public. Perhaps more importantly, the deliberate destruction of state-sanctioned professional jurisdictions during the Jacksonian era signified a general cultural preference for the free-market determination of professional boundaries. Professional jurisdiction therefore rested on battles fought in the workplace and in public opinion. In rural and small-town America, these were the same thing. As I have argued, the professional workplace of such places was simply the locality, and workplace jurisdiction simply meant jurisdiction recognized by the local network of professional practitioners—people aware of one another's practice, possibly through reputation and referral, but not through common work within a division of labor. In short, it was a "professional" public opinion, spread by many of the same mechanisms as the more general public opinion of professionals' clients.[44]

A number of factors helped develop a larger public opinion in late-nineteenth-century America. The lyceum movement recruited professionals as speakers, who familiarized their audiences with both themselves and their professional claims. Touching about one-third of American households in the post–Civil War period, daily newspapers reached nearly two-thirds of the households by 1890, and perhaps over

90 percent by 1900. The same decades saw rapid expansion of the periodical press. More focused public arenas of interprofessional competition emerged in various voluntary societies for social improvement—the American Social Science Association (1865), the National Conference of Charities and Corrections (1873), the American Public Health Association (1872), the various medico-legal societies, and so on. The late-nineteenth-century wave of association not only organized the professions as individual groups, but also brought them together in forums where their boundary disputes could be recognized and decided.[45]

By the time American governments began to consider regulating professions—making the state arena again central—the public one was well established. Lacking the strong executive characteristic of even the French Republics, much less of the Restoration, the July Monarchy, and the Second Empire, American governments began to regulate the professions through legislative action. Thus, when the state finally chose to intervene in professional life, it did so through the branch of government most open to public opinion. To the extent that strong executive government eventually developed, it did so only at the national level, during the New Deal, while the direct regulation of professions remained a state affair. The contingencies of American politics thus conspired to guarantee a central role for public opinion in establishing the limits of professional jurisdiction.

Although the French and American patterns first arose through differences in the sequence of state growth and public opinion development, they have been sustained by enduring differences in both state structure and the media. The French continue their longstanding pattern of ministerial dominance, as the Americans do that of public media. In 1965, when the United States had 1,143 radios per 1,000 population, Great Britain had 294 and France 308. The television figures were United States, 334; Britain, 242; and France, 111. Pervasive media have thus kept the public arena central for professional claims in the United States.[46]

As these figures suggest, Great Britain lies between the extremes of France and the United States, both in the extension of media and in the strength of government. On the one hand, the British press was free of the censorship that often limited the nineteenth-century French press. It also developed more rapidly than did the French press, although not as fast as the American. On the other hand, while the British government lacked the federalism that made general professional policies impossible in America, it also lacked both the will and the ministerial apparatus to carry out the policies that centralized government made possible in France. British regulation of professions has remained a legislative affair, and Parliament has registered only a few professions, preferring to legally protect professional names while leaving jurisdiction to direct (i.e., workplace and public) interprofessional competition and discipline to private qualifying associations. It remains possible for anyone to claim to cure illness in England, although rights to the name "physician" and to payments from the National Health Service are restricted.[47]

There is some evidence that the United States and England are both moving in the French direction. The medical area, often a bellwether of professional life, has long been under intense public control in England and is moving towards such control in the United States. Yet that phenomenon may reflect in part a change in the public audiences for jurisdictional claims, a change from passive to active participation in the negotiation of professional claims. The public, too, is becoming interventionist. This change reflects the double role of professional publics. They are on the one hand judges of general claims made in professional media statements and on the other consumers of professional services. Past theories of professions have often assumed a classic market relation in which atomized clients faced an increasingly organized profession. But in the twentieth century clients have become less atomized. First, organizations have become clients—of lawyers, accountants, architects, librarians, social workers. Second, individual clients have created cartels, usually through insurance companies that negotiate with organized professions in the name of clients. In both cases, the professions face a public whose resources enable it to corporately intervene in interprofessional disputes. Professions have negotiated before active audiences in the workplace for a long time, since other professions have always comprised a substantial portion of the workplace world. Similarly, they have in some times and places faced active audiences within the state. But an active role for the public audience is new.[48]

The changes in American medicine reflect this change as much as they do a move toward the French pattern of state dominance. Since only the state stands above private cartels in America, and since the state operates (in medicare/medicaid) the largest cartel of all, the state will ultimately become the chief negotiator with the American medical profession. But where state interests are less, there is little reason to expect state dominance of interprofessional competition, and the process of private cartelization is more important.[49] Professions like accounting and architecture, which do not involve the welfare state, will not face the state involvement that medicine has faced. Yet the newly organized public audience will play a quite different role in these professions' claims than in the past. As we shall see in chapter 8, the emergence of the profession of data management *within* large corporations entails its development along lines more similar to engineering than to medicine. As with engineering, data management clients are large, well-organized, and dominant over individual professionals. To the extent that more and more professions face such clients, the contest for jurisdiction will be increasingly constrained by organizational forces central to capitalistic enterprises.

The various changes in audiences for professional claims thus imply a quite different pattern of successful competitive structure. We have already seen how the rise of bureaucratic and particularly interprofessional organizations has built a complex arena of workplace competition, independent from the earlier public arena. I have already argued that success in this arena will generally require looser organization than that traditional among the associational professions. At the same time, the presence or emergence of an active state, coupled with the rise of a public newly interventionist in its client aspect, clearly favors quite strong organization. As a consequence, we can expect professions to acquire an explicitly federated character—with subsegments organized to deal with flexible workplace development and loosely linked under a general organization adapted for lobbying. Such indeed is the form of the electrical engineers in the United States—the IEEE being a federation of a dozen or more specialties.

## Co-optable Powers, Oligarchy, and the New Class

Some professions, as chapter 5 argued, employ co-opted external authority in interprofessional competition. We can expect, then, major changes in competition, for the new corporate society has vastly increased the amount of external authority available. This changing balance between professions and external powers is in turn related to another important development, the emergence of dominant, oligarchical professions. Such professions typically control numerous subordinate groups in widely spread jurisdictions and generally rely on co-opted authority. But as fewer and fewer professions control more and more, interprofessional competition becomes less and less important. Studying that history increasingly reduces to studying the development of a few classes of individuals with a common consciousness and social structure. The situation approaches the one portrayed in the well-known "new class" argument. Who does what matters less than the general relation between professionals as a class (or as a single organized occupational group) and external powers.[50]

The issues of external powers, oligarchy, and the new class thus raise a single set of interrelated questions. Is there an emerging oligarchy? If so, is it a response to external powers, a defense against them, or a purely internal phenomenon? Is system competition attenuating as the central focus of professional life moves to the level of class?

Professional dominance is well known. Medicalization has occupied a recent generation of writers, much as scientific management occupied a generation past. Professionally dominated divisions of labor in medicine, law, and accounting have received exacting attention. Within the present analytic scheme, we can define the situation when a few professions control an entire system as a condition of oligarchy. Under oligarchy, that is, new work is not allocated by competition, but simply by power. Presumably this power is exercised within particular areas; accounting, as the emerging oligarch of information, is thus expected to take over providing information to management, and so on.[51]

A closer definition of oligarchy is problematic. Oligarchy may denote the holding of *fully dominant* jurisidiction by a few professions. Yet on such a definition, medicine's extent has not substantially increased in the last century. Its advisory and intellectual jurisdictions are more extensive, and its metaphor has spread to most professional venues. But the medical heartland remains the same, aside from obesity, alcoholism, and a few similar problems. We may then measure dominance by a sum over all a profession's jurisdictions, weighting the extent of each by the degree of control involved. On such an argument American medicine appears much more dominant, for indeed its subsidiary jurisdictions are many, as also are those of American law. But on this definition, the overall situation was little different in the mid-nineteenth century, when law, medicine, the clergy, and the military, with homeopathy and other such minor groups, constituted the whole of American professional life. There was less work to do, but a very small group of professions did it.[52]

We may then measure oligarchy by its effects. As oligarchs grow they should absorb more and more work into themselves; there should be less free-floating work. Yet the clergy, social work, and a host of smaller, younger professions continue to thrive in these interstitial jurisdictions. Perhaps the growth of oligarchy in fact creates a *greater* need for interstitial work, as rigid definitions within dominant jurisdictions fail to comprehend complex problems. Similarly, oligarchy might increase potential boundary conflicts between dominant professions;

with fewer opponents, the oligarchs will fight themselves. Yet the criminal responsibility of the insane and the place of expert testimony in courts kept the nineteenth century American medical and legal professions just as angry at each other as they are today. The battle over taxes between lawyers and accountants is not recent, but dates from the first major tax laws. Although there is no quantitative evidence on border disputes between dominants, they seem no more common now than before, and on their evidence, oligarchy is no more prevalent in America now than one hundred years ago.

Perhaps a more compelling way to conceptualize oligarchy focuses on divisions of labor. As professions develop larger and larger jurisdictions, they develop subordinated groups to accomplish work they direct. If we define dominance as the creation of such divisions of labor, we can measure its extent by shifts in the relative sizes of professions; dominants will shrink as subordinates proliferate. Tables 1 and 2 show the proportion of individual professions in the total of professional, technical, and kindred workers, for the United States and England. Table 3 groups the same data into general jurisdictional areas. Although there are distinct differences between the American and British datasets, the data consistently show dominant professions as a steadily decreasing fraction of this labor force. Medicine and law have fallen rather rapidly, while the share of the medical and business-property areas as a whole has remained roughly constant. If we follow Scott in regarding the clergy as the dominant "social" profession (over social workers and religious workers), then a similar pattern emerges in that area, although the overall area is in slow decline. In design, architects remain small while draftsmen grow, and in science specialized engineers and scientists remain at small levels while unspecialized engineers and technicians grow rapidly. This evidence is only tentative, of course, since we must assume that census categories represent jurisdictional units, and that relative decline signifies division of labor. In fact, decline may signify other things: the place lawyers have lost among the property professions has been taken by accountants, themselves now dominants. Indeed, although some actual subordination took place (e.g., the rise of clerks in British law), the main phenomenon chronicled here is the general expansion of the property-business jurisdiction caused by complex capital exchange and taxation.[53]

The problems of defining oligarchy by jurisdictional extent, system effects, or division of labor can be avoided by a definition of oligarchy in terms of a profession's power, particularly its externally co-opted power. Oligarchy may denote a system in which only a few professions

TABLE 1                Proportion of Professional, Technical, and Kindred Workers
                       in Certain Professions: United States

|  | 1900 | 1910 | 1920 | 1930 | 1940 | 1950 | 1960 | 1970 |
|---|---|---|---|---|---|---|---|---|
| Medicine | 11 | 9 | 7 | 5 | 4 | 4 | 3 | 3 |
| Dentists | 2 | 2 | 2 | 2 | 2 | 2 | 1 | 1 |
| Nursing | 1 | 5 | 7 | 9 | 10 | 10 | 9 | 8 |
| Pharmacy | 4 | 3 | 3 | 3 | 2 | 2 | 1 | 1 |
| Medical technicians | 0 | 0 | 0 | 0 | 0 | 2 | 2 | 2 |
| Law | 9 | 7 | 5 | 5 | 5 | 4 | 3 | 2 |
| Accounting | 2 | 2 | 3 | 6 | 6 | 8 | 7 | 6 |
| Clergy | 9 | 7 | 6 | 5 | 4 | 3 | 3 | 2 |
| Relig./social workers | 1 | 1 | 2 | 2 | 2 | 2 | 1 | 2 |
| Professors | 1 | 1 | 1 | 2 | 2 | 3 | 2 | 2 |
| Teachers | 35 | 34 | 33 | 32 | 28 | 23 | 23 | 23 |
| Architects | 1 | 1 | 1 | 1 | 1 | 0 | 0 | 1 |
| Draftsmen | 1 | 3 | 3 | 3 | 2 | 3 | 3 | 3 |
| Musicians | 7 | 8 | 6 | 5 | 4 | 3 | 3 | 3 |
| Engineers | 3 | 4 | 6 | 7 | 8 | 11 | 12 | 11 |
| Technicians | 0 | 0 | 1 | 1 | 1 | 2 | 4 | 4 |
| Medical area | 1.571 | 0.900 | 0.583 | 0.357 | 0.286 | 0.250 | 0.231 | 0.250 |
| Legal/business area | 4.500 | 3.500 | 1.667 | 0.833 | 0.833 | 0.500 | 0.429 | 0.333 |
| Social area | 9.000 | 7.000 | 3.000 | 2.500 | 2.000 | 1.500 | 3.000 | 1.000– |
| Education | 0.029 | 0.029 | 0.030 | 0.063 | 0.071 | 0.130 | 0.087 | 0.087 |
| Design | 1.000 | 0.333 | 0.333 | 0.333 | 0.500 | 0.000 | 0.000 | 0.333 |
| Engineering |  |  | 6.000 | 7.000 | 8.000 | 5.500 | 3.000 | 2.750 |

*Note:* Figures in the upper part of the table are in percentages. The relevant total is the census total for professional, technical, and kindred workers. The figures are reported in rough work areas. With the exception of musicians, these areas make up the rows of the lower part of the table. Justifications for the groupings are found in the text and notes. In the lower part of the table the figure reported is the ratio of dominant profession (listed first for each area) to the sum of the others.

can co-opt enough external authority to obstruct the competition for work. How could such a limitation arise? First, external authorities may encourage divisions of labor and subordination because they believe them to increase efficiency. Second, oligarchy may support itself, because the initial co-opting professions may control access to external authorities and deny it to others. With respect to the private foundations, for example, American medicine simply "got there first with the most;" the granting committees were already stacked with doctors when the other helping professions arrived for their slice of the pie.[54]

A third reason for expecting limitations on co-optation rests on what I shall call the dilution effect. Strong or unified external authorities

TABLE 2          Proportion of Professional, Technical, and Kindred Workers
                 in Certain Professions: England

|  | 1911 | 1921 | 1931 | 1951 | 1961 |
|---|---|---|---|---|---|
| Medicine | 8 | 5 | 5 | 4 | 3 |
| Nursing |  | 15 | 16 | 19 | 14 |
| Medical technicians |  | 1 | 1 | 5 | 4 |
| Others |  | 1 | 1 | 5 | 4 |
| Law | 6 | 3 | 3 | 2 | 1 |
| Accounting | 2 | 1 | 2 | 3 | 5 |
| Clergy | 12 | 6 | 5 | 3 | 3 |
| Relig./social workers |  | 0.4 | 1 | 2 | 2 |
| Professors | 0.3 | 0.3 | 0.3 | 1 | 1 |
| Teachers | 59 | 38 | 33 | 24 | 22 |
| Medical area |  | 0.294 | 0.278 | 0.138 | 0.136 |
| Legal/business area | 3.000 | 3.000 | 1.500 | 0.667 | 0.200 |
| Social area |  | 15.000 | 5.000 | 1.500 | 1.500 |
| Education | 0.005 | 0.008 | 0.009 | 0.042 | 0.045 |

Source: Routh (1965). Earlier data are discussed in the text and notes.

Note: Figures in the upper part of the table are in percentages. There is no equivalent base total in England, since the census figures have never been made conformable. In the lower part of the table are dominant/subordinate ratios as in Table 1.

maximize their control over the system by preferentially aiding a few actors. The withdrawal of support is then an effective threat. By contrast, if many groups can co-opt power, expertise assumes a general, independent cultural authority precisely because it is so widely supported by external power. The independent legitimation of expertise then *lessens* the role of states, classes, and other external actors as legitimating authorities for professions, a reduction they may well oppose. Only a very powerful external authority (e.g., the French state) can confer equal co-opted authority on all professional groups without suffering a serious loss of authority. When it *does* occur, as in France, such a uniform delegation clearly undermines oligarchy, as this argument predicts. The dilution effect will also prove important in the analysis of the new class.

When measured by external co-optation, oligarchy does increase in the American system of professions; the mid-nineteenth-century period had few co-optable powers, and they have emerged steadily since. Most professions in the United States now have their members trained in universities, often at public expense. Most American professions directly or indirectly exercise state authority over admission to their ranks, which often confers access to legislatively protected monopoly

TABLE 3             Task Areas as Fractions of the Total Professional Labor Force

|  | United States | | | | | | | |
| --- | --- | --- | --- | --- | --- | --- | --- | --- |
|  | 1900 | 1910 | 1920 | 1930 | 1940 | 1950 | 1960 | 1970 |
| Education | 36 | 35 | 34 | 34 | 30 | 28 | 27 | 27 |
| Medical area | 18 | 19 | 20 | 19 | 18 | 20 | 16 | 15 |
| Legal/business area | 11 | 9 | 10 | 11 | 11 | 12 | 10 | 8 |
| Social area | 9 | 8 | 8 | 7 | 7 | 6 | 6 | 4 |
| Design | 2 | 4 | 4 | 4 | 4 | 4 | 4 | 5 |
| Engineering/science | 4 | 5 | 8 | 8 | 9 | 16 | 18 | 17 |
| Print media | 3 | 2 | 3 | 3 | 3 | 2 | 2 | 2 |
| Arts | 11 | 12 | 9 | 8 | 7 | 6 | 5 | |
| Entertainment | 3 | 3 | 2 | 2 | 2 | 2 | 2 | |

|  | England | | | |
| --- | --- | --- | --- | --- |
|  | 1921 | 1931 | 1951 | 1961 |
| Education | 38 | 33 | 25 | 23 |
| Medical area | 24 | 25 | 33 | 25 |
| Legal/business area | 4 | 5 | 5 | 7 |
| Social area | 7 | 6 | 5 | 5 |
| Design | 5 | 7 | 9 | 9 |
| Engineering/science | 7 | 8 | 13 | 25 |
| Print media | 2 | 3 | 3 | 2 |
| Arts | 11 | 10 | 5 | 3 |

Note: Figures are in percentages. For a discussion of totals, see Table 1.

markets. While the British case is considerably different, there too the external authority exercised is considerable. Measuring oligarchy by the extent of co-optable power also defines the French system as oligarchical from at least 1800, since that state has always been amenable to tampering by powerful professions. Yet, on the other hand, the French government has often defended small professions against the oligarchs; co-opted power may thus be a mixed blessing.[55]

This dual role of the French state underscores the generally ambiguous nature of external authority. Even as it assists oligarchs, it undermines them by invoking values other than expertise—public service, political authority, and so on. It also creates relations that can be easily reversed from a borrowing of authority to an imposition of control, as the French professions have long known, and as American medicine is discovering today. Indeed, oligarchy itself plays a similarly ambiguous role. Oligarchy relies heavily on subordinated divisions of labor, which lead ineluctably towards bureaucratization. Bureaucratization in turn drives the dominant group towards administrative status and administrative values, again undermining their direct reliance on expertise. The American psychiatric profession, for example, maintained control of the insane and the groups working with them by becoming more administrators than doctors as the mental hospitals and their specialized occupations grew. Only by portraying administration as therapeutic (and only temporarily) were the psychiatrists able to avoid splitting themselves into administrators and medical men. Nonpsychiatric medicine avoided this situation by encouraging lay administration from the outset, a policy that ultimately located many physicians in divisions of labor they no longer fully controlled.

Co-optation has ultimately transcended oligarchy. In the United States, so much external authority is co-opted into the system of professions that co-optation no longer confers a substantial competitive advantage. This dilution has occurred particularly because the external authorities are themselves no longer unified. Competing professions often fight each other through competing external authorities. The diversity of external allies pits one profession's governmental backers against another's business supporters, and so on. The battles between lawyers and accountants over tax practice illustrate this complexity well. The commercial world would prefer accountant control of the area, and has said so, but the courts and legislatures, with their lawyer staffs, do not agree. Increasing co-optation has ultimately simply meant a new locale for interprofessional competition, the complex terrain of external powers.

Indeed, for all the power of oligarchy, open competitions for professional work are not uncommon. The current information services market is one such competition, and the psychotherapy market another. The entertainment services market in the United States was so fluid in the nineteenth century that individual "professions" of actors, musicians, and "readers" did not really coalesce. Open markets do appear, and dominant oligarchs, as we saw in chapter 5, are not necessarily best situated to seize them.[56] These ambiguous data reflect the ambiguous origins of oligarchy, which resemble those of monopoly capitalism in the Marxist argument. The vulnerability of concrete work drives professions towards abstraction and the consequent enlargement of jurisdiction. Interprofessional competition also leads professions to borrow external authority (to support their power) and to grow (because size permits subordinate and internal divisions of labor, with consequently increased service). Yet all of these forces undermine the system at the same time. The external authority undermines the professions' legitimation by the value of expertise and creates external links that encourage and facilitate external control. Divisions of labor lead to bureaucracy and bureaucratic values, again undermining the value of expertise. Abstraction eventually weakens jurisdiction directly, as chapter 4 argued. Oligarchy is thus a contradictory phenomenon, arising out of internal and external pressures, simultaneously a defense of particular professions and a threat to professionalism itself. It ultimately results in little real change.

Beyond these competitive effects, increasing co-optation has the further consequence of drawing together, not the professions as groups, but professionals as individuals, making them a potential class. This pressure assists a process of class formation with important roots elsewhere. The common interest of professionals in securing effective social and economic returns to their expertise has been well analysed by Djilas, Konrad and Szelenyi, and Gouldner, among many others. This "new class" comprises individuals in the peculiar position of possessing small bits of capital—their knowledge—but forced in most cases to work for wages. The knowledge "capital" is actually controlled by, and largely produced by, the organized professional group and its institutions. This peculiar position, shared by all professionals, serves to define a "class in itself" that some have argued has become a "class for itself." The class consciousness of professionals appears in the ideology of professionalism itself, in the common speech that Gouldner has called the "culture of critical discourse," and in the widespread political beliefs of the new class.[57]

External co-optation furthers class consciousness among professionals through mechanisms related to the dilution effect. Dominants use state power to guarantee that only they hold legally legitimate current jurisdiction and class power to claim that only they have the proper character of professionals. In neither case do these defenses invoke the value of expertise on which the ideology of professionalism and the power of the new class are based. The invocation of external values gives the competitors of dominant oligarchs a common interest in defending the authority of expertise against other forms of authority. This common interest is a class interest—an interest of professionals as individuals rather than of their professions as groups. In classic dialectical fashion, then, the use of external power undermines the competition between subordinates and develops their common interests.

This theoretical argument has ambiguous empirical support. Bledstein correctly argues that the nineteenth-century enthusiasm for professionalism was the first stirring of (new) class consciousness. Certainly the coherent political outlook of professionals indicates a serious awareness of class position. But if certified expertise is the core of new class identification, then class awareness should flower in the defense, by professionals, of the licensed prerogatives of members of *other* professions. Unfortunately, most recent research on licensure comes from economists who assume that the only agents involved are the consuming clients, the producing profession, and the state; the class interests that might lead other professionals to support regulation generally are ignored. We do know that British doctors supported the registration of midwives, but they split deeply over that of nurses. Urban consultants sure of their superiority supported registration for nurses, while rural GPs, fearing competition, opposed it. In the United States, doctors, especially psychiatrists, opposed registration or certification of psychologists, clearly fearing competition. Early CPA legislation in the United States had little opposition, although bankers and others began to speak against it after the rigidly exclusionistic policies had become clear. I can find *no* example of professionals generally supporting a fellow profession's attempts to gain legal protection. The testimony is either from immediately competing professions and negative, or, if positive, from superordinates in a division of labor.[58]

New class mobilization should also appear as general opposition to corporate employers, both commercial and governmental, since the chief modern alternative to the authority of expertise is organizational rationality. Moreover, corporations and governments circumscribe professional authority, organization, and work among their employees. A serious new class movement should coalesce around these issues. Yet there is little evidence that it has. Individual professions, often the most powerful, have opposed government and corporate intervention, but there is no general, class opposition. Why? For one thing, the most powerful professions are those least corporately employed—medicine and law. For another, the corporate employers continuously absorb leading professional employees into management. Furthermore, professional employees usually work in different and often competing divisions of organizations. Physicists in research laboratories will not make common cause with engineers running assembly lines, as doctors in staff organizations will not make common cause with designers in the shop, nor management accountants in an operations division with personnel officers in staff. Although, for example, a dual-hierarchy promotional system would probably favor all these groups, they are extremely unlikely to collectively promote it, but will rather seek special deals.

Thus, while an active new class seems a likely outcome of present trends in the professions, there is little evidence of its arrival. It continues a class-in-itself, a possibility hovering on the edge of the professional world. In the meantime, some expect the combination of increasing oligarchy with greater reliance on external power to destroy competition within jurisdictional areas through bureaucratization's gradual destructuring of the subordinate professional groups. Others see a continuing competition for minor shifts within the generally fixed hierarchies of the jurisdictional areas. Still others believe that technological and organizational change will continuously generate new areas of work—psychotherapy and information being the great midcentury examples—with a consequent continuation of system competition along the familiar lines of part 1.

In the most general sense, indeed, increasing co-optation has not decreased competition but has simply changed its location. Like bureaucratization, co-optation has rearranged the balance of competitive arenas. Bureaucratization has meant more competition in the workplace and the development of the looser form of professional structure more able to succeed in such a competition. Cooptation makes the world of corporate allies another zone of competition, a zone that replaces the class allies used to make certain professions "gentlemanly" in the nineteenth century. Competition is over allies and through allies, rather than direct. Both bureaucratization and co-optation mean more of the same, under different headings. As in inflation, nothing changes but the labels.

The great social changes of the last two centuries have transformed much about the system of professions, but not its central constitution. During the shifts here described, of course, individual professions have been sometimes advantaged, sometimes disadvantaged, sometimes created, sometimes destroyed. This process has been most obvious in the ceaseless building and dismantling of jurisdictions by technological and organizational changes. But the bureaucratization of professional structure, the changing balance of audiences for claims, and the rise of co-optation have ultimately left us where we started. Significant interprofessional competition continues, but in different places and involving different arrangements of "friendly" groups. Changes in knowledge have, in fact, had more drastic effects.

# 7    The Cultural Environment of
Professional Development

The changes so far considered affect the tasks of professions, their organization for work, the audiences for their jurisdictional claims, and the environment of external powers. All these areas concern the social structure of jurisdiction. But great cultural changes have also remade the work of professions, and this chapter discusses three such: the rising amount and complexity of professional knowledge, the new types of legitimacy claimed for that knowledge, and the rise of the university. The new knowledge, the new legitimacy, and the new university are, of course, three facets of one thing, and concepts like Max Weber's *Zweckrationalität* treat them so. But while all three participate in the rise of rationality, they did not by any means add up to a consistent force for change. History, as always, was made by individual conjunctures arising out of the disparities of the various parts of modern rationality.

## Changes in the Organization of Knowledge

Many have written of the increasing amount and complexity of knowledge. Some writers have measured this knowledge "explosion" by the increasing increase of journals and books. Others, believing that publication does not necessarily embody knowledge, have rejected the argument that knowledge *growth* is accelerating, but still accept steady and rapid knowledge growth as a condition of modern life. But in fact some professions face rapidly changing knowledge environments while others do not. The professions of science do; those of social welfare do not. Some professions generate new knowledge within a professionally controlled milieu, as law generates case law. Others receive new

177

knowledge willy-nilly from external sources, as does accounting from regulatory bodies. Finally, some professions work with knowledge that is highly rationalizable, as does engineering, while others, like psychotherapy, do not.[1]

This diversity means that knowledge is another external force shaping interprofessional competition. To the extent that knowledge changes through mechanisms internal to professions, it is of course more an internal resource than an external effect; knowledge so generated can be used against other professions, as I argued in chapter 4. In addition, most adjacent professions face roughly the same knowledge conditions, which therefore have little differential effect. That the restless shift of electronic knowledge contrasts with the relative stability of the law does not affect interprofessional competition because, on the one hand, lawyers and electrical engineers are not often direct jurisdictional competitors, and on the other, the computer designers, physicists, chemists, and others with whom the electrical engineers *are* direct competitors face the same unstable knowledge as do the electrical engineers. But in fact professions adopt different strategies in the face of rapid knowledge change, and those strategies have profound consequences for jurisdiction.[2]

Knowledge change divides into two somewhat contradictory components. One involves the addition of new knowledge; the other, the replacement of old. Addition is the more familiar; in many areas, there are more and more things that individual professionals are expected to know. Previously unknown facts may be recognized through new instruments or concepts. Existing knowledge may be subdivided into more precise categories; detail increases while coverage remains the same. In professions that, like accounting, rest on socially constructed categories, knowledge increase may reflect the rapid generation of new categories by external agencies.

By contrast, knowledge may also change through the replacement of existing facts or methods by new ones. Most familiar in science, this process is nonetheless common to professions in general. The replacement of state commercial law by the Uniform Commercial Code in the 1950s and 1960s outmoded much of lawyers' knowledge of business law. More slow, but no less important, are gradual changes of paradigm or method—the slow replacement of Freudian counseling methods by transactional and other techniques; the move from live to recorded musical performance; the succession of scientific and human-relations management. Perhaps the most striking examples of this slow change occur in the military professions. Occasions of practice may be widely separated, and tactics may gradually but substantially change in inter-

vening years. Since these changes are appreciated by some professionals and not by others, opening campaigns are often grotesquely imbal-
anced, as the Franco-Prussian and Second World Wars show. The First
World War, by contrast, found the officers of both sides stalemated by
tactical developments neither had foreseen.[3]

Replacement of knowledge occurs at several levels, from the replacement of specific facts or methods to that of paradigms or general
approaches. While few firm generalities exist about the relative
changes in these levels in professional knowledge generally, the problem is well-studied in the philosophy and history of science. There,
the traditional argument held that steady, incremental change in specific facts and methods ultimately required general, paradigmatic
change; science advanced like an odometer. By contrast, Kuhn argued
that specifics change very little except during paradigm shifts, when
the lesser changes are entailed by the greater. In the professions, however, where knowledge is actively applied, incremental minor change
seems more frequent than paradigm change. Laws and regulations
change often; jurisprudence and accounting theory do not. Information on drugs and other medical treatment changes weekly; general
approaches to medical care do not.[4]

The two knowledge-change processes—growth and replacement—
have contradictory effects on professions. Growth pressures them to
subdivide, in order to maintain at a constant level the amount of knowledge a given professional must know. Replacement pressures them
towards abstraction, since abstractions will last longer than knowledge
of specific facts and methods. Like any external pressures, these contradictory forces can be resolved by professions in a variety of ways.
Some involve the internal adjustments discussed in chapter 5, particularly adjustment through career patterns, while others involve direct
competitive strategies.

A good illustration of these various forces is the case of electrical
engineering in the United States.[5] The electrical engineers originated
among those working with electricity and telegraphy in the late nineteenth century. The professional association, the American Institute of
Electrical Engineers (founded in 1884), was fairly early dominated by
members interested in power engineering, the specialty involved in
generating, transforming, and distributing electricity. Through their
interest in distribution, the power engineers came to emphasize "commercial engineering" in the 1910s, making an intellectual alliance with
management (one that was echoed by other engineering associations).
Engineers interested in radio—a low-voltage, wireless, signal-amplifi-
cation system—found themselves constrained by the high-voltage,

machinery- and grid-oriented power engineers and agitated for recognition within the AIEE. Failing to receive it, they defected in 1912 to found the Institute of Radio Engineers. IRE members were younger and worked for smaller companies. Furthermore, unlike the AIEE, the IRE was not oriented towards management, but rather towards science and technology. All the same, it was the management-oriented and executive-dominated AIEE that entered World War II as the largest engineering association in the country.

Although the leading organizer of the war research effort, Vannevar Bush, was himself an electrical engineer, he emphasized physics in staffing the war laboratories. Physicists dominated the electronic effort from the MIT Radiation Laboratory, and even the engineering-oriented Radio Research Laboratory employed fully half as many physicists as engineers. But even as it brought physicists into electronics, the war ballooned the electrical engineering societies. The IRE tripled in size and shortly after the war reorganized into a federation of semiautonomous professional groups, each with its own directorate, publications board, and conferences. This decisive step, mimicked by the AIEE a few years later, allowed the IRE to absorb the flood of new engineers and engineering students, and it rapidly became the nation's largest engineering society. The two groups ultimately merged to create the Institute of Electrical and Electronics Engineers (IEEE) in 1963.

No one questions that electrical engineering experienced massive knowledge change throughout its history. But the means of handling that change have varied widely. The first such mechanism was organizational turnover. That the founders of the IRE were younger than the contemporary AIEE leadership shows that the new area of radio engineering was seized by young men looking for work. The enormous centralization of power engineering eventually slowed the growth of the AIEE at precisely the time when demand for radio engineers was sharply rising because of the rapid proliferation of other low-voltage systems. The shift in dominant organizations embodied and articulated the shift of the field.[6]

But succession patterns emerged not only between organizations. Careers themselves developed a pattern, precisely because knowledge change became so rapid. Knowledge replacement becomes a serious career problem when a total turnover of effective knowledge takes less time than the thirty years that span a typical career. Professions respond to such knowledge change with two career strategies: continuing education and career turnover. The latter has always characterized not only electrical engineering, but engineering in general. Surveys of engineers routinely find up to 50 percent of them in management and operations, a fraction that rises with career duration. Research and development work, by contrast, declines steadily through the career. As their own knowledge becomes obsolete, engineers move into fields that do not involve absolute mastery of current techniques.[7]

On the other hand, the intense demand for electrical engineers who did possess current knowledge led many, both within electrical engineering and outside it, to undertake the continuing education necessary to enter or remain in the field. The machinery itself often dictated the path. For example, the replacement of mechanical and pneumatic servomechanisms with electronic process controls led the engineers who worked with those mechanisms to enter electrical engineering through midlife training. A 1928 M.S. in chemical engineering, James Abbott first worked as an operations engineer in a water-driven textile plant. After acquiring another M.S., in electrical engineering, in the 1950s, he completed his career designing and implementing computer-driven process controls for a razor-blade manufacturer.[8]

But organizational and career mechanisms could absorb only so much of the pressure. The intense demand for electrical engineering also pulled bachelor-level workers from other fields. A 1960s study found a larger fraction of bachelor-level physics graduates in engineering than engineering graduates. Indeed, while on the one hand B.S. physics graduates entered engineering as easily as engineering graduates, on the other, Ph.D. physicists dominated the research environments producing new knowledge. Relentlessly abstract training enabled physics graduates to assimilate new techniques and methods to a core of fundamental and largely unchanging abstractions. Faced with such competition, engineers considered making training for their own field considerably more abstract. One version of abstraction—that of the American Society for Engineering Education—emphasized basic sciences and organized "engineering sciences" around the areas of the pure science disciplines. Lewis Terman and others proposed an alternative "abstraction" that emphasized electronics as the creative area "that lies between pure science and traditional engineering." Ultimately, the physicists' hold on the abstractions was too strong; Bell Laboratories and other major research firms continued to hire physics and chemistry Ph.D.'s to do engineering research even after the expansion of engineering Ph.D. programs in the sixties.[9]

The case of electrical engineering illustrates well the fundamentally contradictory forces of knowledge addition and replacement. The intense and wide-ranging demand for state of the art electronics required tens of thousands of electrical engineers versed in the details of particular processes and applications. Yet the state of the art itself changed so fast that these engineers needed reeducation or replacement every ten years. The physicists seized and held the abstract approach to this problem; physicists in engineering could be expected to reeducate themselves as necessary. There thus developed a symbiosis. Abstractly trained physicists generated and supported the fundamental innovations and managed in many cases to remain near the state of the art for a whole career. Individual engineers handled applications, but the profession as a whole dealt with knowledge shift only through reeducation and organizational and career succession. [10]

Where knowledge shift is rapid but not as overwhelming as in electrical engineering, professions develop institutionalized, continuous reeducation. In accounting, where tax and other practice rules change continuously, professional education and development programs have existed since the mid 1950s for the profession at large, as they had for those employed by major firms since considerably earlier. In such professions, there usually exist semiofficial news-services. Law, of course, has the oldest such system in the court reporters, augmented by more recent agencies like the Commerce Clearing House (1937). Such services are sometimes operated by external groups; the pharmaceutical houses (who have published the *Physician's Desk Reference* since 1946), for example, conduct most continuing drug education of doctors. The case of prescription drugs shows another strategy for dealing with rapid knowledge change; an area of rapid change can be almost deliberately separated from the main body of professional activity, thereby leaving a much more constant, and more controllable, remainder. The area of pharmaceutical information, however, is currently being invaded by "clinical pharmacists," an elite group of pharmacists who fear the total deprofessionalization of their profession through automation and who base their new claims on individualized pharmacotherapy. [11]

The changes discussed so far have concerned more the content than the form of professional knowledge. A qualitatively different change has emerged from the artifical intelligence (AI) community, where researchers drawn from a wide variety of professions have developed systems that mimic professional thinking. Expert systems are at present rather specialized competitors with professions. Although incapable of synthetic decisions, they are excellent at sequential, analytic decisions in well-specified areas and thus easily mimic key-based diagnostic systems and corresponding treatment systems. Expert systems are therefore available that mimic diagnosis and treatment in specific medical areas (MYCIN), that perform general medical diagnosis (INTERNIST-1), that control computer configuration (R1), and that interpret mass spectroscopy results (DENDRAL). Efforts are under way in tax laws (TAXMAN), air traffic control (AIRPLAN), resource exploration (PROSPECTOR), and so on. The systems will compete most directly with those professions whose work is to scan large but reasonably well-known bodies of knowledge under a set of specified rules. Medicine is one such example, and medical applications have been among the most successful. By contrast, in synthetic areas dealing with highly individualized cases—psychotherapy and social casework, for example—the systems will have less impact. Professions whose work is largely constructive—architecture and the other "art" professions, general management—are unlikely targets precisely because such professions' jurisdictions are often both general and vague. The systems cannot mimic them; paradoxically, generality and vagueness, which minimize jurisdictional power, maximize defense against expert systems.[12]

But these are general criteria for AI's impact. Its implications for specific interprofessional conflicts depend largely on the structure of interprofessional relations in a particular area. Like other forms of knowledge change, expert systems have little general interprofessional effect, because professions competing with each other will generally compete against the same expert systems.[13] But expert systems will have important interprofessional effects when the knowledge strategies of competing professions vary. Where one competitor works at the level of abstraction and synthesis favored by expert systems, that profession will be at a clear competitive disadvantage. Electrical engineers are already discovering this in the area of circuit design, a considerable portion of which is now accomplished by expert systems (as much drafting is by CAD systems). Similarly, where there is a division of labor, professions will come to rely on expert systems for certain specialized services, rather than on the professions that currently provide them. To the extent that a profession is specialized in such a vulnerable area, it will sustain serious damage from expert systems. A good example might well be the pharmacists just mentioned, whose expansion into "clinical pharmacy" may be blocked by the rather easy computerization of dose response, drug interaction, and other specialized pharmacological knowledge.[14]

More generally, all professions will lose particular portions of their jurisdictions to expert systems. As with rapid knowledge change generally, we can expect professions to isolate those parts of their knowledge vulnerable to expert systems and refound their jurisdictions on nonthreatened areas to the extent necessary. Some good examples are already available. Keyword indexing and computerized bibliographical databases, which date from the 1960s, have stripped reference librarians of many of their classic functions. Were scholars and librarians content with earlier bibliographical services, (performed now in a fraction of the time), reference workers would long since have degenerated into mere custodians of terminals. But in fact this functional elite of librarians treated the online systems as enabling a whole new level of reference service. The only real losers were specialized bibliographers who based their status on massive and detailed knowledge of particular references. General reference librarians gained status—since nearly all of them could now claim access to the kind of expertise only specialists had previously possessed. As service rose, expectation rose with it. Expectation increase will not necessarily protect all fields, however, and the mechanization of professional work cannot but result in an increase in competition. Out-migration into other professions and into administration will also buffer this process somewhat, but the machines will absorb work faster than professions can shrink, and there will inevitably result professions or subprofessions with many members and little work to do, groups that must find work or wither.[15]

Predictions about expert systems thus resemble those for any other form of commodification, but are at a different level. Rather than commodification at the lowest end of professional work, among its most routine aspects, expert systems promise commodification well up the abstraction hierarchy. Yet the same contradictory expectations apply. On the one hand, professional work is replaced by machine work. On the other, the machines enable new forms of professional work and new expectations for professional services. Essentially, the race is between two forms of creativity. The growth of professions to this date shows which has won so far.

### New Forms of Legitimacy

I argued in chapter 4 that, among other functions, the academic sectors of professions exercise that of legitimation. Legitimating work connects professional diagnosis, treatment, and inference to central values in the larger culture, thereby establishing the cultural authority of professional work. But values change. Like other external forces, their changes affect the professions not directly but through the system's structural relations. Sudden value changes affect professions, to be sure, but some are helped and others hindered.[16]

Legitimation justifies both what professions do and how they do it. In the first case, legitimation establishes that the results produced by successful professional work are culturally valued results. Health, justice, and beauty are culturally valued results; they are produced, according to the legitimating claims, by doctors, lawyers, and composers. In the second case, legitimation establishes that results were produced in a culturally approved manner. Efficiency and probity are culturally valued norms of behavior; engineers and accountants acquire legitimacy by following them, although the norms define only the form, not the content, of their professional work.

Legitimation of results is the more familiar of the two types. Military work is legitimate because professionalized force enables the exercise of such central cultural values as nationalism, freedom, and imperialism. Legal work is legitimate because its procedures allow cultural values of fairness, justice, and order to be realized. Doctors intervene in bodily processes to further the cultural value of health. These three examples embody a continuum of instrumentalism. Military work is explicitly instrumental; death and destruction are not normally legitimated in themselves, but what they enable *is*. In law, by contrast, the distance between the immediate result (a "fair trial") and the ultimate value (justice) is considerably less, and moreover the ultimate value is not so much enabled by the activities of lawyers as it is, at least in the legitimation theory of lawyers, carried out to some nearest possible approximation. Likewise, since health itself has often been conceived as absence of disease, the results of medical work are directly legitimate, rather than legitimate as instruments enabling some ultimate value. This continuum finds its limit where professional work is itself a final value, as in the Catholic clergies. Closing his history of Christian liturgy, Gregory Dix says:

So the four-action Shape of the Liturgy was found by the end of the first century. He had told His friends to do this henceforward with the new meaning 'for the *anamnesis*' of Him, and they have done it always since. Was ever another command so obeyed?

The Catholic eucharist is legitimated by revelation; it is grounded in itself. Protestant liturgy, and Protestant ministerial work generally, is by contrast more instrumental; the pastor aims to teach and lead, thereby enabling others to find God.[17]

Professions generally attempt to move towards the consummatory legitimation of the Catholic clergies. Dominant professions become able to publicly define cultural values in terms of sucessful results of their own work. Thus most Americans, and certainly most American lawyers, believe that the adversarial system as practiced in America *is* justice, rather than *is a means to* justice. The common reactions to "inquisitorial" continental procedure testify to this belief. Similarly, while direct medical interventions in disease contribute relatively little to the net health of modern societies, the medical profession has until recently successfully defined health as "not needing to see a doctor." The only major holdout from this movement towards consummatory legitimation has been the military.[18]

Legitimation must draw on cultural values, and cultural values undergo autonomous shifts. Such value shifts can sharply change demand for professional services; secularization provides the most striking example.[19] Despite its occasional recrudescences, concern for salvation has gradually declined in industrialized nations. Other values (often originating in religious thought) have replaced it—happiness, self-actualization, personal independence. This long-run change has undermined the clergy. In Britain, the general irreligion of the 18th century transformed the established clergyman from a religious figure into a local notable serving political and judiciary functions. In the early nineteenth century the clergy, like other gentry, were deeply disturbed by the social dislocations of the Napoleonic Wars and their aftermath, but developed a specifically clerical solution—mass education of a largely religious nature. Both established and dissenting clergy worked extensively in education in the first half of the nineteenth century, although the teaching itself was done by lay people. Later in the century, British clergy, like their American counterparts, entered the field of social melioration. Only the great financial strength of establishment protected the English clergy from the demand consequences of secularization until the twentieth century.[20]

In France clergy were established as state officials under the Concordat of 1802. Expansive and powerful, they dominated education through much of the nineteenth century. In medicine, sisters staffed the hospitals, while rural curés provided state sanctioned medical care. Extensive clergy functions led to expansion in numbers, particularly under the Restoration and the Second Empire. The direct impact of secularization was in fact postponed until the Law of Separation of 1905, which removed all state subsidies of clergy activities and thereby provoked a clerical crisis.[21]

In America, the clergyman's place as director of a local social order disappeared in the Federal period. But the clergy struggled to retain their indirect role in social order by emphasizing order's dependence on personal piety, an emphasis that underlay the evangelical thrust of the Second Great Awakening. Evangelicalism required far more personnel than did the congregationalism of the earlier period, and clergy numbers grew rapidly, as did seminaries and professional associations.

The sudden swing toward secularization after midcentury left the clergy heavily overstaffed. The result was a strong move by Protestant clergy into social melioration and a weaker one into education. (Roman Catholic clergy, by contrast, emphasized the latter.) In both cases the religious legitimation was less direct than that of the evangelical period; the social gospel made Christianity an ethical system as much as a religion. American clergy thus dealt with value change in part by adopting the values replacing their own. Eventually the pastoral care movement brought the new values of adjustment and happiness to many clergymen, making them little more than vaguely deistic counselors.[22]

Value shifts seldom have so differential an effect on demand for professional services. Thus the radical democracy of the Jacksonian era affected all American professions somewhat similarly, opening the markets for legal and medical services to a wider variety of experts. Only a few professions—probably teaching is the most important—were preferentially helped by democratization. In twentieth-century America waves of concern with social or personal problems have occasionally helped certain professions—the social consciousness of the 60s and the "me-decade" of the 70s are examples—but it is not clear whether these phenomena were substantial enough to have had any real impact on social scientists and psychotherapists. The succession of one or another value category may be more apparent than real. Value shifts may occur at a more abstract level, however; some professions legitimate their work with individual values like happiness, health, self-actualization, and personal culture, while others turn to social values like adjustment, justice, orderliness, and amelioration, and still others to political values like democracy, planning, and freedom of information. Indeed, some professions employ the economic legitimations of profit, security, and economic growth, and a few use such extremely general legitimations as the "pursuit of truth" or "ultimate concern." It is difficult to specify any sudden successions among even these value levels in the last two centuries. The gradual emergence of the personal values is probably the most striking change, along with the decline of ultimate concern. As we shall see below, the real change is less in the content of these values than in how they are pursued.[23]

Changing values exercise a second effect on the legitimation of professional results and thereby on competition between professions. Change in values can recast the *meaning* of a profession's legitimation arguments without any change occurring in the arguments themselves. As a consequence, professions continually revise their legitimation systems, particularly as others' positions are improved by the gradual shifts of values. Again the clergy provides a good example. Federalist era clergy, Scott tells us, "embodied and expressed New England communalism:"

The minister purveyed the ideas which connected the town to the broader culture and by which New Englanders interpreted life in all its personal and social dimensions. He performed the rituals that gave the community its common consciousness as well as those that distinguished deviance from conformity, and he dispensed the piety and moralism that shaped the devotional life of the New England people and the public discipline of the New England towns.

Within a communal culture, this position was unassailably legitimate. But when the new politics of party arose in the 1790s, the clergy arguments acquired a different sound. In "pointing out the dangers to order, decrying the apostacy from basic principles, and invoking the time-honored axioms about the nature of office and the role of revealed religion in securing order and liberty," they seemed merely to support the Federalists against the Republicans. Although the clergy opposed a "politics of party," that opposition had itself become a political position and thereby lost the transcendent legitimacy it had possessed. The clergy position hadn't changed; the constellation around it had. Clergy in fact dealt with this situation by spinning off their direct social-order functions into the new moral societies, reestablishing their own legitimacy on purely religious principles.[24]

Similar changes are not uncommon. Typically, such value shifts disrupt professions' attempts at consummatory legitimation, at making their work not a means to a socially valued end, but an end in itself. This redefinition and debunking threatens every profession that possesses consummatory legitimacy. Invading professions claim the same legitimacy as an incumbent in all but some one important feature. This shows the public that alternative groundings exist for professional work, unmasking the fallacy of consummatory legitimacy. To the extent that public value shifts favor change in that one feature, they may shape the competition's outcome. Thus American medicine, which has increasingly relied on the culture's male values of heroism and efficacy to legitimate its interventionist health care, has faced serious challenges from competitors justifying their own presence in the health-care field with the female values of nurturance and forethought.

Changes in the values available to justify professional work may thus affect the actual demand professions face, as well as undermining previously secure jurisdictional claims. Generally these are slow changes, to which professions adjust gradually, although well-endowed professions like the clergy can put off the day of wrath. But professions must legitimate not only what they do, but how they do it. By far the greater impact of value change has been on this legitimation of the means of professional work. People still want beautiful music, healthy bodies, timely information; it is the legitimate means for developing these—the programmable synthesizer, the medical laboratory, the computer database—that have changed.

Legitimation of means begins with the legitimation of professional activity itself—diagnosis, treatment, and inference. In the last century, science, with the broader, related phenomenon of formal rationality, has become the fundamental ground for the legitimacy of professional techniques. In the value scheme on which modern professions draw, science stands for logic and rigor in diagnosis, as well as a certain caution and conservatism in professional therapeutics. It implies extensive academic research based on the highest standards of rationality. The most familiar example of the shift to scientific legitimacy claims is that of nineteenth-century medicine. This change was not as easy as is often thought. In mid-nineteenth-century Britain, in Peterson's blunt words: "medical knowledge was not intrinsically valued, either by medical men or by lay society, and the achievement of professional power involved the evolution of independent power within the sphere of the medical school and the assertion of influence within the hospital." Unlike the mainstream medical institutions, the new specialist institutions outside the medical establishment claimed legitimacy precisely on their technical and scientific expertise. Only the threat of these alternative institutions and the necessity of controlling insubordinate nursing staffs led the medical establishment to move towards a scientific legitimation of medical techniques. In France, by contrast, the high medical establishment had adopted an absolutely scientific basis for legitimacy from the start of the nineteenth century, with the paradoxical consequence that the public believed that it deliberately set medical standards so high in order to deny medical service to most of the country. In the United States, the era of scientific medicine came later, at the end of the century. Mid-century American medicine had fought the homeopaths on the ground that their medicine was *too scientific*. Homeopathy was a rationally consistent and theoretical medicine, while regular medicine was basically a trial-and-error matter. American medicine adopted a truly scientific legitimation only when the manifest results of the bacteriological revolution overwhelmed its faith in personal clinical experience, towards the end of the century.[25]

If science in the narrow sense reshaped many claims, so also did science in the broad sense of rationality and efficiency. Although efficiency had its main effect in transforming the legitimation of professional social structure, it changed legitimation of cultural structure as well. The codification movement in American law invoked the legitimacy of rationalization from the 1880s. Louis Sullivan's "form follows function" attempted a similar task for architecture. Not all professions accepted efficiency as a criterion for their work. Lawyers continued to legitimate their techniques by the tradition of common law. Admittedly inefficient, the cavalry techniques of World War I armies were also legitimated by their hallowed traditions. The Navy, by contrast, chose rational efficiency over tradition; "today all nations start *de novo*" said Admiral Sir John Fisher at the 1906 launching of his technological marvel HMS *Dreadnought*. Most professions, in fact, unhesitatingly adopted efficiency as one basic justification of professional technique. Even in medicine, the careful attention to environment, nutrition, and general health that had characterized mid-nineteenth-century medicine disappeared with the triumphs of specific etiology. Cure was not only scientific, but efficient as well.[26]

Efficiency replaced, in these various cases, a variety of predecessors—tradition, general learning, and the like. These prior legitimations had usually not covered technique alone, but rather all aspects of service provision—the technique of the professional, his individual character, and the occupation's social structure. Nonetheless, general learning, for example, was an important predecessor of efficiency as a specific legitimation of technique. For civil servants in France, England, and even Japan, the possession of generalized ability remained a fundamental ground for legitimacy well into this century. Despite the recent prominence of formal training in specific administrative skills, the French, at least, retain generalism as the foundation of good civil service, and indeed of good management generally. As one member of the French administrative elite told Ezra Suleiman, "To be a good director of a firm, or of any organization, it's good not to have been involved in any particular aspect [of the organization]. It allows you to arrive at an objective synthesis." Freud himself argued that general learning, not specialized psychoanalytic training, provided the surest foundation—for both practitioner and profession—in psychoanalysis.[27]

The replacement of tradition or general learning as foundations for technical legitimacy was a minor matter compared with the larger shift from legitimacy of character to legitimacy of technique. For earlier legitimation systems had spent less effort on technique per se than on character, which in turn would guarantee it. The nineteenth-century

British professions are the best example, particularly those with substantial status in the pre-nineteenth-century period—barristers, physicians, clergymen, and army officers. The work of such men was legitimized largely by their gentlemanliness, their courage, their disinterest. Their competitors chose a more complex justification. The "lower orders" of solicitors and apothecaries based their claims in part on rationalization of their social structure; the new examinations would pick individuals on the basis of skills, the lectures and schools would give a common training. But they claimed as well a character, and a new one at that: a character of probity, rectitude, responsibility. Of such men would Johnston say, at midcentury:[28] "Perhaps in no walk of life in England are there to be found men of such exquisite discretion as these professional advisers of great families. Their legal knowledge constitutes the least part of their value. They have the nicest appreciation of the prudent, the becoming, and the practicable. . . ." In America, the Old Regime tradition was much weaker—the aristocratic approach drowned in the flood of Jacksonian democracy—but character still emerged as a central basis for professional legitimacy, this time bound to the mastery of knowledge. Describing the archetypical nineteenth-century professional, Bledstein writes:

The person with an ideal character was distinctive, intellectually and emotionally confident. He paced life properly, heard the true rhythm of the universe; and chose the real over the illusory, the natural over the artificial. He demonstrated such judiciousness, discretion, equanimity, and balance that right and wrong became clear to him, duly defined, and world matters set straight, perhaps for a life time. . . . The impressiveness of a man's worldly credentials reflectd the strength of his inner character, the permanence of his inner continuity, which corresponded to the outer continuity of a career.

Character was of course central to the Victorian view of the world, and certainly that made it a powerful basis for professional legitimacy. But in the twentieth century, character lost much ground, a fact easily seen in public professional heroes. Schweitzer, for example, gave medicine the legitimacy of altruism, something his successors on *General Hospital* lack. Although the medical profession internally is as concerned with character as ever, its public legitimacy rests completely on science. The military provides the most striking case; gone are the cavalry heroes, the daredevil submariners. The new services sell themselves both to potential recruits and to the public by their activity on the cutting edge of technological innovation. Only the marines are still "looking for a few good men."[29]

Yet character retains a surprising foothold in the legitimation structures of many professions. Dozens of clergymen arrested in civil rights and antiwar demonstrations have witnessed to their profession's altruism, courage, and vocation. The morality play of Watergate presented both positive and negative portraits of the proper character of lawmen—Cox and Sirica against Mitchell and Dean. Another kind of character—that of the colorless team player—supported the legitimacy of middle management's professional claims after the Second World War; this was the celebrated grey flannel man of W.H. Whyte. Yet another form of character emerged as central to the legitimacy claims of the new psychotherapeutic professions. Here legitimacy rested both on successful completion of personal therapy—a model taken from psychoanalysis—and also on wide personal experience, on involvement with one's community, and on a certain broad humanity. Not only in psychiatry, psychology, and social work did this legitimation scheme become important, but also in those branches of the clergy oriented towards counseling.[30]

Finally, a few professions resolutely ground their work on fading values, in particular on character rather than technique. The French army officer corps retained until at least the seventies a legitimation based on tradition, courage, personal glory, service of the *patrie*, and the brotherhood of arms. "In the United States, the symbol of the modern soldier is the helmeted pilot in his 'anti-g' flying suit. . . . In France, it is the muscular tanned paratrooper, the man 'painted' to blend with the jungle, with his chiefs living the same life and sharing the same dangers, disdaining bureaucrats and intellectuals." Other examples of resolute traditionalism in legitimation (as in everything else) are the current English lawyers, both the solicitors and, particularly, the barristers. Both groups have drawn strength from character values and from the traditionality of their techniques.[31]

Character has thus not vanished as a basis for legitimizing professional work. Moreover, the shift from legitimation of character to legitimation of technique was fairly slow. Professions did not lose jurisdiction because values invoked by their legitimation arguments suddenly disappeared. New and competing professions often chose contrasting legitimation values, to be sure. And the conflict of professions dramatized value changes as few other areas did. But the intimate history of jurisdiction depended on more sudden forces—vanishing technologies or new organizations—and the progress of professional generations allowed professions to change their legitimation strategies gradually. The American medical situation at the turn of this century was typical; an older, settled generation urged "aequanimitas" while the younger one preached the "magic bullets" of the new science.[32]

The move from character to technique was complemented by an increasing legitimation through social structure. The social structure of professions was designed by the pioneers of "professionalization" to guarantee on the one hand that practitioners possessed the scientifically or rationally legitimated modes of practice and on the other that they carried them out properly. Neither character nor science was sufficient in itself; social structure provided an additional guarantee and hence a legitimating argument. The structures employed included the familiar steps of professionalization; examinations, licensing or registration, disciplinary committees, accreditation, and ethics codes. Most of these structures served, of course, other purposes as well as that of legitimation—monopoly control being the most important. It is central to recall that legitimation through social structure was pioneered by insurgent groups—apothecaries and solicitors in England—seeking to break the power of traditional dominants. To do so they portrayed the commitment of the profession to certain central values: altruism, discipline, efficiency, accountability. As these values changed, the structures had to change with them or lose their power to help a profession retain its jurisdiction.[33]

The legitimating values involved in professional social structures vary strikingly from country to country, a variation that indeed surpasses their variation over time within given countries. Thus the central legitimation for professional social structure in France has throughout the modern period been association with the state. The form of state regulation matters little and indeed varies little. That French professions legitimate their social structures through association with the state does not, however, sharply affect competition among French professions. Since professions compete within nations, the variation of legitimating values from country to country has no effect. But the particular values of each country shape its competition in particular ways.

Thus, in the United States, the legitimating values for professional structures include their collegiality, their democracy, and increasingly their efficiency. Here efficiency is less a property of techniques than of service delivery. Medical treatment that ignores environmental causes for specific etiology is efficient technically. Medical treatment delivered within a large and differentiated division of labor is efficient organizationally. It is this organizational efficiency that had become, by the third quarter of this century, a central value in the social-structural legitimation of American professions.

The rising value of organizational efficiency directly affects the relative status of professions by forcing most of them to become bureaucratically organized, a trend I have already discussed. Only psychotherapy has successfully avoided taking organizational (or even technical) efficiency as a legitimating value, although the success of behavioral therapy shows that technical efficiency can serve as a legitimating value for groups there as well. But the most striking effect of efficiency in America was indirect. Efficiency (both technical and organizational) emphasized the measurability of output, since efficiency could not be demonstrated with immeasurable outputs. In areas as diverse as engineering, education, and resource and business management, the increasing public popularity of efficiency moved interprofessional competition away from conflict over general values and towards conflict in measurable results. The rise of "educational administrators" reflected not only their ability to persuade the public that schools ought to be run like factories, but also the public's belief that the figures embodying their factory production meant something about education. "Child accounting" told the citizens of Kane, Pennsylvania, that in 1917 their children had "spent 365 years more time in school than they should have." Teachers and others fighting the onset of the administrators did not present opposing numbers because they did not believe in them, which in itself put them at a competitive disadvantage. One characteristic impact of the rise of efficiency as a value has thus been the replacement of substantive criteria of output with more easily measured procedural ones, favoring professions that emphasize the latter.[34]

Varying professional areas have seen the rise of efficiency in various times and by various means. In American business management, efficiency became a central value for legitimation by the first quarter of the twentieth century, imported from engineering. In medicine, efficiency has only occasionally been a successful ground of legitimacy claims; English medical officers of health urged in the 1910s a bureaucratic, salaried medical service and attacked their colleagues on the grounds of inefficient medicine. But in neither England nor the United States has efficiency ever become a central ground for legitimizing services by doctors, however much people may worry about the efficiency of medical services. In most professions, efficiency, like other new values, has become the central claim of insurgent subgroups, usually groups interested in reforming administration of services—thus educational administration, social service administration, administrative psychiatry, and so on. Usually these subgroups eventually become independent professions. Sometimes, as in the case of hospital administration and medicine, the insurgent group comes from outside the existing system. It is clear that efficiency becomes a central legitimacy claim only when science, broadly understood as rational expertise, is not available. Thus medicine, electrical engineering, law, and accounting do not base their chief legitimacy claims on the fact that they work efficiently, although they claim to be "as efficient as necessary." The various forms of civilian and military management, by contrast, make efficiency a central claim, because they have little obvious technical expertise.

The major shift in legitimation in the professions has thus been a shift from a reliance on social origins and character values to a reliance on scientization or rationalization of technique and on efficiency of service. This change reflects value shifts in the larger culture and has steadily pressured professions to move towards these legitimacy bases or face erosion of jurisdiction. Few professions have lost major jurisdiction by refusing to adopt new forms of legitimacy, perhaps because few have in fact retained old forms, and because those few happen to be extremely powerful. Thus, while legitimacy values have shifted markedly over the modern history of professions, and while they differ considerably from country to country, they have surprisingly small effects on the actual history of jurisdiction. New values serve as convenient ideologies for insurgent or new groups, and that appears to be their chief role.

## The Rise of Universities

Among the external developments affecting professions, few have been so discussed as the modern university. Most professional education occurs in universities, and Americans in fact define universities by the presence of professional schools. The association of universities with professions seems to follow ineluctably, because professions rest on knowledge and universities are the seat of knowledge in modern societies.

Joseph Ben-David and Burton Bledstein have pursued this view to its logical conclusion, defining professionalism by association with university-based knowledge. Yet they take different avenues to that conclusion, Ben-David focusing on European, Bledstein on American universities.[35] For Ben-David, professionalism is prefigured in the ancient faculties of theology, law, and medicine. Taking the German system as his model, he treats the university degree as the first step towards professional practice, making all university graduates in the three faculties protoprofessionals. Although admitting the British system to be exceptional, he says bluntly that "higher education . . . [is] the most important element of professionalism."[36] He goes on to argue that the universities hurt the middle classes by drawing "the best of the bourgeoisie" into the professions, away from the class's central activity of commercial endeavor. Professionalism thereby weakened the middle classes and created a "surplus of educated men."[37] Studying the American situation, Bledstein treats professionalism less as entry into a particular skilled occupation than as a general assumption that individuals can, through diligent preparation, acquire knowledge sufficient to a career within a particular form of work. Professionalism is opposed to "office" or "calling," a matter of making oneself through a career, rather than being made by entry into a "preestablished station in life." The university is "the seminal institution within the culture of professionalism" because it rewarded and legitimated the effort, talent, and merit of the bourgeois class, enabling it to defeat a gentry that controlled such other American institutions as state government.[38]

Thus, while both Ben-David and Bledstein emphasize the university-profession connection, their different reasons for doing so belie the functionalist belief that the connection arises in the common association of universities and professions with knowledge. In fact, for both authors the connection arises rather through a class dynamic. Moreover, neither author wishes to deal with the embarrassing British case, despite the professional archetypicality of English medicine, law, and accounting. For none of these three had much association with universities during its "professionalizing" period, and in fact there is precious little such association today. The effects of university growth and development on professions in fact depend on the conjuncture of other forces, as well as on the situation among the professions themselves. Here, too, we must examine each case individually.

Universities can play several roles in professional life. They can serve as legitimators, providing authoritative grounds for the exclusive exercise of expertise. They can house the function of knowledge advancement, enabling academic professionals to develop new techniques outside of practice. They can train young professionals, often in conjunction with the function of research. Finally, universities, like states, may become another arena for interprofessional competition. Often a set of professional techniques is not legally restricted— quantitative techniques for project evaluation are an example—and professions compete by attracting students and monopolizing the teaching of courses in such subjects. The battles of the workplace, court, and public continue into academia itself. These four roles of the university in professional life have dominated at different places and different times. By studying them in Germany, France, England, and the United States, we can see how historical contingencies drastically affected university-profession relations and with them interprofessional competition.

In Germany, universities preceded the professions as powerful institutions.[39] Professional people first acquired formal occupational structures as civil servants, and only later became identified as members of particular occupations; clergymen, lawyers, teachers, and many doctors were largely employed by the state until well into the nineteenth century. While there was professional practice beyond state employment, it was of low status and reward; only after 1848 did such extramural employment become more common. To control professional people, the state instituted meritocratic examinations, for clergymen (seventeenth century), for doctors (1725), for lawyers (1737), and for schoolteachers (1810). By the late nineteenth century there were two sets of examinations, one following university attendance, the other following an extended period of internship (in law or medicine) or seminary (in theology). There were no effective associations of university-trained professionals in Germany before the 1870s, when lawyer and doctor associations appeared. (The clergymen organized in 1892.) State certification, rather than association membership, thus identified professionals in Germany, a situation that persisted long after the appearance of the associations. Since the state examinations assumed university attendance, an assumption increasingly rigid as the nineteenth century passed, the state guaranteed that university schooling defined the professions.

Yet university schooling was in fact little connected with professional practice or knowledge. The two-level examinations reflected in part a differentiation between education and professional training that emerged between 1780 and 1860. These years saw the rise of *Bildung*, a concept variously defined as "cultivation," "a combination of taste, learning, and judgment," or "a curious blend of individualism, idealism, and neo-humanism."[40] *Bildung* entailed a resolutely antiprofessional pedagogy. Preprofessional studies were ridiculed as *Brotstudium* (literally, bread studies). The professors executed their assault on professionalism with vigor. "With few exceptions, the neo-humanists hoped to banish *Brotstudium*, studying for the sake of a career, from the university."[41] Of the higher degrees that emerged throughout the nineteenth century, only the M.D. became necessary to professional practice, although the doctorate had been required for any university teaching since long before. The German faculties were themselves perhaps the most highly professionalized group in Germany. Protected by a state monopoly, organized in independent institutions with considerable rights of self-governance, and dedicated to an ascetic ideal of pure scholarship (*Wissenschaft*), the professors controlled the examinations to their own and other ranks and taught the cultivation of self through scholarship (*Bildung durch Wissenschaft*). Yet this last ideal denied all practicing forms of professionalism but the professoriate's own. Moreover, professors, no matter of what field, owed more allegiance to the professoriate than to the lawyers, doctors, or scientists whose ranks their students would join. Yet at the same time the professoriate increasingly dominated the state examinations and even the new professional associations.

This paradoxical situation had peculiar consequences for interprofessional competition. Despite ever-increasing standards, the prestigious (and in fact preprofessional) tracks of the German universities attracted rapidly increasing numbers of students in the late nineteenth and early twentieth centuries. Although often decried as *Brotstudenten*, these masses of students gave the professoriate an important claim on governmental resources. Thus the professors—the dominant figures in professional life—benefited directly from the swelling numbers, and there grew up, in profession after profession, an enormous oversupply of qualified professionals, quite to the despair of practitioners. (A similar process had happened in the early nineteenth century.) These groups invaded other professional areas. Thus the late nineteenth century saw a steady flow of lawyers into private legal work and business, and of mathematicians into insurance companies. Ben-David himself has analyzed the invasion of philosophy departments by unemployed physiologists.[42]

Meanwhile, outside the universities, there arose a "free" professionalism more like that of England or America, for the nonuniversity professions were much less dominated by the state. Their voluntary associations preceded those of the state professions (the engineers, apothecaries, and dentists organized in the 1850s). Although all of these agitated for state recognition and, increasingly, for university education, they were usually denied. The engineers and commercial professions were educated in *Polytechniken* (later *technische Hochschulen*) that achieved university rank and privileges slowly in the latter half of the nineteenth century. (Faculties of the older universities opposed absolutely any attempt at merger with the *technische Hochschulen*.) The elementary school teachers failed to achieve the recognition accorded their secondary school colleagues and were restricted to academies.

Preceding the professions as powerful social actors, the German universities dominated those professions for which they trained students and ignored the rest, which therefore followed a more American pattern of market development. To the extent that university professors increasingly controlled the state examinations, they controlled the areas of practice to which those examinations gave entrance. But excessive recruitment drove professionals into dozens of new forms of employment. By overproducing in the "learned" professions, German universities seemed to hasten the creation of market-based professions through colonization. But the learned professions did not extend their formal control to areas staffed by the trainees they could not absorb. Rather they left them to create new groups in the new areas. The German university, then, provided the legitimacy and the mechanism for an intensely conservative approach to certain professional jurisdictions, and the freedom and personnel for a rather liberal approach to others.

Until the very end of the nineteenth century, France lacked universities in the German sense.[43] The phrase Université Impériale (or Royale) de France denoted the whole ensemble of secondary and tertiary institutions, under the ultimate control of the Ministry for Public Instruction. Professional training took place partly within this system and partly outside it. Within lay the professional faculties of medicine, law, letters, and science, training students for work in those professions. Outside were the *grandes écoles*, which prepared students for the state service as secondary-school teachers (Ecole Normale Supérieure, 1809), civil engineers (Ecole Polytechnique, 1791, Ecole des Ponts et Chausées, 1747), military engineers (Ecole d'Artillerie et Génie, 1802), and more recently, higher civil servants (Ecole Nationale d'Administration, 1945). (Groups serving the state in these professions comprised the highly prestigious *grands corps d'Etat*.) Other institutions for technical education also emerged outside the "university"—the Ecole Centrale des Arts et Manufactures for industrial engineers (1829), the Ecole Supérieure de Télégraphie (1878), the Ecole Municipale de Physique et Chimie Industrielles (1882), and the Ecole Supérieure d'Electricité (1894). While often private in origin, most of these schools passed eventually into the hands of the state. Like the *grandes écoles* other than Normale, however, they were not controlled by the Minister of Public Instruction. Thus, Polytechnique fell under the Ministries of Interior and War at various times, and when Centrale entered state hands (in 1856) its control fell to the Minister of Commerce. Indeed, Commerce controlled not only Centrale, but also the vast array of lesser technical schools, from the semi-professional Ecoles des Arts et Métiers to local institutes for skilled workers. There were thus at least three educational systems producing professional-type workers in France: the universities, the *grandes écoles*, and the other ministerial schools. These systems were under a variety of ministries, but chiefly under Public Instruction and Commerce.

In 1896, reformer Louis Liard created centralized universities in sixteen cities out of a total of fifty-six separate faculties of medicine, law, letters, and science.[44] However, while the Ecole Normale was officially absorbed into the University of Paris in 1903, the system of *grandes écoles* remains separate from the universities to this day. The dominance and elitism of the *grandes écoles* put the universities in a peculiar position. On the one hand, the orientation of the *grandes écoles* towards professional service in the *corps d'Etat* left research and research training largely up to the university faculties, even in science. On the other, the small size and exclusivity of the *grandes écoles* left much of France without any form of advanced professional or vocational training. Universities were thus simultaneously driven towards academicization on the one hand and direct application on the other. The training of high-status professionals, which reconciled research and application in Germany and later the United States, was largely monopolized by the *grandes écoles*.

As a result, a divided university system developed, with Paris representing the one task and the provincial universities the other. At Paris, there emerged specialized research institutes (Ecole Pratique des Hautes Etudes, 1868; Centre Nationale de la Recherche Scientifique, 1939) which effectively withdrew researchers from general university life. The provincial universities, on the other hand, focused on applied research and vocational preparation, partly because of Liard's belief that they should finance themselves. With cries of overcrowding in law and medicine, technical education and support offered the major avenue of financial expansion. Universities thus initiated dozens of cooperative research programs and developed specific degrees aimed at specific industries. They also sought municipal subsidies, usually tied to specific vocational or industrial goals. In this rapid move into technical education, provincial science faculties came into conflict not only with the *grandes écoles*, but also with the extensive semiprofessional education system of the Ministry of Commerce.[45]

The proliferation of educational modalities, particularly in the newer technical professions, shaped French professionalism decisively. Competition tended to subdivide areas of work. First, the system divided vertically, separating, for example, high-status generalist engineers (the *polytechniciens*) from lower-status applied specialists (the *gadzarts*). Similar divisions split medicine and other professions.[46] Below the generalist level of the *grandes écoles*, other educational institutions competed by carving out a specialized area and creating a degree for it. Sometimes competition was unsuccessful at subdivision; although private commercial schools emerged in the late nineteenth century, the law faculties retained control of social science and commercial training well into the twentieth century, largely as a hedge against their own enrollment problems.[47] But usually the exigencies of university survival reinforced the divisions long characteristic of French educational policy. Even today, the French grant highly specialized *certificats* and *licences* in dozens of subjects. These specialized degrees then form the basis for "professions." The associational professionalism characteristic of Britain and America, with its origins in common work, is largely prevented by this incessant educational subdivision.

In the older professions of law and medicine, the French situation more nearly resembled the German one. Faculties tended to define professional skills and membership and determined the content of the state examinations. On the other hand, they did not, as in Germany, exercise delegated state authority over entire areas of work, nor were they, by the end of the century, still dominant in organized professional life. After a century of effort, the faculties of medicine persuaded the government to abolish the *officiers de santé* only when *syndicats* became powerful enough to offer serious assistance. Similarly, the faculties were forced to absorb the second tier of medical schools as full university schools, Thus while the university and its predecessor faculties played a stronger role in medicine than in technical education, it was still not the determinant one of the German universities.

The developing French system of education thus imposed on the French system of professions an extensive differentiation, both horizontal and vertical. Horizontally it created a world of relatively specialized degrees attached to specialized functions. Vertically it created sharp status differences. This "cartesian order," to use Terry Clark's phrase, undercut the broad foundations that underlay associational professionalism in American and Britain. Professions did not seek university training to legitimate extant activities, but rather were initiated by the new university degrees. Once professions became independently active, they used the educational system less as an external ally than as an arena of competition. Thus, the battle between pharmacy and medicine in the nineteenth century was conducted as much within the universities as in the workplace, the government, or the public media. In the twentieth century, the university's role as site of competition eventually came to overshadow its role as legitimating ally in interprofessional competition.

In England, the relation between professions and universities follows an altogether different pattern.[48] The two ancient universities of Oxford and Cambridge resolutely opposed professional education until well into the twentieth century. The University of London, although it has absorbed many professional schools, remains to this day more a holding company than a university in the German or American sense. The provincial universities of the late nineteenth century follow the American or German pattern more closely, but do not train elite professionals. For their part, many of England's professions, particularly law and accounting, conduct most of their training on their own. Similarly, although many English professions have typically developed, first, educational institutions, then journals and associations, and, much later, disciplinary mechanisms, university education comes at a purely arbitrary point in the development of most English professions. It was relatively early in social work, chemistry, and architecture, relatively late in accounting, medicine, and civil engineering. In short, while England pioneered the form of associational profession regarded by many functionalists as ideal typical, university education is almost completely unrelated to the development of English professions. How are we to explain this anomaly?[49]

A first and central difference between England and America on the one hand and France and Germany on the other is the absence of a strong state during the creation of modern professions. In both France and Germany the state created the institutions that trained professionals in order to provide itself with civil servants. These institutions—the universities of Germany, the faculties and *grandes écoles* of France—defined the boundaries of professions. In England and the United States, on the contrary, the state lacked any real civil service before the latter half of the nineteenth century, and hence had no need for certified professional knowledge. Furthermore, in both countries the unreformed universities gave a vague sort of general education, which proved suitable as professional training only to the clergy. Professions emerged as congeries of men engaged in like activities—doctoring, lawyering, engineering, accounting—rather than as men sharing certain certifications. The idea that *officiers de santé* constituted a second branch of the medical profession, for example, would have offended a nineteenth-century French doctor; they were not a separate branch, but a different tree. The loose ideology of functionalism that enabled English apothecaries to merge with "other doctors" in 1858 simply did not exist in the eyes of French doctors, although it might in those of the ministers. This absence of state interest meant that the evolving professions of England's early nineteenth century had perforce to create their own educational systems, as well as the examinations designed to guarantee professional borders. Only once this process had begun did anyone happen to think of the universities as appropriate for any substantial education at all. Even then, as in Germany, the move towards professional training in university produced a great revulsion.

In unreformed Oxford and Cambridge, success at the honors examinations led to college fellowships that provided income, prestige, and other support while a graduate awaited the call to a clerical living, perhaps, indeed, one in the gift of the college itself. As the professions grew in the early nineteenth century, the prize fellowships also supported graduates in professional education—those reading law and awaiting the call to the bar, for example. At the same time, a variety of forces professionalized university teaching. The increasing importance of examinations encouraged a vast private tutorial system, and the prize fellowships went increasingly to those conducting the coaching, themselves recent honors graduates. These coaches, the nucleus of modern academic teaching, were thus profoundly committed, both by origin and by support, to the traditional pattern of undergraduate education, a pattern emphasizing hard work at a difficult, specialized subject. Paradoxically perpetuated by the professionalization of its dons in the nineteenth century, the Oxbridge system was thus as antiprofessional as the German one. One acquired liberal education (cf. *Bildung*) through the mastery of a specific detailed technique (cf. *durch Wissenschaft*), which would then prepare one to learn anything necessary once one left the university. There was no hint of preprofessional education. The universities repeatedly objected to attempts to move the third year towards specific instruction in law and natural science, and the great J. S. Mill pronounced, on his installation as Rector of Saint Andrews in 1867:

At least there is tolerably general agreement about what an University is not. It is not a place of professional education. Universities are not intended to teach the knowledge required to fit men for some special mode of gaining their livelihood. Their object is not to make skilful lawyers, or physicians or engineers, but capable and cultivated human beings. . . . Men are men before they are lawyers, or physicians, or merchants, or manufacturers; and if you make them capable and sensible men, they will make themselves capable and sensible lawyers or physicians.[50]

This conception was largely unchallenged until well into the twentieth century. Supporters of new subjects simply argued that the new subjects could be as difficult as the old. University education built character and culture; the professions could take care of themselves.

Little wonder, then, that the older English professions continue to administer most of their education outside universities. An honors degree in jurisprudence was established at Oxford in 1871, but drew few students. The Law Society allowed university graduates shorter articles and eventually supported specialized law teaching at the provincial universities. But it still required (and requires) extensive apprenticeship and opposed the broad type of legal instruction characteristic of other nations.[51] The University of London attempted several times to entice barristers and their Inns under the University umbrella, with no success. A university graduate still learns his law in pupilage in barrister's chambers. Medicine is slightly, but not substantially, different.[52] Several provincial universities were created around medical schools, and Cambridge's medical school revived in the first half of the nineteenth century, as Oxford's did in the second. But most clinical training remained in London at the hospital medical schools dominated by the new medical elite. Although eventually absorbed into the University of London, these schools determined their own policies until after the Second World War. Even then, when "the teaching hospitals [were] no longer quite the same family parties which they were before the war," a complex system of reciprocal representation let the doctors determine most school policy. Accounting, too, is an extrauniversity profession. The first university sequence in accounting appeared in 1945, sixty-five years after the founding of the first major accounting association. The vast majority of British accounting students work through correspondence courses. As of the 1950s, the accounting courses involved only three years at university, followed by another three in internship and direct professional instruction. The two are effectively separate.[53]

In science, to be sure, training moved into English universities much earlier. The Imperial College of Science and Technology, another University of London college, was founded in 1907 explicitly for professional education. And Cambridge had instruction in engineering by the last quarter of the nineteenth century. Yet many technical degrees were given by the University of London to students at proprietary schools, technical colleges, and evening institutions, who simply passed a London examination to acquire an "external degree." Originally begun before the turn of the twentieth century, this system still provided one-quarter of English science degrees as of 1950. Here, too, the apparently direct connection between professions and universities belies the reality.[54]

With few exceptions, then, professional education takes place in institutions controlled by the professions, which *may* be affiliated with a university but usually are not. Ben-David's and Bledstein's arguments imply that upwardly mobile groups of professionals should have adopted university education to triumph over rivals. But in England, the universities themselves refused to be co-opted. The most prestigious of them became increasingly antiprofessional as their own teachers professionalized. Although dominated by Oxbridge graduates, law, medicine, and accounting expected university education to provide only character and promise.[55] The Home and Indian Civil Services held the same attitude even more explicitly. The ancient universities did not countenance professional education, and the professions were happy to do it themselves. This pattern clearly influenced the provincial universities as well. Although they flirted with technical education—Manchester with commercial subjects, for example—they generally imitated liberal education on the Oxbridge model. Only in America would conditions favor a synergistic alliance between universities and professions.

In the United States there were no universities, in the German sense, prior to the foundation of Johns Hopkins in 1876, closely followed by Clark in 1887 and the University of Chicago in 1892.[56] Earlier foundations included colleges of the unreformed Oxbridge type, usually training young men for the clergy, schoolteaching, or both, and the post–Civil War state universities, oriented towards the diffusion of useful knowledge and democratic principles. The arrival of mass primary and secondary education had led to the rapid creation of state normal schools for teacher training, but these remained largely separate from the universities until the mid-twentieth century.[57] America also had, in West Point (1802), Rensselaer Polytechnic (1824), Annapolis (1845), MIT (1861), and the Stevens Institute (1870), the rudiments of a separate technical education system. The founding of German-style research universities forced the older institutions to compete, and by the turn of the twentieth century, the modern American university had emerged. The research university of the Germans was married to an American version of *Lernfreiheit*—the elective system—justified for its contribution to "useful" and "democratic" education. At first dominated by preprofessional concerns, undergraduate education under the elective system replaced the English and German ideal of intense discipline in a special area with the idea of liberal culture, an exposure to a systematically broad body of knowledge.

The difference reflected the place of professional education in American universities. Like the continental universities, American universities often included medical or legal faculties. But these rapidly moved towards postbaccalaureate status, with the assistance of the professions themselves. Medical reformers, for example, consistently urged a bachelor's degree prerequisite for entry to medical schools, an entry requirement that spread steadily after the founding of Hopkins. The baccalaureate requirement reflected the less-strenuous character of American collegiate education; thus it made sense to integrate professional schools into universities as postbaccalaureate schools, rather than as alternatives to the letters and science faculties, as in Germany.[58]

At the same time, however, American universities lacked the intense hostility of European universities to the study of "useful" subjects at the undergraduate level. On the contrary, American state legislatures and alumni accepted the new university more for its production of useful citizens than for its production of knowledge. Outside the professions served by preexisting faculties, the universities thus saw little difficulty in founding preprofessional programs. Departments of engineering, business, "domestic science," and physical education proliferated, sometimes as separate schools, but often within general faculties of arts and letters. Such departments were often upgraded to graduate status when the ethic of liberal culture seized the universities around the First World War.

Business schools afford an interesting example.[59] Under the elective system students followed a common curriculum for two years, then a specialized one for two or three more; typically the specialized subjects were organized in "schools" (the Sheffield Scientific School at Yale, for example), and the first separate faculty unit in business education, Pennsylvania's Wharton School, emerged in such a manner in 1881. Routine business education had long been the province of proprietary commercial colleges although the normal schools, private technical colleges, and even public high schools were competing. But education in business moved progressively upward. The California program (1898) and Wisconsin program (1900) were four-year baccalaureates. Dartmouth's Tuck school (1900) required three years of liberal arts work, and Harvard's Graduate School of Business (1908) was explicitly postbaccalaureate. By the twenties, the dominant business degree was postgraduate.

Law schools show a related pattern.[60] The founding of the Association of American Law Schools in 1900 brought together the "reputable" (i.e., university) law schools. The following twenty years, however, saw expansion of the commercial law school sector, which did not require baccalaureate degrees, which had lower fees and standards more generally, and which trained for different types of law. When Alfred Reed proposed formalization of the two-tiered system in 1920, the professional elite threw its weight entirely on the side of the university law schools, hoping to abolish the commercial sector altogether. Although the legal elite, like business and unlike medicine, was unable to accomplish this, it did successfully relegate graduates of the commercial schools to the corners of professional life.

As these examples indicate, the university helped developing American professions in internal battles over professional standards. The new university took shape just as the American professions were recovering from the Jacksonian era, whose democratization had overthrown institutions of professional control in law and medicine and forestalled such institutions in many other professions. By comparison with England, building associational professionalism, even in this less-hostile environment, was very difficult. Professionals were dispersed throughout dozens of locations. The governments controlling their jurisdictions lacked even the weak authority of the English state. As the professions reorganized, they found the university ideally suited to their purposes. It was a new and untainted institution. It stood not only for European culture, but also for democracy and utility. It permitted and encouraged meritocracy. It focused in some loose way on knowledge. In short, it echoed the values of the new professions themselves. Thus while in fact professional education by no means required university affiliation—witness dozens of night law schools and so prestigious a medical school as the Jefferson Medical College—profession after profession turned to the university for help in seizing control of its own educational apparatus. University medical schools, for example, gobbled up the good proprietary schools by the handful and forced the bad ones out of existence. Yet the organized professions by no means conceded control of these university schools; they were in the university but not of it. In many universities, as President Kirkland's old Harvard dictum had it, "each tub [was] on its own bottom"; despite the occasional tiffs between scholars and practitioners, the professors remained professionals first and professors second, a distinct reversal of the German situation. It is noteworthy that Lewellys Barker, Osler's successor as professor of clinical medicine at Hopkins, resigned his position because it paid too little to support his family in proper professional style. Modern-day medical school professors, as every academic knows, are paid doctors' salaries, not professors'.[61]

The use of the university as an external ally in internal professional conflicts had consequences both for university and for profession. For the professions, it facilitated processes of vertical division already under way. In law, it facilitated the split between corporate and personal legal practice; in medicine, between physicians and their subordinate professions. The professions' affiliation with the university thus encouraged professional divisions of labor. But it also had distinct consequences for the university itself. The acquisition of professional schools moved the American university toward the University of London model, making the university a holding company for largely autonomous faculties, usually closer to their professional associations than to a particular university. This pattern now extends into the arts and sciences faculties.

Finally, the simultaneous presence of many professions on campus inevitably made the university an arena of interprofessional competition. In many universities the competition was directly financial. While areas of work were not immediately at stake, differential support could clearly lead to expansion of one profession at the expense of others.[62] Often there *was* competition about areas of work, in the many questions of who would teach what to whom. A 1930 survey of "accounting in the law school curriculum" found that about three-quarters of American lawyers needed knowledge of accounting in their practices, and that most acquired that knowledge by experience.[63] Undertaken by the accounting professor who taught accounting to lawyers at the University of Chicago Law School, the survey and the course that inspired it indicate a deep penetration of accountants into what legal practitioners clearly treated as legitimate legal work. At the same time, commercial law was so important a subject in collegiate *business* schools as to command its own association (American Business Law Assocation, founded in 1924), even though some objected that "the course is made subservient to the professional approach of a purely legal analysis." The fight between lawyers and accountants over who had jurisdiction of this work—work on taxes, estates, financial statements—was fought not only in the open market of practice, but also on college campuses. Throughout the university, there is serious competition in what kinds of courses are offered in which departments, because these courses can shape the disposition of forces in the open markets beyond. A major ally in building the modern, dominant American professions, the university has latterly become a battleground for them.

Three great changes, then, have formed the cultural environment for modern systems of professions. The rapid transformation of knowledge has increased opportunities for competition and even, in the case of artificial intelligence, changed the type of competition involved. While new legitimating values have generally affected professional competition only slightly, they have often facilitated various forms of insurgency. Finally, the rise of universities has tied the professions to a central cultural institution of their societies, although the bond has had many accidental qualities.

It is important to place these changes in perspective; they have often been exaggerated. For example, people have long argued that knowledge was changing "faster than ever"; but as knowledge grows faster and faster, its definition changes. To be sure, in the short run specialization occurs. But in the long run, what had been knowledge becomes rote learning for paraprofessionals or commodities for purchase and sale. Moreover, much of the new "knowledge" is really simply data; not information or technique, but simply undigested facts. Knowledge, in some sense, must thus be conceptualized relatively; it is what the experts alone possess. This conception helps explain why the same competitive mechanisms work today as in the nineteenth century, but should not conceal the fact that the content denoted by "knowledge" has changed sharply in the period.

The same kind of argument applies to legitimacy. We have seen the replacement of social origins and character by rationalization of technique and efficiency of service. But as professions crowd into one end of this range of values, the limited range itself spreads out to fill the same space as the old one. Contrast recreates itself in a smaller compass. People still perceive a difference between the friendly local practitioner and the technocratic hospital specialist, even though the local practitioner makes no house calls, employs the full battery of tests, and dashes from examining room to examining room in a bureaucratized office. The two styles are still distinguished as "character versus technique." Similarly, the legitimation of character revives in attempts to teach ethics to medical students, in courses about the social impact of engineering, in the pin-striped uniforms of the Big Eight accounting firms. To be sure, these evidences would seem little or nothing to a late-nineteenth-century audience. But they witness the enduring validity of the *contrast* of legitimacy modes, and imply that purely technical legitimation of professional work is impossible. We have changed much, but we have not changed at all.

Finally, the university itself obeys the same argument. It has been so successful as to redefine its own meaning. In 1900, when American associational professionalism was in its first full flower, 2 percent of each cohort of twenty-three-year-olds received a bachelor's or first professional degree, and 6 percent *of those* would have another degree in two years. A total of 6 percent of a cohort of seventeen-year-olds finished high school, much less began college. In the United States in 1970, one-quarter of each cohort of twenty-three-year-olds received a bachelor's or first professional degree; one-third of these would have a second professional degree in two more years. Over half of each cohort of eighteen-year-olds started college. [64] But the emergence of the university as mass institution changed the meaning of university certification. The new universities of the late nineteenth century were in fact elite institutions, for all their democratic ideology: small, prestigious, exclusive. Alliance with them was alliance with cultural power and authority. When university certification became common, exclusivity was not spread but simply diluted. The name remained the same; the reality underneath changed quite radically. To be a university-trained profession in 1900 meant something very unique; to be so in 1980 meant nothing unique at all.

In fact the new university was ill suited to permanently absorb the function of professional education. Knowledge change undermined the university's role, for university training assumed that professional knowledge endured a lifetime. By the 1960s, when "professional obsolescence" had become a major issue, nonuniversity institutions—generally the professional associations and the employing corporations—had shouldered the main responsibility for continuing professional education. In 1980 American universities spent about $64 billion. A conservative estimate for *corporate-sector* expenses for education was $40 billion. [65] Although the largest share of corporate educational monies goes to orientation (as do university dollars to undergraduate liberal studies), management courses place second and are basically professional training, since they enable obsolete or mobile professionals to move from profession of origin to management. Professional and technical courses are fourth on the corporate list, a major source of mid-career training. Recently both corporations and consortiums of corporations have created degree-granting programs, an overt threat to the alliance of professions with universities. Continuing education is also sponsored heavily by professional associations in certain professions, particularly accounting. States also provided continuing education for civil and military services. The military, for example, has a unique multitiered system interspersing formal education with practice. First-level staff colleges (the equivalents of postgraduate schools) were founded in Prussia (1810), France (1878), England (1873), and the United States (1885), and several higher levels have followed since. [66]

Ultimately issues of professional education entangle us with the great social changes of the preceding chapter, for corporate capitalism bankrolled (especially) the private, prestigious universities, and the great magnates originally saw them as private preserves. Ezra Cornell wandered around "his campus," and the Stanfords refused to allow "their university" to be tainted by money from other donors. The universities fought and won their independence from this tutelage, partly with the aid of the professions, who provided them with generations of loyal and wealthy alumni in exchange for the protections of legitimacy. But the renewed wave of corporate-university ventures in research and the massive corporate investment in professional education represent a renewed attempt to direct education towards the immediate goals of commerce. It has been accompanied by serious attacks on the utility of university education.[67] This thrust will divide the professions. Those dependent directly on corporate employment—engineering, management, to some extent science and accounting, and perhaps even law—will find themselves seriously torn between the universities that are now the chief supports of their independence and the employers who, although themselves divided, can control them. Professions less dependent on corporate employment—the professoriate, medicine, librarianship, social work, dentistry—will not face the same problem. Although the impact of these forces on particular interprofessional contests is hard to predict, they may well change the nature of competition itself, in particular by attenuating even further the professions' power to directly control their own work and careers.

# III   THREE CASE STUDIES

So far I have addressed the enduring conceptual problems of professionalization theories. But are the corresponding empirical difficulties solved by the approach I propose? To illustrate my model's empirical power, the following chapters present analyses of actual jurisdictional development. An analysis of the American professions involved with information shows how the system vocabulary examines a task area. A discussion of American and British law, in contrast, uses analyses of interprofessional conflicts to answer traditional questions about particular professions. An examination of American psychotherapeutic professions focuses on the creation of a particular jurisdiction, that of "problems with everyday living." The three chapters employ different methodologies, the first being an interpretation of secondary sources, the second a largely quantitative analysis of historical materials, the third an analysis of primary historical data. They also invoke different parts of my theoretical approach. The chapter on information professions examines system disturbances and the resulting contests, following the model of chapters 4 and 5. The study of lawyers views system disturbances from the individual profession's perspective, at the same time exploring the audiences and settlements of professional claims theorized in chapter 3. The analysis of psychotherapy looks primarily at the interplay of subjective and objective jurisdiction, discussed in chapter 2.

Like earlier writers, I have elaborated my model through case studies. A general quantitative test, corresponding to the test of professionalization cited in chapter 1, must wait until the empirical plausibility of the system model is demonstrated. These case studies of jurisdictions, then, correspond to many earlier case studies of professions. They show that one can far better analyze the histories of professions by postulating a system of professions than by assuming a characteristic history of professionalization.

# 8     The Information Professions

In examining the professions involved with information, I shall show how the system model studies a general area of work. Before that examination begins, however, we must ask how a "system story" should be told. As I noted earlier, the professionalization narrative takes the familiar form of a novel of personal development. But narratives of interlocking systems lack such familiar models. How are we to recount them?

According to chapter 4, a characteristic story in the system of professions begins with a disturbance—a new technology requiring professional judgment or a new technique for old professional work. These disturbances undermine the balance between work and professions and lead to a variety of readjustments. Eventually the various parts of the system absorb the disturbance and balance returns. On this analysis, there are three general stages in a system-based historical description: disturbances, jurisdictional contests, and the transformations leading to balance. But the move from theoretical model to practical analysis spoils this clarity. One could, of course, list all the disturbances, then all the consequences, then all the terminal balances. But then the individual sequences would not be followable.[1] If, on the other hand, one followed each disturbance through its effects to its termination, one would assume, incorrectly, that the effects of one disturbance attenuate before the next arrives.[2] I shall therefore tell my story roughly chronologically, tracing disturbances, consequences, and temporary settlements as they arrive. However, where chains of effects seem independent, I shall follow them to their independent terminations, moving forward in time as necessary.

A second preliminary question is how to delimit the object of study.

215

Had I spoken of the professions involved in health, few readers would wonder what was meant. But "information" is less familiar. The area of work, of course, has long existed, but defining it presents two problematic alternatives. On the one hand, we cannot study an area of professional work without loosely delimiting it, and the easiest limits to see are those of existing professions in the area. Yet the specific shapes of these jurisdictions are determined by interprofessional competition; our very language concerning an area is shaped by current incumbents. On the other hand, to identify such an area *without* identifying the professions within it flirts with imperative functionalism. On the functionalist analysis, since people must get their information from somewhere, there must be "institutions" providing it, staffed by corps of specialized experts. Our choice is thus to accept the status quo or to invent an idiosyncratic reality. The Parsonian answer, of course, would be to identify the two halves of the dilemma; having located librarians, accountants, and various others, the functionalist announces that they ."institutionalize the knowledge-providing function."[3] To avoid such reification, yet at the same time to delimit the area of study, I shall consider groups that provide others with information as occupying a general information area of the system of professions, reminding the reader that at any given point in time these groups may control diverse portions of this general area in unique ways. Although I do not claim to have considered all information professions, following the web of competition turns up most of them, and that suits my purposes here.[4]

Some professionals create information that gives clients a basis for action. Prescription by these information professionals is not generally a recommendation for action, but rather a recommendation that certain information, which the professionals may provide, will further actions the client may wish to perform. Some information professionals have moved into providing action recommendations, as we shall see; it is a natural line of expansion. But in general, information professionals help clients overburdened with material from which thay cannot retrieve usable information. On this definition, there have clearly been two general types of information professionals. Qualitative information has generally been the domain of librarians, joined by academics, advertisers, journalists, and others. Quantitative information has seen a larger variety of groups, starting with the cost accountants and management engineers, and coming up through the statisticians, operations researchers, systems analysts, and others to the present. In all these cases, of course, the specific form of the jurisdiction was shaped by culture and context. That is, librarians should not be *identified* with the function of providing qualitative information, but rather should be seen as specializing in *some aspect* of providing qualitative information, an aspect determined both by their own activity defining the jurisdiction and by the social and cultural context within which they work. The first two sections of this chapter cover developments in the two separated sectors, noting the occasions on which the two interpenetrated. Since recent developments seem to be bringing the two halves together, this conjuncture closes the chapter. Within each section, the analysis asks questions generated by the theoretical model of chapters 4 and 5. What were the original jurisdictions created? What external events changed them? How did the changes created by external events reorganize the area and propagate through it? What internal events created disturbances, and what contests ensued? What were the rhetorics of competition between groups?

## The Qualitative Task Area

In qualitative information, a single profession—librarianship—dominated much of the area until recently. Development was generally peaceful, although the parts of librarianship have often fought each other, and although occasional intrusions of unemployed academics have shaken the field. In general, however, this area provides a particularly straightforward demonstration of how system forces shape a profession's development; external and internal forces interact with demographic patterns and, eventually, with some competitors to produce the familiar history of American librarianship.[5]

The first system disturbances in this area were the organization foundings that created the library profession. Although librarians have a long history, the American profession of librarianship originated in a sudden creation of libraries, much as if the medical profession were created to staff hospitals. Libraries arrived in several waves. The public libraries of the latter nineteenth century were followed by the academic and special libraries around the turn of the century. School libraries, particularly in elementary schools, had expanded rapidly from the mid nineteenth century. For the profession, however, the public and academic-special libraries proved particularly important.[6]

Librarians handled the print resources of a community, school, university, or organization; they had physical custody of cultural capital. The use of this capital was left largely up to them, and they had (and have) three basic approaches to it. In the one emphasizing access, the librarian structures the library for retrieval of user-desired information. The two other approaches—emphasizing education and entertainment—are less passive. In both the librarian chooses for clients which information they *should* retrieve. In the educational approach, the criterion of choice is user "improvement;" in the entertainment one, the criterion is user pleasure. The three approaches relate directly to the autonomy of librarians and the amount of work available to them. Mid-nineteenth-century librarians emphasized educational outreach, not only preparing material for retrieval but also defining what ought to be retrieved. Claiming autonomous control of "acquisitions and collections," they fought clients over whether "sensational" fiction was as appropriate reading as "great literature." The librarians ultimately surrendered to the reading public's resilient insistence on light fiction, which embodied the public preference for entertainment over education. Under the influence of Melvil Dewey, the defeated librarians retreated from education and outreach into the technical tasks of cataloging, bibliography, reference, and retrieval, basing the profession on the function of access.[7]

The move towards technical librarianship is generally attributed to Dewey's magnetic influence and his faith in what would later be called scientific management. But demographic forces were equally at work. In the late nineteenth century, library numbers expanded at an extraordinary rate, for reasons not altogether under professional control. For librarians to professionalize under such conditions—that is, for them to seize and maintain effective control of an area of work—it was necessary to rapidly train many workers in professionally controlled techniques. But library schools were few and numbers small. To have insisted on an educational function not only would have flouted public preference, but also would have claimed more work than available professionals could do, and, tangentially, would have confronted the larger and equally growing profession of teaching. The limitation to the access jurisdiction, itself rapidly expanding, avoided these conflicts.[8]

Like most professional groups, the librarians had a highly structured core and a very hazy periphery. At the center stood the college and special librarians, whose separate societies began to appear around the turn of the century. Since they often borrowed one another's resources, these librarians led the drive for standardization in cataloging and bibliography, thereby reinforcing their central professional position. Like the public and school librarians, however, this group also originated in a set of new organizations, the research universities and the reformed professional schools attached to them. This origin had distinct implications. Since research libraries generally had professional academics as clients—academics who emphatically rejected librarians' educational pretensions and who used libraries solely for retrieval—academic librarians specialized in access alone. Since these college librarians were the professional elite, as much through their association with prestigious universities and dominant professions as through their professional activity, their limited view of librarianship's functions received an even stronger emphasis.[9]

The periphery of librarianship consisted of the school librarians, who were often teachers doubling as librarians, and the smaller public librarians, who were organized around statewide library societies and state government library departments. Localist in orientation, these groups retained the outreach and educational aims that the elite had abandoned. (Apparently they had fewer competitors.) Formal organization of the periphery came only in the 1950s, with the School Libraries Section of the ALA and the Association of State Library Agents. In both elite and peripheral settings, librarians' conflicts were generally with clients; only in the university and research settings, however, were those clients other kinds of professionals. This interprofessional competition, much stronger in the universities and research libraries, shaped both the substance and the organizational structure of the overall profession.[10]

Librarians were few; about 4,000 librarians appeared in the United States census of 1900. ALA membership, probably a more representative estimate of the profession's effective size, was only 980 in 1901. Demand for librarians outstripped supply steadily until the thirties, when complaints of oversupply arose. As my theory predicts, at precisely this time of oversupply there recurred the old interest in the librarian as shaper and educator; crowding in the heartland led to attempts at expansion. But jurisdictional change was either not attempted or not feasible. Rather, the profession, whose census level had doubled every ten years between 1900 and 1930, suddenly slowed its growth during the Depression. This decrease was apparently greater on the periphery, for the production of *library school graduates,* who constituted 1 percent of the census figure per annum in 1920, slowed much later, during the Second World War, with the result that by 1950 annual library school graduates numbered about 3 percent of the profession's census figure. As one might expect, things eventually went too far; in the 1950s complaints came of shortages in such low-status areas as children's work and small- and medium-sized public and school libraries generally.[11]

Although shaped decisively by organizational and demographic developments, the qualitative information area has also felt the impact of several major technological events. Developed in 1928, the Recordak process for microfilming seemed to pose a fundamental threat to librarianship. It became common to assert that libraries would soon be replaced by personal collections of microforms. In fact, microforms were not used to create household libraries, but rather to encode vast new amounts of information for existing repositories. Beyond its additive effects—more information meant more demand for librarians—microfilm had two multiplicative ones. First, microforms decentralized the physical capital of knowledge, bringing serious research within the range of those lesser libraries whose clients had previously traveled to major facilities for such work. Second, many of the newly microfilmed materials were not books and monographs, easily cataloged and described, but rather technical writings, conference reports, and previously unpublished raw data. Cataloging and reference suddenly required a new sophistication. Thus, although it is true that outsiders helped introduce the methods (the "documentalists" of the American Documentation Institute, an organization founded in part by vendors and in part by huge libraries anxious to save space), and while the technology did succeed in destroying certain parts of professional work (particularly in exchange of simple materials), microfilm had a net positive effect. It was adopted and supported by members of the professional elites, whose potential market it in fact increased. The ALA itself had a special interest group in documentation from 1936, and a journal appeared in 1938.[12]

The second great technological event was, of course, the development of the computer. Although there had been a few attempts to mechanize library work prior to the 1950s, the Hollerith technology that transformed quantitative information did not have much effect. The computer, however, did. On the one hand, it simplified circulation and rendered catalogs accessible. These were routine, low-status services that seriously professional librarians were happy to lose. But it also required, as the price for these services, near-total standardization in descriptive cataloging and indexing, which deeply invaded the area of judgment that made librarians professionals. Moreover, it could potentially transform the heartland territory of reference. The computer itself did not produce these developments, of course; other professionals did. And as it happened, the "information science" profession was itself largely an offshoot of the librarians, although at an extremely elite level. But the potential for vertical division remains great. Moreover, beyond its impact on qualitative information, the computer also revolutionized quantitative information, and the information science group has sought the unification of the two areas.[13]

A final external event, an idiosyncratic one, had a decisive effect on this area, as on many others. The Second World War created entire information professions, generated technologies with revolutionary information potential, and, perhaps most importantly, generated vast new demands for both quantitative and qualitative information. In the library area, the proliferation of American technical material and the sudden importance of foreign literatures overwhelmed librarians' traditional cataloging and careful bibliography; librarians' rare experiments with automated retrieval systems were clearly inadequate. The war also brought an ideology that information was a crucial national resource; this provided the information professions with a new and powerful legitimation for their work.[14]

External changes like the rise of certain kinds of organizations and technologies are not the only disturbances shaking an area of professional work. The system model also expects disturbance from within—internal developments of knowledge or of professional structure that change the pattern of professional jurisdiction. In librarianship there were several major developments in knowledge. The first was centralized cataloging. The Library of Congress Cataloging Service (from ca. 1900) and various later cataloging manuals commodified much of what had been librarians' expertise. These rules made interlibrary exchange considerably easier—a major goal of the elite librarians—and thereby opened new fields of work to the elite. But their impact on the school and public librarians was much less positive, for they reduced previously professional work at those levels. In fact, however, many peripheral librarians continued to catalog idiosyncratically, and many elite libraries, feeling they had the resources to improve on the Dewey decimal or Library of Congress classifications, retained local systems. Thus, while centralized cataloging threatened to divide librarians into groups accepting and not accepting, the recalcitrance of librarians at several levels prevented this from becoming a sharp vertical distinction of elite and mass.[15]

I argued earlier that internal knowledge and, particularly, structural changes in professions generally aim at changing a profession's competitive position. But other than from clients, librarians in fact faced little competition in their own area. They made a few attempts to invade other areas. Librarians applied their methods to business filing, and Dewey founded in 1882 a commercial concern for that purpose (The Library Bureau). Indeed, at one particularly low point Hollerith sold his tabulating machines through the Bureau. But the bookkeepers and accountants, or rather the firms selling the counting machines these professions used, gained control of this proto-office-information market. For the most part, librarians had more than enough work in their own area. The profession's central problem was rather that of disunity fostered by the diverse organizations for which librarians worked.[16]

When there is little competition, my model predicts that structural change will not be important, as opposed to the professionalization model, which derives structural change from autonomous developmental forces. Librarians had no real incentive for structural change other than a general desire for social repute. Yet that desire required quite different social structures than does competition; professions interested in social repute tend, for example, to emphasize education that is irrelevant to professional practice, rather than examined knowledge in field. We should not be surprised, then, that the ALA began as a kind of elite men's club aimed at educating the masses. The lack of competition also explains the situation of library schools and similar institutions. According to prior theories, these should be central vectors of professionalization. But the first library schools were in fact the personal creation of Dewey and, like most of his work, were wholeheartedly distrusted by the ALA leaders. Licensing—the major competitive strategy of American professionalism—did not come until much later, when the librarians "proper" sought explicit differentiation from the teacher-librarians who staffed the school libraries. The professional social structures that appeared first were schools and journals; in an area where the chief problems were undersupply and overwork, these seem obvious enough. Only later, when the various segments of the profession had drifted far apart, were licenses, academic standing, and other such structures competitively necessary. Perhaps more important still, since librarians, particularly elite librarians, rely so much on each other for services, the truly crucial professional social structures were organizations for work—the centralizing institutions that provided common services. As the amount of material grew, so also did the importance of these structures. The Library of Congress cataloging and card services were the earliest of them, but they have a long series of distinguished followers—from *Choice* and other journals of bibliography, to central depositories and acquisitions agencies like the Midwest Inter-Library Center, down to the great online systems for cataloging (Ohio College Library Consortium, the Research Library Information Network) and reference (MEDLINE, MEDLARS, DIALOG). While the computer has facilitated these structures, librarians have since the profession's beginnings built them with whatever technology was available.[17]

Perhaps more than most professions, the librarians have also relied on corporations to provide the central commodities necessary to this work. This has been particularly true in areas of rapid knowledge change, which threaten jurisdictional strength. (Often, as in the case of Bowker, these outside firms were founded by librarians.) Librarianship's corporate dependence is old; Bowker (1872), H. W. Wilson (1898), and several of great indexing services date from the nineteenth century. These, along with newer firms like Gale Research, publish many of the basic bibliographic tools of librarians. This commodified expertise is necessary to most forms of access, yet, in contrast to the situation in most professions, it seems that the more the reference commodities, the greater the expertise necessary to use them effectively.[18]

The history of librarianship prior to computers was not, however, completely devoid of conflict. Important conflicts arose between the elite special librarians and their clients. The most glaring case involved academics. While expansions and contractions racked the periphery of librarianship, the elite fought academics over the issue of faculty status. Although or perhaps because it brought the conflict between the access and education approaches into clear focus, this conflict has endured unresolved throughout the postwar period. Although many university librarians did achieve faculty status, academics generally still regard them as functionaries, and to add to the injury, by the seventies, unemployed Ph.D.'s in arts and sciences were flooding the ranks of special librarianship. The academic conflict captures a wider pattern characteristic of librarianship and information professions in general. Deciding what is relevant information inevitably embroils the information client and the information professional. The information professions are, *by definition*, involved in continuously negotiated and contested professional divisions of labor.[19]

This general pattern helps explain the conflict between the special librarians and their various scholarly, professional, and industrial clients. The special libraries movement began as an attempt to bring knowledge out of storage and apply it. Arising within the library profession (it was not demanded by clients), it was a fairly broad expansion into government (legislative reference bureaus), industry (technical libraries), and education (the medical and law school libraries). The expanding special librarians employed what I earlier called a gradient rhetoric.[20] My earlier examples involved prevention—psychiatry into neurosis, public accounting into annual reports. By contrast, the special library expansion moved along the gradient that separates information from action. The special librarians claimed that they knew the sources and means to find material that working professionals didn't have the time (and sometimes the ability) to find. They held further that "what you ought to know to solve a problem" could be better defined by a practical knowledge of what the sources make it possible to know than by a theoretical knowledge of what it is in principle necessary to know. This diagnostic decision—about which information is relevant to a problem's solution—is a central part of the claim of professional jurisdiction. The information professions are in some sense specialists in diagnosis and hence represent a general threat to all professions. As we shall see, many other varieties of information professionals besides librarians have tried to expand into their clients' work, similarly claiming an increasing jurisdiction over action itself because "information is prior to action."

The special library expansion took place in the workplace setting, rather than in public or legal ones. Its exact origin is unclear. It may have reflected the internal developments of cataloging, bibliographical, and reference methods, linked to the corporate services that provided indexing for the profession as a whole; on this argument, the expansion was imperialism born of inherent strength. But it may equally have been driven by the gradual failure of the public library's early aim to educate the masses and by the routinization of much professional work by the very corporate services that made expansion possible. The elite had to move or get deskilled with the rest.

More recently the librarians have been faced, ironically, with an invasion through what I have called treatment substitution. In treatment substitution, a profession accepts another's diagnoses and perhaps treatments, while claiming to carry them out faster or more effectively than the other. This attack, of course, involves the computer professions. They have argued that since computers can carry out information retrieval much faster than can other technologies, specialists in the computer area should dominate the information area. But treatment substitution has mixed results, and computer specialists are as likely to be the pharmacists of the information world as its surgeons. I shall return to this topic later in the chapter.

In closing this section on qualitative information prior to the rise of computers, I shall briefly mention two other qualitative information systems. One is a small system within a particular profession, the law.[21] Since the last years of the eighteenth century lawyers have produced for other lawyers an ever-increasing volume of "reported cases." Although the early reporters were simply lists of cases, the nineteenth century saw the rise of extensive indexing, by words, by phrases, by legal concepts, by citation. The legal report system is the oldest continuously maintained database in the United States and exemplifies the great abstracting services—chemistry, psychology, and so on—that provide professional information to particular professions. These services are nearly all under the control of the profession they serve, although usually produced by specialty corporations, and although librarians act as physical custodians and brokers for the material. The pattern shows the characteristic professional defense of separating a rapidly changing but somewhat routinely developed knowledge from a more controllable, because more esoteric, main jurisdiction.

The other qualitative information jurisdiction I wish to mention is that of current information, in particular about general events, which we usually call news, and about consumer products, which we usually call advertising. These jurisdictions have never been completely separated, since American society generally lets the one pay for the other. However, only neoclassical economists regard the information functions of advertising as central, and so I shall consider advertising later, under the heading of marketing.

But the news jurisdiction has steadily grown in size and importance through this century, and the incumbent profession of journalism has come to extraordinary power. The shaping of the news jurisdiction can be summarized as follows.[22] Although news in the modern sense was created by the penny press of the 1830s, the Civil War intensified demand for news coverage and helped push newspapers towards exclusive work in news rather than entertainment. The late nineteenth century saw an invasion of college-trained reporters and consequent improvement in the status, style, and content of reportage. The editorial conception of "facts" in the modern sense had already taken shape by this period, and although Hearst papers made "reporting the facts" a form of entertainment (as opposed to the Ochs conception of facts as information), the news jurisdiction has been founded on providing current "factual" information to the public since the turn of the century.

Journalism remains a very permeable occupation; mobility between journalism and public relations is quite common, as is mobility between journalism and other forms of writing. While there are schools, associations, degrees, and ethics codes, there is no exclusion of those who lack them. Whether journalism's inability to monopolize makes it "not a profession" is not particularly interesting. What matters is that interprofessional competition in fact shaped it decisively. The clearest force driving reporters towards a formal conception of their jurisdiction was in fact competition with hired publicity agents. Journalists of the 1920s were amazed to discover that about 50 percent of the stories in the *New York Times* originated in the work of publicity agents. Reporters saw such stories (correctly) as little better than advertising, and their reaction led on the one hand to a renewed drive for formal professional structures, and on the other to a frank recognition of subjectivity in reporting. Although generational conflicts between editors and junior reporters had long raised the issues of objectivity and facts, journalists began anew to recognize the inherently constitutive nature of their work. Thus, even in so apparently isolated a jurisdiction as the news, competition played a central role in shaping the incumbent group's conception of its work. The structural trappings of professionalization don't determine a profession's history, nor does a failed monopoly make it uninteresting. Competition provides the key to occupational development.

This brief review of qualitative information in the United States demonstrates how much more compelling is the system approach to professional development than are older approaches based on professionalization. By focusing on the determinants of the amount and character of work, on internal and external forces for change, and, where necessary, on competitors, we can make sense of a history that tells us little when we ask about licensing, associations, schools, and so on. In quantitative information, where competition was much keener, the difference is even more striking.

## The Quantitative Task Area

Unlike the qualitative area, the quantitive information area has a complex and contested history. Accountants have warred with engineers, statisticians with economists, operations researchers with cost accountants. Here the consequences of disturbances ramify so rapidly that I shall be able only to outline their beginnings. But again the system model leads us to the right questions: What were the external disturbances and their effects on professional demand and performance? What internal changes in knowledge and structure changed competitive positions? How did internal differentiation interact with system structure to create temporary stabilities?

Although organizational demand built the quantitative information professions of the nineteenth century, these professions did not emerge, as librarians did, through the creation or transformation of jobs in organizations. In Britain, to be sure, accountants emerged through the transformation of receivership into a full-time occupation. But from their beginnings in the last years of the nineteenth century, the American accountants did less bankruptcy and more public accounting.[23] Partly this reflected the colonial nature of American accounting, founded by expatriate Britons imbued with the idea of full-time professional practice. But the difference also reflected the structure of

American demand, particularly for public accounting. The dispersion of American society and capital weakened personal and familistic capital mobilization, forcing an early reliance on public stock and investment. American stockholders and financiers, often far from the objects of their investment, had an enormous need for reliable information on stock companies, a need underscored by the scandals of the robber baron era. By the last years of the century, the government also needed accounting services. Not only did its desire to regularize transportation rates require industry use of standardized accounting, the government itself expected to apply those practices. The late nineteenth century thus saw several constituencies for accurate public accounting. While there was continuity between bookkeeping and accounting, and while accountants' first major business was uncovering fraud and obscurantism, a large new jurisdiction over the attestation of capital was open to the accountants as soon as they could establish their legitimacy.[24]

If the rise of large corporations and the national capital market that fed them helped create the American accounting profession, the rise of interventionist governments built the work of statistics.[25] Statistics, in its then general sense of quantitative social information used by governments, had a long history in America and elsewhere. The more governments intervened, the more they wanted to know about public health, industry, commerce, immigration, and so on. The American Statistical Association, an old (1839) and active body, drew together members of various professions and organizations interested in gathering such figures. Rather like the librarians, these "statisticians" were more interested in compiling numbers than in analyzing them. But again as with the librarians, that stance reflected lack of technique as much as lack of desire. It is striking, however, that statistics did not coalesce as a professional group until the intellectual revolution of inferential statistics. Although one might have expected a process of enclosure here, statistical workers remained identified with their original professions—the great Edward Jarvis being an excellent example. Why statistics did not emerge as a separate profession, when accounting *did*, is an interesting question. Perhaps the diversity of statisticians' objects prevented a common model of professional practice, facilitated in accounting by the common problems of reconciliation, depreciation, and the like.[26]

By the end of the nineteenth century, then, there were two general areas of quantitative information work, one of them a defined jurisdiction held by an active profession, the other a more loosely defined area of work available for potential enclosure. Two great disturbances transformed this situation, one an invention external to the professions involved, the other an intellectual achievement within them.

The invention was that of serious mechanical devices for calculation and tabulation. The most spectacular was the electromechanical tabulating machine of Hermann Hollerith. In 1890 Hollerith machines collated the United States census population figures in about six weeks; the 1880 census had taken about six years. The machines could be rewired to collate any cross-classification of facts, immensely extending the information retrievable. The other inventions—of mechanical computation devices—were less spectacular but more widely used. In 1885 the first Burroughs adding machines appeared, and by 1912 Monroe had produced a mechanical division machine. In 1878 James Ritty had the idea of mechanical cash registers, which appeared shortly thereafter, complete with bell, drawer, and, most importantly, a paper roll recording each transaction.[27]

The impact of these inventions was (1) to create large quantities of accurate data (cash registers), (2) to amalgamate that (and other) data in hundreds of new ways (tabulating machines), and (3) to enable rapid and accurate analysis (calculating machines). These effects revolutionized the quantitative information professions. They routinized a large area of work jointly done by bookkeepers and accountants, sharply dividing the two into the functions of recording and analyzing. They simultaneously enabled accountants to turn clerkship from a task for mature men with families into one for apprentice accountants, and indeed to take fewer of these as time passed. A machine-based division of labor thus combined with career structuring to give accounting an intense control of its work.[28]

Moreover, the machines created, virtually overnight, the field of cost accounting. Strange as it seems today, few turn-of-the-century businesses had any idea which of their products made money, which of their capital was productive, or where in production time, money, and material were lost. Firms had some interest in these unanswerable questions and cost accounts of a sort were kept, usually as signed records by shop foremen. But this data was unusable except in huge firms that could afford the costs involved—chiefly the railroads and largest manufacturing concerns. The Hollerith machinery changed that situation overnight, and by 1919 the National Association of Cost Accountants appeared. (Since cost accounting was a heavily contested area, I shall return to it later.)[29]

Calculating and tabulating machinery had little impact on statistics, however, because that area was being redefined from within, intellectually. It is true that the old-style descriptive statisticians acquired a certain messianic fervor from the tabulating machine. Former census director S. D. North said in 1914,

The world has long been obsessed by the dread of an impending struggle between capital and labor—a titanic conflict involving our entire social system and leading perhaps to another French revolution. And lo, the solution is at hand; for the statistician has appeared, and behind him is an educated public opinion, which demands that equity shall be the basis of compromise, and trusts the statistician to prove mathematically where equity lies.[30]

But despite North's statement, the new field coalesced not around practical applications of statistics to social problems, but around inferential statistics, the comparison of empirical figures with theoretically derived distributions in order to measure factor effects. As often happened in statistics, the revolution came from diverse sources—Galton and Pearson worked with intelligence and Thurstone with psychological data, while Fisher studied crops and Goosen studied beer. Inferential statistics rapidly split statistical workers into a mathematically oriented elite and the traditional, applications-based mass. As Leonard Ayres put it, "Through this evolution a majority of the members of the profession have in this past decade been rendered statistically illiterate. . . ." The elite became the modern profession of statistics, founding the *Annals of Mathematical Statistics* in 1930 and the Institute of Mathematical Statistics in 1935. The mass remained based in other professions, working for whichever employers required the most descriptive statistics—business in the early twenties, government during the New Deal. The ASA journals, true to their eclectic history, long continued to review material from government publications, political science and economics journals, and even accountancy journals.[31]

The situation in quantitative information in the first decades of this century was thus relatively straightforward. There was one well-organized profession, accounting, which had successfully developed and monopolized the function of attesting the worth of publicly traded corporations. A large accounting periphery dealt with attestation of privately held companies, governments, and nonprofit corporations. Accounting had divided vertically from bookkeeping and had differentiated internally to a considerable degree; high-status accountants were obsessed with monopoly through CPA legislation. Beyond the attestation jurisdiction with its accountants, other information areas were considerably more open. Statisticians provided government (and some business) figures, but usually owed allegiance to other professions. The mathematical transformation of statistics was about to divide the field into vertically distinct groups. Outside both professions lay a wide open area—that of analyzing the figures that the new machinery allowed businesses to collect. Although "cost accountants" had appeared to control that area, the one name covered a multitude of groups. This emerging jurisdiction, of internal business information in general and of "costs" and "costing" in particular, has been without question the most heavily contested information jurisdiction in American history.

The manufacturing firm of 1900 knew the importance of cost figures, but had little ability to actually get them. Cost issues had spawned two separate literatures, coming from the two groups one might expect to have responsibility for internal cost information—accountants and engineers. Headed for a collision course over costing, the two professions were quite different. The accountants were a relatively recent British import grafted onto strong American growth. Their public markets were not yet totally defined and their mechanisms of exclusion not yet completed. But the complex internal stratification problems had been somewhat resolved by the merger of the CPA Federation and the American Association of Public Accounting in 1905, and by 1910 accountants were tentatively proposing themselves as a general profession of business administration: "It is only a question of a few years, in our judgment, when the profession of accountancy will be recognized as in full possession of this field."[32]

The engineers—in particular the mechanical engineers—were an older group. The American Society of Mechanical Engineers (ASME) dated to 1880, and schooling in the field had begun to expand in the Civil War period. Born of vertical division, mechanical engineers still worked in shops with machinists, and many had risen through what Calvert calls the "shop culture." But economic expansion pushed demand, leading in turn to the replacement of apprenticeship by formal schooling and a move towards abstract, formal knowledge (the "school culture"), coupled with further rationalization of the machine-shop division of labor. As in many professions, it was the old professional elite—the members of the ASME—who pushed the levers of professionalization and rationalization hardest, even while waxing eloquent about the shop culture that had produced them.[33]

Engineers were not perceived as technical specialists separate from managers. On the contrary, mechanical engineers were expected to supervise shops and higher operations, as well as to design and develop new equipment. Little wonder, then, that the scientific management movement, with its penumbra of systematic management, arose in mechanical engineering. While the heart of this familiar movement was making piece wages rise with output, the system involved a much wider rationalization of management, including time-and-motion studies and flowcharting of production systems. Most especially, scientific management required—and its apostles promised to deliver—complete knowledge of actual and potential costs of production, as well as of actual and potential worker output.[34]

The accountants were simultaneously addressing these problems from the other end. How, for example, did a firm calculate its returns to various pieces of capital? Or a fair wage? Or a fair price? As investors, workers, and an increasingly interventionist government asked these questions, the theory of cost accounting tried to offer some solutions by separating the firm's work into areas of production to which overhead, labor, and material could be directly attributed. At the traditional supervisory levels, the rapid expansion of engineering up from the shop floor crashed head-on into this accountants' penetration from the auditing department. The foreman himself lost most of his power in the battle. His old cost records were outmoded by accountants' Hollerith systems; his flexibility disappeared in the centralized process control sponsored by the engineers.[35]

The battle between the engineers and accountants concerned whether knowledge of actual production processes was more important than knowledge of cost allocation in determining reasonable output and wage standards. Claims for both sides were legion, as indeed befits such an interstitial jurisdiction; it was again a question of knowing the possible cost information (according to the accountants) or the necessary cost information (according to the engineers). Accounting apparently won the war of labels—since the area was called factory (later, cost) accounting, but lost the war of ideas. If one considers all articles on cost and factory accounting listed in the 1923 edition of the *Accounting Index*, which was retrospective to the 1880s, thirty-three individuals were responsible for more than two entries apiece. Ten were accountants, ten were engineers, and four were of some other occupation (the remainder were unidentifiable). Among American authors the engineers had a distinct advantage. While the earlier articles generally appeared in accounting journals, the journal most involved was English (*The Accountant*) and the articles extremely theoretical. American accountants' journals reached their peak role in cost accounting in 1905–9, containing 20 percent of the costing articles. But general business journals, trade journals, and the new "management" journals (e.g., *System*), contained 22 percent each in that period. While the general business journals lost ground later, trade journals and management journals steadily rose, and accountants' journals fell sharply. The initiating ideas in this area thus came from engineering's "systematic managers."[36]

Accountants did, however, manage to monopolize the teaching of general cost accounting, three-quarters of university courses in the subject being taught in accounting or commerce departments. In the long run, therefore, they were able to control the jurisdiction, since only they reproduced themselves. (This victory illustrates the university's new importance as an arena of interprofessional competition.) The scientific managers were in reality a small splinter group from the engineering elite, allied with the loose interprofessional group aiming to professionalize business and industrial management.[37] While this group saw the engineer as central in business management, they did not envision remodeling engineering education to make it education in management. Therefore, as long as engineers produced creative management ideas, they remained a central force, keeping their positions as society's leading efficiency experts by using the figures that cost accountants actually gathered. Indeed, of ASME members in 1930, 19 percent were in technical operations and 17 percent in management. But underneath this leadership, the accountants quietly took over; they had labeled, staffed, and controlled cost accounting. Ironically, since cost accounting took place within organizations, it rapidly lost many of its links with public accounting and became largely independent.[38]

It may seem that routine information about the costs of work is hardly the stuff of professional work, that it requires little judgment and less knowledge. But in fact the central professional task of cost accounting was the creation of "standards," estimates of how much a certain form of production *ought* to cost. Actual variety in production was then analyzed by looking at "variations" from the standards so derived. Estimation of standards required solving the "burden problem" (of allocating overhead costs), smoothing out random fluctuations in shop work, and calculating the effects of fluctuating factors of production. Like most accounting problems, these tasks were gradually solved by complex professional assumptions and conventions. (It was particularly in the area of studying shop variations that engineers contested the area.) These conventions created the crucial judgments that made cost accountants real professionals. As long as cost accounting merely recorded actual costs, it was so much data processing. But the invention of standard costs and the use of those costs for management decision-making firmly established the large new jurisdiction.

While the battle between engineering and accounting raged, demand for cost accounting received a sudden jolt from the First World War. The war's tremendous demand for cost accounting arose particularly over the issue of profiteering and particularly in England. Powerful market position, professional snobbery, and conservative business practice had kept British industry innocent of cost accounting theretofore. But the war required complex price adjustments to prevent profiteering and market manipulation, and the British imported the American S. H. Lever to help in this effort. After the war, English cost accountants immediately formed an institute and set about evangelizing British industry. As the Second World War did for qualitative information, the First also offered a new legitimacy for cost accounting, attaching to what had been simple business efficiency the greater value of patriotism.[39]

While the new maturity of cost accounting might have rebounded on the parent profession of public accounting, the public accountants, as it happened, suddenly lost interest in work within industry. For legislation had created a vast new work area. A series of acts—the Corporate Excise Tax Act of 1909, the Income Tax Amendment and Federal Revenue Act of 1913, and the Excess Profits Tax Act of 1917—opened to the public accounting profession the enormous province of tax work; the area was duly invaded and subdued, not without substantial warfare with lawyers. The growing division of public and cost accounting was furthered by industry's clear desire to differentiate what it told the tax man and the investor, on the one hand, and what it told itself on the other. Even when the consulting divisions of large accounting firms finally elbowed their way into the business market, studies of costs provided little of their business when compared with systems, general management, and personnel services.[40]

Not only were early-twentieth-century businesses ignorant of their internal costs, they also knew little about who bought their products and why. Distribution was a small but growing sector of the economy, commanding only about 6.1 percent of the labor force in 1870, but 8.6 percent by 1900, and 16.4 percent by 1950. Distribution activities grew about three times as rapidly as manufacturing activities between 1870 and 1950, although productivity in the distribution sector grew at only one-third the rate of that in manufacturing.[41] Professional jurisdiction in this area—the jurisdiction now called marketing—was created through a slow process of enclosure. Four groups participated—advertising, economics, journalism, and psychology. For the two academic fields of economics and psychology, marketing was a part-time activity. For advertising, it provided a potential avenue to professional status, one that proved, unfortunately, to be a dead end.

For journalism, marketing provided an ambiguous link between its qualitative information jurisdiction of news and the practical realities of media support. As might be expected, these diverse interests clouded the marketing jurisdiction considerably.

The study of markets was not new in 1900. Trade journals like the *Spectator* had been discussing commercial markets since the Civil War. *Printer's Ink,* the newspaper trade magazine, had discussed the role of advertising in marketing from its foundation in 1888. Shortly after 1900, however, academic psychologist W. D. Scott began to urge the full-scale application of psychological principles in marketing. Well received in business, Scott's ideas horrified those academic colleagues who sought a status independent of the commercial world, although they were enticing to many others. At the same time economists, particularly at Wisconsin, Illinois, Northwestern, Ohio State, and Harvard, developed a more general academic approach to marketing, based on then-popular institutional economics. Working in agriculture and commerce departments more often than in economics, these writers conceived of marketing as embracing not merely the distribution of products, but also sales, advertising, retailing, wholesaling, and even credit. Unlike the psychologists, the economists who entered marketing found businessmen bewildered by their approach, even though some had entered academic marketing after considerable commercial experience.[42]

These moves down out of the academy met head-on with the professionalizing efforts of advertising men. Advertising specialists had created local clubs for some time, and in 1906 these coalesced into the Associated Advertising Clubs of America. The Associated Clubs immediately embarked on serious structural professionalization, with much talk of the "science" of advertising. Proposals for schools of advertising were sent to universities, and when these proved hostile, the Associated Clubs set up its own curriculum. J. E. Kennedy proposed a central advertising research institute to evaluate actual agency work. Although such plans foundered on the agencies' unwillingness to supply proprietary information, advertising research and teaching eventually took root in universities. In the private universities, advertising located in the new business schools, which offered a home that arts and sciences departments refused. In public universities, by contrast, advertising usually ended up in schools of journalism. One version of advertising, therefore, allied with marketing in general, while the other was tied to a particular medium. In fact, neither version achieved a serious monopoly of jurisdiction for its graduates. Most agencies continued to train advertisers in-house, making the occupation extremely permeable.[43]

The journalists not only provided an academic home for advertising, they also created the original institutional structures for the quantitative study and active manipulation of consumers' desires—a specialized area now known as market research. In the 1910s, such publishing companies as the Business Bourse and Curtis Publishing established departments of commercial research that assembled journalists, psychologists, economists, and others to study these issues. As the list shows, this open territory had not wanted for claims or claimants; indeed some who sought to legitimate the new field were later to claim that market research could have stopped the Depression. Like other quantitative information jurisdictions, market research benefited immensely from the new machinery of tabulating and calculating. Unlike some of them, however, market research remained open to members of several professions and was loosely linked with the larger and equally diverse area of marketing. As marketing and market research grew through the thirties and forties, they retained this polyglot character, although increasingly polarizing into psychologists and other social scientists on the one hand and "market analysts" on the other. By 1964 marketing, like statistics before it, had split into a mathematical core—market research—and a nonmathematical periphery—marketing. The split was hastened by the emergence of operations research, which I shall discuss later. In the late seventies, market research would try to enclose its jurisdiction formally, again considering licensure, formal schooling, and other apparatus of formal professionalization.[44]

By the Second World War, the business world could look to several attendant professions for information. Cost accountants monitored the internal flow of labor, material, and capital. Public accountants presented pictures of assets and functioning to investors and the government, under the new and sometimes watchful eye of the Securities and Exchange Commission. Although not held by one particular profession, the marketing jurisdiction occupied members of several professions and provided business with a clearer picture of where its products could go.[45]

Curiously, the new statistics—the powerful inferential statistics—had not yet invaded the rich business jurisdictions. The only exploration was in the area newly called "quality control." Although quality control had long been practiced in some guise (the American Society for Testing and Materials dated from 1898), the scientific managers had generally taken the view that variation could be *eliminated* from production through effective training and automation. (This assumption sustained "variance" analysis in cost accounting.) When two physicists and an electrical engineer at Bell Telephone Laboratories applied the insights of sampling theory to quality control, they assigned a serious meaning to this variation data, which had been treated as mere noise.[46] This effort illustrates perfectly the seizure of residual areas in diagnostic schemes. The system engineers had no use for the information; Shewhart made it central. Characteristically, this first statistical application in business came not from people identified as statisticians but from other professions. From the time of the inferential transformation, statistics itself has always been a small, largely academic discipline that extends vast intellectual jurisdiction by commodiyfying its techniques in texts, formulas, tables, and graphing tools. Although good statistical analysis takes great judgment and substantial expense, statisticians flood their techniques everywhere, let others use them badly, and make a living repairing bad applications and contracting their direct services to the elite clientele. This pattern may, of course, have been forced on the profession by the extreme commodifiability of most of its knowledge, which makes underselling extremely easy and conceals the loss of statistical quality involved. But it may also reflect a chosen elitism. One can easily imagine a large profession like public accounting, but called statistics, that comprised consultants who would swear that statistical analyses meant what the substantive authors claimed they did. In fact, however, this did not happen, for reasons which suggest a deliberate choice. A loose group of workers called financial analysts perform such work in business today; the area seems ripe for enclosure.

The years from 1940 to 1945 transformed the quantitative information professions completely. They created, first, an insatiable demand for quantitative information, which led rather directly to the computers that were later to transform those professions. Second, and much more important in the short run, they saw the creation of techniques that could revolutionize the use of quantitative information in business and government. Most quantitative information professionals in the business area compiled and abstracted figures, which were then used by managers to make decisions on their own grounds. The war produced techniques for making the decisions themselves, giving information professionals a chance to again invade business management itself, this time not only with a scientizing ideology, but also with some very powerful techniques.

The problem of allocating scarce resources under constraint bestrode the boundaries between information and management. Since effective or even plausible techniques for it were unavailable, it had yet to become professional jurisdiction. In most companies the allocation function had previously been handled partly by cost accountants, partly by managers, and partly by lower-level personnel. Not surprisingly, the railroads had the most elaborate system, designed to allocate tracks, stock, and storage so as to maximize some criterion directly related to profit. Although some decisions were made by general managers, much day-to-day allocation was done by dispatchers, who possessed a relatively advanced technology for system control. By 1918 dispatching had become enough of a lifetime occupation to permit formal organization (the ATDA). Like other railroad occupations, however, the dispatchers defined themselves specifically with respect to their work object (the railroad), rather than with respect to their abstract function of resource allocation. There is no evidence that dispatchers developed a theory to aid their work or to enable them, as "professionals," to survive the railroad's demise by moving to another resource allocation job.[47]

During the Second World War, however, scientists and military men developed, first in Britain and later throughout the Allied war effort, a body of theoretical methods for solving allocation problems. Known from their wartime application as operations research (OR), these developments continued after the war, particularly in the American military. Spinning off such organizations as the RAND Corporation (1949), the developing OR community moved into systems work, pioneered cost-benefit analysis, introduced stochastic models for allocation, and developed queuing, gaming, and other relevant theories. (All of these techniques were theoretically computer independent, although the computer made them much more tractable.) The OR professional community thus began as a hybrid between mathematics, various other branches of science, and the occupations within which OR was applied. It illustrates again the process of enclosure, in which a coalition of groups takes over a body of work previously accomplished by members of environing occupations and draws jurisidictional lines around it.[48]

Like the quality controllers and the statisticians, however, practitioners of operations research to some extent avoided becoming a profession. The original Blackett group had contained physiologists, physicists, mathematicians, an astronomer, and a surveyor. Subsequent writers have glorified the multiprofessional approach. As in statistics and market research, however, extreme mathematicization set in during the 1960s and 1970s, concomitant with computer-based commodification of basic professional techniques; older practitioners feared a vertical division of the group. As in both other groups, this development illustrates a professional regression. Once a field becomes self-conscious and professional, practitioners draw their self-respect from other colleagues' admiration. Since the professions are founded on knowledge, admiration peaks when knowledge is most pure, that is, when it is least deformed by actual application. Hence mathematical preeminence.[49]

Professional regression seems to be extremely pronounced in fields like operations research where a small, but very elite, core maintains intellectual control over a much wider jurisdiction. Regression often coincides with standard "professionalization" structures (university schooling, associations, etc.), which have been strong in OR since 1960. Yet the professional elite seems paradoxically to have remained more open (e.g., to applied mathematics) than has the middle level, which is more affected by professionalization and basically involved in applying commodified techniques.[50] We can see this trend in the personnel performing actual OR–management science activities in corporations. Since the fifties, the original enclosers—military men and members of other professions—have rapidly declined, from about 60 percent of OR-MS personnel in 1950–5 to about 20 percent in 1970. OR specialists peaked at slightly over a quarter of the total in the mid-sixties and have fallen since. *Management specialists* (e.g., M.B.A.'s), although invisible in the fifties, made up about a quarter of the 1970 total. Local "organizationals"—inside-trained nonprofessionals, usually with data-processing backgrounds—constituted about a third since 1950, but have recently risen to 40 percent. Several general trends interact here: first, the rise of internal training characteristic of most multiprofessional organizations; second, a strong shift to management, as opposed to professional attitudes (since OR people hope to move into general management); and third, a considerable diffusion of OR techniques throughout firms, with concomitant routinization. These trends again emphasize the central contrast between commodification and mass professionalism as alternate strategies for development. Commodification, serving to maintain intellectual jurisdiction for a small elite, can be contrasted with creation of a mass profession like cost accounting, in which particular individuals carry the profession's techniques to clients but face various kinds of absorption when the clients are large organizations.[51]

The quantitative information professions after World War II were thus a complex and contentious group. Some were sharply defined, others nebulous. Many had generational problems reflecting their recent development. Several were squabbling over basic jurisdictions. I have said little here about the descriptive statisticians, who continued along their earlier patterns, or about the later, continuing roles of cost and public accountants. Nor have I discussed the emerging social sciences as borrowers and competitors in this area, a force that became much greater after the war. But this discussion should give a sense of the complexity of this area of work, of the forces that shaped and re-shaped it, and of the interaction of professional aims with competition and system constraints.

## The Combined Jurisdiction

Two of the central mechanisms resolving interprofessional contests are amalgamation and division, which create professions with knowledge abstract enough to survive objective task change but not so abstract as to render jurisdiction indefensible. The issue of abstraction is particularly crucial in the information area. The 1930s had in fact brought two decisive changes, both to be accelerated by the war. The first was a conception of information science as a coherent whole, embracing qualitative and quantitative information. The other was the concept of computers—machines with which this conception could be made something like a reality. The information professionals who sought to unify organization and retrieval of quantitative and qualitative information under a single paradigm came from several places. Some were involved in the American Documentation Institute (ADI), which transformed itself in the late 1960s into the American Society for Information Science (ASIS). Others came directly from applied mathematics, statistics, and other groups in quantitative information. Yet another strand was rooted in the computer technology that proved central to unification. While the attempt of these diverse groups to unify quantitative and qualitative information is as yet unsuccessful, it has much to tell us about contests for jurisdiction.[52]

Writing about an "unfinished" event is particularly difficult because of a colligation problem. A given *occurrence*—the founding of a licensing board, say—may signify many things, may potentially be part of many different *events*. For example, the Illinois State Board of Health began rating medical schools in the 1880s, and we know now that this was a straw in the wind; licensing in medicine would soon consider degrees and reform of medical education soon emerge. But had we been writing in 1890, we would not have known that the reforms of licensing and education were going to take place, although the Illinois Board ratings would be several years old. Arthur Danto tells a story about Petrarch's ascent of Mont Ventoux to illustrate the same point; Petrarch's brother saw him climb the mountain, but did not see him open the Renaissance.[53] No theory tells us how to assemble occurrences into events to be explained, my own included. For that reason, my examples have usually been drawn from earlier history, where at least the events are agreed upon, if not the explanations. When we reach the current period even the events are not agreed upon; where one writer sees the beginning of an information age, another sees a random deviation, and still another the dominance of a particular profession, differences that of course generally reflect political agendas. What follows is therefore as much a colligation as an explanation of recent events in the information area.

Curiously, intimations of a unified information jurisdiction had long existed in Europe. There, documentation emerged in the early twentieth century as a distinct specialty, separated from librarianship by its work with "documents" rather than books. The central jurisdiction of the documentalists was bibliography (the Fédération Internationale de Documentation was earlier the Institut International de Bibliographie [1895]); they therefore emphasized subject analysis, excluding the collections, descriptive bibliography, general reference, and education tasks performed by American librarians. The Europeans early stressed the importance of classification and developed a basic treatment for the subject analysis problem, the Universal Decimal Classification (UDC). They also developed, in the early years of the century, a mail-order bibliographic database.[54]

In the United States, however, the name documentation was seized by those advocating microfilm for document storage and dissemination in the thirties. The ADI, founded in 1937, was not at first an individual membership organization (it became one in 1952), but rather a publishing house disseminating scientific information on microfilm. Like the Europeans, the ADI envisioned a synthetic data system, but without the European emphasis on retrieval; dissemination was deemed sufficient. It was soon clear that the European definition of documentation made a more viable jurisdiction than did the American one. Since books in fact presented the same bibliographic problems as did microfilms, the American distinction simply reflected physical materials; the important judgment problems concerned effective *intellectual* retrieval rather than dissemination or even physical retrieval. (This focus on intellectual retrieval—on finding information concealed in masses of irrelevancies—would ultimately split the relatively unified American librarians.) The first steps toward formalizing bibliography were taken during the war. As is usual, they were taken by "enclosers" from a variety of professions. The first attempts at mechanical subject indexing, using Hollerith cards, took place in the wartime OSS and the Farm Security Administration. After forty years, qualitative information workers began using the techniques that had transformed quantitative information. Even into the 1950s new methods of coding were being developed using other precomputer technologies. While these methods did not have time to flower before the maturation of the computer, the formal theory of information retrieval had moved to an extremely abstract and formal plane by the early 1950s.[55]

The creation of information science was vastly accelerated by the rise of computers, a technology generated by a consortium of various scientific professions—mostly mathematics, physics, and electrical engineering—under the war's intense demand for quantitative information. (Computers cannot be seen as an event internal to the system of professions; the war demands were an exogenous force, a part of what Braudel calls *événement*.) Although the original computational task had been the generation of ballistics tables, the scientists attacked the problem at the most abstract level possible. There resulted a machine dedicated, like the Hollerith machines, to the assembly of data into information, but allowing complex calculations on the way, and permitting free restructuring of the assembling algorithms. The history of computers since has simply enhanced that freedom and created input-output procedures that made the machines available to first a professional and later a general public. Like many other technologies, the computer spawned a number of potential professions. A sort of computer profession emerged immediately after the war, hybridized out of applied mathematics, electrical engineering, and other environing groups.[56]

This profession was decisively shaped by the rapid development of computer knowledge, a development generated within the profession by and for itself and for the organizations—at first universities, but increasingly vendors of computing machinery—who employed its members. Computing knowledge commodified itself and created new expertise at a phenomenal rate. The structural consequences of this rapid change for the professional groups involved are unclear. In thirty years there have been four or five generations of experts in programming, each one rapidly outmoded by software that made its knowledge a commodity. Those who wrote unique programs directly for the machines were outmoded by fixed programs. Those who wrote fixed programs in octal code were outmoded by the high-level-language compilers. Those who wrote FORTRAN and the other compiled languages were outmoded by "user friendly" canned software. Although these developments took place in less than one occupational generation, it is not clear that actual individuals were outmoded with their knowledge. Many or most of them may have learned new skills and stayed at the front of the profession. Others may have remained at their original levels, coping with the reduced demand for their kinds of programming. Still others may have moved into data-processing administration or consulting. At present, while there is considerable recruiting at several of these levels, bachelor-level programmers writing high-level language are clearly subordinates in a classic profession-internal division of labor. Yet at the same time some programmers at least have managed to work at the most abstract level of programming—the creation of algorithms—throughout several generations of computer knowledge. The fundamentally unchanging nature of the underlying tasks shows well in the enduring importance of central texts like *The Art of Computer Programming*.[57]

Like many technologies, computers were at first perceived as simply doing traditional professional work faster; professional treatments for information problems were accelerated. Thus computers found immediate application within quantitative information—in cost and public accounting, in scientific and engineering calculation, in statistics and operations research. The advent of serious mass memory made them ideal for maintaining large quantitative databases, which multiplied prodigiously in all areas. At the same time, they also speeded treatments applied to *qualitative* information problems, finding rapid application in personnel records and library circulation systems. Despite great storage problems, computers were also used to maintain qualitative databases.[58]

The computer's importance in areas controlled by so many different professions implied, of course, the potential of unifying them. A variety of claimants emerged. The first and, strangely, the least important were the computer specialists themselves, together with their immediate parents, like electrical engineering. The computer specialists saw the unification problem in terms of hardware and software structures—files, variables, sorts. But these changed rapidly through development and commodification. Furthermore, as I have noted in similar situations, takeovers of professional jurisdiction by treatment substitution alone are seldom successful; treatment is not the heart of jurisdiction.

There are in fact two practical claimants to the potential unified information jurisdiction based on computers: on the one hand the information scientists and on the other the public accountants and other consultants specializing in business systems. The two have very different approaches. Information science (IS) is unrelentingly theoretical. The contending banner of accountants—management information systems (MIS)—is, despite its noble sound, largely an amalgam of earlier services in both qualitative (personnel) and quantitative (payroll, operations, cost accounting) tasks. Information science is smaller and dominated by academics. MIS is larger and dominated by large interprofessional organizations that supply contractual services. These distinctions reflected differences in historical origins; information science arose out of an intellectual event unifying an enclosed area of professional work, while MIS arose through the emergence of a structural form (the consulting house). Beyond their general claims, the only real similarity between the two is their equally distant relation to current professions. Information science, although tied to librarianship both historically and through current member affiliations, remains an esoteric field. MIS, although similarly tied to accounting through the preeminence of the Big Eight as MIS consulting houses, is in fact staffed largely by in-house trainees without professional affiliations. Both areas were seeking serious professionalization structures by the 1970s—with library schools changing their names to schools of library and information science, and graduate programs in information systems opening within business schools.[59]

The intellectual approach to unification came from information science. The knowledge supporting the IS claim for unification was extremely abstract; it comprised algorithms for dynamic structuring of information files, for automated indexing and searching of files, and for modeling the active information search of a fairly sophisticated user. Related to artificial intelligence, it employed a broad variety of fairly sophisticated statistical techniques, using computers not simply to speed up conventional storage and retrieval, but rather to reconstruct them altogether. In librarianship, the crucial development proved to be keyword indexing, which, like many such innovations, came originally from hardware vendors. This technique completely restructured indexing and enabled, with considerable practical investment but relatively little theoretical effort, the routinization of a significant portion of what had been special librarianship. Keyword indexing supported the on-line databases that supplemented or replaced earlier corporate structures for qualitative information databases—the published materials of the abstracting services and the old commercial reference houses. Several such databases were indeed produced by long-central library organizations—MEDLINE and MEDLARS by the National Library of Medicine, for example. Others were produced by newer reference services like the Institute for Scientific Information.[60]

The IS approach not only solved certain classical library problems, but also vastly extended the potential role of librarian–information scientists in actual scientific work. Nonetheless it emphasized the retrieval of information, rather than the assembly of information into usable ideas, thereby favoring qualitative over quantitative. This emphasis was reversed in the area of business information. When computer systems arrived in the 1950s, they were put to work speeding the traditional information work in business: cost accounting, personnel, payroll, and, sometimes, operations research. Since businesses adopted computers early their development, they required specialists in translating this work into machine problems, creating the ephemeral occupation of data processing. Often such services were contracted out. With the arrival of compilers and later of canned software, the need for specialists heavily oriented to the computer itself disappeared, but the unification of services remained. New groups arose for providing what came to be called management information services by the late fifties, and these proved heirs to the old cost-accounting, systematic-management, and operations-research jurisdiction of telling managers what to do with their data. This invasion of the actual management area was accompanied, of course, by the sloughing off of associations with purely routine work like personnel records maintenance.[61]

The rise of MIS occurred only through new social structures offering these information resources more efficiently. The equivalents of hospitals and law firms, these organizations offered information services by no means limited to the new technology of computing. Although consulting information services predate the Second World War, large-scale consulting services that install complete information systems for corporate clients have become common only in the last two decades. Like many such areas, this one was invaded by organizations whose common property was their ability to field the multiprofessional teams necessary. Most important were some of the major hardware vendors (Sperry Rand), independent consulting firms (Arthur D. Little), and the new consulting divisions of the giant accounting houses (Arthur Andersen). Additional corporate actors on the information scene are the commercial organizations specializing in market and survey research (NORC, ISR), alliances of major libraries (OCLC, RLG, ARL), and, last but by no means least, vendors of information commodities, both hardware and software. The presence of these large and largely commercial organizations does not make the information area any less of a professional battleground. Many of them are overgrown professional organizations—the accounting firms, many of the consulting houses. Moreover, the place of the dominant vendors—in particular that of Hollerith's Tabulating Machine Company and its successor IBM—differs only in degree from that of the drug firms relative to the pharmaceutical profession, or that of the third-party payers to the medical profession. Indeed, the case of engineers has made familiar the dependence of professionals on large organizations. The information area is no exception to the general rule.

What then is the current structure of professionalism in the information area? While members of various professions continue to enter the area, and while some are trained directly for it, there is no indication of a single group capable of general jurisdiction.[62] Some studies have defined information workers broadly and have seen as many as 1.5 million workers in the field. When so defined, the field is basically industry oriented (70 percent), mainly computer oriented (42 percent involved in computer operations, broadly defined), and about equally divided between information systems design, information systems management, and actual computer operations. The industrial computer work force of 600,000 comprises about one-third systems analysts, one-third operations personnel, one-fourth programmers, and the remainder managers. Of these, the systems analysts have the closest to an effective professional jurisdiction, with programmers subordinate to them. Management information specialists number around 100,000 and clearly originate in a wide variety of fields—marketing, personnel, administration; there is no exclusive or even real attachment between them and a particular body of work.

Elsewhere in the information area, there is also little evidence of coalescence. While many members of the American Society for Information Science have library and information science degrees (34 percent), yet 27 percent have social science degrees, 22 percent science and engineering degrees, and 11 percent arts and humanities degrees; the polyglot pattern of enclosure is still very evident. While bachelor-level computer science degree programs exploded in the 1970s, graduate programs grew slowly. Most Ph.D.-level computer scientists work in the computer area, to be sure, but they make up only about a quarter of the Ph.D.-level work force in that area. Moreover, most of those involved in training computer personnel work in industry (about 22,000), although there are 15,000 training workers in government. Only about 5,000 training workers are in academia—most computer training is thus not formal and academic, but on-the-job training, presumably in particular operations skills.[63]

No coherent set of people has in fact emerged to take jurisdiction in this area. It continues to be extremely permeable, with most training on the job, most expertise readily commodifiable, and careers following wildly diverging patterns. There are certain small and relatively elite groups in the area—the membership of ASIS for example—but even these groups betray their complex origins. Although they have a potential intellectual jurisdiction based on the information science ideology, they have yet to institutionalize coherent training programs and to create secure links of jurisdiction. It seems likely that all the professions in the information area will follow the prior example of statistics, market research, and computing itself. They will end up as small, elite professions with intellectual jurisdictions over large areas. In these areas they will oversee commodified professional knowledge executed by paraprofessionals, serving the elite clients directly themselves. Although a number of writers have seen the emergence of such professional types as "information managers" and "information specialists," in fact such groups will not achieve the mass status of, say, accountants.

This vague summary must close my analysis of the information occupations. I argued before that we know the least, at any given point, about the present, and the information area illustrates that point all too well. However, I did not mean here to give a predictive theory or complete analysis as much as to show how the system approach asks questions about so complex an area of work. Throughout this discussion, I have used the theoretical language of the earlier chapters to emphasize how basic changes in work have shaped the history of the information professions. Sometimes an organization, sometimes a technology has transformed these professions, creating new areas of work, commodifying old ones. Sometimes, too, they have been reshaped by changes in their own organizations and by internal intellectual revolutions. It is striking that nowhere in this history have the structural mechanics of professionalization—the founding of journals, schools, associations—played much more than a subsidiary role. On the contrary, these and other professionalization structures have often coexisted with diverse and complex patterns of jurisdiction. I have followed a number of jurisdictional contests through to their conclusions, tracing how a new idea challenges old professional concepts and perhaps unseats an incumbent profession. I have looked, too, at the rhetorics of competition between groups—the move to abstraction and formalism, the move from information to management. My purpose has been to show how the relations between professions and their work determine the interwoven history of professional development. This case, complex and understudied, shows how such a view can provide a fruitful analysis.

# 9    Lawyers and Their Competitors

Professions' histories are littered with splinter groups and faltering competitors. These are usually ignored in official mythologies, although occasionally recalled as precursors, charlatans, or worse. How can we write a fair history when surviving data pertains largely to successful competitors? When Hobsbawm, Tilly, and other "new social historians" studied the common people of Europe, they faced a similar problem. Common people did not write the memoirs on which history was based, nor were they discussed in the memoirs extant. To find the "people without history," these writers studied the riots by which those people communicated with the governing classes of their time.[1] We can do the same. By studying interprofessional conflict, we can set the successful professions in their real context and correct our theories of their development.

Let us consider, then, a classic problem in the history of professions: how to explain the differences emerging between the legal professions in America and Britain during the critical period from 1880 to 1940. The English solicitors initiated the structural changes of "professionalization" early in the nineteenth century, and had become an effective professional power by 1900. Possessed of secure professional monopolies, particularly of conveyancing, the solicitors seemed to fight only with the barristers, who still excluded them from audience in the higher courts. American lawyers, on the other hand, came to the structural changes of professionalization much later in the nineteenth century and developed a monopolistic ("integrated") bar only in the twentieth. Yet by the mid twentieth century, American lawyers had clearly surpassed their British cousins. Their intense involvement in modern society, both in business and government, contrasted with the solicitors' isolation. Why and how did the English profession lose the preeminence that the American one came latterly to enjoy?

Under my theory, these differences should be traceable to the differing competitors and competitions faced by the two professions. Although we know very little about these competitors, we can use the techniques of the new social history to find them, studying lawyers' complaints of invasion by outsiders. Fortunately, lawyers keep careful records about such "poachers"; these are our basic data. Unlike the preceding chapter, this one will study primary data in serious detail. It will even make predictions about interprofessional differences. Yet the aims remain the same: to illustrate the utility of a system-based theory of professional development. As that theory tells us, however, the lawyers' complaints by themselves are not enough. We must create a framework to interpret them. As Steven Lukes has argued, one cannot infer a system's structure from its conflicts alone. Potential conflicts may be suppressed by dominant groups or hidden by external circumstances. We must therefore first envision the conflicts we might reasonably expect the two legal professions to have, outlining the potential changes in legal jurisdictions in relation to the actual structures of the legal professions.

## Potential Jurisdictional Conflicts of the Legal Profession

Two organizational forms emerged in the late nineteenth and early twentieth centuries that generated enormous demand for legal services—the large commercial enterprise and the administrative bureaucracy.[2] The growth of business practice involved some problems never before encountered—large-scale reorganizations, massive bond issues, tax planning, and, in America, antitrust. There were also vastly increased quantities of traditional business work. Governmental work grew similarly. It often involved practice before new tribunals, tribunals with their own staffs, their own forms of procedure, and their own sense of prerogative. Like business work, government-related work was extremely diverse, ranging from personal matters associated with the welfare state's involvement in housing and education to the corporate business generated by the state's regulatory intrusions into the economy. By contrast with business and government work, matters of land and property did not multiply but merely expanded additively with the population. Indeed a general contraction of this jurisdiction appeared imminent. Many European governments tried to place land ownership under state guardianship through compulsory registration. Although this possible abolition of legal work did not succeed in England, there was for some time serious danger of it. (In the United States, a state-registration threat never developed.)[3]

Potential legal jurisdictions in this period thus grew rapidly. In business and government there appeared qualitatively new areas of work. Even traditional business work expanded very rapidly. In land and property the expansion was slower, but still proportionate to population.

Did the legal profession grow in relation to this changing body of work? Garrison's detailed survey of the Wisconsin bar in the early 1930s estimated the growth in legal work since 1880 using data on deeds filed, civil and criminal cases begun, tax appeals, divorces, probates, and adoptions, as well as data on such indirect measures as population and the value of manufactured and agricultural product. He concluded that for the state as a whole and for nearly every county legal work had vastly outstripped the growth of lawyers; work per lawyer was more plentiful than ever before. Even in urban Milwaukee the increase of lawyers did not keep pace with most of these indicators.[4] Others, however, believed in overcrowding at the bar. In New York City, Isidor Lazarus noted, there were in 1930 264 lawyers per hundred thousand population, about five times the number in England. Indeed, the number of lawyers in the United States increased by over 30 percent from 1920 to 1930 alone. Yet Lazarus too saw large reservoirs of untapped demand in the "lower middle, and the more or less employed or active lower, sections of the community," as well as in "the legal needs of the economically submerged army of the practically unemployed." But he recognized that this demand would be effective only if "the facilities were created for bringing together the supply and demand and adjusting them on an efficient, reasonable, and profitable volume basis."[5]

In America, then, potential legal work apparently increased well beyond the increase of the profession during the entire period. Although there are not similar studies for England, there seems little reason to think the situation there different. The economy grew more slowly, but the ratio of solicitors to population actually fell steadily from 1841 to 1921, increasing only marginally thereafter until the 1970s.[6] On the tentative assumption that output of professional services is a fixed function of professional manpower, we can infer that potential work outstripped potential professional output in both countries, except perhaps in the cities.

In considering such ratios of potential work to potential output, we may envision three types of conflicts between a profession and its competitors. It is important to examine their general character. The first type of conflict arises when potential jurisdiction is expanding relative to potential professional output, either qualitatively (as here in big business and government work) or quantitatively (as here in traditional business work). I shall call this the case of excess jurisdiction. If the incumbent profession does not either expand numerically or increase output per professional, it faces invasion by outsiders. In areas of *quantitative* expansion, where the incumbent already has the kind of cultural jurisdiction discussed in chapter 2 and currently enjoys one of the settlements discussed in chapter 3, invasion means a potential worsening of the settlement, with loss of cultural jurisdiction as a potential long-run consequence. In areas of *qualitative* expansion, the incumbent's cultural control is weak or nonexistent, and invaders have a clearer chance at cultural jurisdiction itself.

A second kind of conflict arises when current jurisdictions are insufficient to support the profession; potential output is expanding faster than jurisdiction. The profession is then looking for work. Expansion (of jurisdiction) may be undertaken either by improving current settlements or by moving into wholly new areas. An overstaffed profession can abolish a clientele settlement, for example, and serve all potential clients itself. (Medicine periodically does this in the area of primary health care.) This necessitates no change in the cultural structure of jurisdiction. A move into a qualitatively new area, by contrast, requires the cultural work to create the new cultural jurisdiction.

These expansion conflicts and professional responses produce characteristic successions of claims for jurisdiction. When expansion reflects insufficient jurisdiction, it occurs first in the workplace and only later becomes established in public and legal eyes. Precisely the reverse happens with sudden quantitative expansion of a jurisdiction relative to professional output; there legal and perhaps public jurisdictions are secure, but workplace control comes to be shared with outsiders. In sudden qualitative expansion of a jurisdiction—as in the case of business and government work—there is no preestablished jurisdictional pattern; the move therefore occurs simultaneously in all three arenas for jurisdictional claims. In practice these patterns mean that we can use the relative extents of legal, public, and workplace jurisdiction to judge a profession's situation. Where workplace jurisdiction exceeds legal or public jurisdiction, there is expansion reflecting excess manpower and output. Where the reverse is true, there is invasion by outsiders, generally reflecting a profession's inability to provide services.

A third general type of conflict is often studied in the literature on professional monopoly—the invasion of a settled jurisdiction by groups providing equivalent services at lower prices. Such invaders generally assault public jurisdiction, usually through an extensive advertising campaign. Attackers may be new to professional work or members of another established profession; they may also use special organizational forms that enable their price cutting. Price-cutting conflicts, like those arising from excessive and insufficient jurisdiction, are ubiquitous. We shall see below all three forms of conflict among professions contesting lawyers' jurisdictions.[7]

Knowing the types of interprofessional conflicts does not tell us where in a profession's jurisdictions these conflicts will appear. Professions normally maintain control of several different areas of work, and which of these are contested is a question of some interest. It seems reasonable to expect that the jurisdictions invaded will be peripheral or weakly held. For example, professions' classifications for diagnosis and treatment always leave considerable residual areas, filled with cases that are neither standard problems nor effectively classifiable along the various dimensions of professional knowledge. Since a profession exercises its weakest subjective jurisdiction over such cases, they should be the most easily poachable. But residuality is not the only aspect of subjective jurisdictional strength. Successful outcome, acceptability of treatments, and legitimation of cultural knowledge are all important. Thus, invaders can seize more central areas if they can clearly provide more effective service or more acceptable or legitimate treatments.

Of the three forms of conflict, two involve the failure to adjust output and demand. In many professions—and the law is one of them—output is closely tied to manpower. This connection provides a first explanation of the difference between American and British lawyers today. In chapter 5 I introduced the concept of demographic rigidity to denote the degree to which a profession's size in the short or long run was determined by its current demography and its career practices. Now both of these may in turn depend on forces other than demand for service; for example, desires for social status or for centralized professional control have often led professions to establish rigid career lines. The professionalization-monopoly model assumes that the more rigidly a profession structures itself, the more powerful it is. In fact, as I argued, a rigid demographic structure leaves a profession quite unable to respond to sudden expansion in demand.

Indeed, the solicitors offer a particularly clear example. The five years of clerkship delayed by at least that time any response to sudden demand increase. More importantly, the necessity of articled clerkship under a certificated solicitor tied the profession's future size directly to its present one. There is an intervening variable, to be sure: the number of such articled clerks taken by a solicitor. But in fact law and professional etiquette prevented the training of multiple clerks, and thus the profession could not expand rapidly with expanding demand. Precisely the mechanisms involved in what Larson calls the "professional project" of advancing solicitors' status were thus mechanisms that made the profession incapable of meeting its demand.

The problem perceived by English solicitors as the unqualified practice problem thus arose through the first type of conflict discussed; an insufficient supply of legal services invited other professions, old and new, to start providing them. The only countervailing factor was the rise of managing clerks who did conveyancing work under solicitors' direction. These clerks enabled an individual solicitor to multiply his effort, breaking the link between numbers and output. Using a subordinate group to respond to demand is a classic solution to the problem of demographic rigidity. Nonprofessionals can have much less structured (and less permanent) careers, since their work acquires its professional quality from the professional himself and from the division of labor in the professional organization (office, hospital). Such work therefore does not require extensive training. One could argue, however, that the resort to these personnel is the best evidence possible of the shortage of solicitors. It seems fair to conclude that the shortage, albeit mitigated by these "unauthorized personnel," was a reality. [8]

Two developments allowed the American profession to avoid this situation. The first was the large firm, whose extensively divided labor accomplished more work with given resources; the Cravath firm, for example, had twenty-five lawyers by 1906 and fifty by 1923. [9] The second was the replacement of clerkship with law school. In 1870, one-quarter of new lawyers had gone to law schools. By 1910, the figure was two-thirds. This shift decoupled the profession's rate of growth from its current size in two ways. First, not only could law schools take extra students more easily than could individual practitioners, but also, since schools were both profitable and prestigious, there was an enormous incentive to found them. There resulted an immense potential for recruitment. Second, the typical law-school career in this period was two years, not five, providing a much shorter response to demand changes. [10]

This rapid expansion was, however, accompanied by a stratification of the American bar, indicated in part by the separation of the night law school graduates from the full-time law school graduates. This stratification has important implications for the interpretation of competition between lawyers and others. Roughly speaking, the night school graduates, along with some day school graduates, dealt with the land and property jurisdiction—individual matters expanding at the rate of population growth. The graduates of the elite full-time schools and their newly huge law firms controlled the qualitatively expanding area of big business practice as well as extensive parts of the new government practice. Work in the traditional business jurisdiction, expanding in amount but not kind, was split between the two groups. Since the majority of the United States lawyer expansion came in night schools and nonelite day schools (whose graduates entered the relatively slowly expanding area of land and property), the American legal profession was moving towards the paradoxical situation of having a lower tier oversupplied with lawyers and an upper one undersupplied.[11]

We can summarize the relation of potential work and output in the two countries as follows. Work in the legal matters of individuals expanded proportionate to population and little more. The amount of business work, on the other hand, grew by orders of magnitude, and in some areas qualitatively new forms of work arose. The same is true of governmental work. In England, the profession's demographic and career structure—adopted to help advance professional status—prevented it from expanding rapidly to meet these demands, although the managing clerks provided some multiplication of professional effort. In the United States, the move to law schools and to the large, differentiated firm made lawyers more able to handle the new work, although at the price of stratification within the profession.

These considerations predict the following patterns of interprofessional conflicts. In England, the lack of solicitors should appear in a general invasion of the basic legal jurisdictions by all kinds of alternative professions. This invasion should occur first in peripheral areas—areas of low client status, of slight economic reward, and of weak cultural jurisdiction. Given the rigid structure of the English profession, it is not unlikely that this invasion might result in some loss of cultural jurisdiction, not just in a move from settlement as dominant to some weaker settlement. Moreover, the qualitatively new jurisdictions of big business and governmental work should be almost completely open to outsiders and hence sites of substantial conflict. In the United States, too, these areas should see serious conflict, but less because of underservice than because of the lack of preexisting cultural jurisdiction, a fact obscured in England by underservice. In addition, the law's move into these areas may have weakened its hold elsewhere, with consequent change in settlements. The demographic power of the American profession, however, should prevent any loss of cultural jurisdiction, despite a possible weakening of settlements. Again, we expect conflicts to appear at peripheral points, and expect differential patterns in the different status levels of the profession.

Having made these rough predictions, we can now survey the jurisdictional squabbles visible in the professional literature. Already, however, we have found a good general answer to the question of why American and English lawyers fared differently during this period. The strong structure of the English profession, however it may have advanced professional status, proved a dangerous strategy in the rapidly shifting work environment. The demographic and institutional flexibility of the American lawyers, so disturbing to the elite WASP lawyers of the East Coast, in fact enabled the Americans to handle the demand expansion with relative ease. But as we shall see, this simple picture is by no means the whole story.

## Complaints about Unqualified Practice and Other Invasions

### GENERAL MATTERS

To study lawyers' interprofessional conflicts, we can study records relating to what the English call "unqualified practice" and the Americans, "the unauthorized practice of the law." This data can be augmented by the study of other, general claims of invasion by outsiders. Formal response to unauthorized practice of course long postdates the practice itself. Outsiders can be impugned for lacking knowledge and character only once there is a credible presumption that insiders in fact possess them, and building this presumption takes time. I have thus tried, where possible, to find sources predating official ones, in order to discover early aspects of the problem. Formal response itself arose at different times in the two countries. In England, the Attorneys and Solicitors Act of 1874 (37 & 38 Vict., c. 68) gave the Law Society powers over those pretending to be solicitors, a power exercised by the Professional Purposes Committee of the Society. The Committee also dealt with professional misconduct. This joint function reflected the importance of solicitors themselves in promoting unauthorized practice, since an early and persistent violation was the employment of uncertificated solicitors and other unqualified personnel to do solicitors' work within the offices of the certificated. This problem was equally common in America.[12]

In the United States, organized concern with unauthorized practice was a later matter.[13] It began with the Committee on Unlawful Practice of Law of the New York County Lawyers Association in 1914, and spread from there to such other urban jurisdictions as Chicago, Nashville, Kansas City, and Memphis. In the late 1920s, unauthorized practice became a serious concern of the American Bar Association, which directed a national attack on it throughout the 1930s. Americans generally handled unauthorized practice and external competition by councils and agreements if possible. Direct legal action, the more usual course in Britain, was a last resort.[14] The delayed beginning of American action reinforces my earlier conclusion that the Americans balanced supply and demand more effectively than the English. Moreover, the urban origins of the first unauthorized practice committees are significant. Since city lawyers were by this time quite stratified, the first conflicts appeared either in the qualitatively new jurisdictions of the upper-tier or in the oversupply of lower-tier lawyers, who were pushing out for new work.

Summary sources permit an approximation of the overall level of enforcement activity in both countries. The Law Society's activity was remarkably constant from 1895 to 1950. There were usually about ten complaints of unqualified practice per year. Acting upon these various complaints was clearly *not* the major work of the Professional Purposes Committee, since complaints by clients against *certificated* solicitors numbered from six to ten times this figure. That American lawyers approached unauthorized practice differently is shown by the higher level of American activity. The New York County Lawyers Association committee reported on ninety-two complaints in 1915 alone, at a time when the population of New York County was about 7 percent that of England. American unauthorized-practice committees characteristically started with large caseloads, then settled down to a lower but fairly steady level of work. "The number of inquiries does not vary much from year to year," said the Pennsylvania Bar Association committee in 1950, speaking of "the routine problems of the relationship between lawyers, bankers, realtors, accountants, justices of the peace, aldermen, and notaries public." This surprisingly constant pattern of activity, common to both countries, implies that enforcement became something of a formality. But still the differences tell us that organized law in England either recognized less conflict or felt that less could be done about it.[15]

Despite the apparent stability of routine enforcement, lawyers' *sense* of the degree of unauthorized practice had definite cycles. Partly this reflected phases natural to any social movement. In both countries interest in the problem would suddenly wax, with violent speeches, excited talk, and often some new kind of organization or interprofessional agreement. But then the newly created enforcement organization would go on to a fairly routine existence, indeed often complaining of lawyers' inattention. Agreements like the code of ethics negotiated between the Pennsylvania lawyers and the Pennsylvania Bankers Association in 1922 could endure a decade of benign neglect before grassroots complaints generated renewed Bar Association action.[16]

## DATA AND METHODS

Neither the steady level of general activity by enforcement committees nor the waves of professional interest in the problem, however, tell us much about the actual content of the professions' conflicts with outsiders. Yet it is these conflicts that in fact shape the two professions. Who did the lawyers fight and why?

For solicitors, I have used two bodies of data to investigate these questions. The first comprises material from the Law Society: (a) the Annual Report of the Council to the membership for the period 1896–1950 and (b) the *Proceedings* of the Annual Provincial Meeting for the period 1875–1911. Since even the provincial meetings were dominated by the London elite, I have sought more broadly representative data. This comes from the *Law Notes*, a monthly legal publication oriented toward the provincial solicitor and edited by Albert Gibson, a Londoner fiercely vigilant of unqualified practice and openly suspicious of the Law Society's position towards it. I have drawn my second body of English data from this journal, for the period 1882–1935.[17]

In America, unauthorized practice issues are handled more locally.[18] Therefore, in seeking comparable data, I turned first to two important urban committees on unauthorized practice, those of the New York County Lawyers Association and the Association of the Bar of the City of New York. I have followed the annual reports of the first of these organizations from its founding in 1916 to 1936, and the second from its founding in 1926 to its disbanding in 1950. As in England, I sought in addition a provincial perspective, and found it in the records of the Pennsylvania Bar Association's statewide committee on unauthorized practice. This material, dating mostly from after 1930, has the advantage of providing the perspective of another state legal system and the disadvantage of not "completing" the New York data series.

The formal data, then, consists of material from six basic sources, which represents metropolitan and provincial concerns in both countries: the New York data and the Law Society data represent the metropolitan concerns, while the *Law Notes* material and the Pennsylvania material represent the provincial ones. (The two metropolitan datasets are pooled in both countries, so that four data series will actually be reported.) From these sources I have taken a coded record of each identifiable complaint of invasion of legal turf by outsiders. Each record contains three simple items of information: the occupation accused of poaching, the area of work invaded, and the year of the occurrence. There are about four hundred mentions each in England and America.[19]

A word is necessary about the interpretation of these data. The presence of complaints in an area signifies two things: (1) that lawyers consider the jurisdiction important enough to fight for it, and (2) that the jurisdiction is open to invasion. As I argued earlier, invasion may mean either that lawyers are too few for their own work or that they are invading someone else's. We can distinguish the two cases only by comparing the relative extent of public and workplace jurisdiction. The absence of complaints is harder to interpret, since it could mean the absence of either condition—importance or openness. In interpreting absence, therefore, we must rely on discursive materials in these records and on other secondary work. Interpretation of change over time is even more difficult. Increasing rates of complaints may indicate either an increase in the level of poaching or an increase in the degree of concern with poaching, possibly arising out of the decreasing availability of work, either in the poached area or elsewhere. Nonetheless, in areas where lawyers have sufficient or excess business, we can assume that increased complaints imply increasing levels of poaching. An increase followed by a decrease seems to be reasonably interpretable as a successful defense of jurisdiction. A steady or episodic level of complaints suggests an unstable border or possibly a settlement by client differentiation. When the nonlawyers step across the client lines—which occurs regularly because of the common skills—the lawyers rush in to enforce the *official* jurisdictional line, which usually gives them complete official control.

AREAS OF CONFLICT

The areas about which lawyers complained included all of the chief legal jurisdictions—business affairs like bankruptcy and companies; property matters such as conveyancing, wills, and trusteeship; advocacy before courts and administrative tribunals; and finally, general advice on business, legal, and personal affairs. In England another area contested was appointment to various positions of national and local administrative or judicial authority, as well as certain kinds of local work (e.g., prosecution) performed for those authorities.[20]

Table 4 shows the distribution of complaints. Advocacy received about the same attention in both countries, with the detailed figures ranging from 10 percent in Pennsylvania to 21 percent in New York.

TABLE 4    Areas of Jurisdictional Conflict

| Dataset | Advoc | Nat | Locp | Locw | Advic | Bus | Land | Gen | N |
|---|---|---|---|---|---|---|---|---|---|
| | | | | Jurisdictions[a] | | | | | |
| New York | 21 | | | | 19 | 34 | 21 | 5 | 154 |
| PABA | 10 | | | | 11 | 14 | 58 | 7 | 101 |
| U.S. total | 17 | | | | 16 | 26 | 34 | 5 | 255 |
| Law Society | 15 | 5 | 6 | 3 | 7 | 23 | 33 | 8 | 150 |
| *Law Notes* | 16 | | | 15 | 2 | 38 | 29 | 2 | 192 |
| England total | 15 | 2 | 3 | 10 | 4 | 31 | 30 | 4 | 342 |

| | | 1880 | 1890 | 1900 | 1910 | 1920 | 1930 | 1940 |
|---|---|---|---|---|---|---|---|---|
| | | By Decades | | | | | | |
| Advocacy: | England | 17 | 4 | 11 | 29 | 27 | 17 | — |
| | U.S. | — | — | — | 15 | 19 | 11 | 38 |
| Advice: | England | 9 | 8 | 2 | 0 | 0 | 0 | — |
| | U.S. | — | — | — | 8 | 17 | 17 | 27 |
| Business: | England | 38 | 34 | 37 | 29 | 9 | 12 | — |
| | U.S. | — | — | — | 28 | 34 | 25 | 8 |
| Land: | England | 26 | 20 | 40 | 20 | 32 | 46 | — |
| | U.S. | — | — | — | 49 | 21 | 40 | 19 |

*Note:* All figures in percentages except *N*.    — means data not available.

[a] Advoc = advocacy; Nat = national offices; Locp = local offices; Locw = local work; Advic = advice; Bus = business; Land = land and property; Gen = general.

The problem of lawyers' monopolies of appointments did not occur in America and made up about 5 percent of the complaints in England. Monopolies of local work again mattered only in England. Problems with legal and other advice, by contrast, were largely an American problem, making up 19 percent of the New York episodes and 11 percent of the Pennsylvania ones. Business matters—liquidation, bankruptcy, making of companies and partnerships, writing threatening letters—comprised from a quarter to a third of the complaints in all data except that on Pennsylvania. Property matters, by contrast, comprised over half of the complaints in that Pennsylvania data, around one-third of them in England, and about one-fifth in New York.[21]

These figures indicate that the invasion of lawyers' jurisdiction was not peripheral, at least in terms of areas. On the contrary, the rates of complaints seem to follow the rates of work. For example, figures from Pennsylvania on distribution of lawyers' actual work show that property matters were the most important work for 62 percent of the Pennsylvania profession outside of Philadelphia and Pittsburgh. The correspondence with the complaints of unauthorized practice in property matters (58 percent) is extremely close. Similarly, the greater level of business complaints in the American cities reflects the equally greater importance of business work there.[22] Of course lawyers are more likely to act on a complaint the more central the area invaded. But still, it is noteworthy that jurisdictional enforcement is not just a matter of professional borders. That this invasion occurred with peripheral *clients*, however, is easily verified from discussions of the complaints. Both in America and Britain the cases often involved small shopkeepers who refused to pay lawyers' rates for enforcing debts, as well as private individuals who sought inexpensive wills and deeds. The conflicts thus involved not change of cultural jurisdiction but largely change of clientele settlements.

The national differences, however, reflect important aspects of jurisdictional claims. Advocacy, the classic heart of lawyers' jurisdiction, was of equal concern to both, as was business, perhaps because of the rapid expansion that had called forth competitors in both countries. (It is notable that business conflicts were urban in the United States and rural in England.) Advice was a different matter. Although the British believed advice to be an important legal function, they never really attempted a dominant settlement in the area.[23] American lawyers did, presumably because their greater numbers made them believe they could reasonably uphold the claim. Finally, land and property conflicts sharply differentiated urban from upstate lawyers in the United States, but not urban from provincial solicitors in England. This indicates a second division among United States lawyers—that between rural and urban attorneys. The two status-tiers discussed before were both largely urban. The extensive competition rural lawyers faced in their basic property jurisdiction suggests possible underlawyering in the countryside, a fact often noted by rural lawyers in debate. Primary and secondary sources confirm this interpretation.[24]

The lower part of the table compares the development of these complaints over time in four areas—advocacy, advice, business, and property. While advice was a decreasing area of concern in British legal work, it was an increasing one in America. There was either less invasion in England, or less ability and inclination to protect the work. Perhaps, too, it was an area of American expansion. Also, in each country problems with business formed a major concern in the first worries about unqualified practice, but fell off as time passed. Apparently these problems could be settled, with effort, and the jurisdiction secured. Problems with advocacy, by contrast, seem episodic in both countries; there are no clear trends. Finally, land and property became increasingly important in England, although the uproar over the Public Trustee Act (6 Edw. 7, c.55, 1906) left its obvious mark on the decade 1900–1910. This indicates both that land and property were becoming increasingly central as solicitors' work and that the jurisdiction was proving hard to settle properly. In the United States, the trend in concern with land and property is unclear.

These national differences become even more pronounced when we consider the detailed figures in table 5. In America concern with land and property seems to be partly an early issue (that is, an issue unauthorized practice committees entered immediately upon their foundation) and partly a rural issue (since it seems so important in Pennsylvania). Advice, conversely, is an urban one and a later one, growing with time. Advocacy, too, seems an urban issue, in the United States, and also seems to increase in importance. Business, although also an urban issue, may have declined as advice and advocacy problems increased. Most of the decline noted in the United States business figures seems to be rural. But such trends may also reflect the upper-tier lawyers' expansion into the new jurisdictions of big business and government, which involve advice and advocacy more than does traditional business work like partnerships and collections. (Advice and advocacy as coded include such areas of government work as practice before the tax courts and other agencies.) Since the jurisdictions were qualitatively new, conflict was inevitable. The conflicts may also reflect expansion in the overlawyered lower tier. Advice may have been a particularly important expansion area there, and as we shall see, business work—in particular collections—was a central issue for lower-status urban lawyers.

Few of these detailed patterns are observed in England. The urban Law Society's concern with unqualified practice in business does decline with time, but the more provincially oriented *Law Notes* shows an enduring and major concern with the issue. The pattern thus reverses the American one. A similar reversal takes place in land and property practice, where the urban group's concern exceeds the provincial one and increases with time. The solicitors' retreat to the solid foundation of conveyancing is clear. Although advice is largely an urban issue, it disappears even there very early. Advocacy still shows no consistent pattern. As for the peculiarly English concerns of national and local offices and work, they too are episodic, if enduring, concerns.

This preliminary survey of conflicts with other groups already tells us much about how the general constraints imposed by the balance of supply and demand for legal services worked themselves out in the

TABLE 5              Areas Invaded by Decades Within Datasets

|  | 1880 | 1890 | 1900 | 1910 | 1920 | 1930 | 1940 |
|---|---|---|---|---|---|---|---|
| **Advocacy** | | | | | | | |
| New York | — | — | — | 19 | 21 | 18 | [43] |
| PABA | — | — | — | [0] | [0] | 7 | [33] |
| Law Society | 8 | 6 | 8 | [36] | 30 | 17 | — |
| *Law Notes* | 21 | [0] | 12 | 26 | — | — | — |
| **Advice** | | | | | | | |
| New York | — | — | — | 10 | 15 | 27 | [36] |
| PABA | — | — | — | [0] | [33] | 10 | [17] |
| Law Society | 23 | 13 | 0 | [0] | 0 | 0 | — |
| *Law Notes* | 3 | [0] | 3 | 0 | — | — | — |
| **Business** | | | | | | | |
| New York | — | — | — | 31 | 34 | 41 | [14] |
| PABA | — | — | — | [18] | [33] | 14 | [0] |
| Law Society | 38 | 35 | 31 | [21] | 0 | 12 | — |
| *Law Notes* | 38 | [32] | 39 | 32 | — | — | — |
| **Land** | | | | | | | |
| New York | — | — | — | 40 | 19 | 10 | [7] |
| PABA | — | — | — | [82] | [33] | 62 | [33] |
| Law Society | 23 | 29 | 42 | [21] | 35 | 46 | — |
| *Law Notes* | 27 | [11] | 39 | 19 | — | — | — |
| **National Office** | | | | | | | |
| Law Society | 0 | 0 | 0 | [0] | 20 | 8 | — |
| *Law Notes* | 0 | [0] | 0 | 0 | — | — | — |
| **Local Office** | | | | | | | |
| Law Society | 4 | 6 | 0 | [0] | 5 | 8 | — |
| *Law Notes* | 0 | [0] | 0 | 0 | — | — | — |
| **Local work** | | | | | | | |
| Law Society | 0 | 3 | 4 | [21] | 0 | 0 | — |
| *Law Notes* | 11 | [58] | 5 | 19 | — | — | — |

*Note:* [ ] = based on $N < 20$. Complaints with unspecified area are omitted. All figures in percentages.

contingencies of actual history. Both professions faced serious external invasions, and in heartland jurisdictions. In both cases the invasion came first with peripheral clients. Both professions regarded advocacy as a central jurisdiction and faced serious competition there. Both faced serious invasions of their traditional work with business.

But beyond these common patterns, the two professions have little in common, as we might expect from their different ability to supply services. American urban lawyers pushed out into advice giving, an area the solicitors rapidly gave up. This expansion occurred both in the upper and lower tiers of the urban profession. These lawyers had

little trouble in land and property, although their country cousins—the few who remained—faced a massive invasion of this heartland jurisdiction. In England, land and property clearly became the
obsession of both urban and provincial solicitors. The reversal of patterns in business practice seems, at this point, to be quite anomalous.

This picture complements and expands the predictions made earlier. A somewhat unsuspected urban-provincial distinction has proven
central, at least in the United States. But the other evidence conforms
to the pattern expected. In the United States, a relatively understaffed
urban upper tier of lawyers pushed into corporate and government
work and found substantial competition there. The overstaffed urban
lower tier perhaps pushed out into general advice and other areas,
looking for work. The rural group was desperately understaffed and
was losing its central monopolies. In England, both provincial and urban solicitors surrendered nonessentials like advice to concentrate on
the heartland of advocacy and land and property, facing substantial
conflict over the latter. The provincials, unlike their urban brethren,
were unable to defend even the traditional business jurisdiction.

The overall pattern thus emerging is one of activity within constraint. Professional groups take certain jurisdictional actions partly for
internal reasons involving their own structure and knowledge base,
partly for external reasons like status and power, and partly because
these actions are constrained by the competitive environment. As yet,
however, we are hardly certain of the directions of jurisdictional expansions and contractions, nor are we aware of which particular areas
of legal work involved especially competent competitors. We can deal
with the first of these questions—the hypothesized directions of
change—by studying extents of jurisdiction in different arenas for professional claims.

## AUDIENCES FOR JURISDICTIONAL CLAIMS

Efforts to curb unqualified practice are efforts to make the workplace
relations of jurisdiction conform to the legal and public ones. As I argued before, if the lawyers have workplace jurisdiction but not public
or legal jurisdiction, then they are expanding into the area. If, by contrast, they have legal and perhaps public jurisdiction, but not workplace jurisdiction, then they are facing an invasion.

The only sources where lawyers are fighting to get legal jurisdiction
established are city sources. Both New York committees had active
legislation and court subcommittees dedicated to solidifying legal control of jurisdictions lawyers had acquired in the workplace. The Law
Society's lobbying activities in Parliament were equivalent. Rural law-

yers tended to demand a very different thing of the courts. They wanted enforcement of the jurisdictions unquestionably established in law and legal precedent. Particularly in England, the provincial lawyers' complaint was that courts would not enforce legal limits in actual workplace practice. There is thus plain evidence that urban jurisdictions were the only sites of lawyer expansion. The rural lawyers of both countries were fighting invasions.

Additional evidence comes from the differing extents of legal and public jurisdiction. On the one hand, what was law for the city was law for the countryside; in the legal arena, lawyers' jurisdiction was theoretically uniform from one place to another. Yet throughout the provincial data from both countries rings the message that the public simply doesn't know lawyers' prerogatives: "There undoubtedly does exist throughout the State in many places, throughout the laymen, a certain reluctance to go to a law office." ". . . the detestation of the law and lawyers evinced by the public, the general unthinking public. . . ."[25]

Such complaints seldom appear in city sources. That the public jurisdiction was less extensive than the legal one in the countryside reemphasizes the interpretation here given—that provincial lawyers were too few for the business and were facing serious invasion. This is further strengthened by the fact, which we know from the actual complaints, that large amounts of legally routine law work—conveyancing and other property matters—were being done by nonlawyers. The workplace jurisdiction was even less extensive than the public one.

In the city, as we have already seen, the arena pattern of jurisdiction shows evidence of expansion. An elegant example of this comes not from the expansion into advice giving and similar areas by the too-numerous lower-status lawyers. Rather it bespeaks an earlier expansion, at the expense of a group called conveyancers. We know that the expansion was old because the uncertainty about jurisdiction was merely at the legal level; the workplace and public jurisdictions, at least in the cities, were secure. The area immediately concerned was the drawing of wills. The legal status of this work was confusing even for lawyers themselves. Thus while most lawyers in both countries assumed that the drawing of wills was a legally established jurisdiction, it was in fact not so. In England, the Stamp Act of 1870 (33 & 34 Vict., c.97) allowed an unqualified person to draw a will, power of attorney, or transfer of stock (provided the transfer contained no trusts or limitations) and to be paid for these activities.[26] In America, when the Pennsylvania Bar Association's brand-new unauthorized practice committee reported in 1932, its chairman, a Philadelphia suburban lawyer, asserted that "the Committee feels that the writing of wills is the practice of law." W. G. Littleton of Philadelphia rose to his feet and thundered:

Is it not a fact that the writing of wills is not only not the practice of the law but in the English system lawyers themselves were not permitted to draw wills until the year 1760, when the exclusive privileges of the English association which formerly had that right were thrown open to members of the Bar, and when I come to speak, my mind running back personally as far back as 1885, when I was thrown in with that class of men who were known as conveyancers, who prepared deeds, mortgages, and other legal instruments, and wrote wills, it would be perfectly astonishing to the lawyer of that day to say that members of the conveyancers' association, whose names you probably know, some of whom I recollect, were violating any law.[27]

This passage is notable not only for its total disagreement about the legally established jurisdiction, but also for its reference to an invisible group of nonlawyer legal professionals, who had in workplace fact been ousted from this jurisdiction within the half century of Mr. Littleton's memory. The new social-history method—studying conflict to find the lost people of history—has produced a lost profession.

The Philadelphia conveyancers had been, in fact, a small, elite group of practitioners, some of whom were lawyers and some of whom were not. They normally both drafted and stored title papers, wills, and other documents. At first employed as hired specialists to abstract titles, they eventually became independent consultants. A family lawyer would consult a conveyancer concerning property to be purchased, and the conveyancer would then abstract the title and take counsel from a consulting real-estate lawyer on the title's encumbrances. As specialists in property documents, the conveyancers naturally handled wills, mortgages, trusts, and related property matters. Apparently they had strong professional structure; as Littleton mentions, they had an association. Other sources report that their examinations were felt by many to be considerably more difficult than those of the lawyers.

Nonetheless, the conveyancers were destroyed, very rapidly, by a convergence of forces. The lawyers were rapidly increasing in numbers and looking for work. This threatened the conveyancers' control of wills, trusts, and similar documents. In their heartland title work, a crucial court case both gave them "professional" stature and destroyed them. In *Watson* v. *Muirhead* (57 PA 161, 1868), the court held conveyancers not liable for bad titles if they had taken reasonable precautions. But this left purchasers without recourse in cases of bad title, a situation the growing business community would not accept. A coalition of exasperated businessmen, lawyers, and conveyancers created in 1876 the Land Title Insurance Company (the first such corporation), to provide a mechanism for pooling the risks of property transfer. In a similar move, lawyers and bankers founded the Fidelity Trust Company to take up work with trusts and other financial matters. As a result of these changes, the conveyancers rapidly disappeared.

The example of the conveyancers shows again how the relative extents of jurisdictional claims can tell us much about the direction of jurisdictional change. For lawyers of the 1930s, the writing of wills was an old expansion jurisdiction, one in which they sought to convert a successful workplace invasion into publicly and legally recognized domination. That the rural public persisted in having wills drawn by banks, trust companies, prothonotaries, and aldermen indicates that this expansion had never had the success in rural areas that it enjoyed in the city.

## COMPETITORS

The lawyers had other antagonists besides the vanquished conveyancers. These antagonists, as I have argued throughout, provide the structure that bends the two professions in different directions. They fall into seven groups. The first are the other free professions—the accountants, the bankers, and others. The second are the other professions affiliated with the law. In America this meant notaries, foreign (out-of-state or out-of-country) lawyers, and disbarred individuals working for other lawyers. In England it meant barristers, law stationers, and solicitor's clerks, and, as in America, uncertificated solicitors. A third group, the land professions, comprises the simple category of real estate agents in the United States, while in England embracing the much wider variety of house agents, estate agents, land agents, valuers, surveyors, and so on. A fourth group is local officials—justices of the peace, magistrates, police, and other municipal authorities, as well as their various clerks. In England this category includes registrars in probate and their clerks. Fifth, a group of negligible importance in the United States, but of great importance in England, is national officials. These included officers of the Board of Trade, of the Office of the Public Trustee, of the Inland Revenue, and of a variety of other administrative bodies. Conversely, the sixth group was more important in the United States—corporations. These include title and trust companies, insurance companies, collection agencies, legal aid societies, trade associations, and various other groups. The seventh category of offenders is a miscellaneous group of outsiders—chiefly "debt collectors" in England and insurance agents in the United States.

Table 6 shows the impact of these competitors. Competition from

TABLE 6              Jurisdictional Competitors

| Dataset | Competitors[a] | | | | | | | |
|---|---|---|---|---|---|---|---|---|
| | Free | Law | Land | Loc | Nat | Orgs | Other | Unsp |
| New York | 5 | 19 | 1 | 0 | 0 | 51 | 7 | 16 |
| PABA | 15 | 9 | 14 | 20 | 1 | 20 | 5 | 14 |
| U.S. total | 9 | 15 | 7 | 9 | 1 | 38 | 6 | 15 |
| Law Society | 11 | 9 | 4 | 11 | 24 | 7 | 11 | 22 |
| Law Notes | 23 | 5 | 18 | 14 | 8 | 11 | 19 | 1 |
| England total | 18 | 7 | 12 | 13 | 15 | 9 | 16 | 10 |

Note: All figures are percentages.

[a] Free = free professions; Law = legal professions; Land = land professions; Loc = local judicial and administrative officials; Nat = national administrative officials; Orgs = corporations; Unsp = unspecified.

other free professions is more common in the provincial than the metropolitan data in both countries, but the general level seems somewhat higher in England. Competition from other legal professionals, by exact contrast, is more common in metropolitan than provincial data, and distinctly more common in the United States. Competition from the land professionals is, as one might expect, largely a provincial concern, and perhaps a little more common in England. Competition from local authorities is purely a rural phenomenon in the United States, although about equally common for both groups in England. A sharp contrast between the two countries arises over competition from officials of national administrative bodies: in the United States, this was negligible, while in Britain it made up nearly a quarter of the Law Society's complaints, and was a substantial problem for the more provincially oriented Law Notes. The figures for competition from organizations—companies of various shapes and sizes—exactly reverse this situation. Companies supply the majority of urban complaints in the United States, and one-fifth of the rural ones. They supply about one-tenth of the English complaints. It is not unfair to summarize these patterns by saying that the English lawyers faced an invasion by officials and other free professionals, and the Americans an invasion by companies and other legal professionals.

This striking contrast raises important questions about the predictions of conflict made above. True, the amount of American jurisdiction in property was expanding with the population, and the business jurisdiction much more rapidly. Yet in both jurisdictions, American lawyers faced competition not from individuals but from specialized corporations—trust companies, title companies, collection agencies.

This competition was directed not against the expanding law firms in the qualitatively new jurisdictions of big business and government, but against individual lawyers and small partnerships working in more slowly expanding areas. This conflict arose out of external invasion of areas under full lawyer jurisdiction, and proceeded by price cutting; it exemplifies the third form of conflict discussed above.

In England the invaders were also organizations, but in that case state organizations. There seems to be clear evidence that the conflict arose through underservice; the state vowed to provide faster and more equitably distributed service. That state work was cheaper was to be a by-product; in fact, it seldom was.[28]

IMPORTANT CONTESTS

To gain a clearer picture of the actual settlements of the major jurisdictional disputes, we may analyze problem areas and competitors in detail. This means replacing general classifications (free professions, national officials, land and property) with actual groups and bodies of work (accountants, the Board of Trade, trusts). I include in this analysis any group or problem responsible for more than ten mentions in the relevant country.

Tables 7 through 10 show this data for problems and competitors respectively. I shall discuss England first, considering first the problems by decade, with the competitors chiefly responsible (table 7) and second the detailed totals for each major competitor, combining all areas of conflict (table 8). In England, the most important areas of conflict, in decreasing order, were the writing of legal threats, prosecution, and general advocacy, followed at some distance by trusts, general probate work, bankruptcy, wills, briefing barristers, writing contracts, general debt work, and general property work.

It is interesting that the writing of threatening letters—the main activity of debt-collecting work—should be the most central problem of British solicitors. The vast majority of these complaints were provincial in origin (forty-one of forty-six), and came from competitors—agents, accountants, debt collectors—who follow a temporal succession. Agents were a general group from whom various land professions officially separated in the late nineteenth century—Chartered Surveyors in 1868, Valuers in 1882, Auctioneers and Estate Agents in 1886, Land Agents in 1902.[29] Each of these groups formed a specialized qualifying association, usually removing itself from debt collection in the process. The provincial accountants continued to do much of it, but accountancy itself became an officially qualified profession in the eighties with the foundings of the Institute of Chartered Accountants

TABLE 7    Problems by Decade with Competitors Involved: England

| Problem | 1880 | 1890 | 1900 | 1910 | 1920 | 1930 | Competitors |
|---|---|---|---|---|---|---|---|
| Advocacy | | | | | | | |
| General advocacy | 15 | 1 | 6 | 8 | | 1 | Accountants, 5 |
| | | | | | | | Debt collectors, 5 |
| | | | | | | | Corporations, 4 |
| | | | | | | | Agents, 3 |
| Briefing | | | 4 | 2 | 4 | 2 | Clerks, local, 5 |
| National positions | | | | | | | |
| National office | 1 | | | | 4 | 1 | Barristers, 3 |
| Local work | | | | | | | |
| Prosecution | 7 | 12 | 5 | 9 | | | Police, 29 |
| Advice | | | | | | | |
| Advising families | 3 | 2 | | | | | |
| Business | | | | | | | |
| Bankruptcy | 5 | 6 | 3 | 1 | | | General officials, 6 |
| | | | | | | | Bankruptcy Office, 5 |
| Liquidation | | 4 | 4 | | | | Bankruptcy Office, 4 |
| | | | | | | | General officials, 3 |
| Winding up estates | 1 | 1 | 3 | | | | |
| Making companies | 1 | | 5 | | | | |
| Threat letters | 16 | 6 | 11 | 10 | 2 | 1 | Debt collectors, 14 |
| | | | | | | | Agents, 10 |
| | | | | | | | Accountants, 7 |
| Contracts | 5 | | 5 | | | 1 | Auctioneers, 4 |
| General debt | 4 | | 5 | 2 | | | Accountants, 4 |
| Land and property | | | | | | | |
| Conveyancing | 1 | | 2 | 1 | 2 | 3 | Building socs., 3 |
| Wills | 5 | | 5 | 1 | 1 | 2 | Corporations, 3 |
| Registration | 2 | 1 | 4 | | | | General officials, 5 |
| Trusts | | 5 | 13 | 1 | | 1 | Public trustee, 17 |
| Leases | 5 | 1 | 2 | | | 1 | House agents, 5 |
| General probate | 4 | | 9 | 4 | | 1 | Law stationers, 4 |
| | | | | | | | Probate registrars, 3 |
| | | | | | | | Inland Revenue, 3 |
| General property | 3 | 3 | 3 | | 1 | | |

*Note:* All figures are counts of mentions. All individual problems with more than five mentions in the full English data are included. Competitors are listed if they have more than three mentions for the particular problem involved.

and of the Society of Incorporated Accountants. While provincial accountants were seldom members of those bodies, accountancy rose in status and standards throughout the period and was also rapidly filling an enormous new jurisdiction generated by the Companies Acts. There was thus less impetus to compete. But the accountants were simply replaced by the "debt collectors," a nondescript group who pro-

TABLE 8          Competitors by Decade: England

| Competitor | 1880 | 1890 | 1900 | 1910 | 1920 | 1930 | N |
|---|---|---|---|---|---|---|---|
| **Free professions** | | | | | | | |
| Accountants | 17 | | 12 | 2 | | | 31 |
| Auctioneers | 5 | 1 | 6 | 4 | | | 16 |
| Bankers | | | 1 | | 1 | 8 | 10 |
| **Law professions** | | | | | | | |
| Barristers | | | | | | | 7 |
| Law stationers | | | | | | | 6 |
| Unadmitted in solicitor | | | | | | | |
| office | | | | | | | 5 |
| **Land professions** | | | | | | | |
| Estate agents | | | | | | | 5 |
| House agents | 2 | 2 | 7 | | | | 11 |
| Agents, general | 16 | 1 | 2 | 1 | 2 | 1 | 23 |
| **Local officials** | | | | | | | |
| Clerks to local | | | | | | | |
| authorities | | | | | | | 5 |
| **National officials** | | | | | | | |
| Bankruptcy Office | | | | | | | 9 |
| Public trustee | | 6 | 13 | | | | 19 |
| Officials, general | 1 | 9 | 9 | 4 | | | 23 |
| **Corporations** | | | | | | | |
| Corporations, general | 6 | | 8 | 4 | | 1 | 19 |
| **Others** | | | | | | | |
| Debt collectors | 1 | 3 | 10 | 9 | | 1 | 24 |

*Note:* Each competitor with more than five mentions in the total English data is listed. Decade figures are given when there are more than ten total mentions.

vided the majority of the later complaints. It appears, then, that this persistent conflict arose from lawyer underservice and a clientele settlement. Solicitors' rates for collection work were simply too high for the provincial merchants.[30]

Police prosecution and general advocacy (usually involving matters of debt collection) were both matters of enduring concern to solicitors. Although lawyers generally like the idea of courts (rather than legislatures) controlling legal practice, in England most judges were barristers or laymen. Solicitors again and again failed to persuade these men to exercise their authority under Section 72 of the County Courts Act of 1888 to forbid lay people to advocate in court. The *Law Notes* went so far as to publish a blacklist of those County Court justices who permitted accountants, debt collectors, and others to practice before them. It also investigated the common provincial practice of hearing the collection professional as witness rather than as advocate. But these practices were apparently never curtailed until the 1920s. Complaints about general advocacy, then, were like those about letter writing: they arose mainly in connection with debt collection and involved the same settlement by division of clientele.[31]

Prosecution by nonsolicitors increased courts' ability to handle minor complaints and so embodied another, equally unacceptable, settlement by clientele differentiation. *Legal* jurisdiction of prosecution was not in fact restricted to solicitors, at least in the lower courts, and indeed as late as 1914 the Home Office was directing chief constables to examine the witnesses in borough police courts in cases where they themselves had laid the information. Solicitors accused police of imprisoning many innocent men and believed justices' clerks favored the police because "they know the procedure of the Court, and save time."[32] But the importance of this jurisdiction to the solicitors was largely symbolic. Criminal prosecution in borough courts was neither a major monetary attraction nor a business source. By serious activity here solicitors hoped to persuade the public of their disinterested wish for public justice. The jurisdictional settlement sought was what I have called intellectual jurisdiction, a claim to control how a particular area is served without in fact having the manpower or the inclination to serve it.

Such disinterest was hardly present in the areas of trusts, general probate, and bankruptcy. These were central areas of solicitors' work, and all three were seriously invaded, not by other professionals, but by Her Majesty's Government. The Bankruptcy Act of 1869 had allowed receivership into the private sector (the work was largely done by accountants), but that of 1883 returned most duties of receivership to the Board of Trade. As if this were not enough, while the Law Society fulminated, the Lord Chancellor (Halsbury) astounded the solicitors by announcing in 1887 his intention of seeking compulsory land registration. (The Law Society noted with some malice that neither Lord Halsbury nor Sir Robert Torrens, inventor of the registration system used in Australia, registered his own titles.) Although the land registration plan was eventually watered down to a limited test of registration in certain districts of London, one of Halsbury's other schemes, for the creation of an Official Trustee, became law as the Public Trustee Act of 1906 (6 Edw. 7, c.55). These developments explain the chief governmental competitors listed in table 7, officials of the Board of Trade, general officials, and the Public Trustee. Two other sets of officials appear in connection with probate work—the registrars, who often did legal work for private parties in connection with their official duties, and the Inland Revenue, who under Section 33 of the Customs and Inland Revenue Act, 1881, and Section 16 of the Finance Act, 1894, had full probate jurisdiction in cases under £500.[33]

This invasion by the government, labeled "officialism" by the solicitors, originated in the impulses that built the welfare state. Services were to be provided to the unserved. Legal delays would be avoided by bureaucratic solutions. The government repeatedly argued its ability to provide these services not only with more rapid and equitable distribution, which solicitors never disputed, but also at less expense, which they emphatically did.[34] Nonetheless, the solicitors were forced to accept coequal jurisdiction with the state in several of these areas, since most bankruptcy remained in state control, trusts became state or private work at the discretion of their principals, and land registration was made voluntary in some areas and compulsory in others. The state, that is, was able to force a jurisdictional settlement by division of labor, rather than merely by client differentiation.

In America, the detailed story of competitors and problems merely verifies a picture we have already surmised from the general data (tables 9 and 10). First, there is a distinct difference between the urban and rural complaints. The rural complaints concern bread and butter property work—wills first and foremost, followed distantly by conveyancing, general property work, the winding up of estates, and trusts. In the city, the specific problems are general debt work, bankruptcy, and advocacy on retainer, followed distantly by legal, tax, and published advice, the writing of threatening letters, wills, and trusts. It is noticeable that the two lists overlap only in wills, trusts, and general property work, and that much of this competition is attributable to one type of competitor—the trust company and the bankers who ran it. The collection agency, by contrast, seems a completely urban phenomenon, as do the title company and other corporations. Local officials are important chiefly in the countryside, while other legal groups have their chief impact in the city, although notaries do cause some problems in the country.

This detailed pattern confirms much about the interpretation of American legal conflicts so far given. The urban bar's lower tier, oversupplied by the night law schools, is fighting to expand into (or perhaps to retain) a collection business that is apparently conceded in the country, where the declining lawyer populations are fighting to defend more central jurisdictions against invasion. The urban groups' most important competitors are corporations offering efficient services. (These corporations, as one might expect from the discussions of chapter 6, were usually multiprofessional in nature; virtually all included

TABLE 9                Problems by Decade with Competitors Involved: United States

| Problem | 1910 | 1920 | 1930 | 1940 | Competitors |
|---|---|---|---|---|---|
| Advocacy | | | | | |
| Government | | | | | |
| advocacy | | 1, | 2, 4 | | |
| General advocacy | 1, | 5, | 1, | | Corporations, 3 |
| Minor tribunals | | | | 3, 2 | |
| Tax appeals | 2, | | 1, 1 | 1, 3 | |
| On retainer | 5, | 4, | 3, | 1, | Collection agencies, 3 |
| | | | | | |
| Advice | | | | | |
| General advice | 1, | | 7, 3 | 1, 1 | Foreign lawyers, 5 |
| Tax advice | 2, | 3, | 1, 3 | 1, | Accountants (PA), 3 |
| Published adv. | 1, | 3, | 4, | 1, | |
| | | | | | |
| Business | | | | | |
| Bankruptcy | 3, | 5, | 6, | 2, | Collection agencies, 7 |
| Winding up estates | 1, | , 2 | , 6 | | |
| Threat letters | 1, | 4, | 4, | | Collection agencies, 4 |
| General debt | 7, | 6, | 4, | | Corporations, 5 |
| | | | | | Collection agencies, 4 |
| | | | | | Unauthorized in lawyer's office, 3 |
| | | | | | |
| Land and Property | | | | | |
| Conveyancing | 2, 3 | , 1 | , 4 | , 1 | |
| Wills | 6, 3 | 3, | 1, 21 | , 1 | Trust companies: NY, 3; PA, 7 |
| | | | | | Bankers (PA), 5 |
| | | | | | Real estate agents (PA), 3 |
| | | | | | Notaries, 3 |
| Trusts | 2, | 3, 1 | 2, 6 | | Trust companies: NY, 5; PA, 5 |
| Mortgages | 2, | | 2, | 1, 1 | |
| Contracts/sale | 1, | 1, | , 3 | | |
| General prop. | 3, 1 | 2, | , 6 | , 1 | Real estate agents (PA), 4 |
| | | | | | Title companies, 3 |

*Note:* All figures are counts of mentions. The figure before the comma is NY, the other figure is PA. All competitors listed are NY unless identified as PA. All individual problems with more than five mentions in the full U.S. data are included. Competitors are listed if they have more than three mentions for the particular problem involved.

lawyers as important, though not dominant, elements.) Having achieved great economies of scale in searching titles, the title companies next sought to construe their right to draft legal instruments directly affecting insurability as a right to draft deeds.[35] The lawyers managed to turn back this attempt to seize a coequal jurisdiction in land affairs—one that would have been fatal to them—but did have to settle for the removal of much title work that had once belonged to them. The same thing happened in collections. The lawyers defeated the collection agencies' bid to seize coequal legal jurisdiction—by denying them the rights to have lawyers on retainer, to write certain

TABLE 10          Competitors by Decade: United States

| Competitor | 1910 | 1920 | 1930 | 1940 | N | NY | PA |
|---|---|---|---|---|---|---|---|
| Free professions | | | | | | | |
| Accountants | 2 | 9 | 4 | 15 | 5 | 10 | |
| Bankers | 4 | 11 | 1 | 16 | 5 | 11 | |
| Law professions | | | | | | | |
| Unadmitted in lawyer office | | | | | 8 | 6 | 2 |
| Foreign lawyers | | 1 | 7 | 4 | 12 | 12 | |
| Notaries | 9 | 5 | 14 | 1 | 29 | 18 | 11 |
| Land professions | | | | | | | |
| Real estate agents | | | 19 | 5 | 24 | 1 | 23 |
| Local officials | | | | | | | |
| Justices of the peace | 3 | 2 | 11 | 1 | 17 | | 17 |
| Aldermen | | 2 | 8 | 2 | 12 | | 12 |
| Corporations | | | | | | | |
| Trust companies | 10 | 7 | 18 | 3 | 38 | 19 | 19 |
| Title companies | 12 | 4 | 3 | 4 | 23 | 19 | 4 |
| Collection agencies | 7 | 9 | 26 | 4 | 46 | 40 | 6 |
| Corporations, general | 10 | 7 | 4 | | 21 | 20 | 1 |
| Insurance companies | | | | | 5 | 3 | 2 |
| Others | | | | | | | |
| Debt collectors | | | | | 7 | 7 | |
| Insurance agents | | | | | 6 | 2 | 4 |

Note: Each competitor with more than five mentions in the total U.S. data is listed. Decade figures are given when there are more than ten total mentions.

kinds of threatening letters, and so on. But the collection agencies in fact performed that centralization of demand which Lazarus had foreseen as necessary and absorbed a considerable amount of demand for legal services in the process. The story was repeated with trust companies. The trust companies' bids to write wills and draft trusts were denied, retaining crucial aspects of property jurisdiction under lawyers' legal control. But the lawyers still lost most administrative work connected with trusts and probate.[36]

In each of these competitions with companies, the lawyers preserved what I have called an advisory jurisdiction. Their competitors' administrative efficiency provided far more effective services in the collection, trust, and title areas than could lawyers. In defense against them, the best the lawyers could manage was to retain legal and public control over the purely legal residual of these areas. The companies took over the administrative work in the workplace and, as time passed, were conceded the public right to it in bar association arguments and the legal right to it in court cases. These jurisdictions proved poachable because, in the terms of chapter 2, the subjective jurisdictions over them were weak; only a small fraction of the traditional work in them actually involved lawyers' special skills. Most of it was administration for which lawyers were neither specially trained nor specially able. Yet all of it had been considered part of trusts, collections, or title work as the case might be. The courts tried for some time to defend the lawyers' view by holding *workplace* jurisdictional standards to apply to lawyers (practice of law includes anything that lawyers have customarily done) while holding *legal* standards to apply to their opponents (practice of title companies includes only what statutes say it does). Ultimately, however, the courts retreated and the poachers relented, satisfied with the lucrative administrative work they could so effectively handle.[37] The result split each of the three old legal jurisdictions in half, giving their administrative portions to the corporations and their legal ones to the lawyers. The meaning of trust, title, and collections as areas of work thus radically changed.

The notaries and foreign lawyers offer two interesting footnotes to unauthorized urban practice. The New York bar attributed the notarial problem to the city's large foreign population. The bar associations attacked "ignorant foreigners coming from countries where the 'notary' is a quasi-lawyer" for supposing that notaries were capable of performing legal actions. Eventually, perhaps because America entered the First World War as France's ally, the committee's remarks became a little less nativistic. The (later) foreign lawyer problem was similar; foreigners arriving in the 1930s often saw fit to advise fellow countrymen concerning the laws of their own land, something the bar association originally tried to attack, but later permitted. But the chief problem with foreign lawyers was their procuring offshore divorces for clients, something which drove the bar committees quite mad. Under the heading of foreign lawyers came also those large law firms from other American cities that opened New York offices. These provide the lone example in these data of a conflict, within the qualitatively new big-business jurisdiction, between members of the upper tier of the profession. Although these invaders were nationally reputable firms, the New Yorkers insisted that they announce on their letterheads their incapability of New York practice. The competition for the new commercial work was so intense as to cause fighting within the profession.[38]

The American rural scene was quite different. There lawyers were scarce and even lawyers were frank about the necessity of nonlawyers doing some legal work. In 1921, half of Pennsylvania's counties had less than forty lawyers apiece, and a quarter had less than twenty. Justices of the peace, aldermen, notaries, prothonotaries, and various other officials and laymen had perforce to do a variety of lawyers' work. Complaints about this practice surfaced most in the smaller cities like Wilkes-Barre, Allentown, and Williamsport, where the clearly defined legal systems of the cities met the locally negotiated divisions of labor characteristic of the true countryside. The rural conflicts concerned basic heartland legal work in land and property and betray all the usual signs of invasion of an underserved jurisdiction. It is striking, by comparison with the urban data, that Pennsylvania shows no sign whatever of the problems associated with collections—complaints about letters, about representation on retainer, about debt work. This too signifies a retreat to heartland work.[39]

Surprisingly, many problems related to the new government business—tax appeals and advocacy before minor and government tribunals—seem to be equally split between urban and rural American lawyers. The presumption that governmental work provided an expansion area mainly for upper-tier urban lawyers may thus be incorrect. The tax advice findings do support it, for that problem is a largely urban matter. But still, the government work may have offered more general opportunities than it seemed at the outset. Perhaps it was the attempt to enter this new jurisdiction that left the rural lawyers so open to invasion in their land and property work.

## Conclusions

This analysis aimed to answer a classic question in the history of professions: how and why did the English solicitors lose the preeminent position that American lawyers rapidly gained in the early twentieth century? The answer here given is a complex one, as befits a complex question. Three things interacted to produce that outcome: the actions of the two professions themselves, the general social environment that produced both new work and new means of doing old work, and a host of competitors trying to control areas centrally important to the legal professions. None of the three can be omitted in a full account; each has its part to play.

The structural cause of the difference lay in the interaction between the two professions' actions and their general environment. The period in general was one of rapid expansion in potential legal work. Yet for reasons largely related to immediate status gains, the solicitors chose a set of rigid professional structures—in particular, clerkship—that sharply limited their ability to expand manpower. Nor did they invent techniques for seriously increasing individual output, although the use of managing clerks helped somewhat. American lawyers had freer professional structures, whether by accident or design, and therefore handled the expansion much more effectively. They grew both in manpower and, in certain areas at least, in output per individual.

This difference in professional action led, given the environment, to a loss of jurisdiction by the solicitors far exceeding that of the American lawyers. The exact course of this retreat to the "heartland" of professional work was determined considerably by the types and numbers of competitors. We have seen several different patterns among rural and urban lawyers, among high-status and low-status lawyers. The competitors have been not only other professions, but also state officials and lay people. Deprofessionalization of certain areas of work occurred extensively in various areas. The actual development of any particular professional subgroup thus comprises a series of events shaped but not determined by constraining factors—the general social environment and the environment of professional competitors. Within these constraints those histories work themselves out somewhat freely. It was virtually certain from the general constraints that solicitors would fall back on some form of basic work. That the basic work would be conveyancing—that 60 percent or more of a modern solicitor's income would come from that source—was by no means foreordained. Rather it reflected the intersection of peculiarly strong legal and public jurisdiction by solicitors with the inability of competitors to produce alternative methods for exchanging property, an inability which the solicitors, of course, used all means in their power to maintain.

The actual decisions made by professions within these constraints reflect many factors discussed in earlier chapters. A profession is likely to fall back on areas in which its subjective jurisdiction is particularly strong, in which its general cultural legitimacy is unquestioned, and in which the work is sufficiently esoteric to justify professional service, but not so esoteric as to make its prescriptions unacceptable or its work unlegitimable. The decision may also reflect external considerations like social status—the solicitors may have chosen conveyancing because of its associations with land, rather than collections with its associations with trade and commerce. The decisions may also reflect the social structure of a profession—the strength of its associations, schools, and work organizations—or the potential of its knowledge base for development. These various internal factors provide the sufficient impetus that chooses a course of action within the necessary constraints imposed by the competitive system surrounding the profession.

At the same time as it opened and closed areas of work, the larger social environment directly shaped the nature of the lawyers' competitors. It is no accident that the solicitors faced officials and American lawyers faced corporations. The rise of interventionist government and of multiprofessional organizations were both noted in chapter 6 as general changes gradually reshaping the nature of competition in the system of professions. Their implications here are clear. In Britain, the government became a major provider of legal services to large sectors of the population. Not content with regulating the professional environment, the government actually entered it as competitor. In America, the new organizations found that they could handle most of the work involved in trusts, titles, and collections at a fraction of the cost of traditional legal service. By separating adminstrative from purely legal work, they deprived lawyers of large areas of traditional jurisdiction. Again, in this case external forces actually invaded the jurisdictional system as competitors, rather than simply changing the nature of competition.

Substantively, then, this chapter has produced a clear and yet suggestive answer to the problem with which we began. It not only tells why American and British lawyers differ today, but suggests a number of questions to ask about other professions. Was the pattern of corporate invasion characteristic of other American professions, and if not, why not? Similarly, is government invasion a general British pattern or a localized one? Do the later arrivals of big government in America and of big business in Britain bring further invasions of legal jurisdictions, and if not, why not? Why were some competitors of the legal profession successful and others not? Can we find reasons for this in the other interprofessional conflicts in which *they* were involved?

This substantive fertility reflects the power of the general theoretical approach taken here. The present chapter has illustrated central parts of that approach. Rather than focus on such structures of professionalization as schools, licenses, degrees, and associations, it focuses on the relation between a profession and its work, the relation of jurisdiction. The analysis of this chapter focuses particularly on different audiences for jurisdictional claims—legal, public, workplace—and on the different jurisdictional settlements achieved before those audiences: by division of labor, by intellectual control, by subordination, by advisory control, and by clientele differentiation. I have pursued these specific aims by a particular method—by outlining the conflicts I expected a particular profession to have, and then investigating them with data on claims of jurisdictional invasion.

This method produced some startling results. It abundantly verified the assumption of extensive interprofessional conflict. It found the vanished conveyancers—an expropriated nonlawyer group of whom I find no mention whatever in standard secondary sources. It discovered the striking differences between the invasions faced by American and British lawyers. It used the differing extents of jurisdiction in legal, public, and workplace environments to verify directions of expansion and contraction. It showed the unforeseen consequence of excessively rigid professionalism in England—inability to handle demand. It emphasized the different invaders of American and British jurisdictions—corporations and government—a difference rich in implications for both professions. In short, the method proved an effective way to answer many of the questions with which we began and produced a number of unexpected benefits.

But there are serious drawbacks, as well. A focus on conflicts means that changes occurring without conflict make very little mark. Yet one of these was in fact central in this period—the quiet loss of the new work in big business by the British solicitors. The financial men of the City, exasperated with the dawdling of the High Courts of Justice, slowly removed most of their disputes from the legal system in this period, settling them either directly or through arbitration. Since no competitor stole this business, nor did it vanish in a clear, abrupt fashion, the change was not noticed by a method aimed mostly at conflict. Another problem is that stable and unconflicted jurisdictions, however important they may be, are eclipsed by more conflicted areas. The concentration on unauthorized practice complaints means a general emphasis on workplace jurisdiction, rather than legal or even public jurisdiction, when the latter may have great long run implications.

These problems can, of course, be met by alternative methods working within the same theoretical approach and the questions it generates. Jurisdictional importance can be assessed directly by studies of the distributions of types of practice. (Indeed, such studies identified the resemblance between areas in which conflict was extensive and areas in which practice was extensive.) Such a measure would capture the invisible withdrawals just mentioned, although in practice only rarely are data specific and reliable enough to differentiate areas of practice as do the unqualified practice complaints. The problem of deemphasizing legal and public jurisdiction is less of a worry than that of biased jurisdictional importance, since these arenas of jurisdictional claims are generally well studied. Yet many of these studies are written by professional participants who mistake their own profession's version of a task for eternal truth. Good studies require a clear conception of the objective task and its possibilities in order to analyze in detail how the subjective jurisdiction was actually constructed. This problem will be investigated in the next chapter.

These methodological quibbles should not obscure the fundamental strengths of the present method. On balance, studying interprofessional conflict provides one of the best possible avenues to analysis of professional development. By studying a familiar question from a new vantage point, the present chapter has shown that interprofessional conflict over work is not simply a peripheral phenomenon, providing detail to the general outline of professionalization. Professions evolve together. Each shapes the others. By understanding where work comes from, who does it, and how they keep it to themselves, we can understand why professions evolve as they do.

# 10     The Construction of the
## Personal Problems Jurisdiction

The two preceding chapters have focused on the interplay of groups and claims. Professional work itself has largely been taken as given, although I have sometimes noted attempts to redefine it. In the present chapter I shall investigate the construction of cultural jurisdiction itself, the shaping of undefined tasks into a series of adjacent jurisdictions. The case studied will be a particularly important modern jurisdiction, that of personal problems.

It is not immediately clear how such an examination should be organized. We might ask who first recognized the personal problems now dealt with by psychotherapy or where modern psychiatry came from. But neither question allows the full range of possibilities; perhaps these problems were hitherto handled under various other names and conceiving them as "personal problems" was simply a new synthesis. Perhaps "modern psychiatry" is itself a new name for an old thing. Furthermore, these questions identify the past in terms of its consequences for a particular present (today), which in fact has no special status other than the arbitrary one of being the latest period we know. Most importantly, such questions confuse rhetoric with analysis. It is mere narrative convenience to organize a historical text around the questions Where did $x$ come from? or What were the results of $x$? We know that the further we go up or down a genealogical tree, the wider the tree gets. This doesn't mean that the whole human race of twenty generations ago was directed towards producing some one individual, any more than it means that one individual twenty generations ago produced all those progeny of today. Rather, each full generation produces the next full generation. Reproduction is a woven net, not a tree.

As with people, so with events. To search for all the causal ancestors, or causal descendants, of a given event is merely a rhetorical convenience. Since history interweaves sequences of events, the combination of two stories with one result prevents their combination with other results. Openings created by one sequence of events may or may not be taken advantage of by another; structural necessities constrain, but sufficient actions determine the outcomes of situations. An analytic rhetoric of narration must preserve this adventitious but structured character. Such a rhetoric must leave events in their immediate temporal context. It must follow the blind alleys as well as the thoroughfares by which history produced the present.

How then can we discuss the origins of professional work with personal problems? The jurisdiction of personal problems was created, split, reattached to other jurisdictions, split in new ways, and reconceptualized a dozen times between 1860 and 1940. Groups associated with it subdivided, joined, then divided along new lines, both ideological and organizational. In principle, one could tell such a story as a series of snapshots: the situation in 1860, in 1870, in 1880, and so on. In all these snapshots would appear the relevant characters, from the start of the story to its end or theirs. Like those who experienced the history, the reader would never know which developing stories would diverge from the immediate subject, never to return. Nor would the reader suspect which other stories, with no initial relevance, would eventually prove central. Such a narration would indeed emphasize the fecund contingency of history; it would also bewilder the reader completely.

I shall, then, follow a middle way. I will move forward and backward, from character to character, emphasizing the interplay between autonomous action and constraining structure. This will not make for a traditionally directed narrative. But history is not a directed narrative but a tissue of contingencies. I hope to make this whole contingent network visible.

## The Status of Personal Problems, 1850–75

In mid- to late-nineteenth-century America, there was no general public conception of problems of living.[1] Nor were angst and maladjustment subjectively real categories of experience. To the extent that such things were experienced at all, they were construed within a vague cultural category of everyday life problems. People might have family or marital quarrels, career difficulties, financial problems, "disappointed affections," chronic minor illness, or even be generally unhappy. But these were seen as diverse exigencies of life, not as forces shaping the quality of life or as encroachments preventing individuals' reaching some highest levels of personal functioning, as they are today. A notion of careers, career success, and career contingencies *had* coalesced by this time, but the ideas of personal adjustment and self-realization had not emerged, under any label. The diverse problems of everyday life were handled by an equally diverse group of agents. Family and friends played a major role. In addition, all of the professions dealt with them, as novels of the time show. Doctor, lawyer, clergyman, all received personal confidences about such problems, and all gave relevant advice. The warrant for this advice was not professional knowledge, but rather the general status accorded settled practitioners in their communities.[2]

Only the clergy had a clear professional construction for everyday life problems. It was not, however, a direct definition of them. Rather, such problems helped clergymen diagnose and treat their flocks' *religious* problems. They were diagnostically important because they were a sign from God telling the individual to address the problem of salvation. They were therapeutically important, and for the ministers as practical professionals this was their more essential role, because they made people willing to take ministers' treatments seriously: "Seasons of sorrow in families are opportunities which ought to be carefully improved by ministers. The providence of God is then preparing the sufferers for the cordial reception of the blessings of the Gospel." Personal problems were not in themselves the objects of clergy work; theologically, there was only the one true problem of salvation. But personal problems helped the clients themselves separate the important from the trivial and provided an overwhelming impetus to follow the specified treatment. In the terms of chapter 2, then, such problems were not part of the clergy's diagnostic or therapeutic classification systems. Rather they helped in colligation and prescription, the brokering processes between actual professional work and client experience.[3]

This situation did not long endure. By the last quarter of the century, external forces made this general area of work more important and more extensive. Sweeping social changes created new problems for individuals and required their solution. The list of these changes is familiar: the emergence of large factories and corporations, the appearance of activist governments, the increase in physical and social mobility, the rise of cities, the immigration of a new underclass. We commonly think of these as social changes, but they were experienced, perhaps in a new way, as personal problems in particular individuals' biographies.[4]

For some individuals, mostly upper- and upper-middle-class males, the new society meant emancipation from traditional relationships. This emancipation was both loved and feared. On the one hand, it brought new opportunities. On the other, it brought a frightening dependence on chance and personal skill. The weight of this dependence was widely recognized.

It is obviously only the obverse of this freedom if, under certain circumstances, one nowhere feels as lonely and lost as in the metropolitan crowd. For here as elsewhere it is by no means necessary that the freedom of man be reflected in his emotional life as comfort.

For many minutes, for many hours, for a bleak eternity he lay awake, shivering, reduced to primitive terror, comprehending that he had won freedom, and wondering what he could do with anything so unknown and so embarrassing as freedom.

It was vital to society that this freedom be successfully endured. As traditional and local bonds unraveled, social solidarity itself came to rest on the ability of these newly free individuals to integrate personally their diverse social roles. An affiliative society depended much more heavily on the integration of the personality than did a traditional one.[5]

For others in the society, however, freedom was not the problem. Lower-class men, and many middle-class men as well, found themselves restricted and constrained by large organizations, in which traditional work habits had little place. The pace, time, and intensity of men's work, the use of their skills, all were determined by the employing organization. Simultaneously, the weakening of such traditional systems of support as the family and local charity and welfare made individual families more dependent than ever on these organizations. At the same time, a contented and effective labor force became vital to employers. There resulted an extensive social and individual interest in the adjustment of individuals to the new working conditions. Since there was little likelihood that conditions would change, the men must be changed to fit them.[6]

A similar loss of control confronted the women of the nineteenth century. The separation of work and home left many women homebound custodians of families, bound to the economic system only by their husbands' jobs and their own unpaid labor as consumers. While some new opportunities arrived within the new women's colleges and in certain sections of the work force, the new "women's sphere" was in fact quite circumscribed. For most higher status women, Sinclair Lewis's words held true: "She was a woman with a working brain and no work. There were only three things which she could do: have children, start her career of reforming, or become so definitely a part of the town that she would be fulfilled by the activities of church and study club and bridge parties." The world of lower-class women was even more limited, although for these women such limitation may have been less of a change.[7]

The new personal problems can also be seen in social activities themselves. That the new society greatly valued the adjustment of person to place is clear from its pervasive interest in social control, which increased in level and detail, and in contexts both formal and informal. The new society defined public drunkenness and other minor misbehaviors as crimes. Its rules of etiquette regulated informal life in community and home. Even sickness was regulated. On the one hand, invalidism lost its legitimacy and sickness was allowed only in hospital. On the other, the regularization of economic life assigned illness a clear economic importance, and for the first time, employers studied work time lost to minor illness.[8]

This rising concern with social order in general was echoed in a corresponding increase in attention to personal "order" in particular. A mass of "positive thinking" movements and psychic cults arose, all aiming to return to the individual a control and security he believed himself to have lost. Club life flowered both among older organizations like the Masons and the Odd Fellows and among the more recent Knights of Pythias, Shriners, and Elks. Not content with these, Americans founded the Knights of Columbus (1882), Moose (1887), Woodmen of the World (1890), Rotary (1905), Kiwanis (1914), and Lions (1917), to mention only major organizations. Fraternal and service organizations explicitly emphasized that they offered men a stability they had lost.[9]

For our purposes here, perhaps the most important evidence of the new personal problems was not the general rise in social control but the professionally defined epidemic of "nerves" and nerve ailments attributed to those problems. Were there no theoretical grounds for expecting a rise in personal problems, nor other evidence of public concern with personal problems, one might suspect this professionally perceived epidemic as a pure invention. But the alternate evidence makes it clear that the professions, too, were identifying a real but inchoate problem. Medically analyzed by Beard, Edes, and many others, the nervous diseases had become a fixture of American experience by 1910. "It used to be believed that only the rich, the well-to-do, and the over-refined discover at last that they have nerves. Now we know that nervousness recognizes no class distinctions." By the 1920s, when the first data is available, Americans were taking hypnotic medications at a rate exceeded only by cough, rheumatism, and stomach remedies. Sodium bromide, a nerve tonic, followed only aspirin and codeine in the list of most common prescription ingredients.[10]

There is, then, clear evidence for a sudden increase in the level and importance of personal problems with life at the end of the nineteenth century. General unhappiness was a new and newly important cultural fact. Like all new areas of work, it had various claimants; clubs and other lay groups absorbed much of it. But like all such problems, it also became the target for professional claims. These claims would give subjective definition to the loose objective reality generated by the great social changes of the nineteenth century, turning them now into everyday life problems, now into nervous diseases, now into emotional problems.

## The First Response to "American Nervousness"

Two professional groups tried to assert cultural jurisdiction over the new personal problems: the clergy and the neurologists. The clergy tried to absorb the work through a slow change in their prior construction of personal difficulties. The neurologists developed new theories to handle particular parts of the area, only later seeking a complete jurisdiction. These two major groups had a number of minor competitors. Among these were a group of "gynecological neurologists," who provide a useful example of failure in jurisdictional competition.

The mid-nineteenth-century clergy's approach to personal problems had been evangelical. God spoke through personal problems; people responded through religious renewal. As the century waned, a new view emerged that one might call pastoral. Sympathy and support should come first; only then should the clergyman evangelize. As one author put it, "Show your sympathy by simply pressing the sufferer's hand rather than by insisting prematurely on any Christian truth, however precious."[11]

This view made personal problems a legitimate, independent element in the clergy's diagnostic classification scheme. No longer were they simply helpful reminders of the important matters of life. Rather, they enjoyed an independent existence and called for treatment in right of that existence. The proper treatment was sympathy and support, coupled with referral to other professionals if it was appropriate—a doctor for chronic pain, a banker for financial problems, and so on. The clergy as yet did not formally separate unhappiness with life from minor illness or financial difficulties; all went under the newly legitimated category of personal problems. To be sure, referral to other professions implicitly categorized these problems. And clergy did see themselves as the appropriate professionals in the case of marital problems and other "purely personal" matters, basing this claim on an intimate knowledge of human nature acquired on the job.

But despite these implicit distinctions, clergy analysis remained primitive. The gradual recognition of personal problems as legitimate categories of professional work did not bring a serious clergy effort to conceptualize them. The clergy's failure to provide any academic foundation for their practice with personal problems ultimately proved their undoing. If another profession should establish relevant diagnostic, therapeutic, and inferential systems and legitimate these in terms of general values, the clergy's simpleminded cultural jurisdiction would be easily usurped. In the period after 1880, another profession made precisely such a foray into the personal problems area. Working specifically with problems of unspecified chronic illness, neurologists laid the foundations of the jurisdiction that would eventually belong to the twentieth century psychotherapeutic professions.

The neurologists' public invasion of personal problems began with the publication of George M. Beard's *American Nervousness* in 1881.[12] A young, colorful, and elite specialty, neurology's roots lay in Civil War field surgery. As neurologists returned to peacetime work, they came to occupy a peculiarly strategic role. In theory, their work was unified by the common factor of association with nerves. In practice, their clienteles were increasingly made up of people who perplexed other doctors. As general medicine acquired serious therapeutic power, it became less patient with those it couldn't cure. Clients with chronic minor problems were referred to consultants, and many of these, for one reason or another, happened to be neurologists. "Nerves" became a general stopgap expression for the medical profession, much as "virus" is today. When neurologists formalized their construction of the personal problems jurisdiction, then, they did so not as an overt act of medicalization, the kind of metaphorical work involved in making, say, obesity a "disease" in the twentieth century. Rather they aimed to rationalize their own knowledge system and make sense of a clientele whose shape was largely out of their control. To understand, then, how the personal problems jurisdiction took shape, we must study the neurologists' knowledge system—the machinery of their subjective jurisdiction—in some detail.[13]

As their situation implied, the neurologists' clientele was not very homogeneous. As long as the theme of nerves entered somewhere—in symptoms, etiology, pathology, or physiology—a disease could be located under the new specialty. Neurologists handled most endocrine diseases because of their spectacular nervous symptoms. They treated inflammatory diseases of nervous tissue like polio, nerve degenerations like Parkinson's disease, and idiopathic brain diseases like epilepsy. They also handled dozens of "occupational neuroses" like the "writers cramp" of pretypewriter clerks, which were the immediate physical results of the new pace of work. Finally, they dealt with a wide variety of so-called functional neuroses—hysteria, neurasthenia, and their relatives.

Academic knowledge of these diseases was itself haphazard. When symptom, picture, and prognosis combined into a recognizable process, texts spoke of a disease. But less than half of a typical nineteenth-century neurology text involved such specifiable diseases. Texts were generally organized by some single dimension of the professional classification system, often site of pathology. Under the various sites would be listed diseases (e.g., polio), symptoms (neuralgia), pathological processes (progressive muscular atrophy), and causes (traumatic neuroses). The heterogeneity of these lists did not signify scientific primitivism, but rather reflected the uneven knowledge characteristic of an active discipline. Academic neurological knowledge accumulated very rapidly but remained in the disassembled state that makes academic knowledge relatively useless for practice. As I argued in chapter 2, academic research typically studies certain dimensions of professional knowledge to the exclusion of the others. In neurology, researchers focused on pathology and differentiation of clinical pictures. Texts were often theoretically unified along one of these dimensions, but were not very coherent as manuals of practice, since they were often written to support an academic argument. The academic discipline of neurology was indeed among the most prestigious in medicine, commanding many of the ablest medical minds of Europe, as well as a brilliant generation of Americans.

The *applied* professional knowledge of this field, however, very much reflected its position as residuary legatee of medicine. For some time it seemed that the criterion for inclusion of a disease under the jurisdiction of neurology was its untreatability. Between 1885 and 1925, neurology lost control over precisely those diseases for which it learned effective treatments—the endocrine diseases and the neurological sequelae of syphilis. Successful or not, most treatment was multiple treatment. There were treatment fads—electrotherapy, rest cures, hydrotherapy, psychotherapy—but each of these treatments was usually employed within a larger and more complex treatment approach.[14]

Neurology's treatments were etiological. Since specific causes were usually unknown, neurology generally fell back on the "predisposing" causes (such qualities as race, climate, lifestyle, and general health) and the "precipitating" causes (specific antecedents of a particular attack—overwork, emotional traumas, masturbation). Treatment meant removing these various causes. Some predisposing causes, of course, could not be removed; the "neurotic diathesis," for example, was a hereditary state thought to dispose individuals to functional neurosis. Precipitating causes might also be ineradicable, like malaria and some other chronic diseases. Removal of predisposing and precipitating causes was, however, supplemented by symptomatic treatment. An extensive array of braces helped the various occupational paralyses, while a vast arsenal of sedatives, hypnotics, and stimulants controlled the general nervous symptoms of elation, sleep disturbance, and depression.[15]

The plodding obtusity of neurological treatment was not repeated in diagnosis. By subtle signs and symptoms, neurologists differentiated dozens of diseases. As specialists in the residuals of a larger jurisdiction, neurologists could not organize their diagnosis as ordinary professions do. Most professions diagnose common problems directly, employing rationalized diagnostic procedures only when common syndromes are excluded. In neurology the situation was nearly reversed. Since there were only a few easily recognized syndromes, the discipline exercised an extremely artful differential diagnosis, based on a proliferating key of signs and symptoms.

The relative untreatability of the nervous diseases meant that diagnosis evolved without reference to treatment. Again this situation reversed that in regular medicine. There, common diseases were increasingly found to have external pathogens whose removal constituted effective treatment. Such treatments directed diagnostic attention to the pathogen itself and away from the body's general state. So unused were neurologists to this feedback between diagnosis and treatment that many were unimpressed by the demonstration of pathogens in tabes and paresis, insisting at least until the mid-1910s on the existence of "nonsyphilitic pseudotabes," and arguing that the spirochete was "not a direct factor but prepares the system for the degenerative process."[16]

This unwillingness to make diagnosis a treatment-based, operational system correlated with the neurologists' holistic inference system. Here, too, no aspect of bodily function was excluded from the analysis. Since most neurological problems were chronic, neurologists had

many chances to handle a problem and possessed, as professions working with such problems usually do, a carefully exclusionary inference
system. The complexity of this system made neurology as much a hermeneutic art as a natural science. As a result, the neurological jurisdiction proved a fertile ground for interprofessional poaching. The nonroutine character of the inferential system permitted no demonstration
of how professional knowledge worked, and the residuality of the clientele meant that in fact it seldom did. It was therefore difficult for
neurology to legitimate itself. As long as there were no alternatives,
such a cultural jurisdiction could stand. When alternatives appeared,
they triumphed quickly.

This ramshackle system of knowledge—powerfully scientific in the
academy but profusely idiosyncratic in practice—constituted neurology's claim to cultural jurisdiction over these problems. It governed a
variegated clientele. About one-quarter of neurologists' patients had
general disease states like epilepsy and hemiplegia; one-tenth had inflammatory diseases like polio and tabes, and a like amount had localized paralyses. Most importantly, about one-quarter to one-third of the
typical patients were diagnosed as having "general nervousness," a
category later labeled as "neurasthenia" and "psychasthenia." Such patients complained of persistent but vague physical discom-
forts—usually gastrointestinal, cardiac, or uterine—and extensive
"nervous" symptoms: the things we now call headache, depression,
anxiety, insomnia, and so on. All of these patients felt themselves to
have serious medical complaints. For us who recognize personal problems as fully legitimate objects of professional jurisdiction, it is hard to
envision milkmaid's spasm, trifacial neuralgia, and general nervousness
as serious medical complaints. Indeed, as the new century wore on,
the level of symptomatology characteristic of neurologists' clienteles
persistently declined. But even the early psychoanalysts—most of
them neurologists by background—treated patients with major physical symptoms like paralyses and localized neuralgia.[17]

The neurologists considered general nervousness to be a "functional" neurosis. Like all nervous diseases, functional neuroses had
both organic and psychic predisposing and precipitating causes. In a
few cases, they ultimately proved to be attributable to physiological
disfunction; myxedema, goiter, tetany, and the other endocrine diseases were all considered functional neuroses in the late nineteenth
century. In most cases, however, such clear origins never appeared.
General nervousness was one such syndrome. Discussions about it
thus included complex theories about both psychic and organic eti-

ology, and indeed about the relation between the two. The disease was treated in equally diverse ways, ranging from Mitchell's celebrated rest cure to electrotherapy and psychotherapy.

Case literature reveals clearly that general nervousness recorded the impact of the great social changes earlier discussed. Dozens of reports attribute medical symptoms directly to social causes—to husbands' being absent on work assignments, to wives' being new to rural life, to family and economic troubles. Responses to these changes were diverse, but not a few individuals reacted to these new situations by identifying diffuse medical symptoms in themselves. They went to local doctors, who found no serious illness and passed the patients on to neurologists if possible. Thus the neurologists' general nervousness was the first serious alternative to the clergy's definition of personal problems.[18]

This alternative construction of personal problems differed from the clergy's in essential ways. First, it was narrower. Many personal problems important to clergymen had no direct interest for neurologists. Financial difficulties, marital problems, and the like became relevant only when they generated or appeared to generate medical symptoms. Second, it was more specific than any clergy definition. There was a syndrome of general nervousness, with signs and symptoms, with causes and mechanisms. If this concept lacked the specific, detailed understanding that came later, neither was it simply a general category of personal problems interpretable by a general knowledge of human nature. Finally, the neurologists had concrete therapies—the rest cure, electrotherapy, psychotherapy—that attacked this problem in particular ways. As I argued in chapter 2, disciplines with specific therapies will generally defeat those with only vague therapies when results are equal. Thus the neurologists, who in fact accomplished little more for general nervousness than did the clergymen, won the day. Although they accomplished no more, they inspected and tested and argued, giving themselves at least the scientific legitimacy of observation and criticism.

A number of other groups invaded the new problem area, and it is instructive to see why they failed. The "gynecological neurologists" provide such an example.[19] This small and loosely identified group attempted to claim all nervous diseases for "real medicine," that is, for the pathogenic model of illness. Like many neurologists, gynecologist H. R. Storer was impressed by the preponderance of women in the nervous population. Unlike them, however, he attributed male nervousness to misdiagnosis and traced female nervous disease, through a complex network of reflexes and endocrines, to the female reproductive organs. Like neurology, gynecology was just establishing itself as a specialty at this point. If neurologists could claim any disease related to nerves, gynecologists could claim any disease related to the female reproductive system, in particular, any nervous diseases related to that system, a relation sometimes conceded or urged by the neurologists themselves.

Treatments reflecting this theory soon appeared. Most were standard gynecological procedures; old therapies with new justifications. But in 1872 R. Battey announced the removal of ovaries in a particularly intractable case of ovarian neuralgia (i.e., menstrual cramps). After ten years of furor, the operation disappeared. But the theory lingered. A new school arose attributing mental disease to gynecological disorders, with a renewed flurry of operations. From 16 to 25 percent of all women in asylums "are there because of the special infirmities of their sex and the disasters and penalties of their lives as wives and mothers," said A. T. Hobbs. But this school, too, passed away rapidly.[20]

Gynecological neurology illustrates well why some attempts at jurisdiction fail. The a priori denial of the male third of the nervous clientele lost the movement any real chance of subjective jurisdiction. First, it created an enormous residual category, which was itself open to invasion by outsiders. Second, and much more important, the lack of a theory tracing *male* nervous disease to *male* reproductive organs lost the group all pretence of comprehensiveness, and hence of scientific legitimacy. In fact, male reproductive organs *had* been removed in cases of neuralgia, but without any theoretical rationale beyond the symptomatic one of removing what hurts. Finally, gynecological neurology's therapy was very weak. On the one hand, it reflected a complex and questionable theory of etiology. On the other, its immediate motivation seemed so trivial (if it hurts, take it out), that clients must have had a hard time perceiving it as scientifically legitimate. Also, of course, it violated general surgical norms about removing healthy tissue.[21]

The gynecological incursion into this area never commanded serious medical attention, beyond the rage over Battey's operation. But it does illustrate the many attempts to enter the personal problems jurisdiction. Ovarian and uterine neuralgia were central complaints in that jurisdiction, as they were in the clienteles of the neurologists. There was thus a vast potential area for jurisdiction. The gynecological seizure failed only because the subjective properties assigned to those problems by the gynecological neurologists were not sufficient foundations for cultural jurisdiction. They were filled with what were even at that time irrationalities and illegitimacies; the gynecologists wanted to bend the objective task further than the culture would let them. There were many other such attempts to enter the personal problems jurisdiction; "focal infection" of dental tissue and lack of proper ophthalmic care both had brief careers as explanations of nervous and mental diseases. Indeed, as it happened, one such group did win the battle for this jurisdiction, not embodying a particular etiological approach, but rather a particular therapy. But psychotherapy was between 1880 and 1920 just another of the competing therapeutic schools, used extensively by a few neurologists but occasionally by nearly all their colleagues and by many nonspecialists as well.[22]

The neurologists' entry into the jurisdiction of personal problems reshaped the area subjectively but did not substantially change workplace practice. The neurologists were a small and elite group, no more than a few hundred in 1900. To protect their prestige, they required members of their association to have rigorous training and to pursue original scientific research. Since the training involved apprenticeship at an elite institution, and since research was largely impossible elsewhere, the neurologists were a demographically rigid group, incapable of rapid expansion.[23]

Yet they had seized an enormous jurisdiction. There were always clients waiting, men and women of all social classes. Thus the actual jurisdictional settlement was not domination, but intellectual jurisdiction. Neurology supplied the ideas that constructed the work, while others supplied most of the service. Clergymen outnumbered neurologists more than five hundred to one, and so maintained their central role in service. Of similar importance were nonspecialist doctors, who equaled the clergy in numbers and distribution. But these nonspecialists were growing less willing to treat personal problems along with medical ones, particularly now that neurology had supplied subjective categories for separating the two. With their withdrawal would come a large workplace demand for service.

Neurology developed first in the cities, and neurologists did achieve workplace control of the medical version of personal problems in New York, Boston, and Philadelphia by the last years of the century. This local *workplace* settlement supported a *public* claim spread more widely by the ever-increasing mass media. Like any intellectual jurisdiction, the neurologists' control of "general nervousness" affected public discourse more than it did either the workplace or the legal definitions of professional work. It is true that the positive-thinking movements vigorously supported lay approaches to personal problems. But the neurologists dominated the professional discussion and much of the public literature.[24]

This domination was serendipitously aided by the clergy's move towards a more explicitly social approach to problems of everyday life. Washington Gladden and other social gospelers attributed many of these personal problems directly to such social causes as poverty, unemployment, and rootlessness. At the same time, Gladden defined the pastor-client relation as one of friendship, strongly opposing "unbending professionalism." Gladden did see the personal problems field as a vast potential: "How much there is, in every community, of anxiety and disappointment and heartbreaking sorrow that never comes to the surface. . . . The pastor has as little reason to complain of it as the doctor has to complain of a multiplicity of patients." But the progressive clergy looked to social structures as the ultimate origin of these problems, and to church-based social welfare agencies as their proper treatment. This new construction of everyday life problems appealed to many legitimating values: to egalitarianism, to efficiency, to altruism. But it made little appeal to science. And its diagnoses more reflected general social criticism than skilled investigations, while its treatments required social changes that elites found unacceptable. Nonetheless, prominent clergy urged this approach to everyday life problems for a decade or more, leaving the individual approaches to them open to the lay mind cure movements and the neurologists.[25]

By the last years of the nineteenth century, then, some of the problems forced on individuals by massive social change had begun to receive formal definition in medical terms. The clergy's earlier definition of personal problems as signposts on the road to salvation was substantially weakened both by the flood of new problems and by the new medical definition. Since the new medical definition embraced only part of the new work, and since the neurologists could serve only a fraction of the work they claimed, personal difficulties were generally dealt with as they had been before, by clergy on the old model or by other professionals on an advice-only, nonprofessional basis. The rapidly rising problems drew other claimants, to be sure, but none of these made a serious mark. The clergy itself met them with a new set of definitions, the social gospel, but this proved unacceptable until secularized—a process that occurred through the withdrawal of social work from its clergy tutelage. Indeed, social work came ultimately to accept the neurologists' approach, as we shall see. For the time being, however, there was a shadowy but immense area of work and only one set of definitions working directly within it.[26]

## The Psychiatric Revolution

At this point, there entered the personal-problems scene a new group, the psychiatrists. Between 1900 and 1920, the psychiatrists gradually merged with the neurologists. The merged groups then split along new lines during the twenties. To follow this transformation, it is necessary that we first turn back into the nineteenth century to find where these invaders came from and why.[27]

Psychiatry was created in the middle years of the nineteenth century by the gradual removal of the insane from workhouses and jails to institutions specially created for them. Transformed by a long history of euphemism from "lunatic asylums" into "mental hospitals" and more recently "mental health centers," these institutions had originated in a lay reform movement. But the medical men who ran them rapidly became a successful profession with dominant jurisdiction. (The medical dominance can, of course, be seen in the first name change.) Although their system of diagnosis was not strong—paresis was perhaps the only accurately specified disease—psychiatrists' treatment was powerfully organized by the ideology of moral therapy, which promised complete cures under the properly detailed regimentation of the activities, the emotions, and the environment of the insane. By the last years of the century, however, moral therapy had proved a clear failure. Although its last defenders blamed the states for expanding hospitals beyond the 250 patients required for effective moral therapy, in fact even small hospitals produced few cures. Although the failure of moral therapy put psychiatrists' jurisdiction in an embarrassing position, there were no real competitors, and psychiatrists retained control by default. But at the same time, the states' decision to house the steadily growing numbers of the insane in massive central hospitals, rather than in dozens of smaller, peripheral ones, transformed the profession. It led to the rapid growth of a subordinate class of physicians, the assistant physicians, who performed the medical work of the asylums under the direction of the superintendents.

At the time when neurologists were first specializing in the residual problems of nonspecialist doctors, the psychiatrists' American Medico-Psychological Association had just officially absorbed the assistant physicians (1885). This made psychiatry a profession based on a body of knowledge, rather than on an organizational location, and freed it for motion in the system of professions. There was good reason to move. The insane had proved resiliently intractable to a half century of serious scientific work. Generations of clinical psychiatry had led to Kraepelin's massive synthesis of the diagnostic literature, but there was still

no decent theory about the origins of insanity. There was much pathological work, but few results. Direct treatment was largely impossible,
and even symptomatic treatment generally hopeless. As a result, psychiatry was a kind of profession in reverse. It controlled an important
jurisdiction with a steadily growing demand but could use little more
than administrative knowledge in its activities. Of its treatments, only
incarceration had any effect, and that made the psychiatrists little different from the jailers they had replaced, despite their legitimation by
reference to the medical model of science, treatment, and cure. It is
little wonder that psychiatrists burned out at an alarming rate; superintendents typically lasted six years in their positions, assistants two or
three. The rapid turnover meant an equally rapid recruitment of new
members. The profession was thus expanding rapidly in potential
membership, but finding its basic work—the cure of the insane—
impossible to accomplish. The profession responded to this crisis with
an intellectual invasion of areas of social control adjacent to that of the
insane. Led by the academic wing of the profession, these assaults
were conducted in public media and interprofessional meetings. Some
of them were accompanied by serious workplace expansions; most
were not.[28]

Psychiatry's intellectual expansion into social control is the first invasion we have seen that began within the academic wing of a profession. The reasons for academic leadership lie in the extreme centralization of the profession's elite. One could identify by 1900 a handful
of organizations dominating the discipline: certain state hospitals
(Utica, Danvers, and Kankakee); the elite private hospitals (McLean,
Bloomingdale, Pratt, and Pennsylvania): and prestigious public facilities (the New York Psychiatric Institute and the federal government's
St. Elizabeth's Hospital). Along with the New York and Massachusetts
state hospital systems, these institutions were the only professionally
exciting locations for the young, academically trained psychiatrist. But
the generation of 1880 to 1900 filled them to capacity, and waiting
times to promotion became insufferably long. Elite institutions trained
many but could hire few. In fact training in institutional psychiatry
proved to be relatively untransferable from state to state, except
among the elite institutions of the East Coast. Elsewhere, political or
home-state appointments were the rule. As a result, a generation of
bright young psychiatrists left these institutions looking for work. They
were but a tiny minority of those considering psychiatry as a career—the majority of those being assistant physicians at peripheral
institutions. But they were an intellectual minority, and while their
numbers could not support a workplace invasion of other professions'

jurisdictions, their minds could mount a very serious assault indeed on the public conceptions of those jurisdictions.[29]

The situation of these psychiatrists can be well contrasted with that of the solicitors and lawyers of the preceding chapter. All three groups were strongly professionalized in the sense of possessing strong professional institutions and organizations. Yet the psychiatrists' elite training institutions produced more graduates than existing work could absorb. The solicitors' slower, but equally elite, apprenticeship system could not produce enough solicitors to serve existing demand. The American lawyers were overproducing, but not in the elite sector of the profession. Only in American psychiatry, therefore, were young leaders driving out into new jurisdictions. Again, adventitious qualities of professional structure had profound system implications.

The general justification for these invasions was prevention. Psychiatrists reasoned that moral therapy failed because insanity reached a chronic state before psychiatrists saw it; one must stop the disease before it began. (Underneath this inference lay the [still] unproved assumption that untreated neurosis would degenerate into psychosis.) Of course, this assumption implied a direct invasion of the neurologists' jurisdictions. The neurologists, however, seem to have welcomed the new interest in prevention. Indeed, some earlier neurologists had themselves pressed the prevention idea in reverse, claiming psychiatry as an extension of neurology and thereby properly subordinate to neurology. The numbers of the psychiatrists, however, and their continuing possession of an independent base in the hospitals had made this claim insupportable. But the coincident interest of the two groups in prevention led to their joint efforts, with lay reformers, in the National Association for the Protection of the Insane and the Prevention of Insanity (1879–84). The association emphasized bodily and mental hygiene—abstinence from alcohol, tobacco, and sex on the one hand, practice of discipline, religion, "laudable emotions," and family life on the other. These emphases drew, of course, on the old "predisposing-cause" vocabulary of the neurologists. For the psychiatrists, such ideas represented a new departure. Psychiatric concepts of causality had emphasized anatomy, possibly to secure an otherwise precarious medical legitimacy. The new emphasis on prevention moved psychiatry away from its scientism by accepting the social origins often attributed to insanity by the public. Psychiatrists had long mocked the public's devotion to such "alleged causes of insanity" as religious fervor, disappointment in love, and so on. The concept of prevention accepted this public knowledge as substantial, bringing with it a tremendous potential for public appeal.[30]

Prevention gave the psychiatrists entrée to the neurological clientele, for psychiatrists considered neurasthenia, general nervousness, and so on as "borderline states" on the road to insanity. Between 1890 and 1920 there was a substantial interpenetration between the elites of the two professions—joint society memberships, careers traversing both specialties. Indeed specialists in the area were generally called "specialists in nervous and mental disease." In the actual workplace, members of both groups applied the psychiatric treatment of institutionalization to a wider variety of diseases than insanity alone. Psychiatrists and neurologists led in the establishment of public institutions for the mentally retarded and for the epileptic. The period 1880–1920 was also the heyday of the private sanitarium for nervous disease; psychiatrists and neurologists founded large numbers of private institutions for the alcoholic and the drug addicted, as well as for the nervous members of the upper and middle classes. Those administering institutions for alcoholism were a particularly adventurous group, venturing into a rich jurisdiction then held by various therapeutic sects, the Keeleyite and "gold cure" therapists. Many of these workplace expansions fell victim to the same kind of limitations that destroyed gynecological neurology. There was little a priori reason to think institutionalization a reasonable treatment for these kinds of problems, and maintaining its legitimacy was difficult. Practitioners, particularly those dealing with the upper classes, had a hard time avoiding client interference; rich relations always knew the diagnosis better than the doctor, and rich patients often refused specific parts of the treatment as well.[31]

While this mixing with neurology proceeded, the most adventurous of the younger psychiatric generation pushed hard on psychiatry's border with the legal profession. Mental-disease specialists claimed a prominent role in celebrated trials, some criminal (Guiteau and Csolgosz), some civil (Eddy and McCormick). From time to time they argued that criminality was a disease and thus ought to be in the jurisdiction of psychiatrists, an argument that met with little success. A more effective public expansion came in the area of juvenile delinquency and other minor behaviors. William Healy, a Chicago neurologist, led this expansion in clinics in Chicago and Boston. By 1920 many large courts were employing psychiatrists to study juvenile offenders, serious foundation support was training young men in the area, and psychiatrists were poised to found a generation of "child guidance" clinics aimed at preventing delinquency.[32]

The reasons for psychiatry's success in establishing intellectual jurisdiction over juvenile delinquency were diverse. On the one hand, its chief competitor, social work, had failed to develop an adequate theory of social treatment to follow its systematization of "social diagnosis." On the other, psychiatry had the advantage of the compellingly brilliant ideas of Freud, for Healy and the others had rapidly swung towards psychoanalysis. Certainly psychiatry was not hurt by the startlingly prominent role it played (in combination with neurology) in the First World War, dealing with shell shock, cowardice, and other psycho-military problems.[33]

Perhaps more importantly, psychiatry had evolved by the twenties a comprehensive theory of adjustment. From its first interest in prevention and indeed from the moral therapy era, psychiatry had been fascinated by the relation of the individual to society. The psychiatric concept of prevention attributed nervous and mental disease to failure of adjustment between individual and society, and assumed successful adjustment would prevent disease. Adjustment underlay every application of psychiatry to social control; young people must be adjusted to the orderly world, soldiers must be adjusted to trench warfare, workers must be adjusted to factories. "Psychiatry," said the Commonwealth Fund, "may do much to adjust human beings, children or adults, to tolerable conditions of life." The implicit assumptions of this theory were (1) that all social factors in nervous and mental disease were important only through their effect on the individual; (2) that any violation of social rules ("the mildest psychopathies, the faintest eccentricities") signified mental problems; and (3) that the proper approach to such problems was individual, not social. These assumptions made psychiatry's general theory of adjustment an enormous popular success. They accepted the new order of society, offered an interpretation for basic social problems, and thereby anchored the borders of the new world. The theory of adjustment rested on a sound combination of legitimating values—science, altruism, individualism, and above all, social orderliness. This combination, coupled with the therapeutic "successes" of the war years, proved sufficient to guarantee psychiatry's intellectual jurisdiction in juvenile delinquency and adjacent areas.[34]

The victory of psychiatry in the public jurisdiction of such social problems did little to handle the everyday problems of everyday human beings. The move of psychiatry into that area came in the workplace and without the public fanfare of the social control expansion. It partook, to be sure, of the same ideologies; adjustment was a central theme. But it was not, fundamentally, an ideological expansion. It was simply a move by psychiatrists into solo outpatient practice in nervous and mental disease.

The neurologists were, in fact, ready for help. L.P. Clark said in 1917: "I would venture to say that at least half the average neurologist's practice is, in its broadest sense, psychologic, if not distinctly psychiatric. . . . If psychiatrists would but more fully realize their obligations . . . it would result in fewer psychologists practicing medicine." In fact, it had become quite clear by 1910 that neurology had claimed far more jurisdiction than it could effectively service. Public assertions were one thing; workplace fact another. Neurology's texts claimed vast areas of medical work; prestigious neurologists like Joseph Collins and Frederick Peterson wrote books and newspaper articles carrying these claims to a larger audience. But in the workplace, neurology could not hope to service all these areas, since it remained small and elite by choice.[35]

This imbalance found its inevitable result in external invasions. The psychologists of whom Clark spoke were not numerous enough to threaten the area until well into the 1920s. A much more serious threat came from within medicine. Late-nineteenth-century medicine produced a number of movements that brought together physicians and laymen interested in a particular therapy or, later, a particular group of diseases. A number of these groups invaded the large neurological jurisdiction of "problems insoluble with standard medical intervention," of which the identified syndrome of "general nervousness" was only a part. The most successful was the group interested in "internal secretions," which involved many neurologists. This group split in the teens from that specialty (and from physiology) to form the specialty of endocrinology. Another protospecialty—dermatology and syphilology—absorbed much of the neurologists' work with syphilis and its sequelae. Less successful than these were a variety of groups organized around therapies. Most of these were physical therapies like electrotherapy, hydrotherapy, and kinesotherapy. (The groups merged in 1910; this merger is an excellent example of a professional group trying to find a defensible level of abstraction.) Because they ceded diagnosis to neurologists and other specialists, however, the physical-therapy groups could not emerge from medical domination.[36]

In their attempt to retain some workplace presence, however, the neurologists were helped by the steady flow of psychiatrists out of the mental hospitals. By 1920, about 2 percent of American physicians living had spent at least one year working in a mental hospital. These doctors undoubtedly served as protospecialists in many localities, their experience guaranteeing referrals of nervous and mental disease cases. This group of nervous and mental disease specialists was both more numerous and more widely distributed than the neurologists. It is this group, identified as psychiatrists by its past affiliation with mental hospitals, that is meant in the phrase "psychiatry moved into working with personal problems in the workplace."[37]

The situation by 1920 was therefore a complex one. Psychiatrists and neurologists were loosely bound together. The AMA, along with the most widespread texts, used the phrase "nervous and mental disease" to denote the joint specialty. Most neurologists were members of the American Psychiatric Association, although relatively few psychiatrists were members of the much smaller American Neurological Association. The prior division remained implicit in the biographies of practitioners and in the continuing existence of separate training, although many self-identified neurologists had had mental hospital experience. For outpatient practitioners, however, the work content of practice was the same regardless of prior career pattern. This delicate merger of psychiatry and neurology rested on theories loosely combining prior neurological knowledge with the new psychiatric theory of adjustment. But no academic ever successfully integrated the two into a synthetic theory, and nervous and mental diseases continued as two largely independent sections in prominent texts, although, of course, the prior neurological texts had never had much synthetic organization in any case. Treatment continued the weakest aspect of the area, with psychotherapy and various forms of physical therapy administered in combinations suggested by the nature of the case.

## The Rise of Psychotherapy

This temporary profession of nervous and mental disease was destroyed by a particular sect, that of psychotherapy. The medical movement supporting psychotherapy was part of a much larger movement that involved large areas of American life. Characterized by Donald Meyer as the "positive thinkers," people like Mary Baker Eddy had argued that minor physical problems as well as a host of other personal difficulties would yield to the disciplined and liberated mind. These mind-cure movements were not primarily professional movements, although they spawned such professional offspring as Christian Science healers and medical psychotherapists. Rather, they were lay movements aimed at securing the personal-problems jurisdiction for a group of loose organizations that looked and functioned like churches, but whose staffs did not resemble regularly organized professions. (A few did. Founded in the nineties, the Unity School had become a standard Protestant sect by the middle of this century.) These movements all explicitly began with laicization and deprofessionalization. The individual was to be architect of her (much more than his) fate.[38]

The laicization of personal problems created less perceived threat to medicine than did the laicization of standard medical work, and the incursion of Christian Science and its relatives into organic medicine of course met overwhelming resistance. In the personal-problems area, however, some doctors collaborated with other professionals and lay people investigating issues. In the societies for psychical research of the 1880s, subcommittees on psychopathology featured several prominent nervous and mental disease specialists. The *Journal of Medical Hypnosis* reported results from a daily clinic and carried advertisements of several psychotherapeutic sanitariums. In the 1890s, the psychic movement strengthened and split, as psychoanalysis was later to do, over the issue of nonmedical psychotherapy. In 1898, the *Journal of Medical Hypnosis* split into the medical *Suggestive Therapy* and the popular *Suggestions*.

Intellectually, these skirmishes on the fringes of neurology's jurisdiction probably had little effect on that profession. Psychotherapy was well known to those familiar with European medicine, and several medical schools taught it. After 1905, the neurologists, and indeed medicine in general, began to pay much more attention to psychotherapy, perhaps because of the visit of the celebrated French neurologist Pierre Janet, perhaps because of the publication of Dubois's *Psychic Treatment of Nervous Diseases*. But the therapy was still just one among many, and was applied to *all* nervous and mental diseases, both those we would presently call organic and those we would not. This polytherapeutics did not imply a disbelief in psychic etiology. On the contrary, as I noted earlier, the neurologists and psychiatrists made such psychic causes as the "stress of modern living" or "disappointed affections" responsible for much of nervous and mental disease. Yet the direct connection between psychic etiologies and psychic treatments was not made. Diseases with both kinds of origins received both kinds of treatment.[39]

But if the academic jurisdiction of the neurologists was not threatened, their public and workplace jurisdictions were. Irregular psychotherapies and laicizers clearly seized the public imagination. Even within the system of professions itself, there eventually came a very visible attempt by mainline clergy to retake the jurisdiction of everyday life problems by amalgamating psychotherapy and religion. The new clergy approach accepted medical diagnoses of the new problems of life, but advocated a religious treatment for them. Named for a Boston church, the Emmanuel Movement began in 1909. E. S. Worcester, an Episcopal rector with a Ph.D. in psychology, advocated using "the Christian religion as a healing power," aiming at the "alleviaton and arrest of certain disorders of the nervous system which are now generally regarded as involving some weakness or defect of character or more or less complete mental dissociation." The list of potential clients included "nervous sufferers, victims of alcohol and other drugs, the unhappy, the sorrowful, would-be suicides, and other children of melancholy." Other Emmanuelists reported seeing mostly neurasthenics and psychasthenics, whom they normally had diagnosed by local physicians. (Worcester's own collaborator was the psychiatrist Isidor Coriat.) The Emmanuel Movement was not a serious workplace threat. But its elite origins and visibility made it a dangerous public threat, particularly to those doctors employing psychotherapy. Afraid of losing legitimacy before medical colleagues, they assaulted the Emmanuelists in a variety of public forums and crushed them within two or three years. For the next forty years legitimate psychotherapy was to be an official, public monopoly of the medical profession.[40]

By the 1920s, the nervous and mental disease specialty also faced newly serious workplace invasions. One came from psychology. Lightner Witmer had long run a children's clinic at the University of Pennsylvania, using psychological testing to discover the origins of personal problems. The psychologists had further demonstrated their independence by splitting away from the Surgeon General's Division of Neurology and Psychiatry during the war and organizing an independent division around mental testing. Most importantly, the war had made testing tremendously visible. The psychologists could argue that many personal and work problems arose in maladjustment of individuals to jobs, something measurable by their tests. While this offered the individual little help, its potential worth to corporations was immense, and psychologists immediately took over most industrial work with employee problems, rapidly expanding into schools as well. The nervous and mental disease specialists, despite a brief attempt, never had much success in this portion of their potential jurisdiction of personal problems.[41]

Another competitor arose within the new demonstration clinics founded by the adjustment school of psychiatrists. There, social workers were finding individual approaches to personal problems far more congenial than the social-diagnosis paradigm bequeathed to them by Mary Richmond. The individual approaches, which they borrowed directly from psychiatry, offered therapeutic answers that casework did not. The social adjustments necessary to treat a typical social work client were often not possible; clients couldn't quit work for a while, agencies didn't have enough spaces for problem children, employers would not change policies. How much more attractive to deal with the individual or family as a self-enclosed unit to be adjusted to society, rather than society to it. Psychiatric social work flourished during the twenties, becoming the most prestigious of the social work specialties. It too represented a potential workplace threat.[42]

Environed by these various competitors and fellow-travelers, the loosely unified nervous and mental disease specialty divided rapidly into two groups with old names but new identities. In the new system, "neurologists" gave organic treatments to patients who had diseases with organic etiology, and "psychiatrists" gave psychic treatments to patients who had diseases with psychic etiologies. To the latter group went the jurisdiction of helping people who were anxious, depressed, and upset with their everyday life. It retained as well the jurisdiction of the insane, with the caveat that any patient with a demonstrably organic psychosis—pellagra psychosis, paresis, and the like—should be treated organically. The proximate cause of this division was, of course, the work of Freud. But the structural cause was the presence of serious external competition for work with people's problems with life—the clergy, the psychologists, the social workers, as well as the not-inconsiderable group of irregular "clergy" associated with the original mind-cure churches—the Unity Church, the New Thought Alliance, Christian Science.

The nervous and mental disease specialty thus survived by restructuring its cultural jurisdiction. In order to make an effective settlement in law, public opinion, and the workplace, it redefined the problems with which it worked. The objective qualities of this work area did not change in the early twentieth century. The chief problems still arose through the dislocations of modern society, the mixture of frightening freedoms with intensifying controls. But the way these problems were constructed by the rapidly splitting profession changed considerably. By the 1930s, a firm subjective structure was created that would not require serious attention until the renewed competition of psychology and social work forced a rebiologizing of personal problems in the late 1970s.

There were four competing versions of the nervous-and-mental-disease construction of personal problems.[43] Each constituted a full model of proper practice; each articulated diagnosis, treatment, and inference in its own way. Two were eclectic paradigms aimed at retaining the unity of the field. The others assumed that the eclectic jurisdiction was illegitimately diverse and divided the jurisdiction between them. The two eclecticisms were essentially generational; there was the old version of C. L. Dana and M. A. Starr and the new version of A. Meyer and E. E. Southard. The divisive pair split over the organic-psychic issue; C. K. Mills, W. G. Spiller, and the other Philadelphia neurologists emphasized organic disease, while W. A. White, A. A. Brill, and the other American Freudians emphasized psychic disturbance. By reviewing these competing views in some detail, we can discover why the dividers were victorious.

Traditional eclecticism defined the neurological jurisdiction as we have already seen. The field was founded on particular syndromes and diseases isolated by extensive clinical practice. Diagnosis employed signs and symptoms to identify a case as a particular syndrome. It seldom led directly to treatment, which generally reflected an independent analysis of predisposing, precipitating, and anatomical causes, and used an extremely diverse armamentarium of cures. Diseases with close diagnosis-treatment linkages tended to be shed from the profession's jurisdiction.

Modern eclecticism, as argued by Adolf Meyer, combined organic, psychic, and environmental causes in a loose but formal system called psychobiology. The ambitious academic program of psychobiology aimed to investigate all these causes in a wide variety of cases and analyze the specific "reactions" involved in each case, ultimately aiming to find the general patterns of "reaction." This laudable but vague program foundered early, and new eclecticism in practice became utterly clinical. Meyer's clinical teaching held that each case was a unique system illustrating unique properties; the clinician's duty was to properly interpret it. Diagnosis ceded most of its professional role in such an approach. No factor was irrelevant, nor was there any publicly accepted classification of the "reactions" although Meyer and others set about slowly finding one. Treatment also atrophied in the face of this absolute preoccupation with professional inference.

By contrast, the organicism of Mills and the Freudianism of White offered specific definitions and approaches. Mills insisted on rigorous standards of diagnosis, increasingly demanding that verifiable signs replace patient symptoms as the foundation for diagnosis. These strict rules of colligation supported an equally strict system of classification; the Mills school sought finer and finer classifications of syndromes, while residualizing most of the unclassifiable area of the functional neuroses. In treatment, Mills was conservatively eclectic, but resolutely opposed the Freudians' "improper" use of psychotherapy, attacking particularly their excessive assumptions about the nature of psychic causality. (That is, he accused the Freudians of overlong and precarious inferential chains.) Not surprisingly, the Mills approach did relatively well with organic nervous diseases possessing evident and rectifiable pathology, while offering little to those whose health complaints were in fact somatizations of personal problems. These were a residual in which the Philadelphia school were uninterested.

The American Freudians, by contrast, offered a hope to precisely those people. They equated three things: (1) diseases displaying psychological symptoms but lacking either organic pathology or signs corroborating the symptoms, (2) diseases of psychic etiology, and (3) diseases amenable to psychotherapy. That is, Freudianism in America applied psychicism as its basic standard in diagnosis, in inference, and in treatment. There was no evidence at the time that separation of psychic from organic nervous and mental disease was logical in terms of then-accepted scientific canons. Indeed, students of "psychosomatic medicine" were soon to argue (with substantial evidence to back them up) that organic pathology and signs could have psychic etiology. Similarly, physicians had known for years that psychotherapy provided effective help for many organic diseases. But the Freudian approach was rigorous and consistent. No longer could endocrine diseases and epilepsy be considered functional neuroses, since they had clear organic signs or pathology. Nor could psychotherapy be legitimately applied to constipation and dyspepsia, nor psychic etiology be adduced in cases of general paresis. The rules of diagnosis and treatment would be rewritten to separate the two realms explicitly.[44]

Perhaps the most important reason for the success of Freudianism, however, was its approach to professional inference. Conservative eclecticism had been organized around syndromes. Since many of these were the residuals of general medicine, few had cures; the link of diagnosis and treatment was adventitious at best, reflecting a clinician's hermeneutic understanding of predisposing and precipitating causes. Meyerian eclecticism was organized around individuals and followed a similarly clinical hermeneutic of the individual reaction. Organic neurology took a conservative, scientific attitude towards inference, arguing that since mechanisms were generally not known, inference was seldom legitimate; treatment could be only palliative. Thus the alternatives to the Freudian inferential system included extreme individualism and conservative nihilism, but little in between.

But Freud gave explicit theories about psychic mechanism. After a few early papers on the traditional syndromes, he wrote chiefly about mechanisms and their relation to symptoms—anxiety, depression, mourning. His papers afforded a new and more logical hermeneutic, supporting an extensive professional inference. Syndromes appeared, but were defined by the causes that generated them—hysteria, obsession, compulsion. The etiologically based syndromes called for an etiologically based treatment, which Freud made a working through of blocked emotional conflicts.

The Freudian system avoided the problems of alternative jurisdictional models. To treat somatized personal problems as a merely residual category—as did Mills and Spiller—was to throw away the jurisdiction willfully. To treat each case as a unique ensemble of causes—as did Meyer—was to make all professional work inferential, which in turn made it impossible to legitimate professional work, since the lay public could not see how the system worked in a simple case. To continue to treat the problem as important and diagnosable but beyond medical understanding—as did the conservative eclectics—was to implicitly surrender the jurisdiction to quacks. Thus, irrespective of its veracity, the Freudian approach offered nearly the only effective solution to the continuous interprofessional competition nervous and mental disease professionals faced.

The functionality of the Freudian system did not guarantee its success, of course. Professional elites have often blocked the spread of reformist ideologies. But in this case it so happened that most of the elite training institutions were led by friends of psychoanalysis or, at the worst, by conservative eclectics who saw in it simply another therapeutic fad. The sheer brilliance of the Freudian system attracted many younger people who could not face the plodding decades required for developing the new eclecticism. As a result, Freudianism in one form or another rapidly became the organizing structure of a new jurisdiction, centered in fact on everyday life problems. Opposed to it was the equally coherent, and equally new, jurisdiction of organic neurology.[45]

Although these jurisdictions were in practice served by psychiatrists and neurologists jointly throughout the 1920s, by the end of the decade the split between the two was nearly complete. The generation of conservative eclectics was dead. The split jurisdictions proved more effectively defensible than had the unified one. Those specializing in the psychic jurisdiction at first treated about equal numbers of patients with minor or chronic medical problems and those without. But as time passed, their clients had fewer substantial medical symptoms; nearly all had anxiety or depression related to some life situation. The diagnostic definitions applied to them by the new "psychiatrists" were not in fact the formal Freudian classification of hysterics, obsessionals, and so on. But Freudian theories of mechanism and the Freudian style of inference dominated the area. Treatment, too, became explicitly psychotherapeutic, if not Freudian in its particulars. The working knowledge system of the new psychiatrists, a mix of eclecticism and Freudianism called "dynamic psychiatry," endured unchallenged until the late 1960s. Throughout this forty-year period it coexisted with the strict Freudianism of the psychoanalysts, who reserved to themselves the most wealthy and "interesting" members of the psychic clientele, most often other mental health professionals.[46]

In the division of psychic and organic work, those who took the psychic side lost much of the legitimacy and jurisdictional strength provided by their close tie to the general medicine. Freud himself saw no reason why therapists had to be physicians, and only the violent opposition of American psychiatrists prevented the International Psychoanalytic Association from following Freud's policy. The American psychiatrists thus had to turn the cultural jurisdiction implicit in Freudian work into a socially structured claim of jurisdiction.

They began by establishing preeminence in the workplace, starting with the juvenile delinquency clinics of the adjustment school. There, the psychiatrists managed to subordinate the psychologists (often women), reversing their successful insubordination during the war. With its limited focus on testing, psychology lacked the all-embracing claims of the psychiatry of adjustment, then drifting from the new eclecticism toward an explicitly Freudian position. When social workers entered the clinics, they, too, functioned under the psychiatrists, who directed the overall clinic division of labor. Often the psychiatrist was a consultant-director who attended the clinic only part-time. The social workers tried to change this situation. In 1927 M. H. Solomon noted with pleasure the growth of independent practice in social work and of psychiatric social workers oriented towards individual therapy. But those preferring subordination to psychiatrists predominated, and supervision by psychiatrists became a central qualification for membership in the American Association of Psychiatric Social Workers. There was, in fact, no independent intellectual basis for the social work jurisdiction, since the ideas came, with few exceptions, from Freud's American psychiatric disciples.[47]

Dominance of these subordinate groups was assured by the practice of personal analysis. Psychoanalysis assumed that therapy must begin with the therapist. By 1923 the New York Psychoanalytic Association required all members to be analyzed. The notion that mental health work required personal therapy rapidly spread to social work, largely through the enthusiastic support of the adjustment-school psychiatrists. Its actual utility irrespective, personal analysis provided absolute professional control of psychotherapy in the workplace. If Freudianism was the only legitimate psychotherapy, and only doctors could

be Freudian analysts, and personal psychotherapy was necessary for
work with personal problems, then the psychiatrists had absolute control of both jurisdiction and knowledge system. This system of workplace control worked successfully until the unprecedented increases in
demand during the 1960s.[48]

Freudianism proved a resounding public as well as workplace success. From the very first, Freudian ideas fascinated American culture.
Their spread was hastened by Freud's own use of analysis as a general
system of cultural interpretation. In a demonstration of professional
imperialism reminiscent of scientific management and medicalization,
psychoanalysis became a method of literary criticism, of political science, of cross-cultural analysis. While it never invaded the actual work
areas of other professions (except for the usual forays against the law
about criminal responsibility), it appeared in an astonishing variety
of guises. This general public success reflected the total dominance of
psychoanalysis as a popular psychology. Although the formalities of
Freudianism may not always have been upheld, the general notions
of ego, unconscious, childhood sexuality, and so on became the foundations of America's perception of its personality.[49]

Psychoanalysis itself was not large enough to serve the enormous
market it in fact succeeded in claiming. Like most professions in that
situation, it retained an intellectual jurisdiction over the entire area,
but allowed most psychotherapy to be done by nonanalyst psychiatrists
and by psychologists and social workers, all of them ultimately under
analytic supervision. At the same time, analysis maintained a particularly powerful clientele settlement. Analysts themselves gave therapy
to their trainees, to members of social elites, and to other mental
health professionals. Their clients thus included those professionals
whose incursions into their work they could most fear; budding revolution by subordinates could easily be defined as "inappropriate rage
against the father." The system was very nearly foolproof.

## Conclusion: The Clergy Surrender

The clergy were in fact the heaviest losers from the creation of the new
psychiatric jurisdiction. They had not lost in workplace fact, for they
outnumbered the mental health professions dozens to one until after
the Second World War. As late as the 1960s, individuals with personal
problems were still seeing clergymen, doctors, and even lawyers before entering the mental health system. But even by the 1920s, the
clergy had lost any vestige of cultural jurisdiction over personal problems. No longer were such problems signs of God's word, or occasions

for thinking about ultimate reality. Rather, they were complete and entire problems unto themselves.[50]

Perhaps nothing makes this clearer than the clergy's acceptance of the possibility, explicit since the Emmanuel movement, that faith might help cure minor physical ailments and other personal problems. The instrumental notion that religion might have a use would have shocked nineteenth-century proponents of the evangelical view. The purpose of religion is worship, and that of the clergy, salvation. To treat religious behavior or belief as a therapy upends the religious hierarchy of purposes. Yet a surprising number of clergy moved to this opinion in the wake of the Freudian revolution. K. R. Stolz wrote in 1932: "The higher integration and expansion of the personality is the governing objective of modern Christian education and pastoral care. . . . [The old style of pastoral visiting] did make for the enlargement of the individual, although vast areas of personal difficulties remained untouched." Indeed, there emerged in this period a clinical pastoral training movement aiming to give young clergymen direct experience with the newly defined personal problems. Seminarians would learn the rudiments of human nature from psychiatrists, psychologists, and social workers who "knew" those rudiments, that is, from the professionals who currently controlled the definitions of them.[51]

Only one figure stood against this clerical surrender to psychiatry. Anton Boisen illustrates with painful clarity what happens to professionals who lead unsuccessful jurisdictional revolutions. Boisen became a mental patient when he was already widely experienced in the world and in his chosen profession. As a patient and a clergyman, Boisen's first reaction to his own and others' mental illnesses was to ask what they meant; what was the religious meaning of the psychotic's fancies? That these ideas had roots in biological events was not grounds for rejecting them; after all, normal ideas have biological roots as well. So Boisen began a painstaking study of religious ideation among psychotics. Daring to ask these questions was risky for a hospitalized psychotic; the psychiatrists said Boisen had lost ground and confined him for several additional months. But he was eventually released and began a career as a guerrilla in the psychiatric heartland. In fact Boisen did not merely analyze the religious meaning of psychotic ideas. He also gave a theory of everyday life problems that was explicitly religious, claiming those problems again for the clergy. Such problems, he argued, lay not in failure to reach a highest level of personal functioning, as the adjustment theorists and Freudians were arguing. Rather they lay in being "unawakened."

These are persons usually fairly well adjusted in the vocational social or sexual fields, who have never really come to terms with their ultimate loyalties. They are those who, passively accepting the faith of their fathers, make no determined effort to bring themselves into conformity with its requirements, but go through life absorbed all too often in the petty, the trivial, the selfish, or even that which makes them loathesome in their own eyes. I am ready . . . to recognize that in order that they may turn and be made whole it may be necessary to disturb their conscience in regard to the quality of life they are living.

Everyday life was problematic not for its unhappiness, but for its triviality. The everyday problems that formed the foundation of the new psychiatric jurisdiction were again merely occasions for asking the fundamental religious questions about ultimate loyalties. Worse yet, adjustment itself was a problem, not a cure.[52]

Few rallied to the flag Boisen raised. He started the pastoral counseling movement to make students contact the challenging religious issues raised by psychotics. But as I noted above, the movement relapsed into the belief that religion would be a means of therapy and ministers lay avatars of psychiatrists. While Seward Hiltner and a few others have carried Boisen's evangelistic flag, the American Association of Pastoral Counselors has become large and powerful precisely by forgetting Boisen's radicalism.[53]

The drift of pastoral counseling towards secular psychotherapy forms a convenient end for this detailed discussion. The contest of professions over personal problems did not, of course, stop in the 1930s. But the general pattern of interprofessional relations then established did not change seriously for three decades. In musical terms, a tonality emerged that organized interprofessional relations until the modulations of the 1960s. Of course the existence of a governing tonality does not bring harmony to a standstill; so also did interprofessional conflict continue within the subjective structure established after the confusions of the 1920s. The basic themes of these later conflicts may be easily sketched.

Psychiatry's heartland jurisdiction—the mental hospitals with their insoluble lunatics—at first grew steadily. In the 1930s, the organic-psychic boundary was recrossed by institutional psychiatrists, who used new somatic therapies to "make patients accessible to" psychic methods of treatment. Convulsive therapies and psychosurgery enjoyed a brief vogue, but were eclipsed after 1953 by ataractic drugs. In the mid 1950s began a slow (and still little understood) depopulation of the mental hospitals. Simultaneously, a coalition of lay reformers and mental health–related professionals led an ideological revolution in favor of "community mental health," despite the lack of evidence that communities would accept ex–mental patients, that the romanticized "communities" of the reformers really existed, or that there were enough facilities or professionals to handle the patients extramurally. The Community Mental Health Act of 1963 speeded hospital declines, which became precipitous when the Supplemental Security Income Amendments of 1973 made deinstitutionalization a financial windfall for the states. (Deinstitutionalization's most profound result has been to create a problem currently called "homelessness," over which yet another group of professions is squabbling.) Although the decline of mental hospitals seemed to threaten psychiatry, trained psychiatrists had in fact long since deserted the state facilities, which were by 1970 staffed largely with unlicensed foreign medical graduates. Psychiatrists had committed their profession to a new heartland, that of psychotherapy. The accidental destruction of their home base thus seemed of little importance.[54]

Psychology, meanwhile, reentered the world of nervous and mental disease through the university. The postwar founding of the National Institute of Mental Health, which should have helped academic psychiatry, in fact became a psychologists' bonanza. By the sixties 50 percent of NIMH investigators were psychologists; only 15 percent were psychiatrists. Experimental and neural psychology overshadowed both clinical research and psychopharmacology in the research budget. The appearance of psychology on the academic frontiers of psychiatry in part echoed their prior conflicts, in particular the contest between preventive and therapeutic approaches to personal problems. From intelligence tests psychology had rapidly evolved personality tests as a new tool for "preventive adjustment." But society's acceptance of psychological testing not only generated an immense market for applied psychology, it also spawned an enormous research enterprise. As an arts and sciences department in universities, psychology was well situated to control this research enterprise and through it to dominate research on the mind. Even more importantly, it could also socialize the burgeoning ranks of college students to the "ownership" of "abnormal psychology" by psychologists. This factor would have profound importance when the postwar college generations looked for help with personal problems. Once again we see the increasing importance of state and university as arenas of interprofessional competition.[55]

The relative dominance of the academy in psychology created internal problems in that profession, leading to an intraprofessional split in the late 1930s. The American Association of Applied Psychology took the clinicians and testers who worked in schools, industry, and private practice, while the APA remained academic. Although the groups rejoined in 1944, the clinical group has gradually come to dominate the general association. By the late 1960s it alone was two-thirds the size of the psychiatric profession.[56]

Although it impugned psychiatrists' legitimacy as custodians of the mind, psychology's dominance of research in that area did not directly undercut the psychiatrists' position as practical psychotherapists. For research on psychotherapy rapidly declined. After taking 20 percent of the NIMH research budget in the immediate postwar period, it fell to 5 percent in the late 1950s. Furthermore, behavioral therapy—a twentieth-century secular version of moral therapy—took an ever-increasing fraction of that small amount, while research on individual psychotherapy withered. Psychotherapy was thus largely an applied field, mainly controlled by the practitioner hierarchy that culminated in the analytic institutes and by the doctors' monopoly on positions as analysts.

The sudden flood of demand for psychotherapy burst this situation open in the 1970s. Since the events are recent, it is impossible to specify accurately the actual causes behind them. The demand may have been generated by the flood of education after the war; use of psychotherapy was strongly correlated with education and there were more educated people. The demand may also have reflected the final wave of secularization; as late as 1967, Freeman and others found people still turning to clergy more than to any other group. (Clergy were followed by "professional counselors," teachers, and doctors.) Perhaps that situation changed at last. Demand may also have been a function of supply; the number of clinical psychologists expanded very rapidly after 1960, as did that of masters-level social workers. Demand undoubtedly also reflected third-party payment schemes for psychotherapy, which had began in the 1950s. Early experiments soured insurance companies on funding psychotherapy; psychiatrists, psychologists, and social workers had used insurance funds to pay for three-year training analyses. But by the mid 1960s about one-quarter of psychiatric outpatient visits were covered by insurance. Psychologists themselves became third-party reimbursable, at first merely for testing services, later for psychotherapy. By 1972, psychologists were collecting from Medicaid in several states, and in 1974 the federal government made clinical psychologists qualified independent providers. The social workers and others pressed hard in pursuit. Not surprisingly, psychiatry fell back on its medical status. The theory of psychogenic mental illness fell into abeyance, and major mental illness, construed in largely biological terms, has become again the center of psychiatric attention. (The profession is also pushing biological interpretations of

major elements of the psychotherapy jurisdiction, in particular depression.) Falling back on its presently secure pharmacological monopoly, psychiatry has virtually conceded the psychotherapeutic world
to its competitors.[57]

In the century following 1860, a new type of professional work
emerged, the work we now call counseling or psychotherapy. I have
tried in this chapter to specify the subjective genealogy of this work.
The great social changes of the late nineteenth century created the set
of tasks from which the work was carved—the new problems of personal life and social control. Early attempts to comprehend these problems within traditional clergy frameworks failed to establish dominant
jurisdiction, although clergymen continued throughout the period to
be the largest group of front-line professionals dealing with these problems. Since some people reacted to personal problems by generating
or recognizing somatic complaints, it was inevitable that consulting
physicians should develop a model for personal problems. This model,
the neurologists' syndrome of general nervousness, construed personal
problems as medical problems, analyzable by medical concepts of causality and governed by medicine's cultural legitimacy. The small elite
of neurology could not handle the demand it so defined, and an expanding psychiatric profession joined it while fleeing the mental hospitals. Under renewed threats from outside professions, the loose neurological construction of personal problems turned into the modern
concept of neurosis as a psychically generated, psychically diagnosed,
and psychically treated phenomenon. This concept has dominated the
personal problems area since, although exigencies of demand have
shifted the groups actually providing the service.

In discussing the details of this history, I have shown how certain
variables determine the exchange of cultural jurisdiction. Characteristics of diagnosis, inference, and treatment determine which of several
rival constructions will become culturally authoritative. As I have repeatedly argued, and as this example well shows, a given cultural jurisdiction is compatible with a wide variety of jurisdictional settlements. The focus here has been on how cultural jurisdiction itself is
created, maintained, and defended. We have watched as social up-
heaval produces undefined tasks that then receive their cultural shape
from the professions confronting them. We can watch, too, as both
accident and design shape the jurisdiction's subsequent history. The
psychiatrists' deliberate invasion of social control under the rhetoric of
prevention, the clergy's willful desertion of its traditional work, the
lucid brilliance of Freudian analysis, the neurologists' self-defeating

elitism, all these interact within a structured ecology of professions to produce the ultimate results we see. To study any of these professions without the others would be to deeply mistake its history. The study of professions must be first and foremost a study of their work, for professions exist to control and execute work. Above all, that study cannot assume the functional identity of profession and task. It must begin, as I have begun here, with a history of tasks and problems. Only then does a history of professions become possible.

# 11    Conclusion

The invention of personal problems returns us to the questions with which I began. When do we use experts? For what? How do we structure and control expertise in society? This closing chapter contains some final comments on these questions. It also discusses the methodology of social history, comparative historical sociology, or whatever else we may wish to call this kind of analysis.

## The System of Professions

I have treated the professions at three general levels. My central focus has been the system of professions, which I have taken to be a structure linking professions with tasks. I have shown these structural relations to so bind the professions that movements of any one affect others. Below the system level, I have investigated differentiation within the professions themselves, less for its intrinsic interest than for its relation to system conditions. Above the system level, I have investigated larger social forces, again focusing on how those forces affect individual professions under certain conditions. I have used the word "profession" very loosely, and have largely ignored the issue of when groups can legitimately be said to have coalesced into professions: when or even how they become groups in the formal sense of acting in subjective concert. I have devoted most of my time to explaining how existing groups are shaped by the three levels of forces and why, but not really how, new groups on occasion arise.[1]

What have been the strengths and weaknesses of this approach? Let me begin with the strengths. I have by this model avoided the focus on particular structures of occupational control—licenses, schools, journals, associations—that has plagued the professions literature for decades. I can therefore explain what happens once all these structures are present, which the professionalization literature cannot, and can analyze as well the many professions that acquire all of these structures in a year or two and the many professions that never acquire them all. My model embraces and explains interprofessional conflicts ignored by the professionalization theorists and the functionalists. It shows how professions both create their work and are created by it. It also notices, where its predecessors ignored, the impact of internal change on external position. At the same time it shows why the general forces of bureaucratization, knowledge change, and so on have not uniform but highly idiosyncratic effects on professions, effects shaped by internal and system forces as well as by professional choices.

My model can also explain why professions sometimes fail—why some become dependent or subordinate and others disappear entirely. More generally, it accounts for, or offers a vocabulary for accounting for, the vast differences in structure and knowledge that continue, against most theories, to characterize the world of experts. It frees us entirely from the ideal-type approach, embracing the myriad deviations so disturbing to Millerson, Cullen, and others. It extends even to the bizarre and counterintuitive, explaining why doctors in training do things they will never do in practice; why the general problem of death is ignored by professions; why professions with elaborate professional structures are sometimes disadvantaged by them. In short, my model fits the historical realities of expert life in the nonsocialist industrialized world.[2]

In accounting for all these things, the system model transcends its predecessors: functionalism, with its naive reification of American society; or monopolism, with its equally naive fear of the dominant classes; or professionalization, with its wistful belief in a sort of corporatist nirvana. These were solid and hopeful models, but the facts we have about professions require their rejection. History is not a simple pattern of trends and development, but a complex mass of contingent forces. The system model achieves a theory of that contingency. Moreover, the model achieves that theory within a much wider context than has been previously theorized. I have not specified "how much" abstraction is enough to enter the system, because that too depends on time and place—on other competitors, larger forces, internal structures. The mechanisms I have sketched work in many different times and places, and, moreover, work within themselves: the model as easily explains relations between medical specialties as relations between law and medicine. Its argument is fractal, reappearing within itself at many levels of measurement.

That fractal quality moves beyond the professions as well. The system approach offers a way of thinking about divisions of labor in general. Perhaps because the professions are so well studied and well defined, it has proved easiest to analyze the division of expert labor. But shorn of the special qualities of professions—in particular occupational competition through abstract knowledge—the system framework suggests an approach to the structuring of work in general.

But one must break eggs to make an omelette. One of these I have already discussed in chapter 5. I have made fairly profound assumptions about the professions' ability to retain and use co-opted power. Some may not find the evidence against that ability as persuasive as I do. I have also given individual professions a strong existence, even a personhood, allowing them to make strategies and plans almost as if they had feelings. Now of course the dominant members of these professions have these qualities. And one can make a strong functional argument that system selection makes the professions appear to behave this way whether they actually do or not. Moreover, rational-actor models offer some powerful advantages once these assumptions are made. But all the same, I *have* underemphasized the problems of coalescence and "groupness," problems implicitly central in the professionalization literature. For example, coalescence is often achieved by one group of practitioners at the expense of others, and while I have some models for the losers (who can become "another profession" as did the British chemists when ditched by the apothecaries in the nineteenth century), there are some problems in my personified approach.

I have also generally assumed that the competition model holds "in the same way" throughout the period discussed—roughly from the Industrial Revolution to the present. I interpret the obvious changes in workplaces and careers of professionals by speaking of competition in new arenas—the workplace, the university, the state. Tied to this is an assumption implicit in the last paragraph—that the "thingness" or degree of coalescence of professions has not changed. Yet the undoubted changes in professional structures for work and association, not to mention the enormous expansion of professional numbers, give the words "medical profession" a quite different meaning in 1986 than in 1886. When 20 percent of the labor force "has expertise," expertise means something quite different than when only 5 percent does, irrespective of whether the 20 percent are lineal descendants of earlier but smaller groups. In part this difficulty is endemic in historical analysis. We must discuss historical subjects as if they themselves stayed constant, while their properties changed. But in fact such essentialism is justified only over limited periods. It may well be that the attentuation of competition, together with its relocation into complex workplaces, in fact vitiates a competitive model for the future of professions.

Finally, many will feel that I have dodged the central and classic problem of defining my fundamental term itself. What *is* a profession? But as I argued in the first chapter, a firm definition of profession is both unnecessary and dangerous; one needs only a definition strong enough to support one's theoretical machinery. My loose definition—professions are somewhat exclusive groups of individuals applying somewhat abstract knowledge to particular cases—works well enough.[3] In fact, profession is not "objectively" definable precisely because of its power and importance in our culture. Take the equally familiar example of education. Is education years in school? Testable knowledge of particular areas? Ability to quickly master new material? Grasp of "classic" texts? Experience of the world? These may indicate education, but they are not the thing itself. When we say "after she left school she began her real education," we show our properly deep ambivalence about the nature of education itself. This ambivalence defines education interstitially, emergently, not as years in school, or experience, or whatever, but rather as their intersection or as something beyond them to which each points. Much the same is true of "profession," which means at once a form of organization, a level of social deference, an association with knowledge, a way of organizing personal careers. Our ambivalent concept holds them all together and, I believe, acquires its power precisely from the yoking of these often-disparate realities. Of "profession's" illocutionary importance there is no doubt. For all our cautions, we are still quick to worry about whether social work really is a profession, or whether professionals are proletarianizing or whatever our hobbyhorse may be. We may not agree on what the term means, but we certainly agree on its importance and centrality. "Profession" thus enjoys a vibrantly real but highly elusive existence, qualities that make it both worthwhile and impossible to discuss objectively.

Overall, I believe that the advantages of my approach outweigh its problems. At the least, it gives us a new set of assumptions from which to triangulate and rectify the old ones. At the best, it gives a wholly new analysis of professional development. Ultimately, the problems with it reflect insoluble dilemmas about discourse on social life: the impossibility of operationally stable definitions of culturally charged terms, the essentialist character of language, the problem of personification.

# History

These methodological questions lead naturally into a larger consideration of how history should be done. Philosophers like to wonder
whether there really is a past, and if there is (or was), how we know it.
Such fundamental epistemological questions surpass me. But this book
embodies an idea of history, and I would like to state it clearly.[4]

History is first and foremost a tangled net of events. Each event lies
in dozens of stories, determined and overdetermined by the causes
flowing through them, yet ever open to new directions and twists. Indeed, given happenings may be seen as parts of different events within
different stories. Because people and groups construct their future by
interpreting their causal environment, the very knowledge of the past
itself shapes the future, even though aggregate regularities and structural necessity simultaneously oblige it. In this book, of course, I have
emphasized the structural necessities—the confining system of the
professions. But I have not ignored such aggregate phenomena as the
swarming of the middle classes into the newly prestigious professions,
nor the intentional action of professions responding to the complex
field of possibilities represented by the system itself.

Such a history is of course an epistemologist's nightmare; direct
cause interacts with structural determination and intention to produce
a succession of futures. But wringing our hands about conflation doesn't
help us write history. The writer must disentangle the threads of determinants, structures, and intentions, then reweave them into an
analysis, and then recount that analysis in some readable form—arduous
tasks indeed. Little wonder, then, that shortcuts abound. There is the
positivistic approach, in which determinate cause floods downhill to an
inevitable present, as if the rocks of structure did not channel events
nor the dams of intentions divert them. There is the gracious art of
narrative, following characters on their pilgrimage to the relevant Can-
terbury, stopping to view now the economic scene, now the social
structure, now the psychology of leaders, but ever marking the flow of
chance and desire. There is textualism, conjuring a whole society from
an artisans' ritual or a stained-glass window, like Proust with his tea-
dipped *madeleine*. These shortcuts are not unproductive. On the contrary, they explore new alternatives for interpreting events and create
new models of causes. But they are inevitably incomplete. Textualism
in fact borrows from elsewhere the vast structure of knowledge it
seems to create from artifacts. Positivism ignores structure and intent.
Narrativism ignores little and assumes little, but chooses its plots more
for literary merit than for analytic propriety.

I have here tried to avoid that plotting, undoubtedly with the occasional consequence of seeming willfully obscure. But plot is a chimera. History does not happen in stories, even if we usually talk about it as if it did. The storylike element enters history itself only because we as historical actors frame our future intentions relative to a past understood in stories. The past stories we consider do assume thereby a special causal importance, although not an importance that can overwhelm either structure or direct determination. For example, if we want to write a history of marriage and divorce in modern America, we must understand American models for relationships, since—right or wrong—these models determine for actors what past is relevant to their decisions to marry or divorce. But we will not therefore ignore determinate forces like race, religion, and class, nor structural ones like the demographic implications of hypergamy.

Narrative works best with certain kinds of events—wars, reform movements, collective actions—that we have learned to perceive narrativistically, as we do not generally perceive the general history of marriage and divorce. Professionalization, of course, is an event we do so perceive. It has been easy to impose the narrative story-structure on the history of professions, a usage we accepted from the professions themselves. Hence we have the "rise of the medical profession," the "rise of the accounting profession," and so on. Indeed, a narrativistic book on medicine recently won the Pulitzer Prize. But the narrative style imposes a continuity that isn't there. The state of modern medicine has more to do with the state of modern nursing, pharmacy, law, and accounting than with that of nineteenth-century medicine. Of course such pseudonarrative continuity may in fact exist. But the rebuttable presumption in the history of professions is that it does not.[5]

But this presumption confronts us with a dilemma; without narrative we have no convenient discourse for a history that includes determinate causality, structural constraint, and intention. In one sense this is not an unusual situation, for the issue of discourse—of how to recount the past—is in any case an issue of genre, and genres do change. After all, our current narratives, heavily marbled with structural and causal analysis, succeeded years of lean and redblooded stories that derived from the deceptive positivism of Ranke's "telling what happened." And this succession itself reflected an episode of professionalization; the new professional history in England and America emphasized social analysis to set itself off from the moralizing stories of the Regius Professors.[6] Our lack of discourse today may signify a similar situation of interprofessional contact, the rich ferment arising from the (renewed) contact of history with the various social sciences. In any case, while the discourse issue can hardly be settled here, I can urge an agenda of problems a new historical discourse must face.

Any viable historical discourse must recognize that human actions are simultaneously determined and chosen, and that human realities are both subjective and objective. While there is much theorizing about these issues, it is of little use to those of us who analyze real historical processes. Our problem is how to allow each side free play, neither romanticizing freedom nor worshipping determinism, accepting both the objective reality of social behavior and the subjective revisions that transform it. Are professions forced towards exclusivism or do they choose it? Obviously they do both. Do professions find their work laid out for them, or do they make it up? Again they do both. In each case, one isn't fully a precondition of the other, nor is one 25 percent true and the other 75 percent true. Rather the two together constitute a composite, interwoven process. The question is how to talk about that process in a way both truthful and humane.

Historical discourse must also recognize the duality of the forces we call determinants. Some exercise their effects directly as sufficient causes, others merely provide constraints, acting as necessary causes. The system structures that have occupied so much of this book exemplify the latter. Like most structures, they contain an implicit record of past events, and generally change more slowly than direct, sufficient causes. These two types of determinism complement intentional action, making the tripartite history that is shortchanged by social-scientific positivism and humanistic textualism. As I have said, narrative history generally recognizes all three moments of the historical process, but gives the predominating role to action. My own discourse has been to elucidate the structure and its properties, then to step back and tell some narratives involving that described structure.

Structure is itself a deceptive reality. Although fixed for the purposes of analysis, it perpetually changes, in myriad little ways, and must eventually be regarded as changed in kind, even though sudden shifts in it cannot be discerned. There is a sense in which structure is simply our conventional name for things that change more slowly than other things, an approach emphasized by Braudel and others of his school. As such, structure has many levels, all changing at different rates, all coming into accidental conjunction, all changing in degree and kind at once. Yet in a contrasting way, structure can also be identified in fundamental oppositions that never change, even though their appearances may seem to. Thus, we think of academic professions competing within the structure provided by universities, and can think of that competition as conditioned by the slow structural metamorphosis that leads to the modern university system. University structure is then a slowly changing fact of competitive life that is eventually transformed, in part by that very competition. But in another sense, the university system has not changed. To identify legal education at the Stanford Law School with nursing education at a normal school that has been renamed as a state university is basically silly; they are as different as nursing education in hospitals and legal education in the Stanford Law School ever were. There is still elite professional education and nonelite professional education; nursing education has been less upgraded than renamed. Structure, in this sense of enduring opposition, indeed denotes things that may never change. It is ultimately meaningless to ask what are the relative extents of the two different kinds of structure in society, however; like the subjective and the objective, the two structures are merely moments, facets, aspects of a single thing.

Central to a new historical discourse, as I have implied, are its assumptions about narrative. Analytic history must reject the story form of discourse, or at least adopt narrative forms reflecting the network character of historical reality. Why should history have been so conservative when fiction, the locus classicus of traditional narrative, has been so robustly experimental? Imagine a scholarly history as written by Proust or Pynchon. At the very least, we must forget the beginnings and ends, and make history the endless succession of middles that it is. There have of course been historical adventurers too: Braudel whose dozens of pages on events meekly follow thousands of pages on structure and conjuncture: Paige mixing aggregate causal analysis with storytelling. But the main change in historical discourse has been the rise of textualism, a method of great literary elegance, but unsuited to other than exploratory analysis.[7]

We must also confront the arbitrary character of our central subjects. Sociology is rich in theory about what makes groups groups—subjective interaction, and so on—but historical studies, this one included, make do with relatively strong assumptions about durability and change: essence endures, qualities change. This strategy, imposed in part by the fixed quality of language, must be unmasked. We require a vocabulary and discourse for the creation and dissolution of protagonists, for the ways in which change in quality creates change in substance, for the disjunction of the two structures noted above. These are not easy changes; they involve naming things we prefer to leave unnamed. But they are necessary to a proper historical discourse.[8]

Finally we require a historical discourse that does not privilege the present. Particularly in fields like the study of professions, the literature takes the present as a terminus ad quem. Of course, future change is expected, but along lines previously seen. In fact, change will go off in strange new directions, and in fact it is not yet clear in what larger events the occurrences of today will take their places. Accounting, for example, is considering postgraduate education. This could be part of a rise of educational standards in accounting, a rise of professional education standards generally, a revulsion against education on the job, a transformation of the university towards vocationalism, a general revolution in the information professions, and so on. It is unknown and unknowable which will prove a century hence to be the proper colligation. About the far past we can at least agree on which are the events to link into stories; about the present we cannot, as a cursory reading of *Time* and *Newseek* shows. That is why I am merely speculating about the future in this chapter. I am much more confident about my interpretation of professionalism around 1900 than about my interpretation of professionalism now; in principle, the present situation is less knowable.[9]

## Theory and the Professions

Like any theory, the system theory of professions addresses a specific question within more general ones. For me the crucial environing question is how societies structure expertise.[10] Professionalism has been the main way of institutionalizing expertise in industrialized countries. There are, as we sometimes forget, many alternatives: the generalized expertise of the imperial civil services, the lay practitioners of certain religious groups, the popular diffusion of expertise characteristic of microcomputing. The contrasting examples show the essence of professionalism: professionalism's expertise is abstract, but not too abstract; it is not generally diffused; its practitioners work full time in particular areas. But professionalism shares with these alternatives the quality of institutionalizing expertise in people. As I have repeatedly argued, expertise is also institutionalized in commodities and organizations. To ask why societies incorporate their knowledge in professions is thus not only to ask why societies have specialized, lifetime experts, but also why they place expertise in people rather than things or rules.

There are many facile answers. Knowledge is too extensive for part-time work. Machines can't make complex decisions. Rules can't envision all cases. But we know that imperial China lasted thousands of years without expert specialization, that artificial intelligence and its predecessors have commodified things that "could never be accomplished by" a form or a material or a machine, that untrained bureaucrats routinely administer complex accounting rules. The question of Why professionalism? is a deeper one, all the more important because its answer can tell us so much about the future of professions.[11]

We have professionalism, in the first place, because our market-based occupational structure favors employment based on personally held resources, whether of knowledge or of wealth. Such employment is more secure, more autonomous, and usually more remunerative, partly because it is organized in "careers," a strategy invented in the nineteenth century to permit a coherent individual life within a shifting marketplace. Professionalism was among the first forms of career. Unlike its contemporary the organizational career, it escaped hierarchical structures whose possibilities narrowed at every level. Professionalism thus offered continuously independent life chances; we should be little surprised that many have taken up that offer.[12]

We have professionalism, secondly, because nearly all kinds of knowledge are organizable as common resources for a body of individuals. We have many times seen that such knowledge must require enough disciplined judgment to be uncommodifiable, that it must enjoy enough success to generate continual demand, and that it must be abstract enough to survive small market shifts, but not so abstract as to prevent monopoly. An open reading of the evidence shows that the human problems susceptible of this professionalized knowledge know few limits. Alcoholism, suicide, aging, building, ultimate meaning, financial advice, "low sexual desire," violence, the environment: all these have seen their professional embodiments. To speak, as some have done, of moral entrepreneurship is to unduly limit the capacity of professions; they seize all sorts of human activities, not just the moral ones.[13]

We have professionalism, third, because competing forms of institutionalization have not yet overwhelmed it. It may seem odd to argue that professionalism itself competes with alternate forms of structuring expertise, in particular, with commodification and organization. But this competition arises in part because the commodities embodying expertise require development, maintenance, and support that increasingly exceed the resources of individual professionals. The commercial organizations and governments that invest in commodified professional knowledge compete directly with professionals for client fees, whether the commodities provide services directly or are simply used by professionals in practice. Commodification is an old process, of course, and one that has not gained substantially on the professions in the last century. But nonprofessionals increasingly own and operate professional commodities, which makes the present competition more dangerous to the idea of professionalism itself.[14]

Organization provides a second, and much more formidable, alternative to professionalism. Many have chronicled how organization destroyed skilled craft labor; a machine-based division of labor allows the unskilled to accomplish highly skilled tasks. The same process, many feel, now applies to the professions.[15] Quite apart from the physical embodiment of professional knowledge in commodities, division of labor has clearly restructured professional work. Multiprofessional firms in accounting, information, and architecture, the team concept in medicine and social services, elaborate professional bureaucracies in engineering and law, all encode professional knowledge in the structures of organization themselves. Much current expertise resides in the rules of these and other organizations of professionals, most of which are either overtly heteronomous or governed by professionals more or less openly identified as professional administrators. These organizations clearly seek to maximize both the quantity of expertise institutionalized in their arrangements and the economic returns to that quantity.

At present, professionalism seems to hold its own. It has stayed ahead of commodification, although many professions and their subgroups have been destroyed in the process. But it may ultimately lose out to organizations. The new hiring patterns of the major information firms and the loose form of organizational professionalism point to a much weaker control of work by the professions themselves. The change involves essential qualities of professionalism, not merely accidental attributes. The forces that first propelled professionalism are still strong today, but other forces may have finally become stronger.[16]

These predictions are weak, but as I said earlier, we know little about the current status of the dynamic process of history. I prefer to close with some recommendations about future studies of professions, choosing the normative over the empirical. We must stop studying single professions—medicine especially—and start studying work. We need histories of jurisdictions—who served them, where they came from, how the market was created, how conflict shaped participants. The most important subjects for such investigations will be understudied professions like accounting and psychology. In particular, the jurisdiction of money requires the kind of attention long received by health. Perhaps sociologists and historians, as biological individuals, concern themselves more with the profession of life and death than with the profession of loss and profit, but surely accounting is today far more socially important than medicine.[17]

There are, of course, strong existing literatures on professional work. The Hughes tradition of observational studies complements the increasing body of historical work on the subject; to these literatures I owe the possibility of this book. But we need larger-scale surveys of actual work, bridging the gap between intimate observation and the general analysis of professional institutions. We need these especially for the past, where surveying actual work means reading case records in hospital archives and rummaging through old accounting memoranda. Such work will support a detailed analysis of processes I have only sketched here.

Sketched is indeed the proper word. For I have written basically as a theorist rather than as a sociologist of professions. Contemporary sociological theory seems to have strayed far from its proper task. Theorists spend whole careers marginalizing classic texts. Those who trespass on empirical ground generally study the entire history of Western capitalism. But the classic thinkers themselves—Marx, Durkheim, Weber, Thomas, and so on—were up to their necks in empirical data: documents, surveys, statistics, and histories, describing dozens of different people and processes. These were not votaries of "classic problems" invented by their predecessors. They wrote theory to explain empirical realities they saw. And they worried less about giving answers, about specific theories of why specific things happened, than they did about creating vocabularies for framing theories, ways of asking questions. I have tried to follow their example. The theories of professionalization and monopolism were basically answers. If the data fit them, fine; if not, they ignored it. But I have accepted the data as given and have designed a theory to account for it, a theory made up not of answers but of questions, the better to help us ask how and why the professions dominate our world.

# Notes

Chapter One

Note: I have tried to ensure that when not specifically labeled otherwise, the professions listed are American.

1. Auerbach (1976); Baritz (1960); Brown (1979).

2. The word "system" is discussed in detail in chapter 4, note 8.

3. The archetypical careers paper is Wilensky (1964). A number of others are extracted in Vollmer and Mills (1966). Virtually any history of an individual profession makes assumptions about sequential development.

4. On the pre-nineteenth-century professions generally, see Holmes (1982). Representative early modern studies are Cipolla (1973), Prest (1981), Weiss (1982), Pégues (1962), Berlanstein (1975), Dewald (1980), Gelfand (1980), Robson (1959), Tackett (1977), and Park (1985). General surveys of the rise of professions in various countries are Ben-David (1963), Reader (1966), Reid (1974), Bledstein (1976), Larson (1977), and Collins (1979).

5. Representative studies of nineteenth-century continental professions are Meyers (1976), LaVopa (1979), Shinn (1980), Royer, Martinage, and Lecocq (1982), Léonard (1981), Chalmin (1957), Serman (1982), Debré (1984), Freeze (1983), and Frieden (1981). English examples are Engel (1983), Rothblatt (1968), Stacey (1954), Duman (1980, 1983), Abel-Smith and Stevens (1967), Lewis (1982), Peterson (1978), M. Lewis (1965), and Spiers (1980). The list of American studies is endless. Weber's discussion is in Weber (1954).

6. Carr-Saunders and Wilson (1933).

7. Millerson (1964).

8. It was Parsons (1954, 1964, 1968) who emphasized the asymmetry of expertise. Other works mentioned are T. J. Johnson (1967), Freidson (1970a, 1970b), and Berlant (1975).

9. Bledstein (1976); Ben-David (1963).

10. The extent of the definitional literature on professions is shown by the extent of the critical literature about it. Exemplary pre-1960 sources are Cogan

(1953, 1955), Gerver and Bensman (1954), and Goode (1957). The major sources (post 1960) are Habenstein (1963), Millerson (1964), T. J. Johnson (1967), Maurice (1972), Chapoulie (1973), Roth (1974), Klegon (1978), and Saks (1983).

11. On self-employment, see the relevant census volumes, for example, table 43 in PC(2), 7A, (U.S. Census 1970). For comparable British figures, see Monopolies Commission (1970). On mobility between professions, see Evans and Laumann (1983). General statistical sources on over-time membership in professions are difficult to find. For the United States, the best source is the census *Historical Statistics* and A. Edwards (1943), on which they are based. The English census changed its definitions several times, and the data series have never been fully reconciled with one another. But see Routh (1965) and especially Perkin (1961).

12. These theoretical arguments against abstract scales explain my ignoring works like Hickson and Thomas (1969) and Cullen (1978) that attempt to derive them. The same arguments explain my willingness to discuss the arts professions, which in some ways are more craftlike than professional, especially performing groups like musicians and actors. Nonetheless, since these professions are related to the more obviously professional creative arts (i.e., musical and dramatic composition) and since these groups have obviously tried to professionalize (e.g., McArthur 1984), I shall include them (cf. Freidson 1986b).

13. This summary derives directly from Wilensky (1964).

14. This summary draws on Caplow (1954: 139–40).

15. Millerson (1964: 182–83).

16. Millerson (1964:86).

17. This section draws throughout on Larson (1977).

18. If two approaches differ in purely formal ways, we tend to see them as theories of different things, rather than as different theories of the same thing, although we still feel they should be reconcilable. Ironically, the proletarianization argument poses a stronger threat to revisionist theories of professionalization like Larson's than it does to conservative ones like Parsons's, because the former make status achievement the driving force of professionalization; therefore a demonstration that status achievement is questionable challenges them directly. Larson would answer that an elite does better while the mass does worse. See also Saks (1983).

19. Carr-Saunders and Wilson (1933); Marshall ([1939] 1965); Parsons ([1939] 1964, 1968). Many other writers lie in the functionalist school, for example, Naegle (1956), Goode (1957), Braude (1961). I have chosen a different classification of professionalization arguments than I used for professionalism because my purpose here is not to give a proper history of professionalization theories—many people have already done a good job of that—but rather to suggest various themes that have divided the literature. As it happens, the classification just given is probably the better description of the schools of writing on professionals, while the earlier one embodies a more defensible set of analytic distinctions. Schools do not always form around the distinctions that seem important to us.

20. Millerson (1964); Wilensky (1964); Caplow (1954).

21. The chief writer of the monopoly school has been Larson (1977). Other works in this tradition are Berlant (1975), Krause (1977), Navarro (1978), Parry and Parry (1976), Auerbach (1976), and Melosh (1982). Most, but not all, monopolist work has concerned medicine. Related but not explicitly monopolist theorists are Johnson (1967) and Freidson (1970a, 1970b). Freidson has lately swung away from his earlier emphasis on dominance (see, e.g., 1986a). For a trenchant critique of monopolist theory, see Saks (1983).

22. The chief writers of the cultural school are Bledstein (1976) and some of the essayists in Haskell (1984). A number of authors have studied the cultural systems of professions, not always from similar perspectives. See, for example, Arney (1982) on obstetrics; Tinker, Merino, and Neimark (1982) on accounting; Strauss et al. (1964) and Castel (1976) on psychiatry; Halmos (1970) on therapists; Hufbauer (1982) on chemists; and MacKenzie (1981) on statistics. Studies of scientists and academics (e.g., Rothblatt 1968, A. J. Engel 1983, T. N. Clark 1973) also tend to follow this approach.

23. The analysis here described is not yet published, having been removed from this book to save space. The problem of finding a hypothesized true order among a body of sequences is the so-called seriation problem, discussed at length in any standard source on multidimensional scaling. A large number of examples may be found in Hodson, Kendall, and Tăutu (1971), and I have myself used the algorithm suggested by A. E. Gelfand (1971) in that book.

24. The problems discussed here have been analyzed at length in Abbott (1984).

25. On deprofessionalization and/or proletarianization see Haug (1973), Toren (1975), Oppenheimer (1973), and Derber (1982). Deprofessionalization is just professionalization in reverse, with many of the methodological and conceptual problems of the original. The proletarianization argument really concerns individual professionals rather than professions as corporate bodies, and hence is not directly relevant to the theoretical questions of how and why professions, as organized bodies, do what they do. On stalled professions, see R. L. Moore (1975) on mediums, Abbott (1982) on railway surgeons, Kraft (1977) on coders, and Litoff (1978) on midwives. On British medicine see Peterson (1978), Reader (1966), and Honigsbaum (1979); and see Seed (1973) and Younghusband (1978) on British social workers, and Lubove (1969) on American. There has always been an undercurrent about "professions in process" in the theoretical literature. Examples are Bucher and Strauss (1961), Bucher (1962), and more recently, Klegon (1978). But while the directional critique of professionalization is well known, even those urging the general idea of professions in process have never really designed a general theoretical scheme, Klegon's paper being perhaps the only such attempt.

26. On medicine, see Bucher (1962), Bucher and Strauss (1961), and Freidson's various works (e.g., 1970a, 1970b, 1975). On American psychiatry, see Abbott (1982, part 4), and on social work, Lubove (1969). On engineers, see Calvert (1967), Layton (1971), and McMahon (1984). On British law and accounting, see E. Jones (1981).

27. On librarianship, see D. Garrison (1979); on engineering, Calhoun (1960); on psychiatry, Grob (1983); and on clergy, Scott (1978) and Youngs (1976). Sociologists have, of course, talked some about work, but generally about its control (e.g., Child and Fulk's otherwise excellent 1982 paper) rather than its actual content.

28. On prestige, see Abbott (1981); on locations, Smigel (1964), Carlin (1962), Wiseman (1970); on power, Heinz and Laumann (1982). Historians connecting internal structure and development are Auerbach (1976), Calvert (1967), and Honigsbaum (1979).

29. Larson (1977), T. J. Johnson (1967).

30. Lest the word "testable" frighten some readers, let me say in advance that this book is mostly theoretical and interpretive. My ultimate "theory" is frankly indeterministic, although recognizing important elements of determinism. In that sense, I am producing not a specific theory, but a framework for describing and analyzing the developments of professions. Given that, "testable ideas" means useful, workable, functional ideas, ideas that help historians and sociologists find ways to viably compare different cases of professional development.

31. The sources on American medicine are overpoweringly rich. The following paragraphs rely on Stevens (1971), Kett (1968), Rothstein (1972), Shryock (1966, 1967), Burrow (1977), Kaufman (1971, 1976), and Vogel and Rosenberg (1979). A recent summary of this huge literature, aimed at a more general audience, is Starr (1982). On osteopaths, see Gevitz (1982), and on chiropractors, Wardwell (1952).

32. The ensuing account relies largely on Abbott (1982), but also on American Psychiatric Association (1944), Grob (1973), and Tomes (1984) for the period before 1880. Sources for after 1930 are Grob (1983), Rogow (1970), and Henry, Sim, and Spray (1971, 1973).

33. The ensuing account is based largely on Abel-Smith and Stevens's magisterial study (1967), as well as on Reader's (1966) account of the nineteenth-century period and G. Holmes's (1982) discussion of the seventeenth and eighteenth. I have also consulted Duman (1980, 1983), Levack (1973), J. R. Lewis (1982), and Robson (1959). I have also made use of William Holdsworth's multivolume *History of English Law*. A current survey of the character of British professions is Monopolies Commission (1970).

34. Recent developments have brought the barristers a little closer to the twentieth century. There is now a central organizing body, for example.

35. The basic sources on English accountancy are Stacey (1954) and E. Jones (1981), although, as with all English professions, one may rely on Carr-Saunders and Wilson (1933) and Millerson (1964) for many of the basics. Excellent studies of English accounting's theoretical knowledge are available, for example, G. A. Lee (1975) and Burchell, Clubb, and Hopwood (1985).

36. There is, to my knowledge, no comprehensive historical study of all the French legal professions. For the current period, I have relied on Abeille (1971), Herzog (1967), and Solus and Perrot (1961). Sources for earlier periods include Berlanstein (1975), Debré (1984), and Young (1869). An excellent de-

scription of the politics of the fusion of 1971 is Raguin (1972), and the current rules for the profession are described in Blanc (1972). In true Cartesian fashion, the French do produce a guide to the current functional, legal, and financial structure of all French liberal professions. This work—Editions Francis Lefebvre 1986—must be the envy of students of professions in any other country. One can only wish it had historical coverage. General sources on the idea of professions in France are Chapoulie (1973) and Maurice (1972). Bodin and Touchard (1959) cover the French "intellectual professions" in a general way. The word *profession* in French means what "occupation" means in English. *Profession libérale* means an occupation whose members work for themselves, (e.g., medicine), although they may under specified conditions be salaried. Some groups Americans would probably consider professionals are *officiers ministériels* (state officers) like the *notaires*. Other salaried professionals are identified by their area of work, for example, *professions sociales*. The situation in German is basically the same. *Beruf* means occupation generally, while *freien Berufe* roughly denotes the American "professions," again with the suggestion of independence. *Profession* is a recent import to Germany. See LaVopa (1980) and Child et al. (1983, on the language of professions in Germany.

37. On railway occupations generally, see Licht (1983). Railway surgeons are discussed in Abbott (1982); see also E. R. Lewis (1894) and Bouffleur (1905). Abbott also discusses electrotherapists, and other now-disappeared therapeutic groups, under the heading of sects, in 1982:part 3. On English dance teachers of the last century, see Flett and Flett (1979). Italian opera impresarios are discussed in a brilliant work by Roselli (1984). Itinerant American singing masters are discussed briefly by G. P. Jackson (1965). The failed profession of architectural sculptors is discussed by Bogart (1984). The ensuing discussion of mediums is based on R. L. Moore (1975).

38. On psychiatry's battles with the spiritualists, see Abbott (1982:part 3), and Gifford (1978).

39. On the medicalization of, for example, obesity, see G. Kolata, "Obesity Declared a Disease," *Science* 227:1019–20, (1985).

## Chapter Two

1. In this chapter, more than in any other, I am relying not only on cited sources and on the theoretical literature on professions, but also on my experience as a field-worker. From April 1972 to June 1973, I spent from two to four hours each weekday doing participant observation in a psychiatric clinic affiliated with a university hospital. In that time I sat in on numerous diagnostic interviews, staffings, and other clinic activities. I also interviewed all staff about their use of psychiatric knowledge, amassing about a thousand pages of field notes. From June 1973 to June 1978 I worked three-fourths time at Manteno State Hospital, in Manteno, Illinois. After about six months full time on two wards, I moved into the evaluation department and spent the ensuing years studying all levels of activities in the hospital, from ward life to patient staffings, staff development, and general operations and management. I also

worked directly with the hospital's forensic group and, to some extent, with the Cook County Criminal Courts. My Manteno material comprises three manuscript boxes, of which probably about a third concerns the lives of the hospital's professionals—doctors, nurses, psychologists, social workers, clergymen, and so on. These two bodies of material provide a foundation on which my ideas about professional knowledge rest.

2. Why and when particular problems are "expertized" in various societies are major questions. Although parts of answers are scattered throughout the book, I have not addressed these questions directly. There is much work on the area, including Fulton (1961) on the expertizing of death, Loseke and Cahill (1984) on that of battered women, Scull (1975a) on madness, Dezalay (1987) on bankruptcy, Wilson (1959) on religious worship, Braude (1961) on religious education, Zander (1978) on the de-expertizing of legal work, and Cipolla (1973) on that of business transactions. Monographs on professions generally consider the taking of work from lay competitors as well. Bonafe-Schmitt (1985) and Roche (1987) consider the use of nonexperts in France and Japan, respectively, for legal functions explicitly expertized in the United States.

3. To say some problems are objectively close to others is not yet to say what determines closeness, what are the dimensions of this space. We know them only operationally—by seeing which aspects of problems seem unchanged by professions' attempts to reconstruct them. We can, of course, expect that some part of our normal map of these problems is based on objective qualities, and that things like technologies, organizations, and natural and cultural facts partially generate these dimensions.

4. The literature on alcoholism is extensive. Two general treatments are Rorabaugh (1979) and Tyrrell (1979), the former covering the Revolutionary and Federal periods, the latter the period of the first temperance movements before the Civil War. The medical and psychiatric approach to alcoholism in the late nineteenth century is studied in Abbott (1982:448ff.), and the legalization and final de-expertization of the problem are well studied in the many works on the late-nineteenth- and early-twentieth-century prohibition movement, for example, Gusfield (1963).

5. A brilliant exposition of the relation of facts and constructions in the related area of drunk driving is Gusfield (1981). Gusfield's concept of "ownership" is cognate with my concept of "jurisdiction."

6. Many authors have addressed this problem. Relatively "objectivist" writers include Russell (1977) on chemists, McMahon (1984) on electrical engineers, and Friedman (1973) on American lawyers, not to mention the vast majority of less sophisticated writers drawn from the ranks of the various professions (e.g., Carey [1969] on accountants). The objectivist position often works with scientific professions and is generally conservative. Relatively "subjectivist" writers include Loseke and Cahill (1984) on "battered women" experts; Tinker, Merino, and Neimark (1982) on accountants; Scull (1975a, 1975b) on nineteenth-century British psychiatrists; Handler (1973 [especially chap. 3]) on social workers; and central to this position, Becker (1963). The subjectivist position is argued most strongly by those studying the social ser-

vice professions and is generally liberal or radical. Fence sitters include MacKenzie (1981) on statistics; Burchell, Clubb, and Hopwood (1985) on accountants, and many of the writers in Vogel and Rosenberg (1979) and Oleson and Voss (1979).

7. The notion that "the further you go the harder you have to try" suggests that good strategy means not going far. But would-be competitors must go far enough to distinguish what they do from what current incumbents do.

8. Outstanding works on the organizational foundations of teaching are Katz's books (1968, 1971). On the similar foundations of social work, see Lubove (1969). On psychiatry, see Grob (1973). On forestry and hydrology, see Hays (1975). On narrators and on property, see Plucknett (1956).

9. On computer history generally see Moreau (1984), and on languages in particular see Wexelblat (1981). On psychiatrists leaving hospitals, see Grob (1983) and Abbott (1982), and on feminization in teaching, see Sugg (1978).

10. The idea of treating diagnosis and prescription as modes of thought (or alternatively the idea of labeling those modes, with which we are familiar, with these terms) comes from Levine (1971), who, I believe, got it from Richard McKeon. A splendid discussion of the medical knowledge system itself is Freidson's classic 1970a:part 3.

11. For a useful introduction to the actual practice of British law (and American, for that matter) see Johnstone and Hopson (1967). Consultant practice in medicine is discussed at length by Honigsbaum (1979) for England and by Stevens (1971) for America. Freidson (1975) has some ethnographic detail.

12. I first encountered the term "colligation" in McCullagh (1978). Whewell coined it in *The Philosophy of Inductive Science*, in 1847.

13. On medical diagnosis, see Freidson (1970a: chap. 12). For a discussion of the celebrated civil-military situation of the Second World War, see Huntington (1957). On the actual practice of architecture, see Gutman (1983) on the use of formulaic designs, and Blau (1984) on practice conditions in firms. There is not, to my knowledge, a case study of small-scale firms equivalent to, say, Carlin's (1962) excellent study of the actual work of solo lawyers. For personal information about small architectural firms, I am indebted to Richard Kalb of Cone and Kalb, AIA. A brilliant and entertaining fictional account can be found in Cresswell (1964).

14. On divorce practice, see O'Gorman (1963), and for a German comparison, Schumann (1985). Carlin (1962:91ff.), however, presents his solo lawyers as enjoying their "marriage broker" roles. The class and type of clients may of course affect colligation; see, for example, Kadushin (1962, 1966). Murphee (1984) discusses the screening of "dirty work" by subordinate personnel, while both B. K. Rothman (1983) and Loseke and Cahill (1984) discuss screening by professionals themselves. Professions sometimes *expand* areas colligated. See for example, K. Jones's (1985) discussion of the inclusion of family in child psychiatric diagnosis, and Duhart and Charton-Brassard (1973) on "nursing diagnosis."

15. For an interesting (but nonsociological) discussion of the diagnosis process in management systems, see McCosh, Rahman, and Earl (1981). Diagno-

sis is often inaccurate; B. Moore (1984) has a brief historical review of relevant studies on medical diagnosis.

16. On the endocrine diseases as nervous diseases, see chapter 10. Having identified manic depression with a biological marker, researchers are now announcing it to be hereditary (Kolata 1987). The earlier redefinition of it as lithium insufficiency was openly visible to me throughout my fieldwork both in clinic and hospital.

17. On architectural practice, see Brain (1984), Gutman (1981), and Boyle (1977).

18. See, for example, Gutman (1983).

19. On chiropractic as specializing in medical residuals, see Cleary (n.d.). Another paper on a residual population is Brumberg's (1982) discussion of "chlorotic girls."

20. There are professions specializing in diagnostic work: clinical psychology in its early days, optometrists, and others. Such groups generally seem to be subordinates in divisions of labor. The "information professions," however, represent a new approach to such specialization. See chapter 8.

21. The treatment system of nineteenth-century British psychiatry illustrates lumping by treatment type (Scull 1975b). Hyperemesis and schizophrenia are both treated by phenothiazine drugs, although of considerably different strengths in the two cases.

22. Delegation is widely studied, and I shall return to it several times. On the general organization of actual legal work see Johnstone and Hopson (1967), Spangler (1986), and Lochner (1975). On medicine see, among many others, Chauvenet (1972), Strauss (1985), and the various essays in Freidson and Lorber (1972).

23. For information on law practice I am indebted to Scott Thatcher.

24. See Lesse (1968) and Stiles, Shapiro, and Elliott (1986).

25. On the danger of nonspecific treatments in, for example, nursing, see Reinhard (1986). A similar conflict between highly mathematicized and naturalistic treatments separates geophysicists from the geologists they are invading (Personal communication, Roger Revelle). On measurability, see, for example, Geison (1980) on medicine. Rosenkrantz (1974) discusses the decline of public health medicine once results became less measurable. On efficacy itself, there is a surprisingly small literature. See Grob (1973, 1983) on nineteenth-century-American psychiatry, and Scull (1975a) on nineteenth-century-British, McKeown (1979) on medicine generally, Cleary (n.d.) on chiropractic, Roeber (1979) on colonial lawyers, and again, Rosenkrantz (1974) on public health medicine.

26. In most professions, cost is a central dimension aspect of treatment decisions. Like medicine with its third-party insurance, law, too, has to some extent avoided the cost problem with the contingent fee. But in most professions—accountancy, psychoanalysis, social work, and above all in industrially employed professions like engineering—cost of treatment is a central issue. Yet if cost has been an absent factor in American medicine, other "profession-

ally irrelevant" client factors—age, general health, emotional outlook, family support—have been as powerful in reshaping treatment there.

27. The correlation of client status and professional status is taken up in chapter 5. More generally, see Abbott (1981). On prediagnosing, see, for example, Kadushin (1962, 1966). Despite the disattractions of brokering, it is extremely necessary, and individual professionals sometimes pride themselves on the sophistication of their brokering knowledge. Schumann (1985) deals with brokering, both in colligation and prescription, among German lawyers.

28. On patient understanding and its impact on medical treatment, see F. Davis (1960) and McKinlay (1976). On costs see, for example, Rothstein's (1972) discussion of competitors underselling regular medicine in the nineteenth century. British lawyers' competitive problems are discussed at length in chapter 9. Client relations in psychotherapy are discussed in Henry, Sim, and Spray (1971).

29. There are surprisingly few studies of actual professional inference— ethnographic accounts of professionals thinking about problems and defining them. Examples are B. K. Rothman (1983), Loseke and Cahill (1984), and Latour and Woolgar (1979). Most writing about professional inference is of course written by professionals themselves. Schön (1983) is an ethnographic and comparative account, but somewhat romanticized. It takes inference as the dominant process in professional work, which belies virtually all other data on practice.

30. On tactics, see R. Holmes (1976), Koenig (1975), Fuller (1961); and on strategy more generally, see Earle (1966). Churchill is said to have remarked that Jellicoe was "the only man on either side who could lose the war in an afternoon."

31. On chiropractic, see Wardwell (1952) and Cleary (n.d.). On neurology, see chapter 10.

32. On inferential chains in architecture, see Gutman (1981) and Boyle (1977). Detailed analyses of inference in medicine are Cebul and Beck (1985) and Engelhardt, Spicker, and Towers (1977). The latter is undoubtedly the finest formal analysis of professional knowledge available. On military inference and its development see Spector (1977) and Fuller (1961).

33. The literature on routine work and deprofessionalization is extensive. See Ritti et al. (1974) on parish assistants, Denzin (1968) on pharmacists, Coe (1970) on anesthesiology, Previts and Merino (1979) on accounting (the ICC issue is discussed on 162; see also Carey 1969:57, 60), and Johnstone and Hopson (1967) on lawyers. The psychiatrist quote is from my own fieldwork. The theoretical literature on this subject is discussed in chapter 5, but the classic citation has been Jamous and Peloille (1970) on the "indeterminacy/technicality ratio."

34. On Meyer, see Abbott (1982:388–93). The occult professions have foundered over precisely this problem. The mediums discussed in the first chapter, the astrologers, and other occult professionals have generally held that every problem must be handled in its own special way. There is no simple

system that can be applied by laymen to professionally trivial cases to illustrate how effective the professional knowledge system is. As a result, occult professions have gradually lost control of jurisdiction over predicting the future, an area in which they were once prominent, to state councillors and, latterly, policy scientists, whose knowledge systems are more easily legitimated, if not always more successful.

35. The contrast between academic and working professional knowledge has had some study. See Montagna (1974: chap. 7) on accounting, Maulitz (1979) on clinical medicine, Kohler (1982) on biochemistry, Sugarman (1986) on British lawyers, and Chauvenet (1973) on French medicine. Dezalay (1986) and Brain (1984) argue that the ambiguous interrelation of the two levels is central to professional life, a conclusion with which I agree.

36. Even academic professions, that is, professions of college and university professors, have "academic" and "practical" sectors. Most research in most academic fields is done at a relatively small number of universities, the knowledge there developed being "applied" (i.e., taught) elsewhere in the system. My argument applies to academics generally, with professors' worries about "relevance" and "classroom presentation" being the colligational and prescriptive problems, and so on. The example of indexing I owe to James Anderson.

37. The legitimating function of academic knowledge is evident to anyone who opens virtually any professional textbook. Sugarman (1986) contains an elegant discussion of the issue in British law. An alternative approach to the relation of theory and practice is Bensman and Lilienfeld (1973), which sees general values as directly implicit in professional work, rather than as consciously developed by academic workers.

38. On music see, for example, Zarlino ([1558] 1983) and Rameau ([1722] 1971), the first arguing, with Castiglione, that music can be understood and composed only through adequate knowledge of all arts and sciences, and the latter preferring modern modes to ancient ones for their greater devotion to that greatest of all 18th-century values, reason. On the later rise of musical critics, see Anthony (1978: chap. 9) on French baroque aesthetics, and more generally, Graf (1971). On literary criticism, see Wellek (1963), who explicitly paints critics as the theorists on literature.

39. On the gentlemanly army, see Harries-Jenkins (1977) and Spiers (1980).

40. On military theory generally, and these authors in particular, see Earle (1966). T. M. Barker (1975) gives an elegant discussion of the relation of thought and practice in the military, although for an earlier period.

41. On psychiatry's attempt to take over criminality, see Tighe (1983, 1985). Weber's discussion is in Weber (1954: chap. 7).

42. There is a great debate about teaching and texts. Texts have dominated teaching in European professions, while practice has the British ones. The American situation lies in the middle. That "real teaching" was done, not from books, but from cases, sharply curtailed the spread of scientific medicine; see, for example, Maulitz (1979), Peterson (1978), and Ludmerer (1983, 1985). A

similar allegiance exists in American law; see Chase (1979) and Robert Stevens (1983). See also Kadushin (1969) on education in music.

43. On faith healers, see chapter 10. On forestry and hydrology, see the discussions scattered throughout Hays (1975). Occasionally clarity is foregone for academic collaboration across disciplines. See, for example, Rado (1987) on the issue of defining death.

44. Throughout the book, I have referred to professions with recognized subjective definitions (diagnoses, inferences, treatments, and academic work) of some objective problem as possessing "cultural jurisdiction." The issue of recognition is taken up in the next chapter.

## Chapter Three

1. To ignore the content of claims, which I shall largely do, is somewhat heretical. But it is without question more important to settle the general how much and where questions before dealing with the fine details of what actually makes up dominant jurisdiction as a social claim. The English theoretical literature on professions has specialized on this subject, particularly on state claims. See Portwood and Fielding (1981), Fielding and Portwood (1980), and T. J. Johnson (1967, 1977).

2. Most monographic studies of professional development contain lengthy discussions of audience (and settlement) issues. I shall generally note only particularly strong cases. A case illustrating all three audiences well is that of British personnel managers; see Timperley and Osbaldeston (1975).

3. Interesting cases are Gieryn (1983) on scientists; Portwood and Fielding (1981) on a variety of professions; and Baker (1985) on an interesting failed group, the country-life professions.

4. On obligation, see Abbott (1983) on professional ethics generally, and Rueschemeyer (1973) on German lawyers. Medicine and public health are the best-studied areas on this subject. See Stone (1980) on German doctors, Burnham (1982) on American medicine, J. L. Brand (1965) on British public health, and Léonard's (1981) lengthy discussion of French doctors.

5. On the public discourse of professional life, see Scull (1975b) on Victorian psychiatrists, Ludmerer (1985) on the Flexner Report, Léonard (1981) on the French medical press, Bancaud (1985) on French lawyers, DeFleur (1964) and Gitlin (1977) on televised professionals, and Scott (1979) on professionals in the nineteenth-century lyceums. Viollet-le-Duc, the great French architect, wrote a charming novelette (1874) for young men on how to build a house. On ethics codes and enforcement, see Abbott (1983).

6. The time jurisdictional claims take is well illustrated in Kobrin's (1966) study of American midwives.

7. On the nature of public discourse, see the sources cited above (n. 5) and also Sussman (1977) and Weisz (1978) on the problems nineteenth-century French doctors had because they were *not* homogeneous.

8. For positive and negative views of hyperkinesis, see Shaffer and Greenhill (1979), negative; Loney (1980), positive; and Aman (1984), positive.

9. On accountants' prerogatives, see Carey (1969, 1970). Lawyers, of course, contest these, see chapter 5, note 39. More generally, good discussions of legal claims are Scull (1975a, 1975b) on Victorian psychiatrists, Voyenne (1959) on French journalists, and Dezalay (1986) on French lawyers.

10. On the *Conseil*, see Rendel (1970), and on the role of French ministries see, among many others, Léonard (1981) and Weisz (1978). Parliament's role is easily traced in Millerson (1964), and the characteristic American style in Gilb (1966) and, for the recent deregulation, Blair and Rubin (1980).

11. On American disestablishment, see Rothstein (1972).

12. On the criminal responsibility of the insane, see Biggs (1955).

13. Reconsideration of the French case makes me revise this judgment later. It may be more correct that legal professional privileges endure in *legislatively dominated* states. Where administrative groups dominate, as in France, legal change can be both sudden and extensive.

14. A good general study of a relatively open task area involving several professions is Henry, Sim, and Spray (1971).

15. Interesting studies of professional services in open markets (what the French call *professions libérales*) are Carlin (1962) on urban lawyers, Handler (1967) on small-city lawyers, Ladinsky (1976) and Lochner (1975) on aspects of legal practice, Wilton-Ely (1977) on British architects, and Melosh (1982) on American and Abel-Smith (1960) on British nursing. Melosh (1982), Carlin (1962), and Fulton (1961), on clergymen and funeral directors, offer discussions of urban competition. British nursing's competition with medicine for primary care was, interestingly, largely rural.

16. The literature on professionals in organizations is vast. Good case studies involving a variety of professions are to be found in Freidson (1970a), Smigel (1964), Montagna (1974), Blau (1984), and Boyle (1977). Negotiations for internal divisions of labor are discussed in Bucher (1962), Schatzman and Bucher (1964), Bucher and Stelling (1969), and Lorber and Satow (1977).

17. Workplace assimilation is discussed in Strauss et al. (1964), Chauvenet (1972), Graham (1931), and E. Jones (1981). The first two, like most workplace studies, involve medical divisions of labor. The latter pair concern absorption of accounting knowledge by lawyers and legal knowledge by accountants. That this happens in open markets indicates that assimilation is a general phenomenon. For another interesting case, see Dhoquois (1985) on the French law of work.

18. Smigel (1964), Montagna (1974) and Owings (1973) discuss elite firms in law, accounting, and architecture, respectively. The mental-hospital example is from my own fieldwork.

19. Coe (1970) presents a good example of a group (anesthesiologists) emphasizing assimilation upward and sharp boundaries downward. Most of these practices were evident in my own fieldwork, both in the university hospital and the state mental hospital. The issue of irrelevant education, however, is widely noted: see LaVopa (1979) and Olesko (1982) on German teachers, Weiss (1982) and Shinn (1978) on French engineers, and Lortie (1959) and Gordon (1980) on American law.

20. See the interprofessional stereotypes discussed in Henry, Sim, and Spray (1971, 1973), as well as the discussion of status strategies in Bosk (1979). Dingwall (1977) gives a splendid discussion of workplace strategies for image maintenance.

21. On television, see, again, DeFleur (1964) and Gitlin (1977). On the American Orthopsychiatric Association, see Abbott (1982).

22. For a more extensive analysis of the origins of modern psychotherapy, see chapter 10.

23. Changes in arenas of competition are discussed extensively in chapter 6.

24. Any monograph about the rise of a dominant profession produces a picture of the claim of full jurisdiction, for example, Parry and Parry (1976), Stevens (1971), Freidson (1970a), Carey (1969, 1970), E. Jones (1981), and so on. Reader (1966) and Larson (1977) cover a number of them at once. An interesting picture of shifting jurisdictional lines (between pharmacy and medicine) is Kronus (1976).

25. By "associational professionalism" I mean professionalism based largely on independent practice, with voluntary associations for exchanging professional knowledge, conducting professional education and regulation, and attempting to co-opt state authority. Such professionalism characterized England from the early nineteenth to the mid twentieth century and the United States from the mid nineteenth to the early twentieth century. I am loosely contrasting it with bureaucratic professionalism, which has always characterized the Continent and which increasingly characterizes the United States. To identify professionalism generally with associational professionalism is to define most of the interesting questions about the institutionalization of expertise out of existence.

26. On scientists and power, see Price (1965).

27. The case of lawyer vigilante groups is considered in chapter 9.

28. Like "jurisdiction," "time immemorial" is another legal metaphor. I am not using it in the technical sense (i.e., A.D. 1189).

29. The standard work on British nursing is Abel-Smith (1960). American nursing (Melosh 1982) had a stronger freelance component; nurses were commonly paid by their patients directly until their successful subordination by doctors. For subordinated divisions of labor under solicitors, see Johnstone and Hopson (1967); under clergymen, Douglass (1926); under architects, Boyle (1977).

30. On fights resulting in subordination, see the nursing sources just cited, as well as Tackett (1977) and Meyers (1976) on clergy and schoolteachers in rural France; Shinn (1978) on various levels of French engineers; Bogart (1984) on architects and architectural sculptors; Léonard (1981) on nineteenth-century French medicine, clergy, and nursing; and Chauvenet (1972) and Duhart and Charton-Brassard (1973) on recent French nursing.

31. On subordinate creation, see Bliss and Cohen (1977), Ford (1975), and especially Schneller (1976), on physician's assistants; and Austin (1978) on social-work paraprofessionals.

32. On the uneasiness of subordination, see the excellent paper by Albrecht (1979) on probation officers.

33. I have used the phrase "division of labor" somewhat ambiguously here, to refer both to situations in which two or more groups do exactly the same work in a jurisdiction and to situations in which they share it through functional interdependence. Generally the former evolve rapidly into the latter, and so I believe the ambiguity is not worrisome. (Kronus 1976, for example, discusses such a case, that of pharmacy and medicine, which ends up in subordination.) An interesting current fight concerns bankruptcy in France, for which lawyers, accountants, and *conseils juridiques* are making attempts (Dezalay 1987). The French teachers, noted above in subordination under rural clergy, eventually became independent notables on their own, achieving a division of labor. On marital counseling, see Nichols (1973) and Prochaska and Prochaska (1978).

34. On architectural practice, see Gutman (1981), Boyle (1977), Wilton-Ely (1977), and for large practices particularly, Owings (1973). Calvert (1967:209) notes that engineers actually thought architects totally irrelevant to building.

35. See Graham (1931), McLaren (1937), and various entries in Carey (1969, 1970) and Previts and Merino (1979).

36. On British accountants and their emergence, see Stacey (1954) and E. Jones (1981). On joint specialties, see, for example, M'Candlish (1889), on accountants and actuaries; and Walton (1909), Meisner (1927) and Griswold (1955), on accountancy and law.

37. On actual use of the insanity defense, see Carnahan (1978).

38. Intellectual jurisdiction is the cultural jurisdiction of chapter 2, recognized socially, but unextended by substantial dominance in service provision. I shall use the terms interchangeably in the sequel. On psychotherapy generally, see chapter 10. A standard source is Henry, Sim, and Spray (1971, 1973). See also books on the individual professions involved, for example, Dorken et al. (1976) and Rogow (1970). The retreat of psychiatry to biology is well known now. Drugs for depression are familiar, and one for obsession has, I believe, recently been announced.

39. On pastoral care generally, see the last section of chapter 10. I have benefited from discussions of this matter with James Colquhoun and James Gill.

40. On advice as expansion see, for accounting E. Jones (1981), for pediatrics Halpern (1982), and for psychiatry Tighe (1985).

41. This "humanistic" legitimacy for pastoral care may have been a passing phenomenon. In the 1970s, many books and articles pointed to the importance of radical movements—most of them radical in their reliance on populist or humanitarian legitimacy—in the professions: Powell (1979), Gerstl and Jacobs (1976), Gross and Osterman (1972), Perrucci (1973). These movements, it seems to me, have not really survived into the 1980s. Changes in legitimacy generally are considered in chapter 7.

42. On client differentiation in nineteenth-century British medicine, see Parry and Parry (1976), Kronus (1976), and Reader (1966); in contemporary

psychotherapy, see Henry, Sim, and Spray (1971); in law, Heinz and Laumann (1982), Auerbach (1976), Carlin (1962, 1966), and Ladinsky (1963); and in architecture, Gutman (1981, 1983) and Wilton-Ely (1977). In several of these cases, client differentiation is a correlate of actual professional differentiation or amalgamation. Client differentiation between professions is indeed homologous with client differentiation within professions. (As I shall reemphasize from time to time, my argument applies as much within professions as between them.)

43. The history of this differentiation can be followed in E. Jones (1981), Stacey (1954), and Carr-Saunders and Wilson (1933).

44. Hidden structures for client settlements are discussed by many writers on many professions, for example, Carlin (1962), O. Hall (1949), and Kadushin (1966). Social-worker differentiation is discussed by Wilensky and Lebeaux (1958).

45. Most monographs on professions contain extensive discussions of major professional associations, and occasionally, as in the case of American accounting (e.g., Lubell, 1980), discuss interrelations between competing associations. Studies of the full organizational life of professions—including all the various groups and societies at several levels, are rarer. Garceau's analyses of librarians (1949) and doctors (1961) are exceptions. Millerson (1964) offers an excellent catalogue of the organizational life of British professions. There is no equivalent, to my knowledge, for the United States. Theoretical works also discuss the various structures of professionalism. Since these are extensively discussed in the opening chapter, I shall not further note them here. I have not discussed (here) unionism among professionals, concerning which there is a large literature. It is clear from France, where professional unions are common after the late nineteenth century, that there is nothing particularly strange in organizing explicit professional associations around issues of self-interest to augment those around issues of discipline or knowledge. The functions are simply run together in the Anglo-American setting. The potential rise of unionism in American professions today generally reflects the bureaucratization discussed in chapter 6 and the change in legitimacy (away from a legitimacy of character) discussed in chapter 7. Some references on professional unions are Hoffman (1976) and Goldstein (1955, 1959) on engineers, Hopkins (1971) on airline pilots, Fisher (1980) on social workers, Murphey (1981) on teachers, McArthur (1984) on actors, and J. M. Clark (1967) on French teachers. Corwin (1965, 1970) treats professionalism (among teachers) itself as a "militant" process.

46. On schooling, see Ludmerer (1985) and Kaufman (1976) on American, and Newman (1957) and Poynter (1966) on British, medicine; Robert Stevens (1983) on American, and Abel-Smith and Stevens (1967) on British, law; Sass (1982) on American, and Whitley, Thomas, and Marceau (1981) on British and French, business; Shinn (1980) and Weiss (1982) on French, and Calvert on American, engineers; and Hughes et al. (1973) on a number of professions. (There are many works also on universities generally, for which see the last section of chapter 7.) On ethics, see Abbott (1983). On licensing and other

forms of regulation, see Shryock (1967) on American medicine, White (1978) on laboratory personnel, McKean (1963) on American lawyers, and general material by Freidson (1984), Angel (1970), and Blair and Rubin (1980).

47. There are, as I have said, many studies of professionals in bureaucracies, but few of professional worksites in general. Sources on both large consolidated worksites and independent practitioners were given earlier, during the discussion of workplace competition (nn. 16–22). New worksites are always appearing; see, for example, Dickson (1984). Professions not only create, but also destroy, social structures in the process of formation. In particular, they have tended to shed direct links with commodity sales. Druggists have tried to separate themselves from retail (Denzin 1968), and opticians have dropped the associations with the photographic and jewelery trades with which they began.

48. On these special sites, there are fine review volumes for the United States (Oleson and Voss 1979) and France (Fox and Weisz 1980).

49. Few studies examine the relation of rank and file to major professional structures. See, however, Abbott (1982) on psychiatrists, Gelfand (1980) on French surgeons, Spano (1982) and Fisher (1980) on social workers, and Garceau (1949) on librarians. On specialization, see Stevens (1971) and Heinz and Laumann (1982). The process is further discussed in the next chapter.

50. See W. L. Smith (1957).

51. See Calvert (1967) on internal subordination in engineering.

52. The role a group plays in interprofessional competition is clearly open to empirical question; coalescence must be measured. In this book, however, brevity will generally force me to take it for granted.

53. On computers and education, see Hunter et al. (1975) and Holden (1984).

54. I will discuss the issue of demand and demography at length in chapter 5.

Chapter Four

1. Of all the classic aspects of professionalization, only licensing had this exclusive quality, and licensing is a poor substitute for the complex reality of jurisdiction.

2. Parsons ([1939] 1954, 1964, 1968), Ben-David (1963), Bledstein (1976), Larson (1977), Freidson (1970a, 1970b).

3. For examples of the carnivorous competitors model, see Parry and Parry (1976), Berlant (1975), and the various works of Ivan Illich.

4. There was some specialization in China, but compared to that in the West it was negligible. See Hartwell (1971a, 1971b). The French have an analogous faith in interchangeability (see Suleiman 1978), and the pattern of weak specialization is repeated in civil services elsewhere (e.g., Kubota 1969).

5. As a sometime student of vacancy chains among college football coaches and mental hospital superintendents, I originally expected to find some actual chains of effects, some real propagation through the system. In fact, there probably is very little such propagation. Task-area boundaries (discussed in the

last section of this chapter) and internal differentiation (discussed in the next chapter) absorb most effects locally. Nonetheless, the vacancy metaphor offers a useful narrative device for organizing the theoretical analysis, and I have retained it for that reason. The major citation on vacancy models is H. C. White (1970). My own work is Smith and Abbott (1983) and Abbott (forthcoming).

6. On interweaving sufficient and necessary causes, see Dray (1978).

7. The phrase "bump chain" is White's.

8. A few colleagues have complained about the word "system," which they feel has dated associations. I use it (in place of the more trendy "structure") because it suggests boundedness and necessary interaction. The idea of chains of effects within a system entails, most importantly, a philosophy of history emphasizing contingency, a philosophy I shall reiterate in the final chapter. Although I fully recognize the great cultural and social forces felt by many to determine the current history of professions, I feel their effects on professions are idiosyncratic, mediated by the system structure discussed here. There are no simple answers about the past and, I will argue in the final chapter, no very simple predictions about the future of professions. I should also note that I am not using system in the Luhmannian sense objected to by Bourdieu (1986). I *am* using it in a sense akin to Bourdieu's *champ*, but Bourdieu means by *champ* what I will later call "task areas," and in any case, "system" implies codetermination and structure, which "field" in English (outside of mathematics) does not. I thank Yves Dezalay for calling Bourdieu's work to my attention.

9. External changes will be discussed in chapters 6 and 7.

10. The serjeants can be traced through the various volumes of Holdsworth's *History of English Law*. The other examples are discussed below.

11. Since writing this chapter, I have come to see cultural changes as more important. Secularization, while too slow for short run effects, has certainly driven the clergy's history for the last two centuries at least. Moreover, professions like accounting face fairly rapid changes in governmental regulations that constitute much of the basis of their work. While, to be sure, these regulations generally reflect organizational shifts, such sudden changes as the 1954 and 1986 Income Tax Acts are clearly to be seen as changes in the (cultural) system of legislation. See, for example, Previts and Merino (1979), E. Jones (1981), Barbier (1972), and Lafferty (1975), on governmental rules in American, British, French, and European accounting, as well as Bancaud and Dezalay (1980) on French law and detailed studies of accounting like Hein (1962). On governmental destruction of professional jurisdiction, see the discussion in chapter 9 of British lawyers and Cipolla (1973) on notaries. A similar role can be assigned to organizational decisions generally; the modern teaching roles at Oxford and Cambridge were created by university decisions to take competitive examinations seriously, which led to privately hired and later publicly supported tutoring (A. J. Engel 1983; Rothblatt 1968).

12. Standard sources on the history of the engineering professions are Shinn (1980), Weiss (1982), Calvert (1967), Calhoun (1960), and McMahon (1984).

13. The case of computer professionals is considered at further length in chapter 9. Today, changes in the technology of deterrence regularly reshape the interprofessional relations of the military, with the Navy returning to an ironic dominance as its submarines prove invulnerable to the air power that humiliated the surface ships of the Second World War.

14. On railway professions, see sources cited in chapter 1. The escape of the telegraphers is evident in the titles of early electrical engineering journals, for example, *Telegraphic Journal and Electrical Review* (1873–91) and *Telegraphic Advocate*, which became *Electric Age* in 1886, *Electrical and Engineering Age* in 1903, and *Electrical Engineering* (merged with *Southern Electrician*) in 1910.

15. The evolution of computing groups is discussed in chapter 8. Basic sources are Kraft (1977), Moreau (1984), Wexelblat (1981), and Pettigrew (1973).

16. On American psychiatry see Grob (1973). On American social work see Lubove (1969), and on Britain, Young and Ashton (1956), Rodgers and Stevenson (1973), and Younghusband (1978). Some other examples: the French social-work professions discussed in Crapuchet (1974), the American librarians discussed by Garrison (1979), and the American teachers discussed by Katz (1968, 1971).

17. On the psychiatric exodus, see Grob (1983) and Abbott (1982). On private practice in social work, see Henry, Sim, and Spray (1973), Cohen (1966), and the sources cited in chapter 10. In France, it is psychologists who are the private-practice profession of counseling (Duflot 1974).

18. On this period of English accounting, see especially E. Jones (1981) and Stacey (1954). The government itself took over most bankruptcy business. The French situation is discussed (tangentially) in Freedeman (1979). I have never managed to find sociological study of *les experts-comptables*.

19. Basic sources on British medicine are Parry and Parry (1976), Reader (1966), and Kronus (1976). The French pharmacists' equivalent attempt (and failure) is chronicled in Léonard (1981), while the relation of French surgeons and physicians (in an earlier period) is discussed by Gelfand (1980). For a clergy example, see the various types of clergy discussed in Pope (1942). The fights between lower- and higher-status French engineers discussed in Shinn (1978) are yet another case. See also Dhoquois (1985) on new groups in the French law of work.

20. Actually, the number of immigrant homeopaths was small, but the knowledge system itself was largely imported. See Kaufman (1971). The internal debate between American and transplanted British accounting is discussed by Previts and Merino (1979). Another interesting case of peripheral attack (in this case on medicine and nursing) is the current "reprofessionalization" in pharmacy (Birenbaum 1982) through the creation of a "clinical pharmacy" focused on individuals' differential reactions to drugs.

21. See Nichols (1973) and Prochaska and Prochaska (1978) on marital counseling. Other examples of enclosure include that of British naval command by seamen and gentlemen (Elias 1950), of British personnel work by

various groups (Timperley and Osbaldeston 1975), of general physiology (Pauly 1984), of biochemistry (Kohler 1982), of "country life" (Baker 1985), and of French legal work for business (Raguin 1972).

22. The general pattern of French state authority over professions is discussed in chapter 6. On the *agréés*, see Herzog (1967), Ripert (1951), and Raguin (1972).

23. Abel-Smith (1960); Garrison (1979).

24. See, on scientific medicine, Vogel and Rosenberg (1979). Operations research and Taylorism are discussed in chapter 8 of this book. The psychiatric claims are discussed in chapter 10. For a strong whiff of economic imperialism, see Hirshleifer (1985). On juvenile delinquency, see Platt (1969).

25. Dozens of sources discuss structural innovations. Reader (1966) and Larson (1977) are probably the best general ones. It is noteworthy that of all professions only the English barristers seem to have completely avoided structural change as a means of protecting jurisdiction, preferring instead absolute monopoly of an increasingly restricted task area.

26. A particularly interesting discussion of the interactions constructing a particular interprofessional border is Larkin (1978) on British radiographers. It is generally difficult to find out from the secondary literature what professionals are actually doing, although actual activity is generally a good guide to jurisdictional shift. Two interesting examples are Calvert (1967:148ff.) and Roy and McNeill (1967: chap.6)

27. On the argument that all social science is economics, see Hirshleifer (1985). On architecture and planning, see the essays in Blau, LaGory, and Pipkin (1983). On hyperactivity, see the sources noted in chapter 3, note 8.

28. I read Gusfield's (1981) brilliant book about drunk driving after writing this chapter, and discovered many similarities in the analyses. His concept of "ownership" closely parallels mine of jurisdiction. The five keys of dramatism are, of course, from Burke (1969).

29. An interesting agency reduction is underway in academics these days, with English departments reminding scientists, social scientists, et al., that since they write their work in texts they are really all under the advisory jurisdiction of the literati. (I thank Bruce Robbins and George Levine for emphasizing this to me.) An earlier episode of the same sort is described by Grafton (1979). The relative hierarchy among the dramatistic ways of organizing jurisdiction clearly explains certain otherwise inexplicable jurisdictional contests. It would be important to consider how cultures determine this hierarchy, and whether serious change is possible. For the moment, my aim is to stress the many possible versions of what I have called reduction. One should note that there are many other aspects to the rhetoric of jurisdictional competition. Contesting professions may focus on the actual or the ideal level of professional work, and on actual skills or purported functions. Combining these dichotomies leads, in teaching, for example, to arguments resting jurisdictional claims on lesson plans (actual level skills), on ability to teach mathematics (ideal skills), on providing education (ideal function), or on "moving 'em through" (actual function). Under different kinds of threats (say from "untrained" teach-

ers, computer education specialists, school administrators) the first three positions might be taken. I can't think of one calling for the fourth. I am indebted
to Alice Fagans, Ann Berkery, and Susan Reinhard for this point.

30. Global metaphors are quite common. On engineering and efficiency,
see Tichi (1987), Hays (1975), Callahan (1962), and Haber (1964). On medicalization, see Fox (1977) and Conrad and Schneider (1980); and on the widespread public health metaphor, Rosenkrantz (1974). The grandiose mental
health metaphors of the seventies are discussed in Dinitz and Beran (1971) and
Wagenfeld and Robin (1976). The vision of electronics as information generally
is discussed in McMahon (1984:231ff.). Halliday (1985) examines such metaphors under slightly different terms.

31. There is no basic history of modern clergy. Merwick (1973) discusses
moves by nineteenth-century Roman Catholic clergy into education and related areas, and various French sources (e.g., Léonard 1981, Meyers 1976)
discuss the clergy's role in health and education there. On the move into social
work, see Lubove (1969) and Douglass (1926); on the move into counseling,
see chapter 10. Ware (1965) gives an excellent discussion of clergymen adapting and not adapting to a new environment.

32. The case of psychiatrists is discussed at length in chapter 10. Gradient
arguments in the broad sense—"our profession should take this over because
it is close to what we do"—are the most common arguments for jurisdictional
change. Thus, nursing tries to take over medical tasks (Melosh 1982), special
education tries to escape medical dominance (Garrier 1983), solicitors move
from conveyancing into land work generally (Miles 1982), and French social
workers, trained in very specific areas, all move towards common and general
involvement in casework (Crapuchet 1974, especially the essays by S. Ginger
and C. Piens and M.-B. Baubrieau). Dentistry is a familiar example of a profession with a prevention rhetoric. It began dealing with fully developed problems, evolved towards prevention, and today is on the brink of putting itself
out of business through all-too-effective prevention (See Gullett 1971 for the
earlier evolution.).

33. The accounting literature has been cited earlier in this chapter (notes
11, 18) and in chapter 1, note 35.

34. Prevention is not the only, but merely the most common, gradient
argument. Gradient arguments are involved when professions take over work
"accessory to treatment"; social workers want to be able to administer routine
psychoactive drugs to "make patients accessible to" their main work (as they
see it) of psychotherapy. Occasionally, groups retreat from prevention, as nursing did from public health work to anchor itself in the medical division of labor.

35. The first time I presented these ideas, Jim Davis asked why they didn't
represent a theory of the division of labor generally. In the following pages I
hope to answer that very challenging question.

36. A general review of recent achievements in AI is Duda and Shortliffe
(1983).

37. Management—business, civil, and military—is an area that lacks any
particular content; that management has not been "professionalized" by any

group that has tried to do so confirms my view of abstraction. Of course, civil and military service are professions, but their identity and above all their ability to reproduce themselves remain tied to the organizations they direct. See, on the professionalization of business Chandler (1977), Sass (1982), and chapter 8 of this book. On civil service, see Kelsall (1955), Kubota (1969), Bendix (1949) and Sharp (1931) and Suleiman (1978) on Britain, Japan, the United States, and France respectively. On the military, see Janowitz (1971), Spiers (1980), and Serman (1982) and Martin (1981) on the American, British, and French armies respectively; see M. Lewis (1960, 1965) on the British Navy.

38. Another profession with "too much" jurisdiction to hold was the American clergy in early Federal times (D. Scott 1978). Another contestant for monumental jurisdiction is nursing, whose current concept of "nursing diagnosis" embraces nearly every aspect of well-being (Reinhard 1986). It will for that reason be untenable. By contrast, the expansion of the various French forms of social work, noted above (note 32), seems to reflect a need to move beyond the artificially restrictive boundaries imposed by the state.

39. The jurisdictional size of a profession of course reflects social-structural pressures as well as cognitive ones. As in many social systems, the underlying, equilibrating forces in the system of professions are often modified by forces like professional power. But since the equilibrium forces are analytically prior, they must be discussed first.

40. Most of these examples have been discussed earlier. It should be noted that the state can enforce levels of function, as in the French creation, in 1971, of the *conseils juridiques* out of previous functions of *agréés* and other sorts of lawyers. The same is occurring today in the developments around bankruptcy (Dezalay 1987). A successful recent amalgamation is the merger of the IRE and AIEE into the IEEE (McMahon 1984), although the IEEE is itself increasingly a federation of separate groups.

41. The issue of engineering's general amalgamation is discussed in Layton (1971). There are several sociological studies of engineering; Gerstl and Hutton (1966), Perrucci and Gerstl (1969), and Prandy (1965). Most focus on the issue of profession and bureaucracy, discussed in chapter 6. On the NAPO's position concerning the BASW, see Younghusband (1978, vol.2:169–70).

42. Division is a very well studied contingency. Theoretical material may be found in Bucher (1962), Bucher and Strauss (1961), Smith (1957), Child and Fulk (1982), and specific to France, Chapoulie (1973). Examples include Rossiter (1979) on agricultural science; Fine (1979:68ff.) on psychoanalysis; Nerot (1974) on French social workers; Léonard (1981) on sectarianism in French medicine; Oldham (1981) and Barbier (1972) on French accountants; Jarvis (1976) on British clergy; Lortie (1959), Ladinsky (1963), Auerbach (1976), and Heinz and Laumann (1982) on American lawyers; and Stevens (1971) on American medicine. Virtually any major monograph on a profession will discuss at least specialization and the forces supporting and retarding it.

43. On mining and civil engineering, see Calhoun (1960) and Calvert (1967: chap.11). The French social work case is again of interest here.

44. In the next chapter, I shall outline the processes of internal differentiation related to vertical division. On apothecaries and grocers, see Kronus (1976). Examples of vertical division, one successful, one so-far unsuccessful, include school superintendents (Callahan 1962) and pharmacy (Birenbaum 1982).

45. I believe the British figures are still correct, although personal communications report increasing gigantism in Britain, except, of course, among barristers. In France, the longstanding restrictions here discussed have definitely been relaxed, at some time in the last decade, to allow much larger firms. With the creation of the *société civile professionelle* in 1966 (Law no. 66-879, 29 November 1966), the government decided to allow to many professions unlimited size, and to others increases beyond then-current limits. Present limits are twelve principals for laboratory directors, ten for doctors and nurses, eight for veterinarians and dentists, seven for surveyors, six for physical therapists, and three for Supreme Court and Council lawyers. To my knowledge there are now no limits for architects, accountants, auditors, or for any type of lawyer or legal advisor (Editions Francis Lefebvre 1986).

46. We don't know whether religious workers actually moved to secular work or the secular profession won through recruitment of the nonreligious. See Douglass (1926) and Abell (1943) on the institutional church. Beyond forces for specialization, division is also sometimes a strategy for intraprofessional competition (Peterson [1978] on Victorian doctors) and sometimes the result of an internal social movement (Ross 1976, M. J. Powell 1979).

47. Numerous properties define this structure. All reflect external social and cultural forces: ideas of legitimate jurisdiction, external constraints on interprofessional competition, and the like. I shall discuss the general history of these forces later; here I am concerned with their impact rather than their origins. My analysis is largely theoretical, since there is no empirical work on the subject.

48. I originally planned to do chapters comparing the actual topologies of this space in America, Britain, and France. However, to lay out even the general task areas seemed so difficult and so controversial that I have not done so, but have merely created a theoretical apparatus for guiding the attempt. Nonetheless, the notion, following Crozier (1964), that systems of professions have a sort of national character seems attractive. The cartesian quality of the French system is striking, although whatever ethnographic data one can find suggests that reality is considerably fuzzier, as Chapoulie (1973) notes. A detailed competitive map of American medical specialties is located in Walter (1967).

49. Delineation of task areas is clearly a central and controversial task. In general, system competition doesn't breach these boundaries. However, while I don't like to suggest that lawyers and engineers fight much about their heartland work, I do think that apparently dissimilar groups—doctors and mechanical engineers, for example—compete (or could compete) more than we think. We must not allow a presentist imperative functionalism to blind us to the plain historical fact that many or most professions have moved around a good

deal in their functions, and that includes, as we shall see in chapter 9, so apparently stable a profession as law. A parallel analysis, noted above, is Bourdieu (1986) on law. Related essays discuss the "fields" of religion (Bourdieu 1971) and science (Bourdieu 1976).

50. Terry Halliday, Stan Katz, and other colleagues have suggested that my model, while all very well and good, applies mostly to the borders of professional work, and that those borders are in fact small areas in comparison to large and stable heartlands. I have two answers. First, understanding the moving borders is essential to understanding changes in the heartland; borders are in fact the central determinants of professional development, as far as I can see. Second, the empirical work in part 3, particularly that on law, convinces me that the heartland is in fact heavily contested as well.

51. Let me here recognize the Hughes school and other direct predecessors to my process view; Hughes (1958), Goode (1960), Bucher and Strauss (1961), Freidson (1970a), Toren (1975), Klegon (1978), Portwood and Fielding (1981), and Child and Fulk (1982).

## Chapter Five

1. There are, of course, other social structures in professions, like licensing and professional organization. But these do not directly differentiate professionals. To the extent that they do so indirectly—which in some professions is considerable—they will behave like the four fundamental structures analyzed here. But these four are structures that explicitly separate the members of a profession—young from old, high from low, bureaucrats from soloists, servants of power from servants of poverty. While they are, of course, important structures in their own right, here I am interested only in how they shape professional development.

2. The argument of this section is detailed, with the relevant evidence on actual hierarchies within professions, in Abbott (1981). The basic argument derives from Douglas (1970). (Many of the sources cited under the topic of vertical division in the preceding chapter are also relevant here.) Hughes et al. (1973) discuss a number of internal stratification systems I had little data on in 1981, particularly clergy and academics. Note that the processes I called colligation and prescription in chapter 2 are basically professional dirty work, filled with impurity through their partial surrender to client control. Dezalay (1986) gives a French perspective on purity in professional knowledge.

3. On psychotherapists see Henry, Sim, and Spray (1971, 1973); on barristers and serjeants, Abel-Smith and Stevens (1967); on foreign medical graduates, Stevens, Goodman, and Mick (1978). Some other examples of regression include Olesko's (1982) German teachers and the various levels of French engineering discussed by Weiss (1982) and Shinn (1980).

4. On medical hierarchies, see Bosk (1979) and O. Hall (1946). On architectural firms, see Owings's (1973) memoir.

5. On the doctors see Walsh (1977) and Morantz-Sanchez (1985). On psychiatrists, see Abbott (1982:236ff.).

6. Although this argument is largely theoretical, it is borne out by my own

field experience and by most of the studies of interprofessional workplaces cited in chapter 3's discussion of divisions of labor.

7. On recent changes in mental health practices, see, for example, Lerman (1982). There is some indication that professionals systematically overestimate their own status, which also may help ease interprofessional status strain (Rettig et al. 1958)

8. I have already discussed client differentiation between professions. The internal phenomenon is largely analogous. See, for example, Carlin's (1962) classic study of lawyers.

9. See O. Hall (1949) on medical clienteles and Heinz and Laumann (1982) on legal ones. The functional and monopolist approaches to professions have so taken professional work for granted that there is surprisingly little study of who actually does what, outside the historians' work. We have a fairly clear picture of client differentiation in medicine and law, but not elsewhere. In heavily divided professions (e.g., British accounting; see Carr-Saunders and Wilson 1933) the subspecialties give a fairly clear map of client differentiation. Larson (1977) attributes client differentiation to the efforts of a professional elite to raise itself above the mass.

10. This connection is emphasized by Auerbach (1976) and such other students of American law as Heinz and Laumann, who have contested my purity interpretation of intraprofessional status (1982:130–32). Other illustrations of the client-intraprofessional status connection may be found in Pope's (1942) clergymen, Austin's (1978) social workers, Léonard's (1981) and Steudler's (1977) French doctors, Meyers's (1976) and LaVopa's (1979) French and German teachers, and Mazerol's (1985) French lawyers.

11. Auerbach (1976) and Pope (1942). On the doctors see especially my discussion of sanitarium practice in Abbott 1982: chap. 3.

12. There is an extensive discussion of librarianship in chapter 8.

13. Michael Powell has informed me that corporate legal departments are starting to retain considerably more work, becoming substantial competitors of the big law firms.

14. On generalists, specialists, and the theory of ecology generally, see Roughgarden (1979). Currently prominent in sociology, the population ecology approach offers a fairly weak analysis of professions because it ignores emergent level forces (i.e., national professional action and cooperation), which are obviously central to professional development. It also assumes professionals and professions to have fewer options for personal and group adaptation than in fact they have.

15. I am basing this judgment on personal field experience.

16. The basic figures on type of employment are available in Evans and Laumann (1983) for America and the Monopolies Commission Report (1970) for England. I have not seen such information for France, although I am sure it exists. Pincemin and Laugier (1959) have figures for medicine, but they predate the invention of sociétés civiles professionelles. As I have noted before (chapter 4, n. 45), the traditional French restrictions on the size of professional partnerships and sociétés have recently been lifted.

17. The usage "heteronomous" and "autonomous" professionals is due to W. R. Scott (1965). R. H. Hall (1967) argues that the two differ less than many analysts feel.

18. Degradation-proletarianization-deprofessionalization is one of the great growth industries of the professions literature. The central citation on degradation generally is Braverman (1976). See also the essays in Derber (1982). On the division of labor in particular professions (recall that this is within a given profession), see Boyle (1977) on architecture, Ritti et al. (1974) on parish clergy, Smigel (1964) on lawyers, and Montagna (1974) on accountants, among many others. On degradation, see, again inter alia, *American Journal of Hospital Pharmacy* (1985) on pharmacists, Calvert (1967) on mechanical engineers, Spangler (1986) on lawyers, Callahan (1962) on teachers, Austin (1978) and Wilensky and Lebeaux (1958) on social work, and Melosh (1982) and Reinhard (1986) on nursing. Theoretical pieces or general reviews include Toren (1975), Haug (1973), Oppenheimer (1973), and Spenner (1983). The first three see major declines in autonomy, skill level, or both, while the last is less sure. Freidson (1986a) provides a characteristically balanced review of this entire literature.

19. On training professionals, see Calvert (1967:150) on draftsmen and engineers, Bosk (1979) on students, interns, and doctors, Smigel (1964) on students, associates, and partners in law firms, and Boyle (1977) on draftsmen and architects.

20. There is a discussion of the computer professions in chapter 8. The chief sources on degradation-deskilling in the area are Kraft (1977), Pettigrew (1973), and Greenbaum (1979).

21. See Callahan (1962), and for the teacher's view, Murphey (1981).

22. Some have undoubtedly gone to administration; some have become the systems analysts of today. We don't know how many have actually suffered personal reduction in work. In teaching, the process is equally unspecified. We know administrators emerged and seized control of a large share of the teaching jurisdiction, but not how many teachers saved themselves by advancing into the administrative positions of the newly bureaucratic schools. On degradation of given professionals, see Markuson (1976) on area bibliographers; see also Steudler (1973) on French, and Kralewski et al. (1985) on American, doctors. The classic example of degradation through hiring of new types of professionals is the hiring of foreign medical graduates; see, for example, Stevens, Goodman, and Mick (1978).

23. Feminization is a major and growing topic in the study of occupations. On feminization in professions see Garrison (1979) on librarians, Melosh (1982) on nursing, and Sugg (1978) and Melder (1972) on teaching. There is a vast literature on women in professions generally, from Etzioni (1969), to Fidell and DeLamater (1971), Grimm (1978), Patterson and Engelberg (1978), and Harris (1981). For an excellent general review, see Brumberg and Tomes (1982). Decline in recruit class, a similar process, is evident in British teaching (Tropp 1957) as in nursing and mechanical engineering, indeed at a time when the latter was all male. Sometimes, the processes of feminization and class

decline are seen in reverse, when women, lower-class men, and other lower-status groups are excluded from upwardly mobile professional groups. Turn-of-the-century American medicine is of course the most familiar example (Walsh 1977, Morantz-Sanchez 1985; see also Parry and Parry [1976] on English doctors), although similar processes are perhaps visible in clinical and applied psychology (where women like Augusta Bronner were early leaders; see Napoli 1981), and authorship (Tuchman and Fortin 1984). In general, degradation itself seems a consequence of other forces in the system of professions and beyond it, and the particular form degradation takes—feminization, class decline, and so on—has, at least in the evidence I see, very little causal effect on the system. Some might argue that the very notion of "profession," both as real-world label and as social-science concept, is gender- or class-based, and that consequently gender and/or class have been the central determinants of professional development since the Industrial Revolution. I disagree. That professions pursue status is obvious. That this may involve class or gender alliance is unquestionable. That these alliances determine the major aspects of professional development is simply wrong. They reinforce, perhaps, but they do not cause. Why they do not is to some extent directly treated later in the chapter. The more important, indirect treatment comes through my offering an alternative theory that allows explanation of so many things a purely class or gender theory of expert labor cannot. For an elegant analysis of feminization coincident with *rise* in status, see Maack (1983), where women librarians lead the French profession's assault on new jurisdictions.

24. Bledstein (1976) extensively discusses the idea of the professional career. On medicine, see O. Hall (1946, 1949); on law see Smigel (1964) and Lortie (1959); and on accounting see Montagna (1974).

25. A good example is the withdrawal of engineers from actual practice into operations and management as their careers advance. See, for example, Perrucci and Gerstl (1969:130ff.), Gerstl and Hutton (1966:88ff.) and Goldberg and Shenhav (1984). Coe (1970) presents the similar example of anesthesiologists.

26. On specialty migration, see the interesting data of the Bureau of Labor Statistics on engineers and chemists—U.S.B.L.S. Reports no.682 (1941) and no.1132 (1953).

27. Demographic rigidity is a widespread phenomenon. Pashigian (1978) uses it to explain slow response to demand by American lawyers. Rigid demographic structures can also lead to *overproduction* if recruitment is not controlled. Kotschnig (1937), Ben-David (1963), McClelland (1983), and many others have written about professions' inability to deal with societally induced excess recruitment in early-twentieth-century Europe, and O'Boyle (1970) has described the same phenomenon a century earlier. Cipolla (1973) saw similar factors in Renaissance notaries, as Sussman (1977) did with nineteenth-century French doctors. On military careers, see Janowitz (1971) and Spector (1977) for the more modern period. Victorian Britain had a purchase system that rendered the career considerably more erratic (Spiers 1980, Harries-Jenkins 1977). Reiss (1955) describes the greater career stability of the "established"

professions, empirically identifying rigidity and dominance. Evans and Laumann's (1983) figures tell much the same story. Léonard (1981) describes the rigid career patterns of French doctors and their implications for service.

28. Calvert (1967) makes a similar argument about the defeat of "shop culture" (apprenticeship) by "school culture" (schooling) in mechanical engineering. The law case is discussed in detail in chapter 9.

29. Examples of unrigid careers can be found among French business managers (Monjardet 1972) and early journalists from France, England, and the United States (Voyenne 1959; A. J. Lee 1976; Schudson 1981). Change is visible in French teachers (Bianconi 1959) whose previously long and stable careers have become noticeably more erratic. Purvis (1973) and Lortie (1975) give classic pictures of the relatively porous career patterns of British and American teachers, respectively, while Hilsum and Start (1974) show the relative rigidity of the bureaucratic structure within which this flux occurs.

30. On accounting, see E. Jones (1981). On American academics, see Cartter (1976) and Solmon et al. (1981). On social work in the Depression, see Fisher (1980) and Spano (1982).

31. The phenomenon of irrelevant education is discussed above in chapter 3, note 19.

32. On the colonization of philosophy in Germany, see Ben-David and Collins (1966). The internal hybridization characteristic of the clergy represents essentially the same phenomenon as out-migration, but without the change of name.

33. The phenomenon of pool professions is very interesting. Journalism has clearly been one (see the sources cited in note 29), as has teaching (Purvis 1973); and users of such pools include clergy (Jarvis [1976] on Britain), as well as arts professions. Through the system of half pay for inactive service, the British military acted until the nineteenth century as a kind of pool profession (Spiers 1980; M. Lewis 1965). See also Fleury (1974:283) on French social work as a second-choice occupation. On music, see chapter 6, note 3.

34. Modern figures on turnover come from Evans and Laumann (1983). On nineteenth-century psychiatrists, see Abbott (1982: chap. 4). On clergymen, see Calhoun (1965).

35. Sociologists' and historians' implicit faith in careers has meant there is little data on interprofessional migration. There is some material on joint careers, which I have already discussed. There is also some evidence on hybridization (Ben-David and Collins [1966] on physiologists in academic philosophy; Bureau of Labor Statistics Bulletin no. 1027 (1951) on various engineering migrations; Holley (1976) on academics in librarianship; and Reissman (1956) on retired Army generals). But of the total linking of groups through migration we have little idea.

36. The impact of French planning is obvious in the work of Shinn (1978) and Day (1978) on the creation and development of various engineering schools in the nineteenth century. In certain of the legal professions, the state maintains absolute control of numbers through a purchase system (*les offices ministériels*). Over the social professions generally, the French government

exercises numerical oversight through *la planification*, the preparation and legislation of official social-economic plans. See, for example, Nizard (1972) for a discussion of plans.

37. There is an extensive literature on levels of time, a subject I have touched on in Abbott (1983). In retrospect, I can see that my theory in this book follows the *annaliste* practice of dividing time into the three levels of *structure, conjoncture*, and *événement*. These parallel my time scales for legal, public, and workplace jurisdiction changes. In this sense, my whole theoretical scheme is an attempt to show how changes at the various levels interact.

38. On managing clerks, see Johnstone and Hopson (1967). They are discussed at some length in chapter 9. As of this writing (June 1987) the solicitors' monopoly of conveyancing has been recently ended (Michael Powell, personal communication).

39. See the various discussions of this battle in Carey (1969, 1970). For a contemporary account of the great case *Agran v. Shapiro*, see Eaton (1955).

40. On the era of heroic treatment, see Rothstein (1972) and especially Pernick's (1985) account of the medical and public reluctance to accept anesthesia as a legitimate technique. Halliday (1985) considers the subject generally, as one aspect of professional power.

41. The journalist example is discussed in chapter 8, and the lawyer example in chapter 9. That courts help the lawyers with more frequency in the United States than in England—where the solicitors have had real difficulties getting senior judges (barristers all) to see their point of view—clearly indicates the direct use of objective power external to the system of professions. The military's direct access to physical force might be a great advantage in interprofessional competition, but it hasn't been used in the countries here studied.

42. Co-optation of state power is discussed in Gelfand's (1980) book on French surgeons of the ancien régime. Any of the standard works on American medicine (e.g., Rothstein 1972; Stevens 1971) discusses similar issues. The British professions' somewhat more lonely stance is discussed in Millerson (1964). On co-optation of foundations, see Brown (1979) on medicine, and Abbott (1982) and Grob (1983) on psychiatry. Until this century American professions seldom tried to derive power from affiliation with universities; indeed the British have only begun to do so since the Second World War. Now, the very universality of these affiliations has degraded their efficacy. It should be noted that incumbent professions are not necessarily in a privileged position vis-à-vis external power. It is theoretically open to all those who wish to acquire it, although, as we shall see, there are reasons why it generally goes to well-situated dominants.

43. Class alliances are heavily studied, as the links between dominant professions and the upper classes are clear in all societies. Reader (1966) offers a survey of the situation in England in the nineteenth century. On psychoanalysis, see Henry, Sim, and Spray (1971, 1973), as well as Oberndorf (1964). On accountants' and lawyers' links to the corporate sector—through the outplacement of those not making partner—see Smigel (1964) and Montagna

(1974). Very many books deal with the class issue, usually under the heading of studying the social origins of professionals. (There are sometimes surprises in this literature. Kelsall [1955] finds a class alliance in the British civil service that Bendix [1949] does not find in America.) A few books focus directly on the issue, for example, Auerbach (1976) on lawyers and Navarro (1978) on medicine.

44. On class in social work see Lubove (1969), Fisher (1980), and Handler (1973).

45. These exercises of power are so ubiquitous as to need little reference. Virtually any serious monograph on a profession will produce dozens of illustrations. Berlant (1975) on medicine in America and Britain is a particularly systematic study.

46. On solicitors and their markets, see chapter 9. The argument for a slow-changing legal-state arena will be somewhat modified in the discussion of France in the following chapter.

47. The oligarchy issue will be treated at length in the next chapter. Treating competition between dominants and subordinates as fundamentally similar to competition between equal dominants may be unwise; see the discussion of degradation above. Feminization illustrates this well. A number of times in America jurisdictions have been split into large routine sections and smaller more "professional" sections; often this process has been accompanied by feminization of the subordinate group. The separation of educational administration out of teaching and of special and university librarianship out of general librarianship are examples. The use of power here was not to prolong or win a jurisdictional contest, but to divide a jurisdiction to the benefit of one group working within it. In the related case of nursing and medicine, power is used to maintain a subordinate relationship in practice that may have lost its subjective justification, again with the same gender concomitant. In the short run, at least, these contests are clearly settled by the exercise of interprofessional power, although in the long run women have begun to reinvade the upper groups.

48. The power of clients has been so clear in the case of engineering, for example, that many analysts have had difficulty treating engineering as a profession, making power over clients a central attribute of professionalism.

49. On the current situation of American medicine, see Stevens (1971) and Starr (1982).

## Chapter Six

1. The great social and cultural changes were not, of course, disconnected developments. Bureaucratization and rationalization, the universities with their new knowledge and the state with its new powers are all part of an overarching event, the rise of industrial societies. By viewing them separately I am giving an appearance of independent explanatory power that may be illusory. This problem is, however, preferable to its alternative; it was precisely viewing these changes as an interconnected whole that produced the functional model in which professions differentiated inevitably into reified ideal social functions.

2. See, for example, Calvert (1967), Calhoun (1960), and McMahon (1984) on mechanical, civil, and electrical engineers. A general reference is Landes (1969).

3. The decadal census figures on musicians as a percentage of the total labor force, are (from 1870) .13, .18, .27, .32, .37, .30, .34, .32, .27, and .29 (in 1960). The increase is steady until 1910, the decrease steady after 1920. It was precisely during the 1920s that radio became a major medium. Kevles (1979:237) cites complaints (in 1929) that talkies put movie musicians out of work. See Faulkner (1971) on the new situation.

4. On surveyors, see Thompson (1968). The history of various English property professions can be followed in Carr-Saunders and Wilson (1933).

5. On information professions, see chapter 8. Chandler (1977) discusses the problem of professional management in its business context. The order of development of private and state management work is discussed in chapter 9, note 2. On civil service, see chapter 4, note 27.

6. On the hiring of professionals in government, see the essays on economists, accountants, engineers, scientists, and mental health professionals in *Public Administration Review* (March-April 1978). Weiss (1982) on French engineers of the *ancien régime* offers an interesting contrast. States can also abolish professional work, of course; the closing of the Admiralty and Arches courts in 1875 put advocates, proctors, and other specialized English legal professionals (if there were any left) out of business permanently. On public relations, see Bernays (1971) and Tedlow (1979). I am assuming that technology and organization act as exogenous causes. While with respect to individual professions this is probably true, with respect to the system as a whole it is probably not. Thus, technology can be invented deliberately (or, more properly, pursued systematically) as a strategy in interprofessional competition; indeed since 1850 most invention has come from professional workers. Organizations (other than those for work) are, I think, less likely to be the actual creations of competing professions.

7. On Hollerith machines, and cost accounting generally, see chapter 8.

8. See, for example, Johnstone and Hopson (1967) on the use of standardized forms in the American construction industry to avoid lawyer involvement. The complaints about law stationers come from the primary materials cited in chapter 9.

9. On CAD programs, see Leesley (1978) and CAD (1978). I describe the statistical situation from personal observation. A general source on the algorithms cited is Stewart (1973); Wilkinson (1965) is the standard technical source. Another interesting study of commodification is Albrecht's (1979) on probation officers. Commodification leads directly to issues of ownership, which in turn embroil professionals with commercial organizations (see Nelkin 1982; R. G. Adler 1984).

10. I shall consider artificial intelligence at more length in the next chapter.

11. Bankers and other business people are still eager to "get information" from professionals, a subject I shall treat in chapter 8. However, they seem less willing to allow those professionals to *act* on that information. See, as an

example, the various applications of operations research and related techniques in Cohen and Gibson (1978), which do indicate a considerably wider role for professionalism in banking than before, possibly along the lines of engineering. Whether those who apply these techniques will try to coalesce as an occupational group is unclear. This difficulty in coalescence holds irrespective of status for groups with explicit business components; pharmacists have faced the same problems (Denzin 1968; McCormack 1956).

12. *Pantouflage*, (literally, walking in one's slippers) is a venerable French tradition, dating at least from the 1880s; see Lalumière (1959:67ff.) and Suleiman (1978:226).

13. Scanning the American division of labor for potentially professional problems that are not professionalized, one can't help recognizing many of them as public goods. Pollution, residence and community planning, public health, quality of life, all are marginally professionalized if professionalized at all. One would predict that they would be more strongly professionalized in France, with its strong state.

14. The problem of adjustment is considered in chapter 10. Major citations are Abbott (1982) and Napoli (1981).

15. A scientifically sound, if rather presentist, account of psychologists' testing of intelligence is Gould (1981). See also Napoli (1981). The French phrase can be found in Crapuchet (1974:291).

16. Again, these "order" professions present problems of colligation. The relation between the problem of order and law enforcement officials is less that of cause and effect than that of whole and part. We recognize the problem of order precisely through people's diverse responses to it; labeling the whole does not thereby explain the part. Nonetheless, the causes of "order problems" can only be hinted at here.

17. Problems identified by social movements and later (sometimes) professionalized are a favorite topic of historians and sociologists. See, for example, Platt (1969) on juvenile delinquency, D. Garrison (1979) on public libraries, Baker (1985) on "country life," Rosenkrantz (1974) on public health, Katz (1968, 1971) on public education, and Grob (1973) on insanity.

18. Larson (1977) makes this change a central focus in her analysis of professionalism, at the cost of ignoring the clergy, the military, and other organizational professions of the past. Millerson's (1964) otherwise complete study of British professions ignores bureaucratization to all intents and purposes. Freidson (1986a) considers the issue at some length. There are a few exceptions to the general trend of bureaucratization. Psychotherapy (see Abbott 1982, M. Cohen 1966) has remained individualized, although founded by the once-bureaucratic psychiatrists. Arts professions have the notion of "creator" as a partial bulwark against bureaucratization, although even so, bureaucratization has been extensive. (See, e.g., Adler [1979] on commercial artists; McArthur [1984] on actors; and, more generally, Freidson [1986b] on arts professions.) Music provides another rare example of debureaucratization— the move of serious composition from the world of patronal bureaucracies in the eighteenth century to the open market in the early nineteenth. One of the

first to move was Mozart, whose initial popularity dwindled with the same rapidity as that of popular musicians today. McArthur (1984) indicates the open and unbureaucratized entertainment market of America's nineteenth century made successful professionalism among actors impossible. Only centralization and increasingly rigid employment structures allowed (briefly) a period of professionalizing before the move to unionization in the 1910s.

19. The "professionals in bureaucracy" literature is enormous. The sources bearing directly on the problem are Glaser (1964), Corwin (1965), W. R. Scott (1965), Prandy (1965), R. H. Hall (1967, 1968), Miller (1968), Montagna (1968), G. V. Engel (1969, 1970), Harries-Jenkins (1970), Ritti (1971), Chauvenet (1972), Engel and Hall (1973), Melosh (1982), Kornhauser (1982), Blau (1984), and Spangler (1986). All agree on the centrality of the issue. Some (e.g., Spangler) think it is more important than others (e.g., Hall, in some of his work). Ference, Goldner, and Ritti (1971), for example, note a countertrend of increasing *professionalism* within a largely bureaucratic organization, something also noted by A. Strauss (1964) among purchasing agents, and by various writers in nursing. Here professionalism seems to be a group strategy to move in the internal division of labor. Zussman (1985), on the other hand, sees professionalism as impossible in precisely the same kind of workplace.

20. On hospitals, see Vogel (1980) on the United States; Abel-Smith (1964), Peterson (1978), and Honigsbaum (1979) on Britain; and Chauvenet (1978) on France. Charles Rosenberg will shortly be publishing a definitive history of the American hospital, collecting his extensive work on this subject. Bureaucracy is also advancing outside the hospital; see, for example, Kralewski, Pitt, and Shatin (1985).

21. The standard sociological study is Smigel (1964). A good historical review is Hobson (1984). See also chapter 9.

22. Boyle (1977), Gutman (1981), and Blau (1984) describe the history, general character, and current sociology of practice in the large architectural firm. Owings's (1973) autobiography gives an unihibited inside view; his discussion of the contract for Oak Ridge, Tennessee, is classic.

23. The basic study of accounting firms is Montagna (1974). On merger, see the firm histories, of which the best is unquestionably E. Jones (1981). External analysis of their role is available in United States Senate, Committee on Governmental Operations (1976).

24. The literature on multiprofessional workplaces is both large and complex. Goldner and Ritti (1967) note bureaucrats' use of professionalism as an ideology to justify halting internal mobility. Gutman (1981) notes the trend to complex, metaprofessional functions, even among supposedly professional organizations. Wagenfeld and Robin (1976) also describe the complex imperialism of such organizations. The situation in France, not surprisingly, is quite different. Even given the new regulations allowing larger professional groupings (*sociétés civiles professionelles*), restrictions on salaried employment (of the official *professions libérales*) and on the corporate structure of multiprofessional firms remain both strong and detailed (Editions Francis Lefebvre 1986).

As in America, the best-studied multi-professional organization in France is the hospital; see, for example, Steudler (1973) and Chauvenet (1978).

25. This division is a basic theme of the professions and bureaucracy literature cited above, and certainly was evident throughout my own fieldwork.

26. Sources concerning railway surgeons are discussed in chapter 1. On the restriction to chief surgeons, see *Railway Surgeon* 1:264; 10:157ff. A common alternative, given the emerging weakness of professional associations to negotiate and control work in multiprofessional organizations, has been the move to unionization with various forms of closed shops. Examples are engineers (Goldstein 1955, 1959), pilots (Hopkins (1971), actors (McArthur 1984), and others (Hoffman 1976, Haug and Sussman 1971). Although Americans find unionization and professionalism opposed, the two have of course long coexisted in France; see, for example, Voyenne (1959) on journalists; J. M. Clark (1967) on teachers; and Léonard (1981) and Steudler (1977) on doctors.

27. In fact, all hiring at major accounting firms is done at the B.A. level with large amounts of training done internally (Montagna 1974). There has been occasional discussion of postgraduate accounting education, (see, e.g., Roy and McNeill 1967), but firms like Arthur Andersen (which bought a college campus for its educational program) do not really need them. I am indebted to H. W. Schlough for information on this matter.

28. To understand expertise generally, we must stop thinking that the main thing to be explained is the peculiar structure exemplified by American medicine at midcentury—relatively independent practice, fee for service, weak and collegial control, active voluntary associations, and above all, hypertrophied autonomy—the phenomenon I have called associational professionalism. The thing to be explained is how expertise is structured in society, the division of expert labor. Denying engineers relevance to that problem by worrying about whether or not they are really a profession is foolish.

29. Callahan (1962). Organizational power, of course, has usually been used in these thefts.

30. Roselli (1984). The impact of capitalization has been noticed most in medicine (see, e.g., Kolata 1980; Culliton 1986), but is in fact quite general (see Faulkner [1971] on musicians; Kevles [1979] and Ravetz [1971] on science) and quite old (Calvert 1967). The boundary between physical and intellectual capital is fluctuating rapidly, and corporations, as one would expect, are emphasizing their rights to as much turf as possible. See Adler (1984) and Nelkin (1982).

31. The dominance of the state is equally clear in Germany; see, for example, Stone (1980) on doctors, Rueschemeyer (1973) on lawyers, and McClelland (1983) for general remarks on German professionals and the state. A good comparative study emphasizing these differences is Béland's (1976) on British and French doctors and engineers.

32. For the *ancien régime* see Franklin (1980). See also Bouteiller (1966), Gelfand (1978), and essays by Ramsey, Goubert, and Fauré in Branca (1977).

33. See Gelfand (1980) on surgeons.

34. On labor under the absolutists and through 1848, see Sewell (1980). Only in professions like accounting, which often specialize in state-required documents, does the state directly shape jurisdiction in England and America as it does in France. See Lafferty (1975) for an excellent comparative analysis of accounting professions and practices in Europe.

35. The history of French medicine in the nineteenth century is superbly discussed in Léonard (1981), on which I have relied heavily. The discussion of malpractice is on p. 58, and the current regulations are given in Editions Francis Lefebvre (1986: sec. 940). See also Pincemin and Laugier (1959) and Herzlich (1982). It is striking that the *official* organization for French medicine, the Ordre National des Médecins, was created only in 1945, although the medical unions date from 1892, and the national voluntary association from 1858. For French law, I have relied on Berlanstein (1975) for the *ancien régime*, and on Young (1869) and Debré (1984) for the nineteenth century. (The latter chiefly concerns political life rather than professional organization.) I have also mined sources on contemporary law for historical points (e.g., Abeille 1971).

36. French doctors first unionized in 1883, but the unions were declared illegal in the following year and not legalized until 1892 (Léonard 1981; Pincemin and Laugier 1959). On the *conventions*, see Steudler (1977). The German situation is discussed by Stone (1980).

37. On the *Conseil d'Etat* see Rendel (1970). On the role of the ministries in medicine, see especially Léonard (1981).

38. The vast reform of French law is described well in Raguin (1972). The postreform situation is detailed in Blanc (1972) and the indispensable Editions Francis Lefebvre (1986). The prehistory of *agréés* and others comes from Abeille (1971), Ripert (1951), and Herzog (1967). As an indication of how long French professions must agitate for state recognition, the issue of recognizing *agréés* was debated as early as 1852 (Dalloz, *Recueil de jurisprudence* 1:127, [1852]). Another interesting case showing the interplay of Ministries, *Conseil*, and profession is that of *assistants sociales*. See the collective note on that profession in Crapuchet (1974:265–68). Perhaps the hardest fact for Americans to understand is the immense power of the education ministry to determine professional policy. Cf. Van den Slik (1983) for a typically horrified American reaction to the prospect of state-regulated education for nurses.

39. On the *délégués*, see the official essay by the Association Nationale des Délégués Permanents à la Tutelle in Crapuchet (1974). On more general social-work jurisdictions, see the essay of Nerot in the same volume. The French have long had the *grands corps d'Etat* to provide professional services in mining, roads and bridges, and other areas, with *grandes écoles* to train for them. Most continental professionals up into this century were rather directly servants of the state. McClelland (1983) discusses the loss of status endured by the first German lawyers to enter full private practice. Teachers, engineers, lawyers, professors, the military, and even the clergy (in Germany; see Bigler 1972, 1974) were state officials throughout the nineteenth century. Many of these groups still are today.

40. On the plans, see Steudler (1973) and, generally, Nizard (1972). On legal aid, see Raguin (1972), and for the comparative English scene, Abel-Smith and Stevens (1967). Planning generally involves planning for professional numbers, as I argued in the preceding chapter.

41. Fees are extensively discussed in Editions Francis Lefebvre (1986), as well as, of course, Steudler (1977). For Germany, see Stone (1980) on doctors and Rueschemeyer (1973) on lawyers. The following discussion relies directly on Steudler (1977).

42. On the medical press, see Léonard (1981).

43. Jamous and Peloille's (1970) oft-cited work on hospitals is an exception, as is Dezalay's (1987) recent work on bankruptcy.

44. On Jacksonianism and its impact on the professions, see especially Rothstein (1972).

45. On the lyceum movement see Scott (1979) as well as the essay by Scott in Geison (1983). The relation of professional and public is also discussed in Calhoun (1965). The newspaper figures come from the *Historical Statistics of the United States*. On the American Social Science Association, see Haskell (1977).

46. These figures are from J. Calman, ed., *Western Europe* (New York: Praeger, [1967]). Of course media coverage has increased in Europe since, but the American preeminence of the public realm, as opposed to the state, seems confirmed by these figures.

47. On censorship in England, see A. J. Lee (1976); and in France, Cobban (1961). The former discusses the late-nineteenth-century English press generally, as does Palmer (1983) the French. On Parliamentary registration, and its rarity, see Millerson (1964).

48. On changes in state regulation, see Freidson (1984), who feels the major change is a move towards formalization of existing controls. Haug and Sussman (1969) discuss the client revolt involving low-status clients—the poor, the black, the students. Starr (1982) and others have discussed the revolt of high-status clients—third party payers, corporations buying legal services, and so on. M. J. Powell (1985) gives a general discussion of the impact of these forces on lawyers.

49. The definition of "state interest" is of course culture-specific. The French definition is considerably wider than the American one. By defining the state's interest in public welfare very broadly, the French set a pattern for a very broad state involvement. Parliament and Congress passed laws requiring independent public accounts of publicly traded corporations only late in the nineteenth century, a belated concession to investors ruined by dozens of bankruptcies. But in mid-nineteenth-century France, a much less commercially advanced country, such risky (because public) capital formation was avoided, and the *Conseil d'Etat* retained direct control over the accounting of capital in enterprises, arguing a general interest to protect stockholders (Freedeman 1979:127). The role for active clients was the less as the state's was the more. Curiously, this particular decision of the French state had the

consequence of retarding the development of an accounting profession in France.

50. General sources on the rise of corporatism in America are Galambos (1970) and Israel (1972). I am indebted to Gosta Esping-Anderson for insisting that class is a central issue.

51. Most of this section is theoretical and concerns examples already referenced elsewhere. I shall give citations only for major matters.

52. State level figures for nineteenth-century American clergy, physicians, and lawyers can be found in appendix B of Haller (1981).

53. The figures for America are from the *Historical Statistics*, while those for Britain are from Routh (1965). Scott's discussion is in D. Scott (1978), although the American census figures corroborate this interpretation of the clergy, having once lumped social and religious workers together (Edwards 1943).

54. See the discussion of co-opted power in the predecing chapter. An example of the foundation connection is Brown (1979) on the Rockefeller Foundation. See also Abbott (1982:257ff.) on the role of Commonwealth Foundation in American mental health.

55. Colvard (1961) describes how the foundations fight back. M. J. Powell (1985) examines lawyers' mixed relations with co-opted power sources.

56. Information and psychotherapy are discussed in later chapters. On the arts professions, see McArthur (1984) on actors.

57. See Djilas (1957), Konrad and Szelenyi (1972), and Gouldner (1981). A straightforward Marxist account of the class position of professionals is Johnson (1977). There is also a general literature on the technical intelligentsia (e.g., Lampert 1979; D. K. Price 1965; Baylis 1974), much of it concerning socialist countries, as indeed does this entire literature. On political views, see Brint (1984). In technical terms, professionals possess not capital, but sectorally specific capital, or, even more properly, capital goods. To the extent that traditional Marxist concepts of class require fully mobile capital, the basis for class formation is weakened. (I am indebted to Doug Nelson for this point.) There is today a burgeoning literature on property rights in ideas, as I noted above in my discussion of physical capital. There is also an immense literature on the social origins of professionals: nearly every major monographic study addresses the question, and writers as politically diverse as Ben-David (1963) and Larson (1977) have made it central to their conceptions of professions. It is also the focus of a general elites literature (e.g., Geiger 1950; Suleiman 1978). Although this question is important on its own, I do not feel that the social origins of professionals have profound implications for the division of professional labor. There are successful competitions by professionals of lower standing (nineteenth-century British apothecaries) and failures (nineteenth-century solicitors). Like feminization, class origins are usually a dependent variable in the division of expert labor. Once established, feminization and similar phenomena have clear consequences, often reinforcing a subordinated status quo. But they are not leading variables.

58. On economic theories of licensure, see Stigler (1971) and various essays in Blair and Rubin (1980). On British doctors, midwives, and nurses, see Abel-Smith (1960:66, 75–78). On American doctors and psychologists, see Reisman (1976:301). On accountants, see Previts amd Merino (1979:147). Zussman (1985) also gives a fairly strongly negative account, seeing not even professionalism, much less serious class interest.

## Chapter Seven

1. D. J. de Solla Price (1963) and Ravetz (1971) argue contrasting sides of the knowledge explosion. Belief in a knowledge explosion has a long history; there is an old joke that Bacon (Goethe, etc.) was the last man to think he knew everything and Leibniz (Pascal, etc.) the last to actually do so.

2. This argument, of course, applies as well to most of the variables discussed in the preceding chapter—bureaucratization, oligarchy, and so forth. Adjoining professions tend to face similar conditions. That is why, ultimately, the central empirical task is to establish the topology of the system of professions.

3. The celebrated debacle of 1914 is discussed in L. Holmes (1976) and Fuller (1961).

4. The sources on knowledge change in science are immense, but certainly Kuhn (1970) and Lakatos and Musgrave (1970) present the basic themes. Much of this literature has concerned social influence over science (e.g., Böhme et al. 1983) a fact which is, I think, generally uncontested in discussions of most professional knowledge. Ravetz (1971) and Böhme et al. (1983) emphasize the Kuhnian insight (or qualifier) that most scientific change consists of addition rather than replacement. Despite this contrast, however, there are many social movements within or involving professions that try to change general approaches—as public interest law does jurisprudence, social accounting does accounting practice, and so on.

5. My general source here is McMahon (1984), which I have supplemented with works on other types of engineering: Calvert (1967); Payne (1960); Perrucci and Gerstl (1969); Gerstl and Hutton (1966); Prandy (1965).

6. Note that technology itself generated this demand. Of course, the people developing the technology were, most of them, engineers themselves, but the demand drew workers from many other fields. This demand is thus in some ways both exogenous and endogenous, both an internal strategy and an external event, to use chapter 4's terms.

7. Surveys on engineering employment can be found in Perrucci and Gerstl (1969:130ff.) and Gerstl and Hutton (1966:88ff.).

8. I thank my father for this information, and for much else.

9. The study cited is from Perrucci and Gerstl (1969:75). On engineering education, see McMahon (1983:234ff.). For information on Bell Labs hiring policies, and for much else, I thank my wife, whose career exemplifies the track here described.

10. On professional obsolescence, see the essays in Dubin (1972). Calvert's

mechanical engineers present a case that upends my theory of abstraction-survival. The "school culture" of abstractly trained engineers ended up doing the routine, conservative work, while the "shop culture" of hands-on, apprenticed engineers developed the innovations. I don't think this situation endured very long, however, since the school culture proved victorious. The shop culture group was older, smaller, and of higher social status (for a brief time). It surrendered, it seems to me, precisely because ultimately it could not compete against the very best of the school culture. It was indeed the shop-culture elite that pushed hardest for schooling. By contrast, in Terry Shinn's (1978, 1980) studies of *polytechniciens*, the small elite of *grandes écoles* graduates actually had training too abstract for application and proved unemployable. Day (1978) found the less abstractly educated *gadzarts* of the Ecole des Arts et Métiers to be more employable than graduates of *grandes écoles*.

11. Continuing education in accounting is extensively discussed in Roy and McNeill (1967). On pharmacy, see Birenbaum (1982).

12. On AI generally, see Duda and Shortliffe (1983) and Feigenbaum and McCorduck (1983).

13. Of course, they will have great impact through the lowering of demand for services—increasing rates of competition—but they will not generally have differential impact, unless one or another profession in an area monopolizes their development and application.

14. See Leesley (1978) and CAD (1978).

15. The library example is discussed in the last section of chapter 8. For another interesting competition—that involving teachers—see Holden (1984) for a recent update. Hunter et al. (1975) is a dated, but general, review of this area. See Perrolle (1985) for the (inevitable) argument that professional life will be completely transformed by AI. This will not happen. Earlier commodifications have always found new demands arising to take up much of the slack. If labor had been being deprofessionalized and dispossessed for as long as this argument and its relatives hold, we would all have been beasts of burden long since. The current division of labor is far from ideal, but it probably involves no more alienation than any other since the general introduction of wage labor.

16. To the extent that I can manage it, there is no hidden ideology about the nature of professions in this section. However, the subject of legitimation brings out those ideologies in both reader and writer.

17. Dix (1945:744).

18. See Ploscowe (1935) on American reactions to continental procedure, especially criminal procedure. On direct medical intervention, see McKeown (1979). The military's instrumentalism stems ultimately from Clausewitz's celebrated dictum on war as policy.

19. I am somewhat arbitrary in calling secularization a matter of value change and hence of legitimation, rather than a matter of simple demand change, in which case it should have been discussed in chapter 4 along with technological and organizational changes. It seemed simpler to keep the value discussion in one place.

20. On British clergy see Reader (1966) and Coxon (1979); on education in

the nineteenth century, see the essay of Laquer in L. Stone (1976), and Laquer (1976). More recently British clergy have, like Americans, entered the counseling movement (Leat 1973; Jarvis 1976).

21. On French clergy, see various references in Cobban (1961) for generalities; see Meyers (1976) and the monumental study of Boutry (1986) for rural details. The medical connection is discussed in Léonard (1981), and laicization of nurses by Cayla (1986).

22. I have followed D. Scott (1978) on early-nineteenth-century Protestant clergy. The move into melioration is familiar from historical sources on social work (e.g., Lubove 1969), and the later move into counseling from current sources like Kleinman (1984). See also chapter 10. On Roman Catholic priests, see Merwick (1973).

23. I have avoided discussing most specific value shifts because they involve controversies too large to begin here. On teaching and democracy see Katz (1968, 1971).

24. The extended quote is from D. Scott (1978:16); the second is from the same source, p. 26. I have followed Scott's account closely here.

25. The extended quote is from Peterson (1978:284), and the discussion of French medicine draws on Léonard (1981). On homeopathy and science, see Kaufman (1971), especially p. 29ff.

26. The Sullivan quote comes from L. H. Sullivan ([1924] 1956:258) and the Fisher one from Koenig (1975:146). On codification, see Friedman (1973:351ff.). The efficiency motif, of course, drew heavily on engineering (Tichi 1987). Even counseling can be legitimated as "scientific" work, when opposed, for example, to traditional clergy work (Leat 1973).

27. The quote is from Suleiman (1978:169). On the general learning of civil servants, see Sharp (1931:143ff.) on France, Kelsall (1955:178ff.) on England, and Kubota (1969:80ff.) on Japan. It should be recalled that Freud lost on the question of lay analysis (Fine 1979:68ff., 142ff.).

28. The following remarks are quoted in Reader (1966:69). Reader is an excellent general source on character in the nineteenth-century English professions (but see also Duman 1979), as G. Holmes (1982) is for the eighteenth-century. Most monographic accounts of particular professions touch on the issue, Peterson (1978) having a particularly strong discussion.

29. The extended quote is from Bledstein (1976:147, 158). On character in medicine, see Bosk's (1979) excellent ethnography of medical training and also Fox and Swazey (1974). Other sources on American legitimation of professions are Janowitz (1971) on the military, Merwick (1973) on the clergy, and Sutton et al. (1962) on business.

30. On the therapeutic character in the clergy, see Kleinman (1984).

31. The extended quote is by J. Planchais, quoted in Martin (1981:184), a brilliant study of the shift to efficiency and management values in the French military. A detailed view of the persistence of military traditions, and thereby of the values they embody, is Vagts (1959). Character remains equally important *within* professions. Indeed, we know from Smigel (1964) and Montagna (1974) that promotion in large law and accounting firms generally reflects char-

acter virtues as much or more than professional accomplishments. Moore's (1984) rather curious note on the "doctors' work ethic" indicates continuity in actual character, if not in character-as-legitimation.

32. Osler ([1889] 1963) discusses "aequanimitas." The "magic bullets" line is from Brandt (1985), who got it from the elder Paul Ehrlich.

33. Reader (1966) is again a source on the use of social structures as legitimation across several English professions. See also Duman (1979) on the service ethic, a legitimation that the monopolist school of professionalization studies has specifically attempted to debunk.

34. The quotes on child accounting are from Callahan's quietly scathing study of efficiency in education (1962:169). Other excellent sources on measurability are Hays (1975), Layton (1971), Bendix (1974), and Honigsbaum (1979).

35. Ben-David (1963); Bledstein (1976).

36. Ben-David (1963:256).

37. See also O'Boyle (1970) and Kotschnig (1937) on this process in various periods.

38. Bledstein (1976). The short quotes are from pages 177 and 120.

39. My basic sources on the German universities and their relation to the professions are Jarausch (1982) and McClelland (1980). I have augmented them with McClelland (1983). Jarausch (1983) contains many interesting and relevant essays.

40. The phrase is Jarausch's (1982:69).

41. McClelland (1980:118).

42. On moves into legal work and insurance, see McClelland (1980:246). Ben-David's discussion is in Ben-David and Collins (1966).

43. My sources on French universities and professional education (both in them and elsewhere) are Weisz (1983), Clark (1973), Fox and Weisz (1980), Shinn (1978, 1980), Weiss (1982), Suleiman (1978), and Ackerknecht (1957).

44. This reform can be followed in the pages of Weisz (1983).

45. On technical education see especially Weisz (1983: chap. 5) and Day (1978).

46. The politics of French medicine in 1900 pitted university professors, who represented elitism as well as scientific medicine, against practitioners and the majority of the medical profession, who were more concerned with clinical work and intraprofessional inequality. See Wiesz's essay in Fox and Weisz (1980).

47. Weisz (1983:188ff.).

48. On English universities, I have largely followed A. J. Engel (1983) and Rothblatt (1968). Since less professional education takes place in universities in England than in other societies, I have relied as well on general monographic sources on various professions. See also Perkin (1961).

49. The information on the order of development of English professions comes from the unpublished study cited in chapter 1, note 23.

50. This marvelous statement is quoted in Rothblatt (1968:248). On objections to changing the third year, see A. J. Engel (1983:39).

51. See Abel-Smith and Stevens (1967:182).

52. I am relying on Poynter (1966) and Newman (1957) for information on medical education.

53. I am relying on Stacey (1954) on accountancy education. The quote on medicine is from Poynter (1966:119).

54. On external degrees, see Payne (1960:167ff.).

55. The content did not matter; the difficulty did. Mathematics and classics were thus the best teaching disciplines because of their supreme difficulty, and the top man in the Cambridge mathematics tripos was so noteworthy as to deserve the sobriquet of "senior wrangler."

56. My general sources on American universities and professional education are Veysey (1965) and Oleson and Voss (1979).

57. The situation was analogous to that in Prussia, although there the schoolteachers were male; they were still excluded from the university.

58. On medical education see Kaufman (1976) and Ludmerer (1985).

59. On business schools see especially Sass (1982) and Sedlak and Williamson (1983).

60. The standard source is Stevens (1983). See also Auerbach (1976).

61. On scholar/practitioner squabbles, see Auerbach (1976:89ff.). On Barker, see his autobiography (Barker 1942).

62. See, for example, Rossiter (1979).

63. Graham (1931).

64. These figures are all from the *Historical Statistics*, pp. 383ff.

65. My basic source on corporate education is Eurich (1985).

66. See Spector (1977).

67. See, for example, Eurich (1985:55, 77).

## Chapter Eight

1. The idea of followability comes from Gallie's (1968) brilliant study of historical writing.

2. That equilibrium never appears does not, however, imply that system thinking is inappropriate, but rather that equilibrating forces exist as never-resolved strains in systems.

3. For example, the Parsonian analyses of law (1954) and medicine (1964).

4. I do not know of any general sociological work on the information professions. Debons et al. (1980) have many numbers but little analysis. I am in part creating the area of information by writing about it in this way. Information is one of those task areas discussed at the end of chapter 4, a domain of professional work.

5. My general sources on the history of American librarianship are D. Garrison (1979) and the essays in Winger (1976). A rather traditional sociological study is Goode (1961).

6. On numbers of libraries, see McMullen (1976) and Holley (1976).

7. I am following Garrison here. Cole (1979) takes a slightly different view. See also Bloom (1976) and Blayney (1977) for later moves back into educational and outreach functions.

8. On library education see, D. J. Davis (1976), Carroll (1970), and Churchwell (1975). What I am calling the access function is called the "doctrine of use" by Cole (1979). On this subject see also Wagers (1978). It is striking that several analysts see the limitation to access as a "positive" move, towards an educational function, at least for research librarians who had been "simply accumulators" of material. I think Garrison is right in her retreat interpretation.

9. On the special and research librarians, see Knapp (1955), Christiansen (1976), Veit (1976), Cole (1979), and Downs (1958). The faculty status issue is discussed by Downs (1958). The one function of librarians that penetrated directly into academic jurisdictions was acquisitions, which has often been done by specialized bibliographers, who are often hybrid by training, being both librarians and academics (Stueart 1972, Holley 1976:198). The relation of academic and general librarians is quite different in Europe, where the two professions are quite separate; see Richards (1985), Rayward (1985), and the essays on French librarians in *Journal of Library History* 19 no. 1. One should also note that the new elite replaced (or allied with) the old "men's-club" elite discussed by D. Garrison (1979).

10. On the localism of school librarians, see Garceau (1949).

11. Supply and demand for librarians in the period up to 1950 are discussed by Reagan (1958) and numerous sources discussed therein. Figures on library school production come from Holley (1976) and Davis (1976).

12. The microfilm process and the development of documentation are discussed by Shera and Cleveland (1977) and Rayward (1985).

13. Sources on library automation are quite extensive. See, for example, L. C. Smith (1983) and Reynolds (1985). The University of Illinois series on library automation dates from 1963. On early mechanization, see Shera and Cleveland (1977); and on computerization, see Markuson (1976) as well. See also Wright (1985) on the relation of librarianship and information science.

14. Markuson (1976) discusses the war impact, particularly in relation to technical material.

15. A general history of cataloging is Henderson (1976). The specific impact of centralized cataloging is discussed by Markuson (1976) and Heisen (1976). Later cataloging developments in librarianship were not originators of disturbances but responses to them. The great "Red" and "Green" books of the postwar period were required by the sudden flood of technical material between Europe and the United States.

16. The Library Bureau is discussed by D. Garrison (1979: 125), and Hollerith's dealings with it by Austrian (1982: 133–34). The history of office work in this period may be found in Davies (1982).

17. On the early men's-club elitism of the ALA, see D. Garrison (1979). As for the mechanics of "professionalization," see P. Sullivan (1976) on associations, Davis (1976) on schools, Danton (1976) on journals, and Holley (1976) on the relation of school librarians to the rest of the profession. The major resources for common work are discussed by Markuson (1976).

18. On the publishers of library resources—the ALA was the dominant

Page 385 of 456

one in the early years—see Danton (1976, especially pp. 171ff.). Even the fact
that all essential reference knowledge has been commodified in a single book
since 1902, (the *Guide to Reference Books,* currently edited by Sheehey), has
not harmed librarians' control of access.

19. On the conflict of academics and special librarians, see Knapp (1955),
Downs (1958), Holley (1976), and the various publications of the Association
of College and Research Libraries Committee on Academic Status. A splendid
quote favoring faculty status is: "Catalogers sit at the fount, as it were, of the
productivity of the human mind, reducing all to order and system. Working at
the frontiers of knowledge, they see and help to order its unfolding" (Carlson
1955:29).

20. The best chronicle of this expansion is Christiansen (1976). The clear
associational achievements of the special librarians are evident in Sullivan
(1976). Their numbers may be found in McMullen (1976).

21. I have been unable to find a secondary history of the development of
law reporters.

22. The following paragraphs draw directly on Schudson (1981). The relation of press agentry and journalists is on pp. 133–44. Competition appears to
have played less of a role in Britain and France. In Britain, journalists of a
slightly earlier period had just experienced a transition similar to American
*librarians'*, losing their educational functions to those of amusement only
(A. J. Lee 1976). Schudson discusses the same changes—the so-called new
journalism—but sees them as contemporaneous rather than sequential in the
United States. In France, the chief developments of the later years of the Third
Republic were, characteristically, unionization and achievement of state recognition and definition (Voyenne 1959), developments that may or may not
have clarified professional boundaries against competition (p. 923).

23. On the history of British accountancy, I have generally followed Stacey
(1954) and especially E. Jones (1981) on types of work. On American accountancy, standard histories are Carey (1969, 1970) and Previts and Merino (1979).
Sources on the current United States situation are Abraham (1978), Montagna
(1974, 1975), Olson (1982), and the celebrated 1976 report of the Senate's
Government Operations Committee, *The Accounting Establishment.* Lubell
(1980) discusses the shaping of American accountancy by external conflicts in
a way strongly suggesting my own conceptual scheme.

24. Sources on the actual work of early American accountancy are Kinley
(1906), Masters (1915), and McLaren (1937) On the relation of bookkeepers
and accountants, see Tipson (1903). Although the attestation function of accounting was well-understood at the time, as was the fact that accountants
were taking over this function from bankers and were becoming go-betweens
with manufacturers (see, e.g., Roberts 1907, Dickinson 1909, Head 1924), the
accountants were as much a necessary condition of the new capital markets as
they were a sufficient result of them. The British accountants in the late nineteenth century were much exercised by their relation to actuaries, some urging merger (Strachan 1888), others urging separation (M'Candlish 1889). Later,
some urged that actuary be to accountant as barrister to solicitor (Phillips

1927). The overwhelming market for British accountants in bankruptcy is shown by the actual rates of commercial failures: eighty-seven in a typical week in 1889 (*The Accountant* 15:548).

25. General sources on the history of statistics qua profession are Mackenzie (1981) on England, and North (1970) and Harshbarger (1976) on the United States.

26. The allegiance of statisticians to their professions of origin persisted well into this century. Thus, in a 1927 review of recent literature, the *Journal of the American Statistical Association* covered articles by political scientists, actuaries, and accountants, as well as the usual government sources (*Journal of the American Statistical Association* [hereafter JASA] 22:546ff.). New members in 1920 included six actuaries, seven securities analysts, seven professors of economics, and five of mathematics. Eighty-two of the 128 new members worked for industry (forty-two in manufacturing and forty in staff.), twenty-two worked in universities, eleven in social service, and only thirteen in government. (I have collected these figures directly from the lists of new members in the *JASA*).

27. On Hollerith, see Austrian (1982). Other machinery is discussed in Harmon (1975). One has only to contrast the complex reporting of the 1890 census with the extensive, but simple, classifications of the 1880 census to see that only the development of programmable computers matched the transformation wrought by Hollerith in quantitative information.

28. On the routinization of bookkeeping, see Tipson (1903) and Lubell (1980). On the decline of clerks through division of labor, see the editorial columns of the *Journal of Accountancy*, for example, 2:283–86 (1906) and 43:365 (1927). The Hollerith technology actually opened up many more areas of work than it closed. To be sure, the simple costing that had hitherto passed for serious analysis was outmoded nearly overnight. But the new possibilities were immense, and it was an accountant—Gershom Smith of Pennsylvania Steel—who became the leading evangelist of Hollerithism. By enabling serious cross-classification of data, the new technology created so much information potential that new kinds of professional judgment were required to control it.

29. As a body of people, cost accounting's history is little known. It can be traced in general works cited above, and, of course, the history of costing ideas is well studied (Solomons 1968a; Garner 1954). I have relied on these two works throughout this section.

30. The quote is from North ([1918] 1970:41).

31. On the inferential revolution, see various essays in Owen (1976). Ayres (1927) gives a blunt account of the vertical split; the quote is from p. 3. On the elite and its own continued eclecticism, see Harshbarger (1976). The ASA had fallen to 35 percent business-employed by 1927 (*JASA* 22:225) from 46 percent in 1920 (*Quarterly Publications of the ASA* 1920:111). A gargantuan 68 percent, however, reported economic matters as their chief interest, while only 11 percent favored statistical method (*JASA* 22:226). The general interest in business strengthened as time passed (*JASA* 24:303ff. [1928]; 25:198ff.

[1930]), although new members were increasingly likely to come from government (51 percent in 1939).

32. Johnson (e.g., 1972) has written a number of papers on early cost accounting. The theme of accountants as general business advisors arose naturally out of accountants' perception of themselves as brokers between bankers and businessmen, noted above. See, for example, the editorial of the *Journal of Accountancy* 2:288–89, (1906), "Accountancy the Profession of Business Administration" (from which the quote is taken). See also Herskowitz (1927), and (one of accounting's legends) Arthur Andersen (1926).

33. I am relying here on Calvert's (1967) account of mechanical engineering. There were 2,500 members of the ASME in 1905 (p. 130).

34. I use the word "engineers" to refer to mechanical engineers throughout this section. There were, of course, three other major engineering bodies by this time, the civil engineers (Calhoun 1960), the chemical engineers (Furter 1982), and the electrical engineers (McMahon 1984). On scientific management, see Haber (1964), Nelson (1974), and Jellinek (1980). The relation of scientific management to costing as a system of ideas and practice (rather than as a group of people) is well discussed by Epstein (1978).

35. On the foreman's loss of power, see Nelson (1974). The theoretical developments in cost accounting in this period are covered by the sources above. I have not discovered who the early members of the National Association of Cost Accountants (founded 1919) were or what profession they thought themselves members of. However, contemporary sources on accountants' role in manufacturing and costing include Hamilton (1918) and Drucker (1928).

36. The accountants were W. R. Bassett, L. R. Dicksee, H. Eggleston, E. T. Elbourne, H. A. Harris, G. C. Harrison, J. L. Nicholson, C. H. Scovell, F. E. Webner, and J. R. Wildman. The engineers were S. H. Bunnell, F. E. Cardullo, H. Dimer, H. A. Evans, B. A. Franklin, H. L. Gantt, H. P. Gillette, H. Hess, C. E. Knoeppel, and H. F. Porter. The remarks about sites of publishing are based on exact analysis of 530 articles by site, quinquennium, and country.

37. On teaching of cost accounting, see Atkins (1928). On professionalizing business, see Diemer (1912), Brandeis (1914), Lowell (1923), and Donham (1927).

38. A general source on the efficiency theme of engineering is Layton (1971). On worksites of mechanical engineers, see Hoover and Fish (1947: 123). While both engineers and accountants contributed to cost accounting, it was accountants who ended up with the work. As we shall see, the area of cost "variations" was ultimately invaded by a statistical theory of production. In the 1920s and 1930s, however, the new Hollerith-based accounting systems and the cost accountants who ran them played the fundamental role in business information.

39. On the British experience in the First World War, see E. Jones 1981:128ff.

40. On the taxation market, see secondary sources like Previts and Merino (1979) and Carey (1970). The latter also deals with lawyer-related problems.

Contemporary sources on this subject are Walton (1909) and Greeley (1927). See also "Lawyer and Accountant," *Journal of Accountancy* 43:360–61 (1927). On the proportions of various types of accounting business, see, for a much later period, United States Senate, Committee on Government Operations (1976:307); and Roy and MacNeill (1967:150–52).

41. The figures on distribution come from Barger (1955:4–15, 37–41).

42. My general sources on marketing and market research are Bartels (1962) and Lockley (1974).

43. On the history of advertising, see, in addition to Bartels (1962), Baur (1949), and especially Schultze (1982), on whom I have relied most strongly here.

44. On market research, I have relied largely on Lockley (1974). On *who* did it, I have considered the specialties of authors of *How to Conduct Consumer and Opinion Research* (New York: Harper, 1946) and the later figures of Twedt (1956). As of 1963, about one-third of AMA members were in marketing research (Kunstler 1963). A surprising 15 percent were in administration. Further information on the split is available in the opening statement of the *Journal of Marketing Research* 1:1 (1964). On late 1970s professionalism, see Coe and Coe (1976) and Murphey and Coney (1976). Note that while the advertising professionalizers failed to successfully control a jurisdiction, they did contribute an important element to the equally permeable jurisdiction of marketing.

45. A contemporary source on accountants and the SEC is Blough (1937).

46. I do not know of a secondary history of quality control. I have relied on the brief historical note in Duncan (1965).

47. A sense of the railroads' allocation problem can be acquired from Riebemack (1893). Change in the structure of railroad labor is discussed by Licht (1983), Cottrell (1970), and, especially on the subject of professionalism, Morris (1973).

48. On the basic history of OR, see Miser (1978) and Trefathan (1954).

49. On mathematicization and professional regression in operations research see Morse (1977) and Klein and Butkovich (1976).

50. On sustained interdisciplinarity, one can consult the opening pages of virtually any textbook in OR, for example, Phillips, Ravindran, and Solberg (1976:3); or, as one writer (T. L. Page) puts it in Flagle, Huggins, and Roy (1969), "Operations research is best considered as the essence of applied science" (p. 121).

51. On current use and staffing of operations work in corporations, see Radnor and Neal (1973). On the quite interesting relation between operations research and its predecessor-rival cost accounting, see Beer (1954) and Churchman and Ackoff (1968).

52. Basic sources on information science are Debons et al. (1980) for numbers and some data on activities; and Rayward (1985), Shera and Cleveland (1977), and Svenonius and Witthus (1981), for historical and sociological overviews of the area. The *Annual Review of Information Science and Technology*

(ed. M. E. Williams) contains a wide variety of relevant papers. I have generally relied on the four sources just listed.

53. Danto (1985:61)

54. This paragraph draws directly on Rayward (1985).

55. See, in addition to Rayward (1985), Wright (1985), Shera and Cleveland (1977), and Markuson (1976).

56. On computers, see Moreau (1984) and Wulforst (1982), the latter on the ballistics issue, the former a more general and theoretical study.

57. There has been much writing about deskilling in the computer and data-processing areas. See Kraft (1977) and Greenbaum (1979). Both regard deskilling as generated not by technology per se, but by management desire for control. Neither attends to the creation of new forms of skilled work outside the computer–data-processing workplace by deskilling within it. Pettigrew (1973) describes a more complex process of negotiation and differentiation. No one, to my knowledge, has any life-course data on what has happened to given individuals over long periods in this industry.

58. For discussions of the new possibilities—subject analysis, quantitative databases, bibliographic systems—see the essays in the *Annual Review of Information Science and Technology* 12, part 2.

59. On graduate programs in MIS, see Dickson and Dock (1975). For a current perspective, see D. Kull, "Should you Hire the Big Eight?" *Computer Decisions*, 29 July 1986. This article has useful comments on personnel policies at the Big Eight accounting houses. For a newer, synthetic view of MIS, see McCosh, Rahman, and Earl (1981), or similar texts.

60. A good introduction to current applications of information science in qualitative work is Salton (1975). Like many such techniques, keyword indexing has undoubtedly created as many opportunities for professional judgment as it abolished. Getting the important information from a keyword database without getting a mass of irrelevancies proved to be a problem requiring professional judgment.

61. This sloughing off is evident by what is missing or deemphasized in any MIS or IS text. McCosh, Rahman, and Earl (1981) is an excellent example. For a somewhat romanticized view of the early days of data processing, see Greenbaum (1979). For a current participant's view, see Nolan (1979).

62. The figures in this paragraph come from Debons et al. (1980), which requires considerable care in interpretation.

63. The figures on ASIS and training are from Svenonius and Witthus (1981).

## Chapter Nine

1. Throughout this chapter certain general sources are referred to by acronym, year, and page. They are as follows:

*ABCNY Annual Report of the Committee on the Unlawful Practice of Law, Association of the Bar of the City of New York*

NYCLA  *The Annual Reports of the Committee on Unlawful Practice of the Law, New York County Lawyers Association*
PABA  *The Annual Report of the Pennsylvania State Bar Association,* including the *Report of the Committee on Practice of Law*
CLS  *The Annual Report of the Council of the Law Society to the Membership*
LN  *Law Notes,* edited by Albert Gibson
APMLS  *The Proceedings and Resolutions of the Annual Provincial Meeting of the Law Society*

This chapter is a slight revision of an article published in the *American Bar Foundation Research Journal* 1986:187–224; I thank the Foundation for permission to republish. Readers wishing further documentation may consult the original paper. Using "people without history" to refer to invisible, common people is a slight misuse of Eric Wolf's felicitous phrase for colonial peoples equally unrepresented in historical records.

2. Curiously, the order of the two was reversed in the two countries. The United States saw the giant integrated railroads by the 1850s; administrative bureaucracies came later, with the Interstate Commerce Commission. In England governmental expansion into daily life preceded the huge commercial organizations (see Chandler 1977:498). Since much of England's capital generation took place within the firm, much of the legal work generated by American industrial expansion was absent (Mathias 1969:383ff.). By contrast, the Board of Trade's renewed involvement in bankruptcy proceedings dates from 1883, the Inland Revenue from 1842, and the administrations associated with welfare state policies from the Liberal administration of 1905–16.

3. The English history of land registration is reviewed in Abel-Smith and Stevens (1967:59–61). The American one is discussed in Johnstone and Hopson (1967:277–84). The English lawyers' attitude to registration is well summarized in W. Golden's statement (*APMLS* 1897:16) "I regard any approach to the registration of land as a public calamity."

4. L. K. Garrison (1935). Since many of Garrison's indicators measure legal work done (wills written, cases begun, etc.) rather than potential legal work (population, agricultural and industrial product), one could argue that fewer lawyers were doing more work—that efficiency was rising. This interpretation seems perfectly reasonable, although the Pennsylvania data I shall later introduce convinces me that much of the legal work done was done by nonlawyers.

5. Lazarus (1937). The quote is from page 22. On lawyer increase, see A. Edwards (1943).

6. Podmore (1980:14). Podmore argues (p. 16) that "Early in this century there were probably too many solicitors for the work available and this was also the case in the 1930s." I do not know the basis for this statement. A cursory glance at the level of unqualified practice suggests that there was plenty of work throughout the period, although solicitors may have set their prices too high to call it forth. On prices, see *CLS* 1914:114ff.; *APMLS* 1884:22ff.; 1886:146ff.

7. Certain forms of jurisdictional change are not evidenced by visible con-

flict. Thus, R. Pennington, president of the Law Society, noted in 1892, "When we met at Nottingham I ventured to call your attention to the fact that the commercial business of the City of London of a legal character had practically left the High Court; and that merchants and others, weary of the delay and not unconscious of the expense attendant on litigation in the High Court, . . . have had recourse to a tribunal constituted by themselves. . . . They prefer even the hazardous chances of arbitration, in which some arbitrator, who knows about as much of law as he does of theology, by the application of a rough-and-ready moral consciousness, or upon the affable principle of dividing the victory between both sides, decides intricate questions of law and fact with equal ease." (*APMLS* 1892:63; see also *APMLS* 1896:25–65). This trend away from legal settlement of disputes, noted as an accomplished fact by Abel-Smith and Stevens (1967) in their interpretaiton of the modern development of English law, results in a loss of jurisdiction without obvious signs of conflict. There might have been a serious attack on arbitrators, but I have found little evidence of it. Nonlawyer dispute resolution is of course common elsewhere; see Roche (1987).

8. There were about seventy-five thousand managing clerks in 1939, about five per solicitor (Abel-Smith and Stevens 1967:396). Johnstone and Hopson (1967:401) put the figure at a much lower thirty thousand as of the 1960s. J. Addison estimated *articled* clerks at five thousand in 1891 (*APMLS* 1891:154), indicating one clerk to three solicitors. The present ratio is about one to two (Zander 1984:7). The Solicitors Act of 1843 (sec. 4) limited solicitors to two articled clerks each (see *APMLS* 1908:238 on this issue). At least one contemporary saw professional overstock early in this century (J. W. Reid in *APMLS* 1908:236–41), which the professional imperialism noted below may confirm. The managing clerks were probably not docile underlings. When the state's invasion of legal jurisdictions began, at least some deserted to the enemy (*APMLS* 1892:96).

9. The figures on the Cravath firm are calculated from the roster of members printed in Swaine (1946). On firm size generally, see Hobson (1984).

10. On site of education, see Auerbach (1976:94). On duration, see Friedman (1973:528), and on law schools generally, Stevens (1983).

11. The internal stratification of American lawyers is discussed by Auerbach, who points out (1976:95) that between 1890 and 1910, full-time day law schools went from fifty-one to seventy-nine, and night law schools from ten to forty-five, a proportionately greater expansion in the lower-status law schools. Indirect evidence for oversupply of lawyers in the lower tier comes from figures on ethics violations. Where conditions are crowded and business scarce, we expect ethics violations as well as interprofessional conflict. The often-observed greater likelihood of ethics violations among lower-tier lawyers is thus explained by simple market forces, rather than by elitist xenophobia (Auerbach 1976:40–44) or by situtational inducement (Carlin 1966.) Indirect evidence of undersupply at the upper level is the ability of upper-tier firms to shed work they found inconvenient or socially awkward. See H. W. Taft on

railroad negligence work (Taft 1938:193). It is important to note that while firms like Cravath specialized in big business and government work, they also absorbed large quantities of routine lower-tier work. See Swaine 1946, vol. 1, p. 370.

12. See *APMLS* 1881:32; 1887:55; *CLS* 1927:43; 1929:54. In America, see *NYCLA* 1932:254.

13. On the early history, see *NYCLA* 1915:197. There are a variety of general sources on unauthorized practice, although there is not to my knowledge a serious historical study of it in the United States. A short legal account is Otterbourg (1951). *Law and Contemporary Problems* devoted an entire issue (5 [Winter] 1938) to the matter, including a characteristically brilliant essay by Karl Llewellyn.

14. For a rare English attempt to urge conciliation and compromise, see *LN* 1909:146. To the extent that interprofessional agreement or compromise ever appeared on the English scene, it took the form of a general assertion of "professional privilege" against all nonprofessionals or officials who "poached" on professional turf. See *LN* 1909:335; 1910:81–82; *APMLS* 1894:28; *CLS* 1906:82, 92, 104, 106. More commonly, the Law Society opposed the registration of other professions (*CLS* 1923:70–79), seemingly on the ground that it kept solicitors' general jurisdictions at maximum extent.

15. The quote is from *PABA* 1950:341. For complaint levels, see *NYCLA* 1915:194; 1917:218; 1926:165; *ABCNY* 1935:230; 1942:279. My English figures are taken from the *Annual Reports* of the Council of the Law Society, generally in the annual report of the Professional Purposes Committee. For the earlier period, see *APMLS* 1887:53. My comments about American committees are based on the New York and Pennsylvania sources cited below.

16. Fine examples of cyclical episodes are found in *Law Notes* during 1887, 1888, and 1908. On lawyer inattention, see *PABA* 1915:143; 1916:147; *LN* 1888:200. On the banker code, see *PABA* 1922:132; 1932:92ff.

17. On Gibson's suspicion, see *LN* 1930:333. The haphazard pattern of dates was only partly dictated by the scarcity of materials. The Council Reports were indeed available to me only from 1896. The Provincial Meetings *Proceedings*, which I used for the earlier period, told me nothing after 1911 that the Council Reports did not. The *Law Notes* were first drawn to my attention by a pejorative reference in *CLS* 1909:38 to "a monthly legal publication." I followed the journal from its beginning in 1882 to the 1930s, although by the 1920s it had come to believe that Council was actually doing a decent job of enforcement (*LN* 1920:242).

18. I have not paid much attention to the interprofessional treaties generally regarded by American lawyers as their chief achievements in relations to other professions. Partly I ignored them because the primary sources indicate that practitioners of those other professions ignore them as well. (At least they ignore the state-level agreements, as the history of recurrent negotiations with bankers and credit men by both the Pennsylvania and New York lawyers makes very clear.) In my data, attempts at local- or state-level negotiations came first, but were ultimately preempted by the American Bar Association efforts that

began in the late 1920s. Once the ABA became involved, the meetings and agreements related largely to legal and public jurisdiction and really had little to do with workplace reality. Dates of official agreements may be found in Otterbourg (1951).

19. I have of course taken much information from my general reading of the material presenting these complaints. There are also numerous problems in sampling and coding these data. Among these, the first is the issue of what constitutes a "mention" of unqualified practice. Is a single sentence equivalent to an entire article? In general, I have tried to count separate episodes, rather than mentions per se, but the data are still not really rigorous. Second, equivalent individuals may receive different names in different places—"accountants" may be "debt collectors" in another place or time. I have rigidly taken the name used in text, with all the problems that implies. Third, sampling is a major issue. With the reports of the practice committees, sampling was not a problem. I simply read the entire report and coded what appeared there. But with other sources—the oral discussions of these reports, the papers of individuals at the Provincial Meetings of the Law Society, the special reports of the Council—I had to scan a large source for anything that looked relevant. Such scanning was my sampling procedure, guided by certain key words and concepts; I traced any mention of either unqualified (unauthorized) practice or of any known competing group. In America, these various records come from lawyers in general, but in England I have studied solicitors only. The English barristers' boundary disputes are well-studied and concern the solicitors almost exclusively. They are thus less interesting for our purposes here.

20. As this list shows, I investigated not only areas where charges of unauthorized practice were made, but also areas where the profession simply asserted its rights of jurisdiction, hoping thereby to have a truer picture of jurisdictional conflict. It should be noted that local work could easily be considered under advocacy, since virtually the only issue was prosecution of criminal cases by the police. This practice, a hobbyhorse of the *Law Notes*, was taken much less seriously by the Law Society.

21. There are fewer than 400 complaints in the tables on areas of competition, because American sources in particular tended to accuse poachers of unspecified errors. I have omitted these when calculating percentages, to achieve comparability. This procedure assumes that specified complaints are a representative sample of the total population.

22. On the Pennsylvania proportions, see *Pennsylvania Bar Association Quarterly* 23:381, 396 (1952). Many sources testify to the rough equivalence between amounts of complaints and amounts of work. For example, the relative dominance of business work in cities is shown in L. K. Garrison (1935), and appears progressively stronger in such later data as Carlin's (1966:12) on area of specialization (45 percent business, 31 percent land and property) and Heinz and Laumann's (1982:40) on percentage of total legal effort (45 percent corporate business, 17 percent land and property, 9 percent regulatory). Carlin's (1962:118) data on lower-tier urban lawyers indicates a closer balance of business with land and property (both 27 percent). This balance is also found

in Handler's (1967:13) data on area of dominant practice (33 percent both in business and in land and property) among the lawyers of a smaller city. The rural dominance of land and property issues is clearly shown by the Pennsylvania data cited in text, as in Graham's (1931) figures for urban specialists (52 percent corporate and 25 percent land and property) and rural ones (39 percent corporate and 50 percent land and property). It thus seems safe to conclude that the gradient from business work to land and property work follows both status lines and urban-rural lines in the United States, and that the parallel it makes with unauthorized practice claims is substantially important.

In England, Miles's (1982) data on rural-eighteenth-century solicitors shows conveyancing the overwhelming leader (40–47 percent), replacing the advocacy (23–29 percent) that had previously dominated. A fair amount of work came from parochial and other local offices. Johnstone and Hopson (1967:372) put the figure two centuries later at 50–60 percent conveyancing for solicitors as a whole, while the National Prices and Incomes Board, speaking in 1968 of the entire profession, put land and property work at about 56 percent of productive time, with advocacy at 25 percent and business matters at 17 percent (cited in Zander 1984). The disappearance of rural collections work at the hands of banks and small debts courts is chronicled in Birks (1960:229–35). The English figures, too, generally parallel complaints about unqualified practice.

23. The British idea of solicitor's advice has a long history, beginning in an era when most of the advice concerned land and property or litigation related to the same. Miles (1982) gives a solid discussion of the eighteenth-century situation. My sources often waxed rhapsodic on the matter: "The physician heals diseases of the body, the lawyer diseases of the mind. How often he is able to heal strife, especially between members of the same family" (*APMLS* 1880:60) "The public convenience is found to be well served by greatly extending the solicitor's duties so as to make him the confidential advisor on all family, legal and business matters, the usual medium of winding up estates, and it seems possible that the entire management of all dealings with land and houses may be in the future (and I think should be) entrusted to the profession" (*APMLS* 1887:103). The importance of personal connection in advice work and legal work generally was a central theme of solicitors' defense against officialism in general and the Public Trustee in particular (*APMLS* 1891:50; 1909:91; see also *APMLS* 1882:129–40 and *LN* 1909:117 for related jurisdictional discussions). As the quote above indicates, solicitors seriously considered expanding their jurisdiction in this period, into auctioneering (*APMLS* 1882:141; 1886:135–39) and into the land professions' jurisdictions generally. They were later to protest much about house agents' and estate agents' invasions. Their equal attempt to oversee all legal professions is noted in *APMLS* 1889:47.

24. See, for example, *PABA* 1916:169. The underlawyering in the countryside may be established by analyzing the relation of lawyers to population in Pennsylvania. Although the rise of the new forms of practice gradually made population a less reliable indicator of demand in this period, it still serves

as an effective baseline. Figures are available for lawyers in 1909 (*PABA* 1909:512) and 1921 (*PABA* 1921:140–41), which may be compared with 1910 and 1920 census materials. There were in 1910 ninety-six lawyers per hundred thousand in Pennsylvania, and in 1920, eighty-six lawyers per hundred thousand. This fall was not equally spaced. The median numbers of lawyers per hundred thousand in the sixty-seven counties (by size) are as follows:

|  | 1910 | 1920 | median decline |
|---|---|---|---|
| less than 10,000 | 85 | 44 | 49.5% |
| 10,000 to 25,000 | 93 | 68 | 23.4% |
| 25,000 to 100,000 | 77 | 58 | 24.0% |
| more than 100,000 | 67 | 59 | 10.4% |

25. Quotes from *PABA* 1934:91 and *LN* 1888:146. It is of course problematic to compare New York urban lawyers with Pennsylvania rural ones. Nonetheless, it is a legal fact that states are governed by uniform law and an empirical fact that complaints of public unwillingness to come to lawyers seem to originate more in the countryside than in the cities.

26. Cf. *LN* 1891:118.

27. *PABA* 1932:110–11. For earlier material on the issue, see *PABA* 1916:168. See, more generally, Coxe (1908:37–47) on conveyancers.

28. See, for example, *CLS* 1906:79–123.

29. For more on these groups see Millerson (1964).

30. On rates of costs see *APMLS* 1884:146–55 and sources cited in note 7. The work of accountancy is best followed through E. Jones (1981), but see also Edey and Panitpakdi (1978).

31. On the County Courts Act, see LN 1980:47. The blacklists are in *LN* 1888:53ff.; 1889:107ff.; 205ff. On witnessing, see *LN* 1909:39. The *Law Notes* at first felt that unqualified practice was largely a phenomenon of the midland courts, then changed its mind to include the whole of the country. Later, it found the midlands again the most problematic area (*LN* 1887:327, 363; 1888:53–55; 1889:205ff.). The intimate relation of lawyers and judges in Anglo-American courts (as opposed to their separation in, for example, French courts) suggests that judges may restrict practices to satisfy their professional cousins. Certainly American law courts, with their lawyer judges, have sided more clearly with lawyers than have British ones, which often have barrister, not solicitor, judges. The celebrated cases on accountants' practice—*Agran vs. Shapiro*, 273 P.2d 619 (1954) and *in re Bercu*, 69 N.Y.Supp. (2d) 730 (1948) are obvious examples. Nonlawyer tribunals clearly don't mind nonlawyer pleading. The Treasury Department itself helped overthrow the legal reasoning of the *Agran* and *Bercu* cases, which was finally demolished by Congress in 1965 (P.L. 89–332 see Carey 1970:2:204–57). More generally, a careful review in 1948 found that only six of twenty-four major federal administrative agencies forbid nonlawyer appearances (*Columbia Law Review* 1948). Of those six, the SEC, the FTC, and the Post Office permitted companies to appear before them represented by their officers—another lawyers' shibboleth. Representation in English administrative tribunals is equally diverse (see Elcock 1969).

As administrative practice has become a larger jurisdiction, the lawyers' hold is correspondingly weaker.

32. The quote is from *LN* 1908:47. On Home Office practice, see *LN* 1914:18; for an earlier perspective, see *LN* 1888:84.

33. On receivership see Stacey (1954:25) and Carr-Saunders and Wilson (1933:210ff.). For Law Society opinions on receivership and registration, see *APMLS* 1886:30ff.; 1889:41ff.; 1891:45ff.; 1893:45. The remark about Halsbury's and Torrens's lands comes in *CLS* 1906:105. On the London scheme, see *CLS* 1906:94–109; for earlier opinion, see *APMLS* 1892:79–114, 1894: 25–59. On registrars, see *CLS* 1914:114ff.; on the Inland Revenue, *CLS* 1909:31. Accountants felt the bankruptcy loss as well. In Ireland, however, accountants succeeded in defeating officials. See Robinson (1983:77ff.)

34. For the Society's ideas about costs, see, for example, *APMLS* 1892:9, 42, 79–91.

35. See *NYCLA* 1920:161–171.

36. In keeping with the openly political character of American public life, much of the battle between the lawyers and the corporations was conducted in the courts and the legislatures, in both of which the lawyers had a strong professional presence that offset their adversaries' financial resources. The NYCLA reported annually on its legislative and legal activities, inevitably reporting the narrow defeat of these wily adversaries. The battle had the usual American features—"sinister and last-minute legislation" (*NYCLA* 1919:166, see also 1916:190–91); the use of ethics rules to deny the opposition legitimate use of lawyers (*NYCLA* 1917:222–23); protestations of disinterest ("This is not a matter of selfish interest to the Bar" *NYCLA* 1919:169; see also 1931:247); telegram campaigns and other organized opposition (*NYCLA* 1922:173, *ABCNY* 1936:248); attributions of vast expenditure by the opposition (*PABA* 1950:530); and dramatic predictions of Armaggedon (*NYCBA* 1922:179). The latter deserve substantial quotation: "All the casual collection agents and advertising sharpers, whose activities your Committee has in substantial measure curtailed in this community, would welcome legislation of the kind sponsored by the Credit Men's association. The passage of such legislation would be but an opening wedge. Debtors would be oppressed, bankruptcies would increase, self-respecting members of the Bar would find their clients cajoled and implored to take other lawyers, strangers to them and to their affairs, courts would be clogged with more unnecessary litigation than exists at present, and the entire practice of the law and the administration of justice dragged down to the plane of unrestricted commercialism." At times, the bar quoted leaders of other professions: "Common sense, common knowledge of human nature, and common experience all teach us the eternal truth of the utterance on the Mount, that 'no man can serve two masters.' That is what trust company lawyers are vainly trying to do when they draw wills for and give legal advice to the customers of their companies" (*NYCLA* 1931:250–51). The lawyers were, however, "doing much . . . to keep abreast of the progressive needs of the mercantile community" (*NYCLA* 1919:166), realizing that "in seeking to preserve professional standards, lawyers must not stand in the

way of legitimate, cooperative endeavor upon the part of business men" (*NYCLA* 1921:171). The result of this was the class-biased decision that trade associations could hold lawyers on retainer, but collection agencies— competitors and employers of lower-tier lawyers—could not (*NYCLA* 1921: 171).

37. On court bias in favor of lawyers, see *NYCLA* 1918:193. For the poachers' satisfaction, see *NYCLA* 1921:174–75.

38. The quote on *notaires* is in *NYCLA* 1916:183. For bar attacks on foreign lawyers giving advice, see *NYCLA* 1924:166; and for the later relenting, *NYCLA* 1941:250. Offshore divorce is discussed in *NYCLA* 1933:262 and *ABCNY* 1936:249. Other American lawyers are discussed in NYCLA 1929:218 and ABCNY 1931:225.

39. Friedman (1973:555–56) suggests that collections had been an important area of work for nineteenth-century rural lawyers. The precarious quality of collection work in the twentieth century is shown by Carlin's (1962:118) data showing how few lawyers specialized in it. It provided some work, but not enough to make a living.

## Chapter Ten

1. My chief source for this chapter is my own dissertation (Abbott 1982) on American psychiatry and neurology between 1880 and 1930. Some of the material below has already been published as Abbott (1980), and I thank the editors of *Sociological Analysis* for permitting its publication in altered form. Readers interested in alternative readings of the period may wish to consult American Psychiatric Association (1944), for the traditional view, and Grob (1973, 1983) for a view centered on psychiatry alone.

2. Good fictional depictions of this role occur in the novels of Oliver Wendell Holmes, Sr.: *Elsie Venner* and *The Guardian Angel*. On the idea of careers, see Bledstein (1976).

3. The clergy concerned are Protestant only. Data on Roman Catholics and Jews are meager, although the only substantial secondary study on American clergy in the mid to late nineteenth century that I know (Merwick 1973) concerns Roman priests. The basic data for this analysis of clergy views come from pastoral counseling texts; I thank the Gardner Sage Library of the New Brunswick Theological Seminary for allowing me to use their magnificent collection. Although texts undoubtedly overstate actual clergy practice, we do have one clergyman's casebooks (Spencer 1858). I thank Seward Hiltner both for calling Spencer's books to my attention and for commenting on this material. Abbott (1982:479ff.) contains an extended version of this argument. The quote is from Murphy (1877:249).

4. A standard work on these late-nineteenth-century developments is Wiebe (1967). A decisive interpretation of the impact of these developments on personal problems is Lears (1981), which unfortunately came to my attention after I had written this analysis. Since my data are generally quite different from Lears's, I have left it unchanged. This analysis draws on Abbott (1982:435–44).

5. The two quotes, with their sophisticated expressions of the problem, are from a somewhat later period: the first from Simmel ([1903] 1946:418) and the second from Sinclair Lewis (1922:109). The notion that personality itself provides solidarity in an affiliative society combines Durkheim's concept of organic solidarity and Simmel's of the web of affiliations.

6. The new structure of work is studied in dozens of sources. A good general source is Rodgers (1978).

7. The quote is from S. Lewis (1920:86). On the role of women, sources are again very rich. A general review is Ryan (1983).

8. On minor misbehavior see Lane (1971); and on etiquette, Schlesinger (1946). On work studies see Abbott (1982:144–45).

9. On mind-cure movements see Meyer (1965). On club life see Ferguson (1937). The Lynds found 97 percent of Middletown's business-class males in clubs and 57 percent of working-class males. For women, the figures were 92 percent and 36 percent, respectively.

10. The quote is from L. C. Powell (1909:10). For the medical evidence, see Fullinwider (1974), Gosling (1976), and Rosenberg (1962). The drug data are from Delgado and Kimball (1932).

11. The quote is from Willcox (1890:147).

12. Although histories exist of neurological thinking, there is no general history of American neurology as a specialty, to my knowledge, other than Abbott (1982). The outpatient- and sanitarium-based careers available to neurologists are discussed in chapter 3, local and national organization in chapters 5 and 6, the knowledge system and education in chapters 8 and 9, and the basic market for services in chapter 11. These discussions are integrated with discussions of psychiatry, since the merging of the two specalties from about 1895–1920 forced me to write the history of both at once. Although I have cited a few major primary sources below, readers desiring serious documentation should look at the dissertation.

13. The discussion of neurological knowledge is based on a general survey of texts and on detailed analysis of changes in successive editions of Church and Peterson's Nervous and Mental Disease (1899–1919, 9 eds.) and Dana's A Textbook of Nervous Disease (1892–1925, 10 eds.). See Abbott 1982:304–16. The impact of European knowledge through postgraduate study and publishing is examined on pp. 324–38.

14. On the loss of diseases, see the various authors writing about "The Training of the Neurologist" in Archives of Neurology and Psychiatry 29: 368–81, 624–32, 862–70 (1933).

15. This discussion of diagnosis, inference, and treatment draws directly on the texts cited above. It is noteworthy that, after seventy-five years of specific pathology, we are today returning to the contextual model of illness urged by the old neurologists.

16. The quotes are from Dana A Textbook of Nervous Disease (New York: Wood, 1908), 516. See the discussion of specific etiology in Abbott (1982:363).

17. Abbott (1982) discusses the neurological clientele on pp. 464–77. Basic data sources include casebooks from various cities and various periods, as well

as a complete survey of both the casebooks and the diagnostic records of the Philadelphia Orthopedic Hospital and Infirmary for Nervous Diseases.

18. A published casebook containing illustrations is G. V. Hamilton (1925). On the relation of general medicine and the specialty of nervous and mental disease, see Abbott 1982:490–95.

19. While various authors have discussed this group, generally with polemical intent, I have relied on my own reading of the primary documents, chiefly the relevant papers in the first fifty volumes of the the the *American Journal of Obstetrics* and the *Transactions* of the American Gynecological Society. For a good survey of the area see Morantz (1974). For a radical view of the area see Haller and Haller (1977), and for a conservative one, Grob (1983). My own discussion is in Abbott (1982:495–98).

20. The quote is from the *American Journal of Obstetrics* 38:171 (1898).

21. One Dr. Peaslee noted, in discussing R. Battey's original paper on his operation, that "the testis has often been removed for mere neuralgia without cure of the pain." See the discussion following Battey's paper, in *Transactions* of the American Gynecological Society 2:279–305.

22. A variety of "sects" carving out parts of this jurisdiction for varying groups are discussed in Abbott (1982:373ff.).

23. On neurologists' organizational structures, see Abbott 1982, chapters 5 and 6.

24. On the distribution of the knowledge of neurologists and, later, specialists in nervous and mental disease, see Abbott (1982:367ff., 402ff.).

25. The quote is from Gladden 1898:177. On the so-called "institutional church", see Douglass (1926) and Abell (1943).

26. On the evolution of social work away from the clergy, see Lubove (1969). There is, to my knowledge, little solid evidence about who people saw about their personal problems in the period 1900–1925. G. V. Hamilton's (1925) casebook reports a variety of techniques towards the end of the period, and Dexter and Dexter (1931) report a substantial clergy presence. One would, of course, infer the latter from numbers alone, as one would the use of general physicians for similar reasons.

27. The standard history of American care for the mentally ill is Grob (1973, 1983), which analyzes psychiatry largely in the context of institutional care. My work not only focuses more on outpatient care and on the interaction of psychiatry and neurology, it also uses different methodologies: collective biography and demographic modeling, case studies of local groups, and formal content analysis of nervous and mental disease literature. Although our differing emphases often lead to different interpretations, Grob and I agree on the areas we cover in common. For an alternative approach to Grob's, see D. Rothman (1971). Psychiatric ideas and practice in the mid nineteenth century are well covered by Dain (1964) and Tomes (1984), respectively. Except where noted, the history that follows is largely standard and can be followed in any of these sources.

28. My analysis of the character and success of inpatient work is standard. Detailed discussions of the roles of superintendent and assistant phsyician may

be found in Abbott (1982), chapter 2. Chapter 4 contains a detailed demo-graphic model of mobility between inpatient and outpatient worlds. See tables 5–19.

29. This network of psychiatric elite institutions is objectively derived from biographical data and analyzed in chapter 5 of Abbott (1982). See especially tables 20–41.

30. On the history of prevention generally, see Abbott (1982:444ff.) and Sicherman (1968). On causes of insanity, see Grob's work, generally, and Abbott (1982:446).

31. The sanitarium has received no serious study to my knowledge. I have discussed sanitarium work in general in chapter 3 of Abbott (1982) and sanitarium work in alcoholism particularly, on pp. 448–50. Borderline states, retardation, and epilepsy are discussed in the same section.

32. A general work on juvenile delinquency in this era is Platt (1969). My discussion of psychiatry and the law, which covers tort liability testimony, criminology, and work failure, as well as juvenile delinquency, is in Abbott (1982:450ff.). (Formal relations of the two professions are discussed on pp. 500–05). I have not discussed here psychiatry's attempt to expand into industry, also considered in that section. The organizational end of the adjustment school, the National Committee on Mental Hygiene, is discussed in Abbott (1982:257–66). General sources on psychiatry and the law can be found in Tighe (1983, 1985).

33. The phrase "social diagnosis" is taken from Mary Richmond's (1917) book of that name. Psychiatry's and neurology's roles in the First World War are discussed in Abbott (1982:266–74, 459–60).

34. On the theory of adjustment, see Abbott (1982:461ff.). The Commonwealth Fund quote is from the *Annual Report* for 1930–31, p. 52, and the quoted phrases are from the work of E. E. Southard.

35. The quotes are from the *Proceedings* of the American Medico-psychological Association 73:375, 377.

36. These smaller groups are briefly discussed in Abbott (1982:374ff.).

37. The calculation of 2 percent is my own, based on a formal birth and death model using demographic parameters from biographical data. It can be found, together with a Poisson estimation of the distribution of these physicians, in Abbott (1982: 130–32).

38. Meyer (1965). My own detailed discussion of pre- and post-Freudian psychotherapy, both lay and medical, in the United States, will be found in Abbott (1982:377–87). Although the sources on psychoanalysis are enormous, the standard sources are still Burnham (1967) and Hale (1971). The latter is unfortunately somewhat progressivist, and both interpret the psychiatric profession through its relation to psychoanalysis. I shall again cite only specific points in the following pages.

39. A detailed content analysis showing the shift of American psychiatric knowledge toward psychotherapy will be found in Abbott (1982:324–30).

40. On the Emmanuel movement, see Abbott (1982:484–86. I thank Sanford Gifford for sharing unpublished material on the movement with me. The Worcester quotes are from Worcester and McComb (1909:48, 53).

41. On psychologists in this period, see Napoli (1981).

42. On psychiatric social work, see Abbott (1982:507–10), and more generally, Lubove (1969). The British psychiatric social workers, who were originally trained in America, assumed the same professional location (Timms 1964).

43. This argument summarizes, in somewhat different order, a discussion of the structure of nervous and mental disease knowledge in the 1920s given in Abbott (1982:380–401).

44. It should be recalled that except where the contrary is specifically stated I am not discussing here what Freud actually said, but Americans' use of what they thought he said. The two were considerably different.

45. That elite training institutions were in the hands of Freudians or open-minded eclectics is an example of the power of contingency in history. To see Freud's ideas as sweeping America otherwise is mistaken. See Abbott (1982: 385, 510).

46. For the state of psychiatric affairs in 1944, when the APA was a century old, see American Psychiatric Association (1944). An insider's history of the psychoanalytic movement in this period is Oberndorf (1964). On lay analysis, see Abbott (1982:510). On the organizational structure of the psychoanalytic end of psychiatry, see Abbott (1982:245–48).

47. On psychiatric social work, see the sources cited earlier. Solomon's remarks were made in her 1927 presidential address to the American Association of Psychiatric Social Workers. See Abbott (1982:508).

48. On personal analysis, see Abbott (1982:509–11). There is, of course, extensive coverage of this topic in general works on psychoanalysis. For an ironic note on psychoanalysis's power even over other schools of therapy, see Lazarus (1971).

49. It is important to recall that central interpreters "Americanized" psychoanalysis. These writers—Sullivan, Horney, White and others—were not academics, but they did serve to legitimate psychoanalysis in the ways I have attributed to academics in chapter 2; they attached it to central American values about maturity, stress, and personal development, often to the horror of more orthodox Freudians like Ernest Jones. Moreover, as major teachers of psychoanalysis, these writers served basically academic functions.

50. For extensive but somewhat unreliable figures on who goes where for counseling, see Freeman (1967).

51. The quote is from Stolz (1932:15, 18).

52. Boisen's life is discussed in his riveting autobiography (1960). The quote is from his long book on the meaning of psychotic ideation (1936:280).

53. On the early history of the pastoral counseling movement, see Kemp (1947). The AAPC was founded in 1963. I am indebted to Seward Hiltner for his comments on this issue. Some commentators emphasize the surrender of the clergy (e.g., Kleinman 1984; Leat 1973), while others emphasize forces holding the clergy together as a coherent group (e.g., Jarvis 1976).

54. This history is standard, although with the latter days of deinstitutionalization I have extensive personal experience. On deinstitutionalization generally, see Lerman (1982). On the more recent psychiatric clientele, see Bahn,

Conwell, and Hurley (1965). On the psychologists' clientele, see Rubinstein and Lorr (1954). On psychotherapy generally, see Henry, Sim, and Spray (1971, 1973).

55. The NIMH figures, here and later on, are from Segal (1975). See pp. 31, 35, 42, 58, 315. On psychology generally see Dorken et al. (1976), Reisman (1976), and Gilgen (1982).

56. See Reed, Myers, and Scheidemandel (1972:29ff.).

57. Freeman (1967). On early psychiatric insurance see Reed, Myers and Scheidemandel (1972:61ff.). On psychologists' collections, see Dorken et al. (1976:82, 121).

## Chapter Eleven

1. Of course, in the discussions of division, enclosure, and attack of chapter 4, I have covered these topics to some extent. But I have not really investigated the issue of coalescence in detail.

2. No historian using this model will have to wonder, as did those employing "professionalization" models, why most of his or her data doesn't seem relevant to a sociological interpretation of the group involved. This was a common complaint during the two years I attended sessions on the history of professions at the Davis Center for Historical Studies. For recent complaints see Kohler (1985) and Pernick (1985).

3. One commentator on this manuscript noted that I do "not really address the issue of why the *special, narrowly defined group* of occupations that Anglo-American scholars have considered professions rose to the position they did." (His emphasis.) That is a fair criticism. I have not limited myself to groups that look like early-twentieth-century American and British law and medicine as discussed in traits theories of professionalism from Carr-Saunders and Wilson in 1933 to, say, Wilensky in 1964. I have tried to deal more generally with the social structuring of expertise in nonsocialist developed countries and have used the word "profession" to cover that investigation. In so doing, I stand in the line of Johnson (1967), Freidson (1983), and dozens of other critics of traits theories, who all aim to refocus the investigation of expertise on this broader issue. My own worries about the concept of profession have to do with the whole notion of group and coalescence, particularly since lifelong careers of basic professional work are less and less common. The exact relation of profession and professional has become much more complex.

4. Two very valuable sources on the philosophy of history have already been cited: Danto (1985) and Gallie (1968). Some of my own thoughts on the matter can be found in my papers on historical sequences (Abbott:1983, 1984). What follows is basically a reflection on historical methods informed by the experience of writing this book and reading much recent (but unrelated) history, historical sociology, and philosophy of history. I have not noted particular sources, since many of the issues are familiar and my own aims are more reflective than scholarly.

5. Parry and Parry (1976) and Carey (1970) are the titles quoted. The Pulitzer Prize was won by Starr (1982).

6. On professionalization in history, see Jann (1985).

7. Braudel (1976); Paige (1975). Brilliant examples of textualism are the works of Natalie Davis and Robert Darnton.

8. I have taken the term "central subjects", along with many insights related to it, from Hull (1975).

9. This point is essential. We must avoid the journalistic fallacy of treating the present as a standard in whose light we view all the past. Good history should recognize both the ephemerality of its current objects of inquiry—in this case the current professions—and the ephemerality of its own world view. This means, of course, that this book, filled as it is with contention against functionalist and monopolist views of professions, will soon enough join them (and earlier versions of interactionism) in the gallery of things to be rejected. That is why—and I say it again, in case I haven't said it enough—I feel that those were good and sound theories whose praises, like those of famous men, we should sing even as we create our own new theories.

10. Eliot Freidson, in a personal comment, disagreed. He feels the environing question is how societies structure work. Jim Davis, Robert Dingwall, and a number of other questioners through the years have raised the same issue: whether I have not given a general theory of the division of labor. While I am flattered by the implication of the question, I think the focus on abstraction limits my study to experts.

11. There was some, but rather limited, specialization among Chinese mandarins; see, for example, Hartwell (1971a, 1971b). On the origins of the British and Indian Civil Services, see Chapman (1970).

12. On this issue see, among many others, Larson (1977), Ben-David (1963), and Bledstein (1976).

13. The phrase "moral entrepreneurship" was invented, as far as I know, by Becker (1963).

14. One might view commodification as a good thing, since it democratizes expertise, microcomputing being an excellent example. On the other hand, that democratization occurs only within a highly structured environment; it probably allows many erroneous applications of the commodified expertise; and it leaves commodity users uninformed when problems are beyond the commodities' abilities.

15. On knowledge in organizations, see Gerver and Bensman (1954) and Wilensky (1967). On deskilling, see Braverman (1976) and many others cited in earlier chapters.

16. Individual and organizational expertise are in some sense structural opposites of the second, absolute kind. That is, there will in some ways always be an opposition between them, even if professions as we currently know them, or as they were construed fifty years ago, disappear. Nonetheless, the fact remains that commodified knowledge seems to create as much new work as it destroys, while the institutionalization of knowledge in organizations does not. See Larson (1980) for an argument more strongly believing that organizations are winning.

17. See Mark 8:35–36, AV.

# References

AICPA. 1966. *Accounting and the Computer.* New York: AICPA.

Abbott, A. 1980. "Religion, Psychiatry, and the Problems of Everyday Life." *Sociological Analysis* 41:164–71.

———. 1981. "Status and Status Strain in the Professions." *American Journal of Sociology* 86:819–35.

———. 1982. *The Emergence of American Psychiatry.* Ph.D. Diss. University of Chicago.

———. 1983. "Sequences of Social Events." *Historical Methods* 16:129–47.

———. 1984. "Event Sequence and Event Duration." *Historical Methods* 17:192–204.

———. forthcoming. "Vacancy Methods for Historical Data." In R. Breiger, ed., *Social Mobility and Social Structure.* Cambridge: Cambridge University Press.

Abeille, J. E. 1971. *Fonctions et professions juridique et judiciaire.* Paris: Librairie Générale de Droit et Jurisprudence.

Abell, A. I. 1943. *The Urban Impact of American Protestantism.* Cambridge: Harvard University Press.

Abel-Smith, B. 1960. *A History of the Nursing Profession.* London: Heinemann.

———. 1964. *The Hospitals 1800–1948.* London: Heinemann.

Abel-Smith, B., and R. Stevens. 1967. *Lawyers and the Courts.* Cambridge: Harvard University Press.

Abraham, S. C. 1978. *The Public Accounting Profession.* Lexington, MA: Heath.

Ackerknecht, E. H. 1957. "Medical Education in 19th Century France." *Journal of Medical Education* 32:148–53.

Adler, J. 1979. *Artists in Offices.* New Brunswick, NJ: Transaction.

Adler, R. G. 1984. "Biotechnology as Intellectual Property." *Science* 224:357–63.

Albrecht, G. L. 1979. "Defusing Technological Change in Juvenile Courts." *Sociology of Work and Occupations* 6:259–82.

Alonso, W. 1971. "Beyond the Interdisciplinary Approach to Planning." *Journal of the American Institute of Planners* 37:169–73.

Aman, M. G. 1984. "Hyperactivity." *Journal of Autism and Developmental Disorders* 14:39–56.

American Journal of Hospital Pharmacy. 1985. "Directions for Clinical Practice in Pharmacy." *American Journal of Hospital Pharmacy* 42:1287–1342.

American Psychiatric Association. 1944. *One Hundred Years of American Psychiatry.* New York: Columbia University Press for the APA.

Ancelin, J. 1976. *Cross-National Studies of Social Service Systems: French Reports,* vol. 1. New York: Columbia University School of Social Work.

Anderson, A. 1926. "The Accountant's Function as Business Advisor." *Journal of Accountancy* 41:17–21.

Angel, J. 1970. *Professional and Occupational Licensing in the United States.* New York: World Trade Academy.

Anthony, J.R. 1978. *French Baroque Music.* New York: Norton.

Arney, W. R. 1982. *Power and the Profession of Obstetrics.* Chicago: University of Chicago Press.

Atkins, P. M. 1928. "University Instruction in Industrial Cost Accounting." *Accounting Review* 3:345–63.

Auerbach, J. S. 1976. *Unequal Justice.* New York: Oxford University Press.

Austin, M. J. 1978. *Professionals and Paraprofessionals.* New York: Human Sciences.

Austrian, G. D. 1982. *Herman Hollerith.* New York: Columbia University Press.

Ayres, L. P. 1927. "The Dilemma of the New Statistics." *Journal of the American Statistical Association* 22:1–8.

Bahn, A. K., M. Conwell, and P. Hurley. 1965. "Survey of Private Psychiatric Practice." *Archives of General Psychiatry* 12:295–302.

Baker, P. 1985. "The Farmer as a Social Problem." Paper Presented to the Organization of American Historians, April 1985.

Bancaud, A. 1985. "L'idéal juridique realisé." *Annales de Vaucresson* No. 23:91–114.

Bancaud, A., and Y. Dezalay. 1980. "La justice face aux restructurations économiques, analyses et stratégies." *Droit social* No. 7–8:357–64.

Barbier, G. 1972. "Accounting in France." *Accountancy* 83: October:10–17.

Barger, H. 1955. *Distribution's Place in the U.S. Economy Since 1869.* Princeton: Princeton University Press.

Baritz, L. 1960. *Servants of Power.* Middletown, CN: Wesleyan University.

Barker, L. F. 1942. *Time and the Physician.* New York: Putnam.

Barker, T. M. 1975. *The Military Intellectual and Battle.* Albany, NY: SUNY Press.

Bartels, R. 1962. *The Development of Marketing Thought.* Homewood, IL: Irwin.

Baur, E. J. 1949. "The Functions of Ceremony in the Advertising Business." *Social Forces* 27:358–65.

Baylis, T. A. 1974. *The Technical Intelligentsia and the East German Elite.* Berkeley: University of California Press.

Becker, H. 1963. *Outsiders.* New York: Free Press.

Beer, S., 1954. "Operations Research and Accounting." *Operations Research Quarterly* 5:1–12.

Béland, F. 1976. "Du paradoxe professionnel: médecins et ingénieurs des années 1800." *Archives européenes de sociologie* 17:306–30.

Ben-David, J. 1963. "Professions in the Class System of Present Day Societies." *Current Sociology* 12:247–98.

Ben-David, J., and R. Collins. 1966. "Social Factors in the Origin of a New Science." *American Sociological Review* 31:451–65.

Bendix, R. 1949. *Higher Civil Servants in American Society.* Boulder: University of Colorado Press.

———. 1974. *Work and Authority in Industry.* Berkeley: University of California Press.

Bensman, J., and R. Lilienfeld. 1973. *Craft and Consciousness.* New York: Wiley.

Berlanstein, L. R. 1975. *The Barristers of Toulouse in the Eighteenth Century.* Baltimore: Johns Hopkins University Press.

Berlant, J. L. 1975. *Profession and Monopoly.* Berkeley: University of California Press.

Bernays, E. L. 1971. "Emergence of the Public Relations Counsel." *Business History Review* 45:296–316.

Bianconi, A. 1959. "Les instituteurs." *Revue française de science politique* 9:935–50.

Biggs, J. 1955. *The Guilty Mind.* New York: Harcourt Brace.

Bigler, R. M. 1972. *The Politics of German Protestantism.* Berkeley: University of California Press.

———. 1974. "Social Status and the Political Role of the Protestant Clergy in Pre-March Prussia." Pp. 175–90 in Wehler 1974.

Birenbaum, R. 1982. "Reprofessionalization in Pharmacy." *Social Science and Medicine* 16:871–78.

Birks, M. 1960. *Gentlemen of the Law.* London: Stevens.

Blair, R. D., and S. Rubin, eds. 1980. *Regulating the Professions.* Lexington, MA: Heath.

Blanc, E. 1972. *La nouvelle profession d'avocat.* Paris: Librairie du Journal des Notaires et des Avocats.

Blau, J. 1984. *Architects and Firms.* Cambridge: MIT Press.

Blau, J. R., M. LaGory, and J. S. Pipkin, eds. 1983. *Professionals and Urban Form.* Albany: SUNY Press.

Blayney, M. S. 1977. "Librarians for the Millions." *Journal of Library History* 12:235–49.

Bledstein, B. J. 1976. *The Culture of Professionalism.* New York: Norton.

Bliss, A. A., and E. D. Cohen, eds. 1977. *The New Health Professionals.* Germantown, MD: Aspen Systems Corporation.

Bloom, H. 1976. "Adult Services." Pp. 379–98 in Winger 1976.

Blough, C. G. 1937. "The Relation of the SEC to the Accountant." *Journal of Accountancy* 63:23–39.

Bodin, L., and J. Touchard. 1959. "Les intellectuels dans la société française contemporaine." *Revue française de science politique* 9:835–59.

Bogart, M. H. 1984. "In Search of a United Front." *Winterthur Portfolio* 19:151–76.

Böhme, G., W. van den Daele, R. Hohlfeld, R. Krohn, and W. Schäfer. 1983. *Finalization in Science.* Dordrecht: Reidel.

Boisen, A. T. 1936. *The Exploration of the Inner World.* Chicago: Willett, Clark.

————. 1960. *Out of the Depths.* New York: Harper.

Bonafe-Schmitt, J. P. 1985. "Pour une sociologie du juge prud'homal." *Annales de Vaucresson* No. 23:27–50.

Bosk, C. 1979. *Forgive and Remember.* Chicago: University of Chicago Press.

Bouffleur, A. I. 1905. "Company Associations." *Railway Surgical Journal* 11:13–15.

Bourdieu, P. 1971. "Genèse et structure du champ religieux." *Revue française de sociologie* 12:295–334.

————. 1976. "Le champ scientifique." *Actes de la recherche en sciences sociales* No. 2–3.

————. 1986. "La force du droit." *Actes de la recherche en sciences sociales* No. 64.

Bouteiller, M. 1966. *Médecine populaire d'hier et d'aujourd'hui.* Paris: Editions G.-P. Maisoneuve et Larose.

Boutry, P. 1986. *Prêtres et paroisses au pays du curé d'Ars.* Paris: Editions du CERF.

Boyle, B. M. 1977. "Architectural Practice in America, 1865–65." Pp. 309–44 in Kostof 1977.

Brain, D. K. 1984. *The Discipline of Design.* Ph.D. diss., Harvard University.

Branca, P., ed. 1977. *The Medicine Show.* New York: Science History Publications.

Brand, B. E. 1983. "Librarianship and Other Female Intensive Professions." *Journal of Library History* 18:391–406.

Brand, J. L. 1965. *Doctors and the State.* Baltimore: Johns Hopkins University Press.

Brandeis, L. 1914. *Business: a Profession.* Boston: Small, Maynard.

Brandt, A. 1985. *No Magic Bullet.* New York: Oxford University Press.

Braude, L. 1961. "Professional Autonomy and the Role of the Layman." *Social Forces* 39:297–301.

Braudel, F. 1976. *The Mediterranean.* 2 vols. New York: Harper.

Braverman, H. 1974. *Labor and Monopoly Capital.* New York: Monthly Review Press.

Brint, S. 1984. "New Class and Cumulative Trend Explanations of the Liberal

Political Attitudes of Professionals." *American Journal of Sociology* 91: 30–70.

Brown, R. E. 1979. *Rockefeller Medicine Men: Medicine and Capitalism in America*. Berkeley: University of California Press.

Brumberg, J. J. 1982. "Chlorotic Girls, 1870–1920." *Child Development* 53:1468–77.

Brumberg, J. J., and N. Tomes. 1982. "Women in the Professions." *Reviews in American History* 10:275–96.

Bucher, R. 1962. "Pathology: A Study of Social Movements within a Profession." *Social Problems* 10:40–51.

Bucher, R., and J. Stelling. 1969. "Characteristics of Professional Organizations." *Journal of Health and Social Behavior* 10:3–16.

Bucher, R., and A. Strauss. 1961. "Professions in Process." *American Journal of Sociology* 66:325–34.

Burchell, S., C. Clubb, and A. G. Hopwood. 1985. "Accounting in its Social Context: Towards a History of Valued Added in the United Kingdom." *Accounting, Organizations, and Society* 10:381–413.

Burke, K. 1969. *A Grammar of Motives*. Berkeley: University of California Press.

Burnham, J. C. 1967. "Psychoanalysis and American Medicine, 1894–1918." *Psychological Issues* 5:4 (special issue).

———. 1982. "American Medicine's Golden Age." *Science* 215:1474–79.

Burrow, J. G. 1977. *Organized Medicine in the Progressive Era*. Baltimore: Johns Hopkins University Press.

CAD. 1978. "CAD: The Next Ten Years." *CAD* 10:347–49.

Calhoun, D. 1960. *The American Civil Engineer*. Cambridge: MIT Press.

———. 1965. *Professional Lives*. Cambridge: Harvard University Press.

Callahan, R. E. 1962. *Education and the Cult of Efficiency*. Chicago: University of Chicago Press.

Calvert, M. A. 1967. *The Mechanical Engineer in America*. Baltimore: Johns Hopkins University Press.

Caplow, T. 1954. *The Sociology of Work*. Minneapolis: University of Minnesota.

Carey, J. L. 1969, 1970. *The Rise of the Accounting Profession*. 2 vols. New York: American Institute of Certified Public Accountants.

Carlin, J. 1962. *Lawyers on Their Own*. New Brunswick NJ: Rutgers University Press.

———. 1966. *Lawyers' Ethics*. New York: Russell Sage.

Carlson, W. H. 1955. "The Trend Towards Academic Recognition of College Librarians." *College and Research Librarians* 16:24–29.

Carnahan, W. A. 1978. "The Insanity Defense in New York." New York Department of Mental Hygiene.

Carr-Saunders, A. P., and P. A. Wilson. 1933. *The Professions*. Oxford: Oxford University Press.

Carroll, C. E. 1970. *The Profession of Education for Librarianship*. Metuchen, NJ: Scarecrow.

Cartter, A. M. 1976. *Ph.D.'s and the Academic Labor Market*. New York: Mc-Graw Hill.

Castel, R. 1976. *L'ordre psychiatrique*. Paris: Editions de Minuit.

Cayla, J.-S. 1986. *La profession infirmière*. Paris: Sirey.

Cebul, R. D., and L. H. Beck, eds. 1985. *Teaching Clinical Decision-Making*. New York: Praeger.

Chalmin, P. 1957. *L'officier français de 1815 à 1870*. Paris: M. Riviere.

Chandler, A. D. 1977. *The Visible Hand*. Cambridge MA: Harvard University Press.

Chapman, R. A. 1970. *The Higher Civil Service in Britain*. London: Constable.

Chapoulie, J.-M. 1973. "Sur l'analyse sociologique des groupes professionels." *Revue française de sociologie* 14:86–114.

Chase, A. 1979. "The Birth of the Modern Law School." *American Journal of Legal History* 23:328–48.

Chauvenet, A. 1972. "Professions hospitalières et division du travail." *Sociologie du travail* 13:145–63.

———. 1973. "Idéologies et status professionnels chez les médecins hospitaliers." *Revue française de sociologie* 14:(supp):61–76.

———. 1978. *Médecines au choix, médecine de classes*. Paris: Presses Universitaires de France.

Child, J., M. Fores, I. Glover, and P. Lawrence. 1983. "A Price to Pay? Professionalisms and Work Organization in Britain and West Germany." *Sociology* 17:63–78.

Child, J., and J. Fulk. 1982. "Maintenance of Occupational Control." *Work and Occupations* 9:155–92.

Christiansen, E. B. 1976. "Special Libraries." Pp. 399–416 in Winger 1976.

Churchman, C. W., and R. L. Ackoff. 1968. "Operational Accounting." Pp. 80–89 in Solomons 1968.

Churchward, L. G. 1973. *The Soviet Intelligentsia*. London: Routledge.

Churchwell, C. D. 1975. *The Shaping of American Library Education*. ACRL Monograph. Chicago: ALA.

Cipolla, C. 1973. "The Professions—the Long View." *Journal of European Economic History* 2:37–51.

Clark, J. M. 1967. *Teachers and Politics in France*. Syracuse: Syracuse University Press.

Clark, T. N. 1973. *The French University and the Emergence of the Social Sciences*. Cambridge: Harvard University Press.

Cleary, P. D. N.d."Chiropractic Use." Rutgers University Graduate School of Social Work.

Cobban, A. 1961. *A History of Modern France*. Harmondsworth: Pelican.

Coe, R. 1970. "The Process of the Development of Established Professions." *Journal of Health and Social Behavior* 11:59–67.

Coe, T. L., and B. J. Coe. 1976. "Marketing Research: The Search for Professionalism." Pp. 257–59 in K. L. Bernhardt, ed., American Marketing Association *Educator's Proceedings* No. 39.

Cogan, M. L. 1953. "Towards a Definition of Professions." *Harvard Educational Review* 23:33–50.

———. 1955. "The Problem of Defining a Profession." *The Annals* 297: 105–111.

Cohen, D. C. 1952. "London Scriveners and the Estate Market in the Later Seventeenth Century." *Economic History Review* 2s 4:221–30.

Cohen, K. J., and S. E. Gibson, eds. 1978. *Management Science in Banking.* Boston: Warren, Gorham and Lamont.

Cohen, M. 1966. "The Emergence of Private Practice in Social Work." *Social Problems* 14:84–93.

Cole, J. 1979. "Storehouses and Workshops." Pp. 364–85 in Oleson and Voss 1979.

Collins, R. 1979. *The Credential Society.* New York: Academic Press.

Columbia Law Review. 1948. "Proposed Restriction of Law Practice Before Federal Administrative Agencies." *Columbia Law Review* 48:120–30.

Colvard, R. 1961. "Foundations and Professions: The Organizational Defense of Autonomy." *Administrative Science Quarterly* 6:167–84.

Conrad, P., and J. W. Schneider. 1980. *Deviance and Medicalization.* Saint Louis: C. V. Mosby.

Corwin, R. 1961. "The Professional Employee: A Study of Conflict in Nursing Roles." *American Journal of Sociology* 66:604–15.

———. 1965. "Militant Professionalism, Initiative and Compliance in Public Education." *Sociology of Education* 38:310–31.

———. 1970. *Militant Professionals.* New York: Appleton.

Coser, L. 1965. *Men of Ideas.* New York: Free Press.

Coser, L., C. Kadushin, and W. W. Powell. 1982. *Books.* New York: Basic.

Cottrell, F. W. 1970. *Technological Change and Labor in the Railroad Industry.* Lexington MA: Heath.

Coxe, R. D. 1908. *Legal Philadelphia.* Philadelphia: W. J. Campbell.

Coxon, A. P. M. 1979. *The Fate of the Anglican Clergy: A Sociological Study.* London: Macmillan.

Crapuchet, S., ed. 1974. *Sciences de l'homme et professions sociales.* Toulouse: Privat.

Cresswell, H. B. 1964. *The Honeywood File.* London: Faber and Faber.

Crozier, M. 1964. *The Bureaucratic Phenomenon.* Chicago: University of Chicago Press.

Cullen, J. B. 1978. *The Structure of Professionalism.* New York: Petrocelli.

Culliton, B. J. 1986. "McLean-AMI Agree on Joint Venture." *Science* 231: 1363–64.

Dain, N. 1964. *Concepts of Insanity in the United States.* New Brunswick NJ: Rutgers University Press.

Danto, A. 1985. *Narration and Knowledge.* New York: Columbia University Press.

Danton, J. P. 1976. "The Library Press." Pp. 153–76 in Winger 1976.

Davies, M. W. 1982. *Woman's Place is at the Typewriter.* Philadelphia: Temple University Press.

Davis, D. J. 1976. "Education for Librarianship." Pp. 113–33 in Winger 1976.

Davis, F. 1960. "Uncertainty in Medical Prognosis: Clinical and Functional." *American Journal of Sociology* 66:41–47.

Day, C. R. 1978. "The Making of Mechanical Engineers in France." *French Historical Studies* 10:439–60.

Debons, A., D. King, U. Mansfield, and D. Shirey. 1980. *Manpower Requirments for Scientific and Technical Communications*. Final Project Report, NSF, Div Info Sci/Tech, Grant DSI 7727115, NTIS.

Debré, J.-L. 1984. *Les republiques des avocats*. Paris: Librarie Académique Perrin.

DeFleur, M. 1964. "Occupational Roles as Portrayed on Television." *Public Opinion Quarterly* 28:57–74.

Delgado, F. A., and A. A. Kimball. 1932. "Prescription Department Sales Analysis in Selected Drug Stores." Washington: GPO, Domestic Commerce Series No. 61.

Denzin, N. K. 1968. "Incomplete Professionalization: The Case of Pharmacy." *Social Forces* 46:375–81.

Derber, C., ed. 1982. *Professionals as Workers: Mental Labor in Advanced Capitalism*. Boston: G. K. Hall.

Dewald, J. 1980. *The Formation of a Provincial Nobility*. Princeton: Princeton University Press.

Dexter, E. W., and R. C. Dexter. 1931. *The Minister and Family Troubles*. New York: R. R. Smith.

Dezalay, Y. 1986. "From Mediation to Pure Law." *International Journal of the Sociology of Law* 14:89–107.

———. 1987. "From Bankruptcy to the Reorganization of Failing Firms." Paper presented to the Law and Society Association, Washington, D.C., 12 June 1987.

Dhoquois, R. 1985. "La vulgarisation du droit du travail." *Annales de Vaucresson* No. 23:15–26.

Dickinson, A. L. 1909. "The Relation Between the Accountant and the Banker." *Journal of Accountancy* 8:55–57.

Dickson, D. 1984. "Science Shops Flourish in Europe." *Science* 223:1158–60.

Dickson, G. W., and V. T. Dock. 1975. "Graduate Professional Programs in Information Systems." *Interfaces* 6:38–43.

Diemer, H. 1912. "Industrial Management." *Journal of Accountancy* 13:272–78.

Dingwall, R. 1977. "Atrocity Stories and Professional Relationships." *Work and Occupations* 4:371–96.

Dingwall, R., and P. Lewis, eds. 1983. *The Sociology of the Professions*. London: St. Martin's.

Dinitz, S., and W. Beran. 1971. "Community Mental Health as a Boundaryless and Boundary Busting System." *Journal of Health and Social Behavior* 12:99–107.

Dix, G. 1945. *The Shape of the Liturgy*. London: Dacre.

Djilas, M. 1957. *The New Class*. New York: Praeger.

Donham, W. B. 1927. "The Emerging Profession of Business." *Harvard Business Review* 5:401–5.

Dorken, H., et al. 1976. *The Professional Psychologist Today*. San Francisco: Jossey Bass.

Douglas, M. 1970. *Purity and Danger*. London: Penguin.

Douglass, H. P. 1926. *1000 City Churches*. New York: Doran.

Downs, R. B. 1958. *The Status of College and Research Librarians*. Chicago: ALA, ACRL Monograph No. 22.

Dray, W. H. 1978. "Concepts of Causation in A.J.P.Taylor's Account of the Origins of the Second World War." *History and Theory* 17:149–74.

Drucker, A. P. R. 1928. "The Accountant as an Efficiency Expert." *Accounting Review* 3:364–68.

Dubin, S. S., ed. 1972. *Professional Obsolescence*. Lexington, MA: Heath.

Duda, R. O., and E. H. Shortliffe. 1983. "Expert Systems Research." *Science* 220:261–68.

Duflot, C. 1974. "Le psychologue." Pp. 362–73 in Crapuchet 1974.

Duhart, J., and J. Charton-Brassard. 1973. "Reforme hospitalière et soin infirmier sur ordonnance médicale." *Revue française de sociologie* 14:(supp): 77–101.

Duman, D. 1979. "The Creation and Diffusion of a Professional Ideal in Nineteenth Century England." *Sociological Review* 27:113–38.

———. 1980. "Pathway to Professionalism: The English Bar in the 18th and 19th Centuries." *Journal of Social History* 13:615–28.

———. 1983. *The English and Colonial Bars in the Nineteenth Century*. London: Croon Helm.

Duncan, A. J. 1965. *Quality Control and Industrial Statistics*. Homewood, IL: Irwin.

Earle, E. M., ed. 1966. *The Makers of Modern Strategy*. New York: Atheneum.

Eaton, M. C. 1955. "What Did Mr. Agran Do?" *Journal of Accountancy* 99:6:33–39.

Edey, H. C. T., and P. Panitpakdi. 1978. "British Company Accounting and the Law." Pp.356–79 in A. C. Littlejohn and B. Yamey, eds., *Studies in the History of Accounting*. New York: Arno.

Editions Francis Lefebvre. 1986. *Memento pratique Francis Lefebvre—professions libérales 1986*. Paris: Editions Francis Lefebvre.

Edwards, A. 1943. *Comparative Occupational Statistics for the United States 1870–1940*. Washington: Government Printing Office.

Edwards, J. D. 1960. *History of Public Accountancy in the United States*. East Lansing, MI: Michigan State University Press.

Elcock, H. J. 1969. *Administrative Justice*. London: Longman's.

Elias, N. 1950. "Studies in the Genesis of the Naval Profession." *British Journal of Sociology* 1:291–309.

Engel, A. J. 1983. *From Clergyman to Don*. Oxford: Oxford University Press.

Engel, G. V. 1969. "The Effect of Bureaucracy on the Professional Autonomy of the Physician." *Journal of Health and Social Behavior* 10:30–41.

————. 1970. "Professional Autonomy and Bureaucratic Organization." *Administrative Science Quarterly* 15:12–21.

Engel, G. V., and R. H. Hall. 1973. "The Growing Industrialization of the Professions." Pp. 75–88 in *The Professions and Their Prospects*, ed. E. Freidson. Beverly Hills, CA: Sage.

Engelhardt, H. T., S. F. Spicker, and B. Towers, eds. 1977. *Clinical Judgment*. Dordrecht: Reidel.

Epstein, M. J. 1978. *The Effect of Scientific Management on the Development of the Standard Cost System*. New York: Arno.

Etzioni, A. 1969. *The Semi-professions and Their Organization*. New York: Free Press.

Eurich, N. P. 1985. *Corporate Classrooms*. Princeton: Carnegie Foundation for the Advancement of Teaching.

Evans, M., and E.O. Laumann. 1983. "Professional Commitment: Myth or Reality." *Research in Social Stratification and Mobility* 2:3–40.

Faulkner, R. R. 1971. *Hollywood Studio Musicians*. Chicago: Aldine.

Feigenbaum, E. A., and P. M. McCorduck. 1983. *The Fifth Generation*. Reading, MA: Addison Wesley.

Ference, T. P., F. H. Goldner, and R. R. Ritti. 1971. "Priests and Church." *American Behavioral Scientist* 14:507–24.

Ferguson, C. W. 1937. *Fifty Million Brothers*. New York: Farrar and Rinehart.

Fidell, L. S., and J. DeLamater. 1971. *Women in the Professions*. Beverly Hills, CA: Sage.

Fielding, A., and D. Portwood. 1980. "Professions and the State." *Sociological Review* 28:23–53.

Fine, R. 1979. *A History of Psychoanalysis*. New York: Columbia University Press.

Fisher, J. 1980. *The Response of Social Work to the Depression*. Cambridge, MA: Schenckman.

Flagle, C. D., W. H. Huggins, and R. H. Roy, eds. 1969. *Operations Research and Systems Engineering*. Baltimore: Johns Hopkins University Press.

Flett, J., and T. Flett. 1979. *Traditional Step Dancing in Lakeland*. London: English Folk Dance and Song Society.

Fleury, D. 1974. "Profession et formation des éducateurs specialisés (justice)." Pp. 278–90 in Crapuchet 1974.

Ford, A. S. 1975. *The Physician's Assistant*. New York: Praeger.

Fox, R., and G. Weisz, eds. 1980. *The Organization of Science and Technology in France 1808–1914*. Cambridge: Cambridge University Press.

Fox, R. C. 1977. "The Medicalization and Demedicalization of American Society." *Daedalus* 106:9–19.

Fox, R. C. and J. P. Swazey. 1974. *The Courage to Fail*. Chicago: University of Chicago Press.

Franklin, A. 1980. *La vie privée d'autrefois: les médecins*. Geneva: Editions Slatkine.

Freedeman, C. E. 1979. *Joint-Stock Enterprise in France*. Chapel Hill, NC: University of North Carolina Press.

Freeman, H. A. 1967. *Counseling in the United States*. Dobbs Ferry: Oceana.

Freeze, G. L. 1983. *The Parish Clergy in Nineteenth Century Russia*. Princeton: Princeton University Press.

Freidson, E. 1970a. *Profession of Medicine*. New York: Dodd Mead.

———. 1970b. *Professional Dominance*. Chicago: Aldine.

———. 1975. *Doctoring Together*. Chicago: University of Chicago Press.

———. 1983. "The Theory of Professions." Pp. 19–37 in Dingwall and Lewis 1983.

———. 1984. "The Changing Nature of Professional Control." *Annual Review of Sociology* 10:1–20.

———. 1986a. *Professional Powers*. Chicago: University of Chicago Press.

———. 1986b. "Les professions artistiques comme défi à l'analyse sociologique." *Revue française de sociologie* 27:431–43.

Freidson, E., and J. Lorber, eds. 1972. *Medical Men and Their Work*. Chicago: Aldine.

Frieden, N. M. 1981. *Russian Physicians in an Era of Reform and Revolution*. Princeton: Princeton University Press.

Friedman, L. M. 1973. *A History of American Law*. New York: Simon and Schuster.

Fuller, J. F. C. 1961. *The Conduct of War*. London: Eyre and Spottiswoode.

Fullinwider, S. P. 1974. "Neurasthenia: The Genteel Caste's Journey Inward." *Rocky Mountain Social Science Journal* 11:1–9.

Fulton, R. L. 1961. "The Clergyman and the Funeral Director." *Social Forces* 39:317–23.

Furter, W. F., ed. 1982. *A Century of Chemical Engineering*. New York: Plenum.

Galambos, L. 1970. "The Emerging Organizational Synthesis in Modern American History." *Business History Review* 44:279–90.

Gallie, W. B. 1968. *Philosophy and the Historical Understanding*. New York: Schocken.

Garceau, O. 1949. *The Public Library in the Political Process*. New York: Columbia University Press.

———. 1961. *The Political Life of the AMA*. Hamden, CN: Archon.

Garner, S. P. 1954. *The Evolution of Cost Accounting to 1925*. Tuscaloosa: University of Alabama Press.

Garrier, J. G. 1983. "Masking the Social in Educational Knowledge." *American Journal of Sociology* 88:948–74.

Garrison, D. 1979. *Apostles of Culture*. New York: Free Press.

Garrison, L. K. 1935. "A Survey of the Wisconsin Bar." *Wisconsin Law Review* 10:131–69.

Geiger, T. 1950. "An Historical Study of the Origins and Structure of the Danish Intelligentsia." *British Journal of Sociology* 1:209–20.

Geison, G. 1980. "Science and Efficacy in the History of Professions." Paper presented to the Davis Center for Historical Studies 9 May 1980.

Geison, G., ed. 1983. *Professions and Professional Ideologies in America*. Chapel Hill: University of North Carolina Press.

————. 1984. *Professions and the French State*. Philadelphia: University of Pennsylvania Press.

Gelfand, A. E. 1971. "Rapid Seriation Methods." Pp. 186–201 in Hodson, Kendall, and Tăutu 1971.

Gelfand, T. 1978. "Medical Professionals and Charlatans." *Histoire sociale* 11:62–97.

————. 1980. *Professionalizing Modern Medicine*. Westport, CN: Greenwood.

Gerstl, J., and G. Jacobs, eds. 1976. *Professions for the People*. Cambridge, MA: Schenkman.

Gerstl, J. E., and S. P. Hutton. 1966. *Engineers: The Anatomy of a Profession*. London: Tavistock.

Gerver, I., and J. Bensman. 1954. "Towards a Sociology of Expertness." *Social Forces* 32:226–35.

Gevitz, N. 1982. *The D.O.'s*. Baltimore: Johns Hopkins University Press.

Gieryn, T. F. 1983. "Boundary Work and the Demarcation of Science from Non-science." *American Sociological Review* 48:781–95.

Gifford, S. 1978. "Medical Psychotherapy and the Emmanuel Movement." Pp. 106–118 in G.E. Gifford ed, *Psychoanalysis, Psychotherapy, and the New England Medical Scene*. New York: Science History Publications.

Gilb, C. 1966. *Hidden Hierarchies*. New York: Harpers.

Gilgen, A. R. 1982. *American Psychology since World War II*. Westport, CN: Greenwood.

Gitlin, T. 1977. "The Televised Professional." *Social Policy* 8:94–99.

Gladden, W. 1898. *The Christian Pastor and the Working Church*. New York: Scribners.

Glaser, B. G. 1964. *Organizational Scientists*. Indianapolis: Bobbs Merrill.

Goldberg, A. I., and Y. A. Shenhav. 1984. "Research and Development Career Paths." *IEEE Transactions on Engineering Management* EM-31: August: 111–17.

Goldner, F. H., and R. R. Ritti. 1967. "Professionalism as Career Immobility." *American Journal of Sociology* 72:489–503.

Goldstein, B. 1955. "Some Aspects of the Future of Unionism Among Salaried Professionals in Industry." *American Sociological Review* 20:199–205.

————. 1959. "The Perspective of Unionized Professionals." *Social Forces* 37:323–27.

Goode, W. J. 1957. "Community within a Community." *American Sociological Review* 22:194–200.

————. 1960. "Encroachment, Charlatanism, and the Emerging Profession." *American Sociological Review* 25:902–14.

————. 1961. "The Librarian: From Occupation to Profession?" *Library Quarterly* 31:306–18.

Gordon, R. W. 1980. "Approaches to the Study of Legal Thought and Legal Practice in Late Nineteenth-Century America." Paper presented to the Davis Center for Historical Studies, 8 February 1980.

————. 1983. "Legal Thought and Legal Practice in the Age of Enterprise." Pp. 70–110 in Geison 1983.

Gosling, F. 1976. *American Nervousness*. Ph.D. diss., University of Oklahoma.

Gould, S. J. 1981. *The Mismeasure of Man*. New York: Norton.

Gouldner, A. W. 1981. *The Future of Intellectuals and the Rise of the New Class*. New York: Oxford University Press.

Graf, M. 1971. *Composer and Critic*. New York: Norton.

Grafton, A. 1979. "How Classics Became a Profession." Paper presented to the Davis Center for Historical Studies, 13 April 1979.

Graham, W. J. 1931. "Accounting in the Law School Curriculum." *American Law School Review* 7:215–17.

Greeley, H. D. 1927. "Professional Cooperation between Accountants and Attorneys." *National Association of Cost Accountants Bulletin* 8:18:838–51.

Greenbaum, J. M. 1979. *In the Name of Efficiency*. Philadelphia: Temple University Press.

Grimm, J. W. 1978. "Women in Female-Dominated Professions." Pp. 293–315 in Stromberg and Harkess, eds., *Women Working*. Palo Alto: Mayfield.

Griswold, E. W. 1955. "A Further Look at Lawyers and Accountants." *Journal of Accountancy* 100:6:29–35.

Grob, G. N. 1973. *Mental Institutions in America*. New York: Free Press.

————. 1983. *Mental Illness and American Society, 1875–1940*. Princeton: Princeton Unviersity Press.

Gross, R., and P. Osterman, eds. 1972. *The New Professionals*. New York: Simon and Schuster.

Gullett, D. W. 1971. *A History of Dentistry in Canada*. Toronto: University of Toronto Press.

Gusfield, J. 1963. *Symbolic Crusade*. Urbana: University of Illinois Press.

————. 1981. *The Culture of Public Problems*. Chicago: University of Chicago Press.

Gutman, R. 1981. "Architecture as a Service Industry." *Casabella* 474–5: 28–32. (trans).

————. 1983. "Architects in the Home Building Industry." Pp. 204–23 in Blau, LaGory, and Pipkin 1983.

Guy, M. E. 1985. *Professionals in Organizations*. New York: Praeger.

Habenstein, R. W. 1962. "Sociology of Occupations: The Case of the American Funeral Director." Pp. 225–46 in A. M. Rose., ed., *Human Behavior and the Social Process*. Boston: Houghton Mifflin.

————. 1963. "Critique of 'Profession' as a Sociological Category." *Sociological Quarterly* 4:291–308.

Haber, S. 1964. *Efficiency and Uplift*. Chicago: University of Chicago Press.

Hale, N. 1971. *Freud and the Americans*. New York: Oxford University Press.

Hall, O. 1946. "The Informal Organization of the Medical Profession." *Canadian Journal of Economic and Political Science* 12:30–44.

————. 1949. "Types of Medical Careers." *American Journal of Sociology* 55:243–53.

Hall, R. H. 1967. "Some Organizational Considerations in Professional-Organization Conflict." *Administrative Science Quarterly* 12:461–78.

———. 1968. "Professionalization and Bureaucratization." *American Sociological Review* 33:92–104.

Haller, J. S. 1981. *American Medicine in Transition, 1840–1910.* Urbana: University of Illinois Press.

Haller, J. S., and R. M. Haller. 1977. *The Physician and Sexuality in Victorian America.* New York: Norton.

Halliday, T. 1985. "Knowledge Mandates." *British Journal of Sociology* 36: 421–47.

Halmos, P. 1970. *The Faith of the Counsellors.* New York: Schocken.

Halmos, P., ed., 1973. *Professionalization and Social Change.* Keele, England: University of Keele. Sociological Review Monograph No. 20.

Halpern, S. A. 1982. *Segmental Professionalization Within Medicine: The Case of Pediatrics.* Ph.D. diss., University of California.

Hamilton, G. V. 1925. *An Introduction to General Psychopathology.* Saint Louis: Mosby.

Hamilton, G. W. 1918. "A Plea for the Cost Accountant." *Industrial Management* 55:446.

Handler, J. F. 1967. *The Lawyer and His Community.* Madison: University of Wisconsin Press.

———. 1973. *The Coercive Social Worker.* Chicago: Rand McNally.

Harmon, M. 1975. *Stretching Man's Mind.* New York: Mason-Charter.

Harries-Jenkins, G. 1970. "Professionals in Organizations." Pp. 51–107 in Jackson, 1970.

———. 1977. *The Army in Victorian Society.* London: Routledge.

Harrigan, P. J. 1975. "Secondary Education and the Professions in France." *Comparative Studies in Society and History* 17:349–71.

Harris, B. 1981. *Beyond Her Sphere: Women and the Professions in American History.* Westport, CN: Greenwood.

Harshbarger, B. 1976. "History of the Early Developments of Modern Statistics in America (1920–1944)." Pp. 133–45 in D. B. Owen, ed., *On the History of Statistics and Probability.* New York: Marcel Dekker.

Hartman, M., and L. W. Banner, eds. 1974. *Clio's Consciousness Raised.* New York: Harper.

Hartwell, R. M. 1971a. "Financial Expertise, Examinations, and the Formulation of Economic Policy in Northern Sung." *Journal of Asian Studies* 30:281–314.

———. 1971b. "Historical Analogism, Public Policy, and Social Science in 11th and 12th Century China." *American Historical Review* 76:692–727.

Haskell, T. L. 1977. *The Emergence of Professional Social Science.* Urbana: University of Illinois Press.

Haskell, T. L., ed. 1984. *The Authority of Experts.* Bloomington: Indiana University Press.

Haug, M. R. 1973. "Deprofessionalization." Pp. 195–212 in Halmos 1973.

————. 1976. "The Erosion of Professional Authority." *Health and Society, the Milbank Memorial Fund Quarterly* 54:8–104.

Haug, M. R., and M. B. Sussman. 1969. "Professional Autonomy and the Revolt of the Client." *Social Problems* 17:153–61.

————. 1971. "Professionalization and Unionization." *American Behavioral Scientist* 17:525–41.

Hays, S. P. 1975. *Conservation and the Gospel of Efficiency.* New York: Atheneum.

Head, W. W. 1924. "The Relationship Between Banker and Accountant." *Journal of Accountancy* 38:1–6.

Heimer, C. A. 1984. "Organizational and Individual Control of Career Development in Engineering Project Work." *Acta Sociologica* 27:283–310.

Hein, L. W. 1962. *The Impact of the British Companies Acts Upon the Major Areas of the Practice of Accountancy in Britain.* Ph.D. diss., UCLA.

Heinz, J. P., and E. O. Laumann. 1982. *Chicago Lawyers.* New York: Russell Sage. Chicago: ABF.

Heisen, T. M. 1976. "Early Catalogue Code Development in the United States, 1876–1908." *Journal of Library History* 11:218–48.

Henderson, K. L. 1976. "Descriptive Cataloging in the United States, 1876–1975." Pp. 227–71 in Winger 1976.

Henry, W. E., J. H. Sim, and S. L. Spray. 1971. *The Fifth Profession.* Ann Arbor: Books on Demand.

————. 1973. *The Public and Private Lives of Psychotherapists.* San Francisco: Jossey Bass.

Herskowitz, H. 1927. "The Accountant as a Forecaster of Business." *American Accountant* 12:6:52–53.

Herzlich, C. H. 1982. "The Evolution of Relations between French Physicians and the State 1880–1980." *Sociology of Health and Illness* 4:241–53.

Herzog, P. E. 1967. *Civil Procedure in France.* The Hague: Martinus Nijhoff.

Hickson, P. J., and M. W. Thomas. 1969. "Professionalization in Britain." *Sociology* 3:37–54.

Hilsum, S., and K. B. Start. 1974. *Promotion and Careers in Teaching.* Slough, Berkshire: NFER publishing.

Hirshleifer, J. 1985. "The Expanding Domain of Economics." *American Economic Review* 75:53–68.

Hobson, W. K. 1984. "The Emergence of the Large Law Firm, 1875–1930." Pp. 3–27 in G. W. Gewalt, ed., *The New High Priests.* Westport, CN: Greenwood.

Hodson, F. R., D. G. Kendall, and P. Tăutu, eds. 1971. *Mathematics in the Archeological and Historical Sciences.* Edinburgh: University of Edinburgh Press.

Hoffman, E. B. 1976. *Unionization of Professional Societies.* New York: The Conference Board.

Holden, C. 1984. "Will Home Computers Transform Schools?" *Science* 225:296–97.

## 404    References

————. 1987. "Is Alcoholism Treatment Effective?" *Science* 236:20–22.

Holley, E. G. 1976. "Librarians, 1876–1976." Pp. 177–207 in Winger 1976.

Holmes, G. 1982. *Augustan England: Professions, State and Society 1680–1730*. London: Allen and Unwin.

Holmes, R. 1976. *Epic Land Battles*. Secaucus, NJ: Chartwell.

Honigsbaum, F. 1979. *The Division in British Medicine*. New York: St. Martin's.

Hoover, T. J., and J. C. L. Fish. 1947. *The Engineering Profession*. Stanford: Stanford University Press.

Hopkins, G. E. 1971. *The Airline Pilots*. Cambridge: Harvard University Press.

Hufbauer, K. 1982. *The Formation of the German Chemical Community 1720–1795*. Berkeley: University of California Press.

Hughes, E. C. 1958. *Men and Their Work*. New York: Free Press.

————. 1963. "Professions." *Daedalus* 92:655–68.

Hughes, E. C., B. Thorne, A. M. DeBaggio, A. Gurin, and D. Williams. 1973. *Education for the Professions of Medicine, Law, Theology, and Social Welfare*. New York: McGraw Hill.

Hull, D. L. 1975. "Central Subjects and Historical Narratives." *History and Theory* 14:253–74.

Hunter, B., C. S. Kastner, M. L. Rubin, and R. J. Seidel. 1975. *Learning Alternatives in U.S. Education*. Englewood Cliffs, NJ: Education/Technology Publications.

Huntington, S. P. 1957. *The Soldier and the State*. New York: Vintage.

Israel, J. 1972. *Building the Organizational Society*. New York: Free Press.

Jackson, G. P. 1965. *White Spirituals in the Southern Uplands*. New York: Dover.

Jackson, J. A., ed. 1970. *Professions and Professionalization*. Cambridge: Cambridge University Press.

Jamous, H., and B. Peloille. 1970. "Changes in the French University Hospital System." Pp. 111–52 in Jackson 1970.

Jann, R. 1985. *The Art and Science of Victorian History*. Columbus: Ohio State University Press.

Janowitz, M. 1971. *The Professional Soldier*. New York: Free Press.

Jarausch, K. H. 1982. *Students, Society, and Politics in Imperial Germany*. Princeton : Princeton University Press.

Jarausch, K. H., ed. 1983. *The Transformation of Higher Learning, 1860–1930*. Chicago: University of Chicago Press.

Jarvis, P. 1976. "A Profession in Process." *Sociological Review* 24:351–64.

Jellinek, M. 1980. "Towards Systematic Management." *Business History Review* 54:63–79.

Johnson, H. T. 1972. "Lyman Mills: Early Cost Accounting for Internal Management Control in the 1850s." *Business History Review* 46:466–74.

Johnson, T. J. 1967. *Professions and Power*. London: MacMillan.

————. 1977. "The Professions in the Class Structure." Pp. 93–110 in Scase 1977.

Johnstone, Q., and D. Hopson. 1967. *Lawyers and Their Work*. Indianapolis: Bobbs-Merrill.

Jones, E. 1981. *Accountancy and the British Economy 1840–1980*. London: Batsford.

Jones, K. 1985. "Straightening the Twig." Paper presented to the Organization of American Historians, April 1985.

Kadushin, C. 1962. "Social Distance Between Client and Professional." *American Journal of Sociology* 67:517–31.

———. 1966. "The Friends and Supporters of Psychotherapy." *American Sociological Review* 31:781–802.

———. 1969. "The Professional Self-concept of Music Students." *American Journal of Sociology* 75:389–404.

Katz, M. B. 1968. *The Irony of Early School Reform*. Boston: Beacon.

———. 1971. *Class, Bureaucracy, and the Schools*. New York: Praeger.

Kaufman, M. 1971. *Homeopathy*. Baltimore: Johns Hopkins University Press.

———. 1976. *American Medical Education*. Westport, CN: Greenwood.

Kelsall, R. K. 1955. *The Higher Civil Servants in Britain*. London: Routledge.

Kemp, C. F. 1947. *Physicians of the Soul*. New York: Macmillan.

Kett, J. 1968. *The Formation of the American Medical Profession (1780–1860)*. New Haven: Yale University Press.

Kevles, D. J. 1979. *The Physicists*. New York: Vintage.

Kinley, D. 1906. "The Field of Accountancy." *Journal of Accountancy* 2: 187–93.

Klegon, D. 1978. "The Sociology of Professions." *Sociology of Work and Occupations* 5:259–83.

Klein, D., and P. Butkovich. 1976. "Can the Professions of Operations Research/Management Science Change and Survive?" *Interfaces* 6:47–51.

Kleinman, S. 1984. *Equals before God: Seminarians as Humanistic Professionals*. Chicago: University of Chicago Press.

Knapp, P. B. 1955. *The College Librarian: Sociology of a Professional Specialty*. College and Research Libraries 16:66–72.

Kobrin, F. E. 1966. "The American Midwife Controversy." *Bulletin of the History of Medicine* 40:350–63.

Koenig, W. 1975. *Epic Sea Battles*. Secaucus, NJ: Chartwell.

Kohler, R. E. 1982. *From Medical Chemistry to Biochemistry*. New York: Cambridge University Press.

———. 1985. "History of Professions and Historians of Science." Paper presented to the Organization of American Historians, April 1985.

Kolata, G. 1980. "NMC Thrives Selling Dialysis." *Science* 208:379–82.

———. 1987. "Manic Depression." *Science* 232:576–77.

Konrad, G., and I. Szelenyi. 1972. *The Intellectuals on the Road to Class Power*. New York: Harcourt Brace.

Kornhauser, W. 1982. *Scientists in Industry*. Westport, CN: Greenwood Press.

Kostof, S. K., ed. 1977. *The Architect: Chapters in the History of a Profession*. New York: Oxford University Press.

Kotschnig, W. M. 1937. *Unemployment in the Learned Professions*. London: Oxford University Press.

Kraft, P. 1977. *Programmers and Managers*. New York: Springer.

Kralewski, J., L. Pitt, and D. Shatin. 1985. "Structural Characteristics of Medical Group Practices." *Administrative Science Quarterly* 30:34–45.

Krause, E. A. 1977. *Power and Illness*. New York: Elsevier.

Kronus, C. 1976. "The Evolution of Occupational Power: Task Boundaries, Physicians and Pharmacists." *Journal of Work and Occupations* 3:3–37.

Kubota, A. 1969. *Higher Civil Servants in Postwar Japan*. Princeton: Princeton University Press.

Kuhn, T. S. 1970. *The Structure of Scientific Revolutions*. Chicago: University of Chicago Press.

Kunstler, D. A. 1963. "AMA Membership in 1963." *Journal of Marketing* 27:4:51–54.

Ladinsky, J. 1963. "Careers of Lawyers, Law Practice, and Judicial Institutions." *American Sociological Review* 28:47–54.

———. 1976. "The Traffic in Legal Services." *Law and Society Review* 11:207–24.

Lafferty, M. 1975. *Accounting in Europe*. Cambridge, England: Woodhead and Faulkner.

Lakatos, I., and A. Musgrave, eds. 1970. *Criticism and the Growth of Knowledge*. Cambridge: Cambridge University Press.

Lalumière, P. 1959. *L'inspection des finances*. Paris: Presses Universitaires de France.

Lampert, N. 1979. *The Technical Intelligentsia and the Soviet State*. New York: Holmes and Meier.

Landes, D. S. 1969. *The Unbound Prometheus*. Cambridge: Cambridge University Press.

Lane, R. 1971. *Policing the City*. New York: Atheneum.

Laquer, T. N. 1976. *Religion and Respectability*. New Haven: Yale University Press.

Larkin, G. V. 1978. "Medical Dominance and Control: Radiographers in the Division of Labour." *The Sociological Review* n.s.26:843–58.

Larson, M. S. 1977. *The Rise of Professionalism*. Berkeley: University of California Press.

———. 1980. "Proletarianization and Educated Labor." *Theory and Society* 9:131–75.

Latour, B., and S. Woolgar. 1979. *Laboratory Life*. Beverly Hills, CA: Sage.

LaVopa, A. 1979. "Status and Ideology: Rural Schoolteachers in Pre-March and Revolutionary Prussia." *Journal of Social History* 12:430–56.

———. 1980. "The Language of Profession." Paper presented to the Davis Center for Historical Study, 1980.

Layton, E. T. 1971. *Revolt of the Engineers*. Baltimore: Johns Hopkins University Press.

Lazarus, A. A. 1971. "Where Do Behavior Therapists Take Their Troubles?" *Psychological Reports* 28:349–50.

Lazarus, I. 1937. "The Economic Crisis of the Legal Profession." *National Lawyers' Guild Quarterly* 1:17–24.

Lears, J. 1981. *No Place of Grace.* New York: Pantheon.

Leat, D. 1973. "Putting God Over." *Sociological Review* 21:561–72.

Lee, A. J. 1976. *The Origins of the Popular Press in England.* London: Croon Helm.

Lee, G. A. 1975. "The Concept of Profit in British Accounting 1760–1900." *Business History Review* 49:6–36.

Leesley, M. E. 1978. "The Uneven Acceptance of CAD." *CAD* 10:227–30.

Léonard, J. 1981. *La médecine entre les savoirs et les pouvoirs.* Paris: Aubier Montaigne.

Lerman, P. 1982. *Deinstitutionalization and the Welfare State.* New Brunswick, NJ: Rutgers University Press.

Lesse, S. 1968. *An Evaluation of the Results of the Psychotherapies.* Springfield, IL: Thomas.

Levack, B. P. 1973. *The Civil Lawyers in England.* Oxford: Oxford University Press.

Levine, D. N. 1971. "Facing our Calling: Sociology and the Agon of Liberal Education." Paper presented at the American Sociological Association, Denver, 1971.

Lewis, E. R. 1894. "The Evolution of Railway Surgery." *Railway Surgeon* 1:227.

Lewis, J. R. 1982. *The Victorian Bar.* London: Robert Hale.

Lewis, M. 1960. *Social History of the Navy 1793–1815.* London: Allen and Unwin.

———. 1965. *The Navy in Transition, 1814–1864.* London: Hodder and Stoughton.

Lewis, S. 1920. *Main Street.* New York: Harcourt Brace.

———. 1922. *Babbitt.* New York: Harcourt Brace.

Licht, W. 1983. *Working for the Railroad.* Princeton: Princeton University Press.

Light, D. N., S. Liebfried, and F. Tennstedt. 1986. "Social Medicine versus Professional Dominance." *American Journal of Public Health* 76:78–83.

Litoff, J. B. 1978. *American Midwives.* Westport, CN: Greenwood.

Lochner, P. R. 1975. "The No Fee and Low Fee Legal Practice of Private Attorneys." *Law and Society Review* 9:431–73.

Lockley, L. C. 1974. "History and Development of Marketing Research." Pp. 1:3–1:15 in R. Ferber, ed., *Handbook of Marketing Research.* New York: McGraw Hill.

Loney, J. 1980. "Hyperkinesia Comes of Age." *American Journal of Orthopsychiatry* 50:28–42.

Lorber, J., and R. Satow. 1977. "Creating a Company of Unequals: Sources of Occupational Stratification in a Ghetto Community Mental Health Center." *Sociology of Work and Occupations* 4:281–302.

Lortie, D. C. 1958. "Anesthesia: From Nurses' Work to Medical Specialty."

Pp. 405–41 in E. G. Jaco, ed., *Patients, Physicians, and Illness*. Glencoe, IL: Free Press.

———. 1959. "Laymen to Lawmen." *Harvard Educational Review* 29: 352–69.

———. 1975. *Schoolteacher*. Chicago: University of Chicago Press.

Loseke, D. R., and S. E. Cahill. 1984. "The Social Construction of Deviance: Experts on Battered Women." *Social Problems* 31:290–310.

Lowell, A. L. 1923. "The Profession of Business." *Harvard Business Review* 1:129–31.

Lubell, M. S. 1980. *The Significance of Organizational Conflict on the Legislation Evolution of the Accounting Profession*. New York: Arno.

Lubove, R. 1969. *The Professional Altruist*. New York: Atheneum.

Ludmerer, K. M. 1983. "The Plight of Clinical Teaching in America." *Bulletin of the History of Medicine* 57:218–29.

———. 1985. *Learning to Heal: The Development of American Medical Education*. New York: Basic.

Maack, M. W. 1983. "Women Librarians in France." *Journal of Library History* 18:407–49.

MacKenzie, D. A. 1981. *Statistics in Britain 1865–1930*. Edinburgh: Edinburgh University Press.

Markuson, B. E. 1976. "Bibliographic Systems, 1945–1976." Pp. 311–28 in Winger 1976.

Marshall, T. J. [1939] 1965. "The Recent History of Professionalism in Relation to Social Structure and Social Policy." Pp. 158–79 in *Class, Citizenship, and Social Development*. Garden City, NY: Anchor.

Martin, M. L. 1981. *Warriors to Managers*. Chapel Hill: University of North Carolina Press.

Masters, J. E. 1915. "The Accounting Profession in the United States." *Journal of Accountancy* 20:349–55.

Mathias, P. 1969. *The First Industrial Nation*. New York: Scribners.

Maulitz, R. C. 1979. "Physician vs. Bacteriologist." Pp. 91–107 in Vogel and Rosenberg 1979.

Maurice, M. 1972. "Propos sur la sociologie des professions." *Sociologie du travail* 13:213–25.

Mazerol, M. T. 1985. "Justice des mineurs, justice mineure." *Annales de Vaucresson* No. 23:175–90.

M'Candlish, J. M. 1889. "Accountants and Actuaries." *The Accountant* 15: 518–20, 528–30.

McArthur, B. 1984. *Actors and American Culture 1880–1920*. Philadelphia: Temple University Press.

McClelland, C. 1980. *State, Society, and University in Germany, 1700–1914*. Cambridge: Cambridge University Press.

———. 1983. "Professionalization and Higher Education in Germany." Pp. 306–20 in Jarausch 1983.

McCormack, T. H. 1956. "The Druggists' Dilemma." *American Journal of Sociology* 61:308–15.

McCosh, A. M., M. Rahman, and M. J. Earl. 1981. *Developing Managerial Information Systems*. New York: Wiley.

McCullagh, C. B. 1978. "Colligation and Classification in History." *History and Theory* 17:267–84.

McKean, D. D. 1963. *The Integrated Bar*. Boston: Houghton Mifflin.

McKeown, T. 1979. *The Role of Medicine*. Princeton: Princeton University Press.

McKinlay, J. B. 1976. "Who is Really Ignorant—Physician or Patient?" *Journal of Health and Social Behavior* 16:3–11.

McLaren, N. L. 1937. "The Influence of Federal Taxation Upon Accountancy." *Journal of Accountancy* 64:426–39.

McMahon, M. 1984. *The Making of a Profession*. New York: IEEE.

McMullen, H. 1976. "The Distribution of Libraries Throughout the United States." Pp. 23–53 in Winger 1976.

Meisner, H. H. 1927. "Is Joint Practice of Accounting and Law Advantageous?" *American Accountant* 12:2:12–15.

Melder, K. 1972. "Women's High Calling." *American Studies* 13:2:19–33.

Melosh, B. 1982. *The Physician's Hand*. Philadelphia: Temple University Press.

Merwick, D. 1973. *Boston Priests, 1848–1910*. Cambridge: Harvard University Press.

Meyer, D. 1965. *The Positive Thinkers*. Garden City, NY: Doubleday.

Meyers, P. V. 1976. "Professions and Social Change: Rural Schoolteachers in Nineteenth Century France." *Journal of Social History* 9:542–58.

Miles, M. 1982. "Eminent Practitioners: The New Visage of Country Attorneys, 1750–1899." Pp. 470–503 in G. R. Rubin and D. Sugarman, eds., *Law, Economy, and Society*. Abingdon, Oxon: Professional Books.

Miller, G. A. 1968. "Professionals in Bureaucracy." *American Sociological Review* 32:755–68.

Miller, J., J. R. Lincoln, and J. Olson. 1981. "Rationality and Equity in Professional Networks." *American Journal of Sociology* 87:308–35.

Miller, K. S. 1980. *The Criminal Justice and Mental Health Systems*. Cambridge, MA: Oelgeschlager, Gunn, and Hain.

Millerson, G. 1964. *The Qualifying Associations*. London: Routledge.

Miser, H. J. 1978. "The History, Nature, and Use of Operations Research." Pp. 3–24 in J. J. Moder and S. E. Elmaghraby, eds., *Handbook of Operations Research*. New York: Van Nostrand.

Monjardet, D. 1972. "Carrières des dirigeants et contrôle de l'enterprise." *Sociologie du travail* 13:131–44.

Monopolies Commission (Great Britain). 1970. *Professional Services* (Report in two volumes). HMSO 4463–1, 1970.

Montagna, P. 1968. "Professionalization and Bureaucratization in Large Professional Organizations." *American Journal of Sociology* 74:138–45.

———. 1974. *Certified Public Accountancy*. Houston: Scholars Book Co.

———. 1975. "The Public Accounting Profession." *American Behavioral Scientist* 14:475–91.

Moore, B. 1984. "Historical Notes on the Doctor's Work Ethic." *Journal of Social History* 17:547–72.

Moore, R. L. 1975. "The Spiritualist Medium." *American Quarterly* 27: 200–21.

Morantz, R. 1974. "The Lady and Her Physician." Pp. 38–53 in Hartman and Banner 1974.

Morantz-Sanchez, R. M. 1985. *Sympathy and Science.* New York: Oxford University Press.

Moreau, R. 1984. *The Computer Comes of Age.* Cambridge: MIT Press.

Morris, S. 1973. "Stalled Professionalism." *British Historical Review* 47: 317–34.

Morrison, C. 1972. "Kinship in Professional Relations." *Comparative Studies in Society and History* 14:100–35.

Morse, P. M. 1977. "ORSA Twenty-Five Years Later." *Operations Research* 25:186–88.

Murphee, M. C. 1984. "Brave New Office: The Changing World of the Legal Secretary." Pp. 140–59 in K. B. Sachs and D. Remy, eds., *My Troubles are Going to Have Trouble With Me.* New Brunswick, NJ: Rutgers University Press.

Murphey, J. H., and K. A. Coney. 1976. "Accreditation of Marketing Researchers?" Pp. 260–65 in K. L. Bernhardt, ed., American Marketing Association *Educator's Proceedings* No. 39 (1976).

Murphey, M. 1981. *From Artisan to Semi-professional.* Ph.D. diss., University of California at Davis.

Murphy, T. 1877. *Pastoral Theology.* Philadelphia: Presbyterian Board of Publication.

Naegle, K. D. 1956. "Clergy, Teachers and Psychiatrists." *Canadian Journal of Economic and Political Science* 22:46–62.

Napoli, D. S. 1981. *Architects of Adjustment.* Port Washington, NY: Kennikat.

Navarro, V. 1978. *Class Struggle, the State, and Medicine.* New York: Prodist.

Nelkin, D. 1982. "Intellectual Property." *Science* 216:704–08.

Nelson, D. 1974. "Scientific Management, Systematic Management, and Labor, 1880–1915." *Business History Review* 48:479–500.

Nérot, S. 1974. "Les professions du travail social." Pp. 255–63 in Crapuchet 1974.

Newman, C. 1957. *The Evolution of Medical Education in the Nineteenth Century.* Oxford: Oxford University Press.

Nichols, W. C. 1973. "The Field of Marriage Counseling." *Family Coordinator* 22:3–13.

Nizard, L. 1972. "La planification." *Sociologie du travail* 14:369–87.

Nolan, R. L. 1979. "Managing the Crisis in Data Processing." *Harvard Business Review* 57:2:115–26.

North, S. N. D. [1918] 1970. "Seventy-five Years of Progress in Statistics." Pp. 15–49 in J. Koren, ed., *The History of Statistics.* New York: Burt Franklin.

Oberndorf, C. P. 1964. *A History of Psychoanalysis in America.* New York: Harper.

O'Boyle, L. 1970. "The Problem of an Excess of Eduated Men in Western Europe, 1800–1850." *Journal of Modern History* 42:471–95.

O'Gorman, H. 1963. *Lawyers and Matrimonial Cases*. New York: Free Press.

Oldham, K. M. 1981. *Accounting Systems and Practice in Europe*. Aldershot, Hants.: Gower.

Olesko, K. 1980. *The Emergence of Theoretical Physics*. Ph.D. diss., Cornell University.

———. 1982. "'Physiker' von Beruf." Paper for Conference on *Wissenschaft als Beruf*, Princeton, 3 April 1982.

Oleson, A., and J. Voss, eds. 1979. *The Organization of Knowledge in Modern America, 1860–1920*. Baltimore: Johns Hopkins University Press.

Olson, W. E. 1982. *The Accounting Profession*. New York: AICPA.

Oppenheimer, M. 1973. "The Proletarianization of the Professional." Pp. 213–28 in Halmos 1973.

Osler, W. [1889] 1963. *Aequanimitas and Other Papers*. New York: Norton.

Otterbourg, E. M. 1951. "A Study of the Unauthorized Practice of Law." *Unauthorized Practice News*, special issue, September 1951.

Owen, D. B. 1976. *On the History of Statistics and Probability*. New York: Marcell Dekker.

Owings, N. A. 1973. *The Spaces in Between*. New York: Houghton Mifflin.

Paige, J. M. 1975. *Agrarian Revolutions*. New York: Free Press.

Palmer, M. B. 1983. *Des petits journaux aux grandes agences*. Paris: Aubier Montaigne.

Park, K. 1985. *Doctors and Medicine in Early Renaissance Florence*. Princeton: Princeton University Press.

Parry, N., and J. Parry. 1976. *The Rise of the Medical Profession*. London: Croon Helm.

Parsons, T. [1939] 1954. "The Professions and Social Structure." Pp. 34–49 in *Essays in Sociological Theory*. New York: Free Press.

———. 1964. *The Social System*. New York: Free Press.

———. 1968. "Professions." Vol.12, Pp.536–47 of *International Encyclopedia of the Social Sciences*. New York: Macmillan.

Pashigian, B. P. 1978. "Number and Earnings of Lawyers." *American Bar Foundation Research Journal* 1:5–82.

Patterson, M., and L. Engelberg. 1978. "Women in Male-Dominated Professions." Pp. 266–92 in Stromberg and Harkess, eds., *Women Working*. Palo Alto: Mayfield.

Pauly, P. 1984. "The Appearance of Academic Biology in Late 19th Century America." *Journal of the History of Biology* 17:369–97.

——— 1987. "General Physiology and the Discipline of Physiology, 1890–1935." Pp. 195–207 in *Physiology in the American Context*. Bethesda, MD: American Physiological Society.

Payne, G. L. 1960. *Britain's Scientific and Technological Manpower*. Stanford: Stanford University Press.

Pégues, F. J. 1962. *The Lawyers of the Last Capetians*. Princeton: Princeton University Press.

412    References

Perkin, H. 1961. "Middle Class Education and Employment in the 19th Century." *Economic History Review* 14:122–30.
———. 1969. *Key Profession*. London: Kelley.
Pernick, M. 1985. *A Calculus of Suffering*. New York: Columbia University Press.
Perrolle, J. A. 1985. "Intellectual Assembly Lines: The Rationalization of Managerial, Professional, and Technical Work." Paper presented at the American Sociological Association, Washington, D.C., 1985.
Perrucci, R. 1973. "In the Service of Man: Radical Movements in the Professions." Pp. 179–94 in Halmos 1973.
Perrucci, R., and J. Gerstl. 1969. *Profession Without Community*. New York: Random House.
Peterson, M. J. 1978. *The Medical Profession in Mid-Victorian London*. Berkeley: University of California Press.
Pettigrew, A. 1973. "Occupational Specialization as an Emergent Process." *Sociological Review* 21:255–78.
Phillips, D. T., A. Ravindran, and J. J. Solberg. 1976. *Operations Research*. New York: Wiley.
Phillips, E. W. 1927. "The Actuary in Commerce and Industry." *The Accountant* 76:587–94.
Pincemin, J., and A. Laugier. 1959. "Les médecins." *Revue française de science politique* 9:881–900.
Platt, A. M. 1969. *The Child Savers*. Chicago: University of Chicago Press.
Ploscowe, M. 1935. "The Expert Witness in Criminal Cases in France, Germany, and Italy." *Law and Contemporary Problems* 2:504–09.
Plucknett, T. F. T. 1956. *A Concise History of the Common Law*. Boston: Little, Brown.
Podmore, D. 1980. *Solicitors And the Wider Community*. London: Heinemann.
Pope, L. 1942. *Millhands and Preachers*. New Haven: Yale University Press.
Portwood, D., and A. Fielding. 1981. "Privilege and the Professions." *Sociological Review* 29:749–73.
Powell, L. C. 1909. *The Emmanuel Movement in a Small Town*. New York: Putnam.
Powell, M. J. 1979. "Anatomy of a Counter-Bar Association." *American Bar Foundation Research Journal* 1979:501–41.
———. 1985. "Developments in the Regulation of Lawyers." *Social Forces* 64:281–305.
Poynter, F. N. L., ed. 1966. *The Evolution of Medical Education in Britain*. Baltimore: Williams and Wilkins.
Prandy, K. 1965. *Professional Employees*. London: Faber.
Prest, W., ed. 1981. *Lawyers in Early Modern Europe and America*. New York: Holmes and Meier.
Prevet, F. 1955. *La moralité professionelle des origines à nos jours*. Paris: Sirey.

Previts, G. J., and B. D. Merino. 1979. *A History of Accounting in America.* New York: Wiley.

Price, D. J. de Solla. 1963. *Little Science, Big Science.* New York: Columbia University Press.

Price, D. K. 1965. *The Scientific Estate.* London: Oxford University Press.

Prochaska, J., and J. Prochaska. 1978. "Twentieth Century Trends in Marriage and Marital Therapy." Pp. 1–24 in T. J. Paolino and B. S. McCrady, eds., *Marriage and Marital Therapy.* New York: Brunner Maazel.

Purvis, J. 1973. "Schoolteaching as a Professional Career." *British Journal of Sociology* 24:43–57.

Radnor, M., and R. D. Neal. 1973. "The Progress of Management-Science Activities in Large U.S. Industrial Corporations." *OR* 21:427–73.

Rado, L. 1987. "Cultural Elites and the Institutionalization of Ideas." *Sociological Forum* 2:42–66.

Raguin, C. 1972. "L'indépendance de l'avocat." *Sociologie du travail* 13:164–84.

Rameau, J.-P. [1722] 1971. *Treatise on Harmony (1722).* New York: Dover.

Ravetz, J. R. 1971. *Scientific Knowledge and its Social Problems.* New York: Oxford University Press.

Rayward, W. B. 1985. "Library and Information Science: An Historical Perspective." *Journal of Library History* 20:120–36.

Reader, W.J. 1966. *Professional Men.* New York: Basic.

Reagan, A. L. 1958. *A Study of Factors Influencing College Students to be Librarians.* ACRL Mongraph No. 21. Chicago: ALA.

Record, J. C. 1957. "The Marine Radioman's Struggle for Status." *American Journal of Sociology* 62:353–59.

Reed, L. S., E. S. Myers, and P. L. Scheidemandel. 1972. *Health Insurance and Psychiatric Care.* Washington: American Psychiatric Association.

Reid, D. M. 1974. "The Rise of Professions and Professional Organizations in Modern Egypt." *Comparative Studies in Society and History* 14:71–96.

Reinhard, S. 1986. "Is Nursing's Jurisdiction Eroding or Expanding?" Course Paper, Rutgers University, Department of Sociology.

Reisman, J. M. 1976. *A History of Clinical Psychology.* New York: Irvington.

Reiss, A. J. 1955. "Occupational Mobility of Professional Workers." *American Sociological Review* 20:693–700.

Reissman, L. 1956. "Life Careers, Power, and the Professions: The Retired Army General." *American Sociological Review* 21:215–21.

Rendel, M. 1970. *The Administrative Functions of the French Conseil d'Etat.* London: LSE/Weidenfeld and Nicolson.

Rettig, S., et al. 1958. "Status Overestimation: Objective Status and Job Satisfaction Among Professions." *American Sociological Review* 23:75–81.

Reynolds, D. 1985. *Library Automation.* New York: Bowker.

Richards, P. S. 1985. "Professional Transformations in Early 20th Century Europe." *Journal of Library History* 20:81–85.

Richmond, M. 1917. *Social Diagnosis.* New York: Russell Sage.

Riebemack, M. 1893. "Railway Statistics as Applicable to the Earnings of Passenger Trains." *Quarterly Publications of the American Statistical Association* 3:519–32.

Ripert, G. 1951. *Traité élémentaire de droit commerciale*. Paris: Librairie Générale de Droit et Jurisprudence.

Ritti, R. R. 1971. *The Engineer in the Industrial Corporation*. New York: Columbia University Press.

Ritti, R. R., T. P. Ference, and F. H. Goldner. 1974. "Professions and Their Plausibility." *Sociology of Work and Occupations* 1:25–51.

Robbins, B. 1987. "Disciplinary Aesthetics." Rutgers University, Mimeo.

Roberts, G. E. 1907. "The Public Accountant and the Banker." *Journal of Accountancy* 5:114–18.

Robinson, H. W. 1983. *A History of Accountants in Ireland*. Dublin: Institute of Chartered Accountants of Ireland.

Robson, R. 1959. *The Attorney in Eighteenth Century England*. Cambridge: Cambridge University Press.

Roche, J. 1987. "Institutionalizing Mediation." *Law and Society Review* 21: 243–66.

Rodgers, B. N., and J. Stevenson. 1973. *A New Portrait of Social Work*. London: Heinemann.

Rodgers, D. T. 1978. *The Work Ethic in Industrial America*. Chicago: University of Chicago Press.

Roeber, A. G. 1979. "Justices and Lawyers in Virginia." Paper presented to the Davis Center for Historical Studies, 27 April 1979.

Rogow, A. A. 1970. *The Psychiatrists*. New York: Delta.

Rorabaugh, W. J. 1979. *The Alcoholic Republic*. New York: Oxford University Press.

Rorem, C. R. 1928. "Social Control through Accounts." *Accounting Review* 3:261–68.

Roselli, J. 1984. *The Opera Industry in Italy from Cimarosa to Verdi*. Cambridge: Cambridge University Press.

Rosenberg, C. E. 1962. "The Place of George M. Beard in 19th Century Psychiatry." *Bulletin of the History of Medicine* 36:245–59.

Rosenkrantz, B. G. 1974. "Cart Before Horse: The Practice and Professional Image in American Public Health." *Journal of the History of Medicine and Allied Sciences* 29:55–74.

Ross, R. J. S. 1976. "The Impact of Social Movements on a Profession in Process." *Sociology of Work and Occupations* 3:429–54.

Rossiter, M. W. 1979. "The Organization of the Agricultural Sciences." Pp. 211–48 in Oleson and Voss 1979.

Roth, J. A. 1974. "Professionalism: The Sociologist's Decoy." *Sociology of Work and Occupations* 1:6–51.

Rothblatt, S. 1968. *The Revolution of the Dons*. New York: Basic.

Rothman, B. K. 1983. "Midwives in Transition." *Social Problems* 30:262–71.

Rothman, D. 1971. *The Discovery of the Asylum*. Boston: Little, Brown.

Rothstein, W. G. 1972. *American Physicians in the Nineteenth Century*. Baltimore: Johns Hopkins University Press.

Roughgarden, J. 1979. *Theory of Population Genetics and Evolutionary Ecology*. New York: Macmillan.

Routh, G. 1965. *Occupation and Pay in Great Britain, 1906–60*. Cambridge: Cambridge University Press.

Roy, R. H., and J. H. McNeill. 1967. *Horizons for a Profession*. New York: AICPA.

Royer, J.-P., R. Martinage, and P. Lecocq. 1982. *Juges et notables au XIXe siècle*. Paris: Presses Universitaires de France.

Rubin, M. R. 1986. *The Knowledge Industry in the United States, 1960–1980*. Princeton: Princeton University Press.

Rubinstein, E. A., and M. Lorr. 1954. *Survey of Clinical Practice in Psychology*. New York: International Universities Press.

Rueschemeyer, D. 1973. *Lawyers and Their Society*. Cambridge: Harvard University Press.

Russell, C. A. 1977. *Chemists by Profession*. Milton Keynes, England: Open University Press.

Ryan, M. 1983. *Womanhood in America*. New York: F. Watts.

Saks, M. 1983. "Removing the Blinders." *Sociological Review* 31:1–21.

Salton, G. 1975. *Dynamic Information and Library Processing*. Englewood Cliffs, NJ: Prentice-Hall.

Sass, S. A. 1982. *The Pragmatic Imagination*. Philadelphia: University of Pennsylvania Press.

Scase, R., ed. 1977. *Industrial Society: Class Cleavage and Control*. London: Allen and Unwin.

Schatzman, L., and R. Bucher. 1964. "Negotiating a Division of Labor Among Professionals in the State Mental Hospital." *Psychiatry* 27:266–77.

Schlesinger, A. 1946. *Learning How to Behave*. New York: Macmillan.

Schneller, E. S. 1976. "The Design and Evolution of the Physician's Assistant." *Sociology of Work and Occupations* 3:455–77.

Schön, D. A. 1983. *The Reflective Practitioner: How Professionals Think in Action*. New York: Basic.

Schudson, M. 1981. *Discovering the News*. New York: Basic.

Schultze, Q. J. 1982. "'An Honorable Place': The Quest for Professional Advertising Education, 1900–1917." *Business History Review* 56:16–32.

Schumann, C. 1985. "La gestion juridique de problèmes emotionnels." *Annales de Vaucresson* No. 23:115–35.

Scott, D. 1978. *From Office to Profession*. Philadelphia: University of Pennsylvania Press.

———. 1979. "The Popular Lecture and the Creation of a Public." Paper presented to the Davis Center for Historical Studies, 9 February 1979.

Scott, W. R. 1965. "Reactions to Supervision in a Heteronomous Professional Organization." *Administrative Science Quarterly* 10:65–81.

Scull, A. 1975a. "From Madness to Mental Illness." *Archives européenes de sociologie* 16:218–51.

———. 1975b. "Mad-doctors and Magistrates." *Archives européene de Sociologie* 17:279–305.

Sedlak, M. W., and H. F. Williamson. 1983. *The Evolution of Management Education.* Urbana: University of Illinois Press.

Seed, P. 1973. *The Expansion of Social Work in Britain.* London: Routledge.

Segal, J. 1975. *Research in the Service of Mental Health.* Rockville MD: NIMH. DHEW publication (ADM) 75–236.

Serman, W. 1982. *Les officiers français dans la nation.* Paris: Aubier Montaigne.

Sewell, W. H., Jr. 1974. "Etat, Corps, and Ordre." Pp. 49–68 in Wehler 1974.

———. 1980. *Work and Revolution in France.* Cambridge: Cambridge University Press.

Shaffer, D., and L. Greenhill. 1979. "A Critical Note on the Predictive Validity of 'the Hyperkinetic Syndrome.'" *Journal of Child Psychology and Psychiatry* 20:61–72.

Sharp, W. R. 1931. *The French Civil Service.* New York: Macmillan.

Shera, J. B., and D. B. Cleveland. 1977. "History and Foundations of Information Science." Pp. 249–75 in M. E. Williams, ed., *Annual Review of Information Science and Technology* 12.

Shinn, T. 1978. "Des corps de l'Etat au secteur industriel." *Revue française de sociologie* 19:39–71.

———. 1980. *L'école polytechnique 1794–1914.* Paris: Presses de la Fondation Nationale des Sciences Politiques.

Shortell, S. M. 1974. "Determinants of Physician Referral Rates." *Medical Care* 12:13–31.

Shryock, R. H. 1966. *Medicine in America.* Baltimore: Johns Hopkins University Press.

———. 1967. *Medical Licensing in America 1650–1965.* Baltimore: Johns Hopkins University Press.

Sicherman, B. 1968. *The Quest for Mental Health in America.* Ph. D. diss., Columbia University.

Simmel, G. [1903] 1946. *The Sociology of George Simmel,* K. Wolff, ed. New York: Free Press.

Smigel, E. O. 1964. *The Wall Street Lawyer.* New York: Free Press.

Smith, D. R., and A. Abbott. 1983. "A Labor Market Perspective on the Mobility of College Football Coaches." *Social Forces* 61:1147–67.

Smith, H. L. 1958. "Contingencies of Professional Differentiation." *American Journal of Sociology* 63:410–14.

Smith, L. C. 1983. *20th Clinic on Library Applications of Automation: Professional Competencies.* Urbana: University of Illinois CSLIS.

Smith, W. L. 1957. "Psychiatry in Medicine: Intra- and Interprofessional Relations." *American Journal of Sociology* 63:295–89.

Solmon, L. C., L. Kent, N. L. Ochsner, and M.-L. Hurwicz. 1981. *Underemployed Ph.D.'s.* Lexington, MA: Heath.

Solomons, D. 1968a. "The Historical Development of Costing." Pp. 3–49 in Solomons 1968b.

Solomons, D., ed. 1968b. *Studies in Cost Analysis.* Homewood, IL: Dorsey.

Solus, H., and R. Perrot. 1961. *Droit judiciaire privée.* Paris: Sirey.

Sorensen, J. E., and T. L. Sorensen. 1974. "The Conflict of Professionals in Bureaucratic Organizations." *Administrative Science Quarterly* 19: 98–106.

Spangler, E. 1986. *Lawyers for Hire.* New Haven: Yale University Press.

Spano, R. 1982. *The Rank and File Movement in Social Work.* Washington, D.C.: University Press of America.

Spector, R. 1977. *Professors of War.* Newport, RI: Naval War College Press.

Spencer, I. S. 1858. *A Pastor's Sketches.* New York: Dodd (2d series, 1859).

Spenner, K. I. 1983. "Deciphering Prometheus." *American Sociological Review* 48:824–37.

Spiers, E. M. 1980. *The Army and Society 1815–1914.* London: Longmans.

Stacey, N. A. H. 1954. *English Accountancy.* London: Gee.

Stans, M. H. 1955. "Tax Practice Problems." *Journal of Accountancy* 100: 6:36–43.

Starr, P. 1982. *The Social Transformation of American Medicine.* New York: Basic.

Steinberg, A. 1981. "The Spirit of Litigation." Paper presented at the Social Science History Association, Nashville, 1981.

Steudler, F. 1973. "Hôpital, profession médicale, et politique hospitalière." *Revue française de sociologie* 14:(supp):13–40.

———. 1977. "Médecine libérale et conventionnement." *Sociologie du travail* 19:176–98.

Stevens, R. 1971. *American Medicine and the Public Interest.* New Haven: Yale University Press.

Stevens, R., L. W. Goodman, and S. S. Mick. 1978. *The Alien Doctors.* New York: Wiley.

Stevens, Robert. 1983. *Law School: Legal Education in America from the 1850s to the 1980s.* Chapel Hill: University of North Carolina Press.

Stewart, G. W. 1973. *Introduction to Matrix Operations.* New York: Academic Press.

Stigler, G. 1971. "The Economic Theory of Regulation." *Bell Journal of Economics* 2:3.

Stiles, W. B., D. A. Shapiro, and R. Elliott. 1986. "Are All Psychotherapies Equivalent?" *American Psychologist* 41:165–80.

Stolz, K. R. 1932. *Pastoral Psychology.* Nashville: Cokesbury.

Stone, D. A. 1980. *The Limits of Professional Power.* Chicago: University of Chicago Press.

Stone, L. ed., 1976. *Schooling and Society.* Baltimore: Johns Hopkins University Press.

Strachan, T. Y. 1888. "The Accountant and the Actuary." *The Accountant* 14:244–48.

Strauss, A. 1985. *Social Organization of Medical Work.* Chicago: University of Chicago Press.

Strauss, A., L. Schatzman, R. Bucher, D. Ehrlich, and M. Sabshin. 1964. *Psychiatric Ideologies and Institutions.* New York: Free Press.

Strauss, G. 1964. "Work Flow Frictions, Interfunctional Rivalries, and Professionalism." *Human Organization* 23:137–49.

Stueart, R.D. 1972. *The Area Specialist Bibliographer.* Metuchen, NJ: Scarecrow.

Sugarman, D. 1986. "Legal Theory, the Common Law Mind, and the Making of the Textbook Tradition." Pp. 26–61 in Twining, ed., *Legal Theory and the Common Law.* Oxford: Basil Blackwell.

Sugg, R. 1978. *Motherteacher.* Charlottesville: University Press of Virginia.

Suleiman, E. N. 1978. *Elites in French Society.* Princeton: Princeton University Press.

Sullivan, L.H. [1924] 1956. *The Autobiography of an Idea.* New York: Dover.

Sullivan, P. 1976. "Library Associations." Pp. 135–52 in Winger 1976.

Sussman, G. 1977. "The Glut of Doctors in Mid-Nineteenth-Century France." *Comparative Studies in Society and History* 19:287–304.

Sutton, F. X., S. E. Harris, C. Kaysen, and J. Tobin. 1962. *The American Business Creed.* New York: Schocken.

Svenonius, E., and R. Witthus. 1981. "Information Science as a Profession." Pp. 291–316 in M. E. Williams, ed., *Annual Review of Information Science and Technology* 16.

Swaine, R. T. 1946. *The Cravath Firm and Its Predecessors.* New York: Privately Printed.

Tackett, T. 1977. *Priest and Parish in Eighteenth Century France.* Princeton: Princeton University Press.

Taft, H. W. 1938. *A Century and a Half at the New York Bar.* New York: Privately Printed.

Tedlow, R. S. 1979. *Keeping the Corporate Image.* Greenwich, CN: JAI Press.

Thompson, F. M. L. 1968. *Chartered Surveyors.* London: Routledge.

Tichi, C. 1987. *Shifting Gears.* Chapel Hill: University of North Carolina Press.

Tighe, J. 1983. *A Question of Responsibility.* Ph. D. Diss., University of Pennsylvania.

———. 1985. "The 'Science' of Responsibility." Paper presented to the Organization of American Historians, April 1985.

Timms, N. 1964. *Psychiatric Social Work in Great Britain 1939–1962.* London: Routledge.

Timperley, S. R., and M. S. Osbaldeston. 1975. "The Professionalization Process: A Study of an Aspiring Occupational Organization." *Sociological Review* 23:607–27.

Tinker, A. M., B. D. Merino, and M. D. Neimark. 1982. "The Normative Origins of Positive Theories: Ideology and Accounting Thought." *Accounting, Organizations, and Society* 7:167–200.

Tipson, F. S. 1903. "The Relation of the Auditor to the Bookkeeper." *Accountant and Bookkeeper* 2:41–43.

Tomes, N. 1984. *A Generous Confidence*. Cambridge: Cambridge University Press.

Toren, N. 1975. "Deprofessionalization and Its Sources." *Work and Occupations* 2:323–37.

Trefathan, F. N. 1954. "A History of Operations Research." Pp. 3–35 in J. F. McCloskey and F. N. Trefathan, eds., *Operations Research for Management*. Baltimore: Johns Hopkins University Press.

Tropp, A. 1957. *The Schoolteachers*. New York: Macmillan.

Tuchman, G., and N. E. Fortin. 1984. "Fame and Misfortune." *American Journal of Sociology* 90:72–96.

Twedt, D. W. 1956. "Who is the AMA?" *Journal of Marketing* 20:385–89.

Tyrrell, I. R. 1979. *Sobering Up*. Westport, CN: Greenwood.

United States Senate, Committee on Government Operations. 1976. *The Accounting Establishment*. Washington: Government Printing Office.

Vagts, A. 1959. *A History of Militarism*. New York: Free Press.

Van den Slik, J. R. 1983. "State Regulation as a Threat to Nursing Education." *State Government* 56:105–11.

Veit, F. 1976. "Library Services to College Students." Pp. 361–78 in Winger 1976.

Veysey, L. 1965. *The Emergence of the American University*. Chicago: University of Chicago Press.

Viollet-le-Duc, E. L. M. 1874. *The Story of a House*. trans. G. M. Towle. Boston: Osgood.

Vogel, M. 1980. *The Invention of the Modern Hospital 1870–1930*. Chicago: University of Chicago Press.

Vogel, M. J., and C. E. Rosenberg, eds. 1979. *The Therapeutic Revolution*. Philadelphia: University of Pennsylvania Press.

Vollmer, H., and D. M. Mills, eds. 1966. *Professionalization*. Englewood Cliffs, NJ: Prentice-Hall.

Voyenne, B. 1959. "Les journalistes." *Revue française de science politique* 9:901–34.

Wagenfeld, M. O., and S. S. Robin. 1976. "Boundary Busting in the Role of the Community Mental Health Worker." *Journal of Health and Social Behavior* 17:112–22.

Wagers, R. 1978. "American Reference Theory and the Information Dogma." *Journal of Library History* 13:265–81.

Walsh, M. R. 1977. *Doctors Wanted: No Women Need Apply*. New Haven: Yale University Press.

Walter, C. 1967. "Who's Infringing on Whose Specialty?" *Medical Economics* 44:77–102.

Walton, S. 1909. "The Relation of the Commercial Lawyer to the CPA." *Journal of Accountancy* 7:205–13.

Wardwell, W. I. 1952. "A Marginal Professional Role: The Chiropractor." *Social Forces* 30:339–48.

Ware, C. F. 1965. *Greenwich Village*. New York: Harper.

Weber, M. 1954. *On Law in Economy and Society.* New York: Simon and Schuster.

Wehler, H.-U. 1974. *Sozialgeschichte Heute.* Göttingen: Vandenhoeck and Ruprecht.

Weiss, J. 1982. *The Making of Technological Man.* Cambridge: MIT Press.

Weisz, G. 1978. "The Politics of Medical Professionalization in France 1845–1848." *Journal of Social History* 12:1–30.

———. 1983. *The Emergence of Modern Universities in France, 1863–1914.* Princeton: Princeton University Press.

Wellek, R. 1963. *Concepts of Criticism.* New Haven: Yale University Press.

Wexelblat, R. L. 1981. *History of Computer Languages.* New York: Academic.

White, H. C. 1970. *Chains of Opportunity.* Cambridge: Harvard University Press.

White, W. D. 1978. "The Impact of Occupational Licensure of Clinical Laboratory Personnel." *Journal of Human Resources* 13:91–102.

Whitley, R., A. Thomas, and J. Marceau. 1981. *Masters of Business: Business Schools and Business Graduates in Britain and France.* New York: Tavistock.

Wiebe, R. L. 1967. *The Search for Order.* New York: Hill and Wang.

Wilensky, H. L. 1964. "The Professionalization of Everyone?" *American Journal of Sociology* 70:137–58.

———. 1967. *Organizational Intelligence.* New York: Basic.

Wilensky, H. L., and C. W. Lebeaux. 1958. *Industrial Society and Social Welfare.* New York: Russell Sage.

Wilkinson, J. H. 1965. *The Algebraic Eigenvalue Problem.* Oxford: Oxford University Press.

Willcox, G. B. 1890. *The Pastor Amidst His Flock.* New York: American Tract Society.

Williams, M. E., ed. Annual. *Annual Review of Information Science and Technology* White Plains, NY: Knowledge Industry Publications.

Wilson, B. R. 1959. "Pentecostal Ministers." *American Journal of Sociology* 64:494–504.

Wilton-Ely, J. 1977. "The Profession of Architect in England." Pp. 180–208 in Kostof 1977.

Winger, H. W., ed. 1976. "American Library History: 1876–1976." *Library Trends* 25:1 (special issue).

Wiseman, J. P. 1970. *Stations of the Lost.* Chicago: University of Chicago Press.

Wolpe, P. R. 1985. "The Maintenance of Professional Authority." Paper presented to the American Sociological Association, Washington, D. C., August 1985.

Worcester, E. S., and S. McComb. 1909. *The Christian Religion as a Healing Power.* New York: Moffat, Yard.

Wright, H. C. 1985. "Shera as a Bridge between Librarianship and Information Science." *Journal of Library History* 20:137–56.

Wulforst, H. 1982. *Breakthrough to the Computer Age*. New York: Scribner.

Young, A. 1869. *An Historical Sketch of the French Bar*. Edinburgh: Edmiston and Douglas.

Young, A. F., and E. T. Ashton. 1956. *British Social Work in the Nineteenth Century*. London: Routledge.

Younghusband, E. 1978. *Social Work in Great Britain 1950–1975* 2 vols. London: Allen and Unwin.

Youngs, J. W. T., Jr. 1976. *God's Messengers*. Baltimore: Johns Hopkins University Press.

Zander, M. 1978. *Legal Services for the Community*. London: Temple Smith.

———. 1984. *The State of Knowledge about the English Legal Profession*. Chichester, Sussex: Barry Rose.

Zarlino, G. [1558] 1983. *On the Modes*. New Haven: Yale University Press.

Zussman, R. 1985. *Mechanics of the Middle Class*. Berkeley: University of California Press.

# Index